# The Expositor's Bible
## The Acts Of The Apostles
## Vol. 1

*By*

George Thomas Stokes

# The Expositor's Bible
## The Acts Of The Apostles
## Vol. 1
### by George Thomas Stokes

ISBN: 978-93-61154-27-0

Published by

# DOUBLE 9 BOOKS

2/13-B, Ansari Road
Daryaganj, New Delhi – 110002
info@double9books.com
www.double9books.com
Tel. 011-40042856

# ABOUT THE AUTHOR

George Thomas Stokes was an Irish church historian. He was the eldest son of John Stokes of Athlone and Margaret Forster, his wife, and was born on December 28, 1843, in Athlone, Ireland. He attended Galway Grammar School, Queen's College, Galway, and Trinity College, Dublin, where he earned a B.A. in 1864. He went on to get his M.A. in 1871, B.D. in 1881, and D.D. in 1886. In 1866, Stokes was ordained for the curacy of Dunkerrin in the diocese of Killaloe in the then established Church of Ireland, and in the following year was sent to the curacy of St. Patrick's, Newry. In 1868, he was appointed first vicar of the newly established charge of All Saints, Newtown Park, County Dublin, a position he held until his death. Stokes began studying Irish church history after joining All Saints. Dr. Reichel nominated him as his deputy in the chair of ecclesiastical history at the University of Dublin; Stokes succeeded him in 1883. Ireland and the Celtic Church, published in 1886, was an immediate success. It was followed in 1888 by his Ireland and the Anglo-Norman Church, which explored the history of Irish Christianity in greater depth. Stokes was married twice: first to Fanny, daughter of Thomas Pusey of Surbiton, Surrey, and then to Katherine, daughter of Henry J. Dudgeon of the Priory in Stillorgan, County Dublin.

# CONTENTS

# PREFACE

This volume contains an exposition of the Acts of the Apostles down to, but not including, the conversion of St. Paul and the baptism of Cornelius. There is a natural division at that point. Prior to these events, the inspired narrative is engaged with what the late Bishop Lightfoot of Durham called great "representative facts," prophetical or typical of the future developments of the Church, whether among Jews or Gentiles;[1] while the subsequent course of the history deals almost entirely with missionary work among the heathen and the labours of St. Paul.[2]

We are dependent for the story of these earliest days of the Church's life upon the Acts of the Apostles. I have endeavoured, however, to illustrate the narrative by copious references to ancient documents, some of which may appear of dubious value and authority, such as the *Acts of the Saints* and the writings of the mediæval Greek hagiologist, Simeon Metaphrastes, who lived in the tenth century.[3] The latter writer has been hitherto regarded as more famous for his imagination than for his historical accuracy. This age of ours is a noted one, however, for clearing characters previously regarded as very doubtful, and Simeon Metaphrastes has come in for his own share of this process of rehabilitation. The distinguished writer just referred to, Dr. Lightfoot, as we have shown in a note on p. 218, has proved that Metaphrastes embodied in his works valuable early records, dating back to the second century, which in critical hands can shed much light upon primitive Christian history.[4] In fact, students of Holy Scripture and of early Christianity are learning every day to look more and more to ancient Greek, Syriac, and Armenian writers, and to the libraries of the Eastern Churches, for fresh light on these important subjects. It is only natural we should do so. Writers like Simeon Metaphrastes and Photius, the student Patriarch of Constantinople, lived a thousand years nearer the apostolic times than we do. They flourished in an age of the highest civilization, when precious literary works, in hundreds and thousands, which are no longer known amongst us, lay all around them and at their command. These men and their friends gathered them up and extracted them, and common sense alone teaches that a critical study of their writings will reveal to us somewhat of the treasures they possessed. The libraries of the East again form a great field for investigation. During the last fifty years we have paid some little attention to them, which has been amply rewarded. The recovery of the complete works of Hippolytus and of Clement of Rome, the discovery of the *Teaching of the Apostles* and of the *Diatessaron* of Tatian, are only specimens of what we may yet hope to exhume from the dust of ages.

The testimony, too, borne by these finds has been of the greatest importance. The *Diatessaron* alone has formed the most triumphant reply to the argument against the Gospels, specially against St. John's Gospel, formulated some years ago by the author of *Supernatural Religion*. And the process of discovery is still going on. I have said something in the notes to the final lecture of the present volume concerning the latest discovery of this kind which throws some light upon the composition of the Acts. I refer to the lost *Apology* of Aristides, which has just been brought to light. Let me very briefly tell its story and show its bearing on the age and date of the Acts. Eusebius, the historian of the fourth century, mentions in his *Chronicle*, under the year 124, the two earliest apologies written in defence of Christianity; one by Quadratus, a hearer of the Apostles, the other by Aristides, a philosopher of Athens. Now this year 124 was about twenty years after St. John's death. These apologies have hitherto been best known by this historian's notice, though Eusebius says they were widely circulated in his time. The *Apology* or defence of Aristides has often been sought for. In the seventeenth century it was said to have been extant in a monastery near Athens,[5] but no Western had ever seen it in a complete shape in modern times. Two years ago, however, Professor J. Rendel Harris, M.A., of Cambridge and of Haverford College, Pennsylvania, discovered it in a Syriac version in the library of the convent of St. Catharine on Mount Sinai, whence he has published it with an English translation in a new series of *Texts and Studies in Biblical and Patristic Literature*, the first number of which has appeared at Cambridge within the last few weeks.[6]

I need not go farther into the story of the recovery of this document, which raises high our expectations of others still more interesting. The *Apology* of Quadratus would be even more important, as it bore direct testimony to the miracles of our Lord. The brief extract from it which Eusebius gives in his *History*, book iv., chap. 3, proves how precious would be the complete work. "The deeds of our Saviour, says Quadratus, were always before you, for they were true; those that were healed, those that were raised from the dead, who were seen, not only when healed and when raised, but were always present. They remained for a long time, not only whilst the Saviour was sojourning with us, but likewise when He had been removed. So that some of them have also survived to our own times."

In the *Apology* of Quadratus we should obtain a picture of the popular theology of the Church during that dark period which elapsed between the days of Clement of Rome and Ignatius, and those of Justin Martyr. The *Apology* of Aristides which has been found reveals something indeed in the same direction, but is more occupied with an attack upon paganism than in a statement of the Christian faith. Here, however, consists its bearing on the Acts of the Apostles, not directly, but by way of contrast. Let me explain what I mean. In lecture xvii., when treating of the story of Simon Magus, I have shown how the simple narrative of the Acts concerning that man became elaborated in the second century till it formed at last a regular romance; whence I conclude that if the Acts had been written in the second century the story of Simon Magus would not be the simple matter we read in St. Luke's narrative. Now our argument for the date of the Acts derived from the *Apology* of Aristides is of much the same kind. This document shows us what the tone and substance of second century addresses to the pagans were. It is the earliest of a series of apologies extending over the whole of that century. The *Apology* of Aristides, the numerous writings of Justin Martyr, specially the *Oratio* and the *Cohortatio ad Græcos* attributed to him, the *Oration* of Tatian addressed to the Greeks, the *Apologeticus* and the treatise *Ad Nationes* of Tertullian, the *Epistle to Diognetus*, the writings of Athenagoras, all deal with the same topics, the theories and absurdities of Greek philosophy, the immoral character of the pagan deities, and the purity of Christian doctrine and practice.[7] If the Acts of the Apostles had been composed in the second century, the address of St. Paul to the Athenians would have been very different from what it is, and must necessarily have partaken of those characteristics which we find common to all the numerous treatises addressed to the heathen world of that date. If the Acts were written in the second century, why does not the writer put arguments into St. Paul's mouth like those which were current among the Christian apologists of that time? The philosophical argument of Aristides, which is followed by Justin Martyr[8] and the later apologists, when contrasted with the simplicity of St. Paul, is a conclusive proof of the early date of the composition of the Acts.[9] But this is not the only argument of this kind which modern research furnishes. Aristides shows us what the character of Christian controversy with the pagans was in the generation succeeding the Apostles. We can draw the same conclusion when we examine Christian controversy as carried on against the Jews of the same period.

We have a number of treatises directed against the Jews by Christian writers of the second century: the *Dialogue* of Justin Martyr with Trypho the Jew, of Jason and Papiscus, and the treatise of Tertullian directed *Ad Judæos*. When compared with one another we find that the staple arguments of these writings are much the same.[10] They were evidently framed upon the model of St. Stephen's address at Jerusalem, of St. Paul at Antioch in Pisidia, and of the Epistle to the Galatians. They deal with the transitory and temporary character of the Jewish law, they enter very largely into the fulfilment of Old Testament prophecy, and they notice Jewish objections. The second century works are, however, elaborate treatises, dealing with a great controversy in a manner which experience had showed to be far the most effective and telling. The Jewish controversy in the Acts, whether in the mouth of St. Peter, St. Stephen, or St. Paul, is treated in a much simpler way. The speakers think, speak, write, like men who are making their first essays in controversy, and have no experience of others to guide them. Had the Acts been written in the second century, the writer must have composed the addresses to the Jews as well as those to the Gentiles after the model of the age when he was writing. The more carefully, however, we examine and contrast these two controversies, as conducted in the Acts and in the writings of the second century respectively, the more thoroughly shall we be convinced of the apostolic date of St. Luke's narrative, of its genuine character, and of its historic worth.

I have written this book from my own standpoint as a decided Churchman, but I hope that I have said nothing which can really hurt the feelings of any one who thinks otherwise, or which may tend to widen those differences between Christians which are such a terrible hindrance to the cause of true religion and its progress in the world.

I have tried to use the Revised Version consistently throughout my expositions, but I fear that my attempt has been but vain. In my formal quotations I think I have succeeded. But then, in commenting upon Scripture, a writer constantly refers to and quotes passages without formal reference. Here is where I must have failed. The Authorized Version is so bound up with all our earliest thoughts and associations that its language unconsciously colours all our ideas and expressions. Any one who at present makes such an attempt as I have done will find illustrated in himself the phenomena which we behold in writings of the fifth and sixth centuries. St. Jerome published a Revised Version of the Latin translation of the Scripture about the year 400 A.D. For hundreds of years afterwards Latin writers are found using indiscriminately the old Latin and the new Latin translations. St. Patrick's *Confession*, for instance, was composed about the middle of the fifth century. Quotations from both versions of the New Testament are found in that document, affording a conclusive indication of its date; just as the mixture of the Revised and Authorized Versions will form a prominent feature in theological works composed towards the close of the nineteenth century.

I have to acknowledge the kind assistance of the Rev. H. W. Burgess, LL.D., who has patiently read all my proofs, and called my attention to many a solecism or mistake which might have otherwise disfigured my pages; and of Mr. W. Etienne Phelps, B.A., deputy keeper of Primate Marsh's Library, who has compiled the index.

GEORGE T. STOKES.

All Saints' Vicarage, Blackrock,
*May 27th, 1891.*

# CHAPTER I
# THE ORIGIN AND AUTHORITY OF
# THE ACTS OF THE APOSTLES

"The former treatise I made, O Theophilus, concerning all that Jesus began both to do and to teach, until the day in which He was received up, after that He had given commandment through the Holy Ghost unto the apostles whom He had chosen." — Acts i. 1, 2.

These words constitute the very brief preface which the writer thought sufficient for the earliest ecclesiastical history ever produced in the Church of God. Let us imitate him in his brevity and conciseness, and without further delay enter upon the consideration of a book which raises vital questions and involves all-important issues.

Now when a plain man comes to the consideration of this book one question naturally strikes him at once: How do I know who wrote this book, or when it was written? What evidence or guarantee have I for its authentic character? To these questions we shall apply ourselves in the present chapter.

The title of the book as given in our Bibles does not offer us much help. The title varies in different manuscripts and in different ancient authors. Some writers of the second century who touched upon apostolic times call it by the name our Bibles retain, The Acts of the Apostles; others call it The Acts of the Holy Apostles, or at times simply The Acts. This title of "Acts" was indeed a very common one, in the second and third centuries, for a vast variety of writings purporting to tell the story of apostolic lives, as an abundance of extant apocryphal documents amply proves. The Acts of Paul and Thecla, the Acts of St. Thomas, of St. Peter, and of St. John, were imitations, doubtless, of the well-known name by which our canonical book was then called. Imitation is universally acknowledged to be the sincerest form of flattery, and the imitation of the title and form of our book is an evidence of its superior claim and authority. One of the oldest of these apocryphal Acts is a document celebrated in Christian antiquity as the Acts of Paul and Thecla. We know all about its origin. It was forged about the year 180 or 200 by a presbyter of Asia Minor who was an enthusiastic admirer of the Apostle St. Paul. But when we take up the narrative and read it, with its absurd legends and its manifold touches and realistic scenes drawn from the persecutions of the second century, and well known to every student of the original records of those times, we can at a glance see what the canonical Acts of the Apostles would have been had the composition been postponed to the end of the second century. The Acts of Paul and Thecla are useful, then, as illustrating, by way of contrast in title and in substance, the genuine Acts of the New Testament which they imitated.[11]

But then, some one might say, how do we know that the genuine Acts of the Apostles existed prior to the Acts of Paul and Thecla and the time of Tertullian, who first mentions these apocryphal Acts, and tells us of their forged origin? The answer to that query is easy enough. Yet it will require a somewhat copious statement in order to exhibit its full force, its convincing power.

Tertullian is a writer who connects the age of apostolic men, as we may call the men who knew the Apostles—Ignatius, Polycarp, Clement of Rome, and such like—with the third century. Tertullian was born about the middle of the second century, and he lived till the third century was well advanced. He was one of those persons whose chronological position enables them to transmit historical facts and details from one critical point to another. Let me illustrate what I mean by a modern example. Every unprejudiced thinker will acknowledge that the Rev. John Wesley was a man who exercised an extraordinary religious influence. He not only originated a vast community of world-wide extent, which calls itself after his name, but he also imparted a tremendous impetus to spiritual life and work in the Church of England. After the departure of Mr. Wesley from this life his mantle fell upon a certain number of his leading followers, men like Adam Clarke, the commentator; Jabez Bunting, the organizer of modern Wesleyanism; Thomas Coke, Robert Newton, and Richard Watson, the author of the *Institutes of Theology*. Several of these men lived far into this century, and there are at the present day thousands still alive who recollect some of them, while there are many still alive who can recollect all of them. Now let us draw a parallel with all reverence, and yet with perfect fairness. John Wesley began his life at the beginning of the eighteenth century as our Lord began His human life at the beginning of the first century. John Wesley's immediate disciples perpetuated their lives till the middle of the present century. Our Lord's apostles and immediate followers perpetuated their lives in some cases till well into the second century. At the close of the nineteenth century there are hundreds, to say the least, who remember Adam Clarke and Thomas Coke, who in turn were personally acquainted with John Wesley. In the last quarter of the second century there must have been many still alive—apostolic men, I have called them—whose youthful memories could bear them back to the days when the Apostle St. John, and men like St. Mark, and St. Luke, and St. Ignatius, still testified what they had personally seen and heard and known. Why, the simple fact is this, that in the year 1950 there will be still living numerous persons who will be able to say that they have personally known many individuals who were the friends and acquaintances of John Wesley's immediate disciples. Four long lives of ninety years, the one overlapping the other, will easily cover three centuries of time.

Let us dwell a little more on this point, for it bears very directly on Tertullian's witness, not only to the canon of the New Testament, but also to the whole round of Christian doctrine. It is simply wonderful what vast tracts of time can be covered by human memory even at the present day, when that faculty has lost so much of its power for want of exercise, owing to the printing-press. I can give a striking instance from my own knowledge. There is at present an acquaintance of mine living in this city of Dublin where I write. He is hale and hearty, and able still to take the keenest interest in the affairs of religion and of politics. He is about ninety-five years of age, and he has told me within the last twelve months that he remembers quite well a grand-aunt of his born in the reign of Queen Anne, who used to tell him all the incidents connected with the earliest visits of John and Charles Wesley to Ireland about 1745. If Tertullian's experience was anything like my own, he may quite easily have known persons at Rome or elsewhere who had heard the tale of St. Paul's preaching, labour, and miracles from the very men whom the Apostle had converted at Antioch, Damascus, and Rome. I can give a more striking instance still, which any reader can verify for himself. Mr. S. C. Hall was a writer known far and wide for the last seventy years. About the middle of this century Mr. Hall was at the height of his popularity, though he only passed to the unseen world within the last year or so. In the year 1842 he, in union with his accomplished and well-known wife, composed a beautifully-illustrated work, published in three volumes, called *Picturesque Ireland*, which now finds an honoured place in many of our libraries. In the second volume of that work Mr. Hall mentions the following curious fact bearing on our argument. He states that he was then (in 1842) staying at the house of a gentleman, Sir T. Macnaghten, whose father had commanded at the siege of Derry in 1689, one hundred and fifty-three years before. Yet vast as the distance of time was, the explanation which he offered was easy enough. The Macnaghten Clan was summoned to assist in the celebrated siege of Derry. They refused to march unless headed by their chief, who was then a boy of seven. The child was placed on a horse and duly headed his clan, who would follow him alone. That child married when a very old man, and his eldest son attained to an equally patriarchal age, carrying with him the traditions of Jacobite times down to the reign of Queen Victoria. I could give many other similar instances, illustrating my contention that vivid and accurate traditions of the past can be transmitted over vast spaces of time, and that through persons who come into living contact with one another.[12]

Tertullian must have had ample means, then, of ascertaining the facts concerning the books of the New Testament from living witnesses. There is again another point we must bear in mind, and it is this: the distance of time with which Tertullian's investigations had to deal was not so vast as we sometimes imagine. It was by no means so great as the spaces we have just now referred to. We naturally think of Tertullian as living about the year 200, and then, remembering that our Saviour was born just two centuries before, we ask, What is the value of a man's testimony concerning events two centuries old? But we must bear in mind the exact point at issue. We are not enquiring at all about events two centuries old, but we are enquiring as to Tertullian's evidence with respect to the canonical Gospels and the Acts; and none of these was one hundred years old when Tertullian was born, about 150 A.D., while the Gospel of St. John may not have been more than sixty years old, or thereabouts, at the same date. Now if we take up the writings of Tertullian, which are very copious indeed, we shall find that the Acts of the Apostles are quoted at least one hundred times in them, long passages being in some cases transcribed, and the whole book treated by him as Scripture and true history. If we accept the ordinary view, that the Acts were written previously to St. Paul's death, the book was only a century old at Tertullian's birth. But we can come nearer to the apostolic times.

The Muratorian Fragment is a document which came to light by chance one hundred and fifty years ago. It illustrates the age of the Acts, and shows what wondrous testimonies to the New Testament scriptures we may yet gain. Its story is a very curious and interesting one for ourselves. St. Columbanus was an Irish missionary who, about the year 600 A.D., established a monastery at Bobbio, a retired spot in North Italy. He gathered a library there, and imparted a literary impulse to his followers which never left them.[13] Some Irish monk a hundred years later than Columbanus employed his time in copying into a book an ancient manuscript of the second century giving a list of the books of the New Testament then received at Rome. This second-century manuscript enumerated among these the four Gospels, the Acts of the Apostles, and thirteen Epistles of St. Paul. Concerning the Acts of the Apostles, the Roman writer of this document, who lived about A.D. 170, says: "The Acts of all the Apostles are written in one book. Luke explains to the most excellent Theophilus everything which happened in his presence, as the omission of Peter's martyrdom and of Paul's journey into Spain manifestly proves;" a passage which clearly shows that about the middle of the second century the Acts of the Apostles was well known at Rome, and its authorship ascribed to St. Luke.[14] But this is not all. We have another most interesting second-century document, which proves that at the very same period our canonical book was known and authoritatively quoted far away in the south of France. It is hard to exaggerate the evidential value of the Epistle of the Churches of Lyons and Vienne written about the year 177, and addressed to their brethren in Asia Minor. That letter quotes the books of the New Testament in the amplest manner, and without any formal references, just as a modern preacher or writer would quote them, showing how common and authoritative was their use. Leader-writers in the *Times* or the *Saturday Review* often garnish their articles with a scriptural quotation; the late Mr. John Bright, in his great popular orations, loved to point them with an apt citation from Holy Writ; but he never thought it necessary, nor do journalists ever think it necessary, to prefix a formal statement of the place whence their texts have been derived. They presume a wide knowledge and a formal recognition of the text of the Bible. So it was in this epistle written from Lyons and Vienne, and in it we find an exact quotation from the Acts of the Apostles—"According as Stephen the perfect martyr prayed, Lord, lay not this sin to their charge."

But this is not the whole of the argument which can be derived from the Epistle of the Lyonnese Christians, which is given to us at full length in the fifth book of the *Church History* of the celebrated historian Eusebius. Their incidental notice of the Acts involves a vast deal when duly considered. The Epistle from Lyons implies that the Acts were received as authoritative and genuine in the churches of towns like Ephesus, Philadelphia, Smyrna, Miletus, where the memories and traditions of the Apostles were still vivid and living. Then, too, the Bishop of Lyons had suffered in this persecution. His name was Pothinus. He was the first Bishop of the Church of Lyons, and he died when he was more than ninety years of age, and may have been a disciple of an apostle, or of one of the first generation of Christians. At any rate, his memory would easily carry him back to the days of Domitian and the times of the first century; and yet the Church over which this first-century Christian presided accepted the Acts of the Apostles. The testimony of Pothinus helps then to carry back the Acts of the Apostles to the year 100 at least. But we can go farther still, and closer to apostolic times.

The Gospel of St. Luke and the Acts of the Apostles are, we may say, universally admitted to be by the same writer. The reference of the Acts to the Gospel, the unity of style and tone of thought, all demonstrate them to be the production of one mind. Any circumstance therefore which proves the early existence of the Gospel equally proves the existence of the Acts of the Apostles. Now we have proof positive that the Gospel of St. Luke occupied an authoritative position and was counted an apostolic and sacred writing at Rome in the early years of the second century, say between 100 and 150, because when Marcion, whom we might call a primitive Antinomian, wished to compile a gospel suited to his own purposes, he took St. Luke's Gospel, cut out whatever displeased him, and published the remainder as the true version. The perversion and mutilation of St. Luke's work shows that it must already have held a high position in the Church at Rome, or else there would have been no object in mutilating it. Marcion's treatment of St. Luke proves the use and position the Gospel and the Acts must have occupied in days when the converts and companions of the Apostles were still alive.[15] That is as far as we can go back by external testimony. But then we must remember what these facts involve—that the Gospel and the Acts occupied authoritative positions in various parts of the world, and specially in Rome, Gaul, Africa, and Asia Minor, in the generation next after the Apostles. Then let us take up the Book of Acts itself, and what does this book, known at Rome and throughout the Christian world at that early period, tell us? It informs us that it was the work of the writer of the Gospel, and that the writer was a companion of the Apostle Paul throughout the portion of his career sketched in the latter part of the book. The Christian Church has never pinned its faith to the Lukian authorship of either the Gospel or the Acts. The question of the authorship of these books is an open one, like that of the Epistle to the Hebrews. The Acts has been attributed to Silas, to Timothy, to Titus; but I may say, without going into any further details on this question, that every attempt to ascribe the Acts to any one else save to the beloved physician has failed, and must fail, because he was the real author, well known to the living tradition of the Church of Rome in the early part of the second century, as that tradition is handed down to us in the language of the Muratorian Fragment.

If we were writing a critical treatise, we should of course have to enter upon the full discussion of many questions which might here be raised. The Acts of the Apostles in its latter chapters plainly claims to be the work of an eye-witness. In its opening words, placed at the head of this dissertation, it claims to be the work of the author of the Gospel. All the facts fall into a simple, natural order if we accept the traditional testimony of the Church that the Acts and the Gospel were both of them written before the martyrdom of St. Paul, and were indited by the hands of St. Paul's companion St. Luke. Any other solution is forced, unnatural, and involves inconsistencies on every side. We may turn aside from this brief outline of the critical question, to some more purely spiritual reflections, simply referring those who desire more information on the questions of date and authorship to such exhaustive works as those of Dr. Salmon's *Introduction to the New Testament*; Dr. Westcott on the *New Testament Canon*; Dr. Charteris on *Canonicity*, or Meyer's *Introduction to the Acts*.

First, then, it may strike the intelligent reader, how comes it that we have not much fuller testimony in early Christian writers to the Acts of the Apostles, and to all the books of the Old Testament? How is it that the writings of Polycarp, Ignatius, Clement of Rome, do not abound with references, not merely to the Acts, but also to the four Gospels and to the other works of the New Testament? How is it that we have to depend on this obscure reference and that dubious quotation? These are questions which have often puzzled my own mind before I had investigated, and must often have raised anxiety and thought in other minds sincerely desirous of being rooted and grounded in the truth. But now, after having investigated, and thought, I think I can see solid reasons why things are as they are; clear evidences of the truth of the Christian story in the apparent difficulties. Historic imagination is one of the necessary requisites in such an investigation, and historic imagination is one of the qualities in which our German cousins, from whom most of the objections to the canon of the New Testament have been derived, are conspicuously deficient. They are gifted with prodigious industry, and an amazing capacity for patient investigation. They live secluded lives, however, and no one is a worse judge of practical life, or forms wilder conclusions as to what men actually do in practical life, than the academic pure and simple. A dear friend, now with God, himself a distinguished resident of a well-known college, used often to say to me, "Never trust the opinion of a mere college fellow or professor upon any practical point; they know nothing about life." This dictum, begotten of long experience, bears on our argument. German thought and English thought offer sharp and strong contrasts on many points, and on none more than in this direction. English students mix more in the world, are surrounded by the atmosphere of free institutions, and realize more vividly how men spontaneously act under the conditions of actual existence. The German thinker evolves his men of the past and the facts of their existence out of his own consciousness, without submitting them to the necessary corrections which experience dictates to his English brother; and the result is, that while we may be very ready to accept the premises of the Germans, we should be in general somewhat suspicious of their conclusions. Scholarship alone does not entitle a man to pronounce on questions of history. It is only one of the elements requisite for the solution of such problems. Knowledge of men, experience of life, enabling a man to form a just and true mental picture of the past and of the motives by which men are influenced, —these are elements equally necessary. Now let us try and throw ourselves back by an effort of historical imagination into the age of Polycarp, Ignatius, and Clement of Rome, and I think we shall at once see that the omission of such abundant references to the New Testament as men at times desiderate was quite natural in their case.

Let us reflect a little. The manner in which the early Christians learned the facts and truths of Christianity was quite different from that which now prevails. If men wish now to learn about original Christianity they resort to the New Testament. In the age of Polycarp they resorted to the living voice of the elders who had known the Apostles, and had heard the truth from their lips. Thus Irenæus, who had the four Gospels before him, tells us: "I can recall the very place where Polycarp used to sit and teach, his manner of speech, his mode of life, his appearance, the style of his address to the people, his frequent references to St. John and to others who had seen our Lord; how he used to repeat from memory the discourses which he had heard from them concerning our Lord, His miracles, and His mode of teaching; and how, being instructed himself by those who were eye-witnesses of the Life of the Word, there was in all that he said a strict agreement with the Scriptures." And it is very natural that men, though possessed of the Gospels, should thus have delighted in the testimony of elders like Polycarp. There is a charm in the human voice, there is a force and power in living testimony, far superior to any written words. Take, for instance, the account of a battle contributed to a newspaper by the best-informed correspondent. Yet how men will hang on the lips and follow with breathless attention the narrative of the humblest actor in the actual contest. This one fact, known to common experience, shows how different the circumstances of the early Christians were as touching the canonical books from those which now exist, or existed in the third and fourth centuries. Again, we must remember that in the age of Polycarp there was no canon of the New Testament as we have it.[16] There were a number of books here and there known to have been written by the Apostles and their immediate followers. One Church could show the Epistle written by St. Paul to the Ephesians, another that written to the Colossians. Clement of Rome, when writing to the Corinthians, expressly refers them to the First Epistle to the Corinthians, which possibly was treasured by them as their one sacred document of the new covenant; and so it was doubtless all over the Christian world till well-nigh the close of the second century. The New Testament was dispersed in portions, a few leading Churches possessing perhaps all or most of the books, and a few remote ones probably only a few detached epistles, or a solitary gospel. A Greek document found in the National Library at Paris within the last few years illustrates this point. The Scillitan martyrs were a body of Africans who sealed their testimony to the faith by suffering martyrdom in the year 180, about three years after the sufferings of the Christians of Lyons and Vienne. North Africa, now the chosen home of the false prophet, was then the most fruitful field for the religion of the Crucified, yielding doctors, saints, confessors, in multitudes. The document which has now come to light tells the story of these north Africans and their testimony to the truth. The details of their judicial examination are there set forth, and in one question, proposed by the heathen magistrate, we have an interesting glimpse of the very point upon which we are insisting, the scattered and detached nature of the New Testament writings at that period. The President of the Roman Court, in the course of his examination, asks the leader of the martyrs, St. Speratus, "What are those books in your cases?" "They are," he replied, "the epistles of that holy man Paul." So that apparently the Scillitan Church depended for instruction, in the closing years of the second century, upon the Epistles of St. Paul alone.[17]

The canon of the New Testament grew up by degrees somehow thus. While the Apostles and their followers and the friends of their followers lived and flourished, men naturally sought after their living testimonies, consulting doubtless such documents as well which lay within their reach. But when the living witnesses and their friends had passed away, the natural instinct of the Church, guided by that Spirit of Truth which in the darkest times has never wholly left Christ's Spouse, led her to treasure up and dwell with greater love upon those written documents which she had possessed from the beginning. It is no wonder, then, that we do not find large quotations and copious references to the canonical books in the earliest writers—simply because it was impossible they should then have occupied the same place in the Christian consciousness as they now do. Rather, on the contrary, we should be inclined to say that, had they been largely quoted and frequently referred to by Polycarp, Ignatius, or Clement, men might naturally have derived therefrom a forcible argument against the genuine character of the works of these primitive Fathers, as such quotations would have been contrary to the principles of human nature. It is very important for us to remember these facts. They have a very clear bearing upon present-day controversies. Friends and foes of Christianity have often thought that the truth of our religion was bound up with the traditional view of the canon of the New Testament, or with some special theory of inspiration; forgetting the self-evident truth that Christianity existed at the beginning without a canon of the New Testament, that the early Christians depended upon personal testimony alone, and that if the Apostles and their friends had never written a line or left a solitary document behind them, yet that we should have abundant information concerning the work and teaching of our Lord and His Apostles in the writings of the successors of the Apostles, compared with and fortified by contemporaneous pagan testimony. Men have sometimes thought and spoken as if the New Testament descended from heaven in its present shape, like the image that fell down from Jupiter which the Ephesians worshipped, forgetting the true history of its upgrowth and origin. The critical theories that have been advanced in abundance of late years would have troubled a second-century Christian very little. If the Johannine authorship of the fourth Gospel were denied, or the Pauline authorship of Colossians or Ephesians questioned; what does it matter? would have been his reply. These documents may have been forgeries, but there are plenty of other documents which tell the same story, and I have myself known many men who have suffered and died because they had embraced the truths, from the lips of the Apostles themselves, which they have taught me. The simple fact is, that if all the books of the New Testament were proved impudent forgeries except the Epistle to the Romans, the two Epistles to the Corinthians, and the Galatians, which every person admits, we should have ample and convincing statements of Christian truth and doctrine. The devout Christian may, then, make his mind easy, certain that no efforts and no advances in the field of biblical criticism are likely to ruffle even a feather of the faith once delivered to the saints.

But then, some one may come forward and say, is not this a very uncomfortable position for us? Would it not have been much more easy and consoling for Christians to have had the whole canon of Scripture infallibly decided by Divine authority once for all, so as to save all doubts and disputations on the whole subject? Would it not have been better had the Acts of the Apostles expressly named St. Luke as its author, and appended ample proofs that its statement was true? This objection is a very natural one, and springs up at times in every mind; and yet it is merely part and parcel of the larger objection, Why has Revelation been left a matter of doubt and disputation in any respect? Nay, it is part of a still wider and vaster question, Why has truth in any department, scientific, philosophical, ethical, or historical, been left a matter of debate? Why has it not shone forth by its own inherent light and compelled the universal consent of admiring mankind? Why has not the great fundamental truth of all, the existence and nature of God, been made so clear that an atheist could not possibly exist? A century and a-half ago Bishop Butler, in his immortal *Analogy*, disposed of this objection, which still crops up afresh in every generation as if that work had never been written.[18] God has placed us here in a state of probation, and neither in temporal nor in spiritual matters is the evidence for what is true, and right, and wise so clear and overwhelming that no room is left for mistake or error. As it is in every other department of life, so is it especially with reference to the canon of Scripture. It would doubtless be very convenient for us if the whole question were settled authoritatively and no doubts possible, but would it be good for us? would it be wholesome for our spiritual life? I trow not. We have, indeed, a living and speaking example of the blessings of uncertainty in the state of the Roman Catholic Church, which has tried to better the Divine method of training mankind, and banish all uncertainty. That communion undertakes to settle infallibly all questions of theology, and to leave nothing in doubt; and with what result? The vast body of the laity take no interest whatsoever in theological questions. They regard theology as outside their sphere, and belonging to the clergy exclusively. The clergy in turn believe that the Pope, in his office of infallible and universal pastor and teacher, has alone the right and authority to settle doctrines, and they leave it to him. They have made a solitude, and that they call peace, and the pretence alone of an authority which undertakes to release man from doubt and the need of investigation has paralysed theological inquiry among Roman Catholics.

The same results on a vastly larger scale must have happened throughout the Christian world had God made His revelation so clear that no doubt could arise concerning it. Man is a lazy animal by nature, and that laziness would at once have been developed by the very abundance of the light vouchsafed. Religion would have been laid aside as a thing settled once for all. All interest would have been lost in it, and human attention would have been concentrated on those purely mundane matters where uncertainty arises, and therefore imperiously demands the mind's thought and care. The blessings of uncertainty would offer a very wide topic for meditation. The man of vast wealth whose bread is certain can never know the childlike faith whereby the poor man waits upon his God and receives from Him day by day his daily dole. The uncertainties of life hide from us much future sorrow, teach us to walk by faith, not by sight, and lead us to depend completely on the loving guidance of that Fatherly Hand which does all things well. The uncertainties of life develop the spiritual life of the soul. The doubts and questions which arise about religion bring their own blessings with them too. They develop the intellectual life of the spirit. They prevent religion becoming a matter of superstition, they offer opportunities for the exercise of the graces of honesty, courage, humility, and love; and thus form an important element in that Divine training by which man is fitted here below for the beatific vision which awaits him hereafter. Human nature ever craves with longing desire to walk by sight. The Divine method evermore prescribes, on the contrary, that man must for the present walk by faith. Very wisely indeed, and with truest spiritual instinct, the poet of the *Christian Year* has sung, in words applicable to life and to theology alike:—

"There are who, darkling and alone,
Would wish the weary night were gone,
Though dawning morn should only show
The secret of their unknown woe:
Who pray for sharpest throbs of pain
To ease them of doubt's galling chain:
'Only disperse the cloud,' they cry,
'And if our fate be death, give light and let us die.'

"Unwise I deem them, Lord, unmeet
To profit by Thy chastenings sweet,
For Thou wouldst have us linger still
Upon the verge of good or ill,
That on Thy guiding hand unseen
Our undivided hearts may lean,
And this our frail and foundering bark
Glide in the narrow wake of Thy belovèd ark."[19]

The thoughts with which we have hitherto dealt connect themselves with the opening words of the text with which we have begun this chapter, "The former treatise I made, O Theophilus." There are two other points in this passage which are worthy of devout attention. The writer of the Acts took a thoroughly historical view of our Lord's life after the resurrection as well as before that event. He considered that our Lord's person, no matter how it may have been modified by His death and resurrection, was still as real after these events as in the days when He ministered and wrought miracles in Galilee and Jerusalem. His whole life was continuous, from the day of the birth in Bethlehem "until the day He was taken up."

Then again St. Luke recognises the dual personality of our Lord. As we shall afterwards have frequently to notice, St. Luke realized His Divine character. In the opening verses of this book he recognises His complete and perfect humanity—"After that He had given commandment through the Holy Ghost unto the Apostles." There was an ancient heresy about the nature of our Lord's person, which denied the perfection of our Lord's humanity, teaching that His Divinity took the place of the human spirit in Christ. Such teaching deprives us of much comfort and instruction which the Christian can draw from a meditation upon the true doctrine as taught here by St. Luke. Jesus Christ was God as well as man, but it was through the manhood He revealed the life and nature of God. He was perfect Man in all respects, with body, soul, and spirit complete; and in the actions of His manhood, in the exercise of all its various activities, He required the assistance and support of the Holy Ghost just as really as we ourselves do. He taught, gave commandments, worked miracles through the Holy Ghost. The humanity of the Eternal Son required the assistance of the Divine Spirit. Christ sought that Divine aid in prolonged communion with His Father and His God, and then went forth to work His miracles and give His commandments. Prayer and the gift of the Spirit and the works and marvels of Christ were closely connected together, even before the open descent of the Spirit and the wonders of Pentecost. There was a covenant blessing and a covenant outpouring of the Spirit peculiar to Christianity which was not vouchsafed till Christ had ascended. But the Divine Spirit had been given in a measure long before Christ came. It was through the Spirit that every blessing and every gift came to patriarchs, prophets, warriors, teachers, and workers of every kind under the Jewish dispensation. The Spirit of God came upon Bezaleel and Aholiab, qualifying them to work cunningly for the honour and glory of Jehovah when a tabernacle was to be reared. The Spirit of God came upon Samson, and roused his natural courage when Israel was to be delivered. The Spirit of God could rest even upon a Saul, and convert him for a time into a changed character. And just as really the Holy Ghost rested upon the human nature of Jesus Christ, guiding Him in the utterance of those commandments, the outcome and development of which we trace in the book of the Acts of the Apostles.

# CHAPTER II
# THE CONVERSATIONS OF THE GREAT FORTY DAYS

"They therefore, when they were come together, asked Him, saying, Lord, dost Thou at this time restore the kingdom to Israel? And He said unto them, It is not for you to know times or seasons, which the Father hath set within His own authority. But ye shall receive power, when the Holy Ghost is come upon you: and ye shall be My witnesses both in Jerusalem, and in all Judæa and Samaria, and unto the uttermost part of the earth." —Acts i. 6-9.

The conversations and intercourse between our Lord and His apostles during the forty days which elapsed from the resurrection to the ascension must have been of intensest interest, yet, like so much that we should esteem interesting concerning the heroes of Scripture and their lives, these things are wrapped round with thickest darkness. We get a glimpse of the risen Christ here and there. We are told He was conversing with His disciples touching the things concerning the kingdom of God. And then we are practically referred to the Acts of the Apostles if we wish to know what topics His resurrection discourses dealt with. And when we do so refer to the Acts we find that His disciples moved along the line of Christian development with steps sure, unfaltering, and decided, because they doubtless felt themselves nerved by the well-remembered directions, the conscious guidance of the Eternal Son of God, vouchsafed in the commandments given by Him in the power of the Holy Ghost.

Let us reflect for a little on the characteristics of Christ's risen appearances to His disciples. I note then in the first place that they were intermittent, and not continuous,—here and there, to Mary Magdalene at one time; to the disciples journeying to Emmaus, to the assembled twelve, to five hundred brethren at once, at other times. Such were the manifestations of our Lord; and some may feel inclined to cavil at them, and ask, Why did He not dwell continuously and perpetually with His disciples as before His resurrection? And yet, reading our narrative in the light of other scriptures, we might expect the resurrection appearances of Christ to have been of this description. In one place in the Gospel narrative we read that our Lord replied thus to a section of His adversaries: "In the resurrection they neither marry nor are given in marriage, but are as angels in heaven." Now we often read of angelic appearances in Holy Scripture, in the Old and New Testament alike. We read too of appearances of Old Testament saints, as of Moses and Elias on the Mount of Transfiguration. And they are all like those of our Lord Jesus Christ after His resurrection. They are sudden, independent of time or space or material barriers, and yet are visible and tangible though glorified. Such in Genesis was Abraham's vision of angels at the tent door, when they did eat and drink with him. Such was Lot's vision of angels who came and lodged with him in wicked Sodom. Such was Peter's vision when an angel released him, guided him through the intricate mazes of Jerusalem's streets; and such were Christ's appearances when, as on this occasion, His disciples, now accustomed to His risen and glorified form, tested Him as of old with the question, "Lord, dost Thou at this time restore the kingdom to Israel?"

I. *Now let us here notice the naturalness of this query concerning the restoration of the kingdom.* The Apostles evidently shared the national aspirations of the Jews at that time. A large number of books have come to light of late years, which show what a keen expectation of the Messiah's kingdom and His triumph over the Romans existed at the time, and prior to the time, of our Saviour. The book of Enoch, discovered one hundred years ago in Abyssinia, and translated into English in the beginning of the present century, was written a century at least before the Incarnation.[20] The book of Jubilees was written in Palestine about the time of our Lord's birth; the Psalter of Solomon dates from the same period. All these works give us clearest glimpses into the inner mind, the religious tone, of the Jewish nation at that time.[21] The pious unsophisticated people of Galilee were daily expecting the establishment of the Messianic kingdom; but the kingdom they expected was no spiritual institution, it was simply an earthly scene of material glory, where the Jews would once again be exalted above all surrounding nations, and the hated invader expelled from the fair plains of Israel. We can scarcely realize or understand the force and naturalness of this question, "Dost Thou at this time restore the kingdom to Israel?" as put by these Galilean peasants till one takes up Archbishop Laurence's translation of the book of Enoch, and sees how this eager expectation dominated every other feeling in the Jewish mind of that period, and was burned into the very secrets of their existence by the tyranny of Roman rule. Thus, let us take the forty-seventh chapter of the book of Enoch, which may very possibly have been in the thoughts of the Apostles as they presented this query to their Lord. In that chapter we read the following words, attributed unto Enoch: "There I beheld the Ancient of Days, whose head was like white wool; and with Him another, whose countenance resembled that of man. His countenance was full of grace, like that of one of the holy angels. Then I inquired of one of the angels who went with me, and who showed me every secret thing concerning this Son of Man, who He was, whence He was, and why He accompanied the Ancient of Days. He answered and said to me, This is the Son of Man, to whom righteousness belongs, with whom righteousness has dwelt, and who will reveal all the treasures of that which is concealed. For the Lord of Spirits has chosen Him, and His portion has surpassed all before the Lord of Spirits in everlasting uprightness. This Son of Man whom thou beholdest shall raise up kings and the mighty from their couches, and the powerful from their thrones; shall loosen the bridles of the powerful, and break in pieces the teeth of sinners. He shall hurl kings from their thrones and their dominions, because they will not exalt and praise Him, nor humble themselves before Him, by whom their kingdoms were granted to them. The countenance likewise of the mighty shall He cast down, filling them with confusion. Darkness shall be their habitation, and worms shall be their bed; nor from that their bed shall they hope to be again raised, because they exalted not the Name of the Lord of Spirits." This is one specimen of the Messianic expectations, which were just then worked up to fever pitch among the Galileans especially, and were ever leading them to burst out into bloody rebellion against the power of the Romans. We might multiply such quotations fourfold did our space permit. This one extract must suffice to show the tone and quality of the religious literature upon which the souls of the Apostles had fed and been sustained, when they proposed this query, "Dost Thou at this time restore the kingdom to Israel?" They were thinking simply of such a kingdom as the book of Enoch foretold.

This very point seems to us one of the special and most striking evidences for the inspiration and supernatural direction of the writers of the New Testament. Their natural, purely human, and national conception of the kingdom of God was one thing; their final, their divinely taught and inspired conception of that kingdom is quite another thing. I cannot see how, upon any ground of mere human experience or human development, the Apostles could have risen from the gross, material conceptions of the book of Enoch, wherein the kingdom of the Messiah would have simply been a purified, reformed, and exalted copy of the Roman Empire of that day, to the spiritual and truly catholic idea of a kingdom not of this world, which ruled over spirits rather than over bodies.[22] Some persons maintain that Christianity in its doctrines, organisation, and discipline was but the outcome of natural forces working in the world at that epoch. But take this doctrine alone, "My kingdom is not of this world," announced by Christ before Pilate, and impressed upon the Apostles by revelation after revelation, and experience after experience, which they only very gradually assimilated and understood. Where did it come from? How was it the outcome of natural forces? The whole tendency of Jewish thought was in the opposite direction. Nationalism of the most narrow, particular, and limited kind was the predominant idea, specially among those Galilean provincials who furnished the vast majority of the earliest disciples of Jesus Christ. Our minds have been so steeped in the principles of Christian liberalism, we have been so thoroughly taught the rejection of race-prejudice, that we can scarcely realize the narrow and limited ideas which must have ruled the minds of the first Christians, and therefore we miss the full force of this argument for the Divine character of the Christian religion. A Roman Catholic peasant from Connaught, an Ulster Orangeman, a Celtic Presbyterian Highlander, none of these will take a wide, tolerant, generous view of religion. They view the question through their own narrow provincial spectacles. And yet any one of them would have been broad, liberal, and comprehensive when contrasted with the tone and thought of the Galilean provincials of our Lord's day. They lived lonely, solitary lives, away from the din, the pressure, and the business of daily life; they knew nothing of what the great outside world was thinking and doing; they fed their spirits on the glories of the past, and had no room in their gloomy fanaticism for aught that was liberal and truly spiritual. How could men like them have developed the idea of the Catholic Church, boundless as the earth itself, limited by no hereditary or fleshly bonds, and trammelled by no circumstances of race, climate, or kindred? The magnificence of the idea, the grandeur of the conception, is the truest and most sufficient evidence of the divinity of its origin. "In Christ Jesus there is neither Jew nor Greek, bond nor free, male nor female," the rapt expression of an inspired and illuminated Apostle, when compared with this query, "Dost Thou at this time restore the kingdom to Israel?" the darkened utterance of carnal and uninspired minds groping after truth, furnishes to the thinking soul the clearest evidence of the presence of a supernatural power, of a Divine enlightenment, vouchsafed to the Apostles upon the Day of Pentecost. If this higher knowledge, this nobler conception, this spiritualised ideal, came not from God, whence did it come?

I do not think we can press this point of the catholicity and universality of the Christian idea and the Christian society too far. We cannot possibly make too much of it. There were undoubtedly Christian elements, or elements whence Christian ideas were developed, prevalent in the current Judaism of the day. Many a clause of the Lord's Prayer and of the Sermon on the Mount can be paralleled almost word for word from the Jewish teachers and writings of the times immediately preceding our Lord. There was nothing in Christ of that petty vanity of little minds which craves after complete originality, and which will be nothing if not completely new. He was indeed the wise and the good householder, who brought forth out of His treasures things old as well as things new. Many a teacher and thinker, like Philo, whose ideas had been broadened by the Divine training of banishment and enforced exile in Alexandria or in Asia Minor, had risen to nobler and wider views than were current in Palestine. But it was not among these, or such as these, that the catholic ideas of the gospel took their rise. Christianity took its rise among men whose ideas, whose national aspirations, whose religious hopes, were of the narrowest and most limited kind; and yet, amid such surroundings and planted in such a soil, Christianity assumed at once a world-wide mission, rejected at once and peremptorily all mere Judaic exclusiveness, and claimed for itself the widest scope and development. The universality of the Gospel message, the comprehensive, all-embracing character of the Gospel teaching, as set forth in our Lord's parting words, is, we conclude, an ample evidence of its Divine and superhuman origin.

II. *In this passage again there lies hidden the wisest practical teaching for the Church of all ages.* We have warnings against the folly which seeks to unravel the future and penetrate that veil of darkness by which our God in mercy shrouds the unknown. We have taught us the benefits which attend the uncertainties of our Lord's return and of the end of this present dispensation. "It is not for you to know times or seasons." Let us endeavour to work out this point, together with the manifold illustrations of it which the history of the Church affords.

(*a*) The wisdom of the Divine answer will best be seen if we take the matter thus, and suppose our Lord to have responded to the apostolic appeal fixing some definite date for the winding-up of man's probation state, and for that manifestation of the sons of God which will take place at His appearing and His kingdom. Our Lord, in fixing upon some such definite date, must have chosen one that was either near at hand or else one that was removed far off into the distant future. In either of these cases He must have defeated the great object of the Divine society which He was founding. That object was simply this, to teach men how to lead the life of God amid the children of men. The Christian religion has indeed sometimes been taunted with being an unpractical religion, turning men's eyes and attention from the pressing business and interests of daily life to a far-away spiritual state with which man has nothing to do, at least for the present. But is this the case? Has Christianity proved itself unpractical? If so, what has placed Christendom at the head of civilization? The tendencies of great principles are best shown in the actions of vast masses. Individuals may be better or worse than their creeds, but if we wish to see the average result of doctrines we must take their adherents in the mass and enquire as to their effect on them. Here, then, is where we may triumph. The religions of Greece and of Rome are identical in principle, and even in their deities, with the paganism of India, as the investigations of comparative historians have abundantly shown.[23] Compare Christendom and India from the simply practical point of view, and which can show the better record? The paganism of India, Persia, and Western Asia was the parent of the paganism of Greece and Rome. The child has passed away and given place to a noble and spiritual religion, while the parent still remains. And now what is the result? Can the boldest deny that while barbarism, decay, and death reign over the realms of Asiatic paganism, though starting with every advantage upon its side, concerning the religion of the Cross, which is taunted with being an unpractical religion, and concerning that religion alone, can it be said in the language of the rapt Jewish seer, "Wheresoever the waters of that river have come, behold there is life," and that the fair plains, and crowded cities, and the massive material development and civilisation of Europe and of America alike proclaim the truth, that Christianity has the promise of the life which now is as well as of that which is to come?

(b) Our Lord's answer to His Apostles was couched in words suited to develop this practical aspect of His religion. It refused to minister to mere human curiosity, and left men uncertain as to the time of His return, that they might be fruitful workers in the great field of life. And now behold what ill results would have followed had He acted otherwise! The Master in fact says, It is not well for you to know the times or seasons, because such knowledge would strike at the root of practical Christianity. Uncertainty as to the time of the end is the most healthful state for the followers of Christ. Christ holds out the prospect of His own return for a twofold purpose: first, to comfort His people under the daily troubles of life—"Rejoice in the Lord alway: again I will say, Rejoice. Let your forbearance be known unto all men. The Lord is at hand;" "Whatever our hope or joy or crown of glorying, are not even ye, before our Lord Jesus Christ at His coming;" "If we believe that Jesus Christ died and rose again, even so them also that are fallen asleep in Jesus will God bring with Him,"—these and dozens of other passages, which will recur in a moment to every student of St. Paul's writings, prove the power to comfort and sustain exercised by the doctrine of Christ's second coming. But there was another and still more powerful influence exercised by this doctrine. It stirred men up to perpetual watchfulness and untiring care. "Watch, therefore, for ye know neither the day nor the hour;" "Therefore be ye also ready, for in an hour that ye think not the Son of man cometh;" "The night is far spent, the day is at hand; let us therefore cast off the works of darkness, and let us put on the armour of light,"—these and many a similar exhortation of the Master and of his chosen Apostles alike, indicate to us that another great object of this doctrine was to keep Christians perpetually alive with an intense anxiety and a sleepless watchfulness directed towards the person and appearing of Christ. The construction of the gospel narrative shows this.

(c) There are in the New Testament, taken as a whole, two contrasted lines of prophecy concerning the Second Coming of Christ. If in one place the Lord Jesus speaks as if the date of His coming were fixed for His own generation and age, "Verily, I say unto you, this generation shall not pass away till all these things shall be fulfilled," in the very same context He indicates that it is only *after a long time* that the Lord of the servants will return, to take account of their dealings with the property entrusted to them. If St. Paul in one place seems to indicate to the Thessalonians the speedy appearing of Christ and the end of the dispensation, in another epistle he corrects such a misapprehension of his meaning. If the Revelation of St. John in one place represents the awful Figure who moves amid the Churches, watching their works and spying out their secret sins, as saying, "Behold, I come quickly," the same book pictures a long panorama of events, extending over vast spaces of time, destined yet to elapse before the revelation of the city of God and the final triumph of the saints. The doctrine of Christ's second appearing is like many another doctrine in the New Testament. Like the doctrine of God's election, which is undoubtedly there, and yet side by side with election appears as really and truly the doctrine of man's free will; like the doctrine of God's eternal and almighty love, side by side with which appears the existence of a personal devil, and of an abounding iniquity and sorrow which seems to contradict this doctrine; like the doctrine of the Godhead itself, where the Unity of the Divine Nature is most clearly taught, yet side by side therewith appears the manifold personality of Father, Son, and Holy Ghost as existing in that Nature,—so too is it in the case of the doctrine of Christ's Second Coming. We have a twofold antinomy. In one line of prophecy we have depicted the nearness and suddenness of Christ's appearing; in another line we behold that tremendous event thrown into the dim and distant future. And what is the result upon the human mind of such opposite views? It is a healthy, useful, practical result. We are taught the certainty of the event, and the uncertainty of the time of that event; so that hope is stirred, comfort ministered, and watchfulness evoked. We can see this more clearly by imagining the opposite. Suppose Christ had responded to the spirit of the apostolic query, "Dost Thou at this time restore the kingdom to Israel?" and fixed the precise date of His coming? He would in that case have altogether defeated the great end of

His own work and labour. Suppose He had fixed it a thousand years from the time of His Ascension. Then indeed the doctrine of Christ's Second Coming would have lost all personal and practical power over the lives of the generation of Christians then living, or who should live during the hundreds of years which were to elapse till the date appointed. The day of their death, the uncertainty of life, these would be the inspiring motives to activity and devotion felt by the early Christians; while, as a matter of fact, St. Paul never appeals to either of them, but ever appeals to the coming of Christ and His appearing to judgment as the motives to Christian zeal and diligence. But a more serious danger in any such prediction lurks behind. What would have been the result of any such precise prophecy upon the minds of the Christians who lived close to the time of its fulfilment? It would have at once defeated the great end of the Christian religion, as we have already defined it. The near approach of the great final catastrophe would have completely paralysed all exertion, and turned the members of Christ's Church into idle, useless, unpractical religionists. We all know how the near approach of any great event, how the presence of any great excitement, hinders life's daily work. A great joy or a great sorrow, either of them is utterly inconsistent with tranquil thought, with steady labour, with persistent and profitable exertions. The expectation of some tremendous change, whether it be for happiness or misery, creates such a flutter in the spirit that steady application is simply out of the question. So would it have been in our supposed case. As the time fixed for the appearance of our Lord drew nigh, all work, business, labour, the manifold engagements of life, the rearing of families, the culture of the ground, the development of trade and commerce, would be considered a grand impertinence, and man's powers and man's life would be prostrated in view of the approaching catastrophe.

(*d*) Again and again has history verified and amply justified the wisdom of the Master's reply, "It is not for you to know times or seasons." It was justified in apostolic experience. The Second Epistle to the Thessalonians is a commentary on our Lord's teaching in this passage. The Christians of Thessalonica imbibed the notion from St. Paul's words that Christ's appearance to judgment was at hand. Perhaps St. Paul's words in his first Epistle led them into the mistake. The Apostle was not infallible on all questions. He was richly inspired, but he knew nothing of the future save what was expressly revealed, and beyond such express revelations he could only surmise and guess like other men.[24] The Thessalonians, however, were led by him to expect the immediate appearance of Christ, and the result was just what I have depicted. The transcendent event, which they thought impending, paralyzed exertion, destroyed honest and useful labour, scandalized the gospel cause, and compelled St. Paul to use the sternest, sharpest words of censure and rebuke. The language of St. Paul completely justifies our line of argument. He tells us that the spirits of the Thessalonians had been upset, the natural result of a great expectation had been experienced as we might humanly have predicted. The beginning of the second chapter of his Second Epistle proves this: "Now we beseech you, brethren, touching the coming of our Lord Jesus Christ, and our gathering together unto Him; to the end that ye be not quickly shaken from your mind, nor yet be troubled, either by spirit, or by word, or by epistle as from us, as that the day of the Lord is present." See here how he dwells on mental perturbation as the result of high-strung expectation; and that is bad, for mental peace, not mental disturbance, is the portion of Christ's people. Then again he indicates another result of which we have spoken as natural under such circumstances. Idleness and its long train of vices had followed hard upon the mental strain which found place for a time at Thessalonica, and so in the third chapter of the Epistle he writes, "Now we command you, brethren, in the name of our Lord Jesus Christ, that ye withdraw yourselves from every brother that walketh disorderly;" and then he defines the disorderliness of which he complains, "For we hear of some that walk among you disorderly, that work not at all, but are busybodies." Or, to put the matter in a concise shape, and interpret St. Paul into modern language, the expectation of the near approach of the judgment and the personal appearing of Christ had upset the spirits of the Thessalonians; it had so fluttered them they could not attend to ordinary business. Human nature then asserted itself. Idleness resulted from the mental disturbance. Idleness begot gossip, disorder, and scandals. The idlers indeed professed that they ceased from labour in order to give their whole attention to devotion. But St. Paul knew that there was no incompatibility between work and prayer, while he was convinced there was the closest union between idleness and sin. Idleness put on an appearance of great spirituality, but St. Paul effectually met the difficulty. He knew that an idler, no matter how spiritual he pretended to be, must eat, and so he strikes at the root of such mock religion by laying down, "If any will not work, neither let him eat," — a good healthy practical rule, which soon restored the moral and spiritual tone of the Macedonian Church to its normal condition.

(e) The experiences of Thessalonica have been often repeated down through the ages till we come to our own day. I remember a curious instance that I once read of exactly the same spirit, and exactly the same method of cure, as St. Paul used, in the case of an Egyptian monastery in the fifth century. The monks were then divided into two classes. There were monks who laboured diligently and usefully in communities, and there were others who lived idle lives as solitaries, pretending to a spirituality too great to permit them to engage in secular pursuits. A solitary one day entered a monastery presided over by a wise abbot. He found the monks all diligently employed, and, addressing them from his superior standpoint, said, "Labour not for the meat that perisheth." "That is very good, brother," said the abbot. "Take our brother away to his cell," he said to one of his attendants, who left him there to meditate. Nature, after a time, began to assert its sway, and the solitary became hungry. He heard the signal for the midday meal, and wondered that no man came to summon him. Time passed, and the evening meal was announced, and yet no invitation came. At last the solitary left his cell and proceeded in search of food, when the wise abbot impressed on him the Pauline rule that it was quite possible to unite work and worship, labouring for the bread that perisheth while feeding on the bread that is eternal.

The tenth century again verified the wisdom of the Divine denial to reveal the future, or fix a date for Christ's second coming. The year 1000 was regarded in the century immediately preceding it as the limit of the world's existence and the date of Christ's appearing. The belief in this view spread all over Europe, and the result was just the same as at Thessalonica. Men abandoned all work, they left their families to starve, and thought the one great object worth living for was devotion and preparation for their impending change. And the result was widespread misery, famine, disease, and death, while, instead of working any beneficial change upon society at large, the terror through which men had passed brought about, when the dreaded time had gone by, a reaction towards carelessness and vice, all the greater from the self-denial which they had practised for a time. And as it was in the earlier ages so has it been in later times. The people of London were, in the middle of the last century, deluded into a belief that on a certain day the Lord would appear to judgment, with the result that the business of London was suspended for the time. The lives of John Wesley and his fellow-evangelists tell us how diligently they seized the opportunity of preaching repentance and preparation for the coming of Christ, though they shared not the belief in the prediction which gained them their audience. While again in the present century there was a widespread opinion about the year 1830 that the coming of Christ was at hand. It was the time when the Irvingite and Darbyite bodies sprang into existence, in which systems the near approach of the Second Coming forms an important element. Men then thought that it was a mere matter of days or weeks, and in consequence they acted just like the Thessalonians. In their ardour their minds were upset, their business and families neglected, and, as far as in them lay, the work of life and of civilisation was utterly destroyed. While when again we come to later times experience has taught that no men have been more profitless and unpractical Christians than the numbers, by no means inconsiderable, who have spent their lives in vain attempts to fix now for this year, and again for that day, the exact time when the Son of Man should appear. The wisest Christians have acted otherwise. It is told of a foreign bishop, eminent for his sanctity and for the wise guidance which he could give in the spiritual life, that he was once engaged in playing a game of bowls. One of the bystanders was of a critical disposition, and was scandalized at the frivolity of the bishop's occupation, so much beneath the dignity, as it was thought, of his character. "If Christ was to appear the next moment, what would you do?" he asked the bishop. "I would make the next stroke the best possible one," was the wise man's reply. And the reply involved the true principle which the Lord Himself by His refusal to gratify the Apostles' curiosity desired to impress on His people. The uncertainty of the time of Christ's coming, combined with the certainty of the event itself, should stir us up to intensity of purpose, to earnestness of life, to a hallowed enthusiasm to do thoroughly every lawful deed, to think thoroughly every lawful thought, conscious that in so doing we are fulfilling the will and work of the great Judge Himself. Blessed indeed shall be those servants whom the Lord when He cometh shall find so doing.

III. Christ, after He had reproved the spirit of vain curiosity which strikes at the root of all practical effort, then indicates the source of their strength and the sphere of its activity. "Ye shall receive power after the Holy Ghost is come upon you." They were wanting then, as yet, in power, and the Holy Ghost was to supply the want. Intellect, talent, eloquence, wit, all these things are God's gifts, but they are not the source of spiritual power. A man may possess them one and all, and yet be lacking in that spiritual power which came upon the Apostles through the descent of the Spirit. And the sphere of their appointed activity is designated for them. Just as in the earliest days of Christ's public ministry He spake words indicative of the universal spirit of the gospel, and prophesied of a time when men from the east and west should come and sit down in the kingdom of God, while the children of the kingdom should be cast out, so, too, one of His few recorded resurrection sayings now indicates the same: "Ye shall be My witnesses, both in Jerusalem, and in all Judæa, and Samaria, and unto the uttermost part of the earth." Jerusalem, Judæa, — the Apostles were to begin their great practical life of witnessing at home, but they were not to stay there. Samaria was next to have its opportunity, and so we shall find it to have been the case; and then, working from home as centre, the uttermost parts of the earth, a distant Spain from Paul, and a distant India from Thomas, and a barbarous Scythia from Andrew, and a frigid, ocean-girt Britain from a Joseph of Arimathæa,[25] were to learn tidings of the new life in Christ.[26]

# CHAPTER III
# THE ASCENSION OF CHRIST, AND ITS LESSONS

"When He had said these things, as they were looking, He was taken up; and a cloud received Him out of their sight."—Acts i. 9.

In this passage we have the bare literal statement of the fact of Christ's ascension. Let us now consider this supernatural fact, the Ascension, and meditate upon its necessity, and even naturalness, when taken in connection with the whole earthly existence of Incarnate God, and then strive to trace the results and blessings to mankind which followed from it in the gift of the new power, the covenanted gift of the Spirit, and in the spread of the universal religion.

I. The ascension of our Lord is a topic whereon familiarity has worked its usual results; it has lost for most minds the sharpness of its outline and the profundity of its teaching because universally accepted by Christians; and yet no doctrine raises deeper questions, or will yield more profitable and far-reaching lessons. First, then, we may note the place this doctrine holds in apostolic teaching. Taking the records of that teaching contained in the Acts and the Epistles, we find that it occupies a real substantial position. The ascension is there referred to, hinted at, taken as granted, pre-supposed, but it is not obtruded nor dwelt upon overmuch.[27] The resurrection of Christ was the great central point of apostolic testimony; the ascension of Christ was simply a portion of that fundamental doctrine, and a natural deduction from it. If Christ had been raised from the dead and had thus become the firstfruits of the grave, it required but little additional exercise of faith to believe that He had passed into that unseen and immediate presence of Deity where the perfected soul finds its complete satisfaction. In fact, the doctrine of the resurrection apart from the doctrine of the ascension would have been a mutilated fragment, for the natural question would arise, not for one age but for every age, If Jesus of Nazareth has risen from the dead, where is He? Produce your risen Master, and we will believe in Him, would be the triumphant taunt to which Christians would be ever exposed. But then when we closely examine the teaching of the Apostles, we shall find that the doctrine of the ascension was just as really bound up with all their preaching and exhortations as the doctrine of the resurrection; the whole Christian idea as conceived by them just as necessarily involved the doctrine of the ascension as it did that of the resurrection. St. Peter's conception of Christianity, for instance, involved the ascension. Whether in his speech at the election of Matthias, or in his sermon on the day of Pentecost, or in his address in Solomon's Porch after the healing of the crippled beggar, his teaching ever presupposes and involves the ascension. He takes the doctrine and the fact for granted. Jesus is with him the Being "whom the heavens must receive until the times of restoration of all things." So is it too with St. John in his Gospel. He never directly mentions the fact of Christ's ascension, but he always implies it. So too with St. Paul and the other apostolic writers of the New Testament. It would be simply impossible to exhibit in detail the manner in which this doctrine pervades and underlies all St. Paul's teaching. The ascended Saviour occupies the same position in St. Paul's earliest as in his latest writings. Is he speaking of the lives of the Thessalonians in his First Epistle to that Church: "they are waiting for God's Son from heaven." Is he pointing them forward to the second advent of Christ: it is of that day he speaks when "the Lord Himself shall descend from heaven." Is he in Rom. viii. dwelling upon the abiding security of God's elect: he enlarges upon their privileges in "Christ Jesus, who is at the right hand of God, making intercession for us." Is he exhorting the Colossians to a supernatural life: it is because they have supernatural privileges in their ascended Lord. "If ye then were raised with Christ, seek the things above, where Christ is seated on the right hand of God." The more closely the teaching of the Apostles is examined, the more clearly we shall perceive that the ascension was for them no ideal act, no imaginary or fantastic elevation, but a real actual passing of the risen Saviour out of the region and order of the seen and the natural into the region and order of the unseen and supernatural. Just as really as they believed Christ to have risen from the dead, just as really did they in turn believe Him to have ascended into the heavens.

II. But some one may raise curious questions as to the facts of the ascension. Whither, for instance, it may be asked, did our Lord depart when He left this earthly scene? The childish notion that He went up and up far above the most distant star will not of course stand a moment's reflection. It suits the apprehension of childhood, and the innocent illusion should not be too rudely broken; but still, as the advance of years and of wisdom dispels other illusions, so too will this one depart, when the child learns that there is neither up nor down in this visible universe of ours, and that if we were ourselves transported to the moon, which seems shining over our heads, we should see the earth suspended in the blue azure which would overhang the moon and its newly-arrived inhabitants. The Book of the Acts of the Apostles does not describe our Saviour as thus ascending through infinite space. It simply describes Him as removed from off this earthly ball, and then, a cloud shutting Him out from view, Christ passed into the inner and unseen universe wherein He now dwells. The existence of that inner and unseen universe, asserted clearly enough in Scripture, has of late years been curiously confirmed by scientific speculation. Scripture asserts the existence of such an unseen universe, and the ascension implies it. The second coming of our Saviour is never described as a descent from some far-off region. No, it is always spoken of as an Apocalypse,—a drawing back, that is, of a veil which hides an unseen chamber. The angels, as the messengers of their Divine Master, are described by Christ in Matt. xiii. as "coming forth" from the secret place of the Most High to execute His behests.[28] What a solemn light such a scriptural view sheds upon life! The unseen world is not at some vast distance, but, as the ascension would seem to imply, close at hand, shut out from us by that thin veil of matter which angelic hands will one day rend for ever. And then how wondrously the speculations of that remarkable book to which I have referred, *The Unseen Universe*, lend themselves to this scriptural idea, pointing out the necessity imposed by modern scientific thought for postulating some such interior spiritual sphere, of which the external and material universe may be regarded as a temporary manifestation and development.[29] The doctrine of the ascension, when rightly understood, presents then no difficulties from a scientific point of view, but is rather in strictest accordance with the highest and subtlest forms of modern thought. But when we advance still closer to the heart of this doctrine, and endeavour, quite apart from all mere carping criticism, to realize its meaning and its power, we shall perceive a profound fitness, beauty, and harmony in this mysterious fact. Laying apart all carping criticism, I say, because the critical spirit is not appreciative, it is on the look-out for faults, it necessarily involves a certain assumption of superiority in the critic to the thing or doctrine criticised; and most certainly it is not to the proud critic, but to the humble soul alone, that the doctrines of the Cross yield of their sweetness, and make revelation of their profound depths. We can perceive a fitness and a naturalness in the ascension; we can advance even farther still, and behold an absolute necessity for it, if Christ's work was to be perfected in all its details, and Christianity to become, not a narrow local religion, but a universal and catholic Church.

III. The ascension was a fitting and a natural termination of Christ's earthly ministry, considering the Christian conception of His sacred Personality. When the Second Person of the Eternal Trinity wished to reveal the life of God among men, and to elevate humanity by associating it for ever with the person of Him who was the Eternal God, He left the glory which He had with the Father before the world was, and entered upon the world of humanity through a miraculous door. "The Son, which is the Word of the Father, begotten from everlasting of the Father, the very and eternal God, and of one substance with the Father, took Man's nature in the womb of the blessed Virgin, of her substance." These are the careful, accurate, well-balanced words of the second Article of the Church of England, in which all English-speaking Christians substantially agree. They are accurate, I say, and well-balanced, avoiding the Scylla of Nestorianism, which divides Christ's person, on the one side, and the Charybdis of Eutychianism, which denies His humanity, on the other. The Person of God, the Eternal Word, assumed human nature, not a human person, but human nature, so that God might be able, acting in and through this human nature as His instrument, to teach mankind and to die for mankind. God entered upon the sphere of the seen and the temporal by a miraculous door. His life and work were marked all through by miracle, His death and resurrection were encompassed with miracle; and it was fitting, considering the whole course of His earthly career, that His departure from this world should be through another miraculous door. The departure of the Eternal King was, like His first approach, a part of a scheme which forms one united and harmonious whole. The Incarnation and the Ascension were necessarily related the one to the other.

IV. Again, we may advance a step further, and say that not only was the ascension a natural and fitting termination to the activities of the Eternal Son manifest in the flesh, it was a necessary completion and finish. "It is expedient," said Christ Himself, "that I go away; for if I go not away the Comforter will not come to you." For some reason secret from us, but hidden in the awful depths of that Being who is the beginning and the end, the source and the condition of all created existence, the return of Christ to the bosom of the Father was absolutely necessary before the outpouring of the Divine Spirit of Life and Love could take place. How this can have been we know not. We only know the fact as revealed to us by Jesus Christ and affirmed by His Apostles. "Being therefore by the right hand of God exalted, and having received of the Father the promise of the Holy Ghost, He hath poured forth this which ye see and hear," is the testimony of the illuminated Apostle St. Peter on the day of Pentecost, speaking in strict unison with the teaching of Jesus Christ Himself as reported in St. John's Gospel. But without endeavouring to intrude into these mysteries of the Divine nature, into which even the angels themselves pry not, we behold in the character and constitution of Christ's Church and Christ's religion sufficient reasons to show us the Divine expediency of our Lord's ascension.

Let us take the matter very plainly and simply thus. Had our Lord not ascended into the unseen state whence He had emerged for the purpose of rescuing mankind from that horrible pit, that mire and clay of pollution, immorality, and selfishness in which it lay at the epoch of the Christian era, He must in that case (always proceeding on the supposition that He had risen from the dead, because we always suppose our readers to be believers) have remained permanently or temporarily resident in some one place. He might have chosen Jerusalem, the city of the great King, as His abode, and this would have seemed to the religious men of His time quite natural. The same instinct of religious conservatism which made the Twelve to tarry at Jerusalem even when persecution seemed to threaten the infant Church with destruction, would have led the risen Christ to fix His abode at the city which every pious Jew regarded as the special seat of Jehovah. There would have been nothing to tempt Him to Antioch, or Athens, or Alexandria, or Rome. None of these cities could have held out any inducement or put forward any claim comparable for one moment with that which the name, the traditions, and the circumstances of Jerusalem triumphantly maintained. Nay, rather the tone and temper of those cities must have rendered them abhorrent as dwelling-places to the great Teacher of holiness and purity.

At any rate, the risen Saviour, if He remained upon earth, must have chosen some one place where His presence and His personal glory would have been manifested. Now let us contemplate, and work out in some detail, the results which would have inevitably followed. The place chosen by our Lord as His visible dwelling-place must then have become the centre of the whole Church. At that spot pilgrims from every land must necessarily have assembled. To it would have resorted the doubter to have his difficulties resolved, the sick and weak to have their ailments cured, the men of profound devotion to bathe themselves and lose themselves in the immediate presence of Incarnate Deity. All interest in local Churches or local work would have been destroyed, because every eye and every heart would be perpetually turning towards the one spot where the risen Lord was dwelling, and where personal adoration could be paid to Him. All honest, manly self-reliance would have been lost for individuals, for Churches, and for nations. Whenever a difficulty or controversy arose, either in the personal or ecclesiastical, the social or political sphere, men, instead of trying to solve it for themselves under the guidance of the Divine Spirit, would have hurried off with it to the Fount of supernatural wisdom, as an oracle, like the fabled pagan ones of old, whence direction would infallibly be gained. Judaism would have triumphed and the dispensation of the Spirit would have ceased.

The whole idea, too, of Christianity as a scheme of moral probation would have been overthrown. Christ as belonging to the supernatural sphere would of course have been raised above the laws of time and space. For Him the powers of earth and the terrors of earth would have had no meaning, and heavenly glory, shooting forth from His sacred Person, would have compelled obedience and acceptance of His laws at the hands of His most deadly and obstinate foes. Sight would have taken the place of faith, and the terrified submission of slaves would have been substituted for the moral, loving obedience of the regenerate soul. The whole social order of life would also have been overthrown. God has now placed men in families, societies, and nations, that they might be proved by the very difficulties of their positions. The probation which God thereby exercises over men extends not to those alone who are subject to government, but to those as well who are entrusted with government. God by His present system tries governors and governed, kings and subjects, magistrates and people, parents and children, teachers and pupils, all alike. Any one who has ever made the experiment knows, however, how impossible it is to give full play to one's power and faculties, whether of government or of teaching, when overlooked by the conscious presence of one who can supersede and control all the arrangements made or all the instructions offered. Nervousness comes in, and paralyzes the best efforts a man might otherwise make. So would it have been had Christ remained upon earth. Neither those placed in authority nor those set under authority would have done their best or played their part effectually, feeling there was One standing by whose all-piercing gaze could see the imperfection of their noblest actions. A modern illustration or two will perhaps exhibit more plainly what we mean. London, with its enormous and ever-growing population, constitutes in many respects a portentous danger to our national life. But thoughtful colonists often see in it a danger which does not strike us here at home. London has a tendency to sap the springs of local interest and local self-reliance. Every colonist who attains to wealth and position feels himself an exile till he can get back to London, which he regards as the one centre of the empire worth living at; while the colonies, viewing London as the centre of England's wealth, power, and resources, feel naturally inclined to fling upon London the care and responsibility of the empire's protection, in which all its separate parts should take their proportionate share.

Or again, let us take an illustration from the ecclesiastical sphere. M. Renan is a writer who has depicted the early history of the Church from a sceptical point of view. He has done so with all the skill of a novelist, aided by the resources of immense erudition. Before Renan became a sceptic he was a Roman Catholic, and a student for the priesthood in one of those narrow seminaries wherein exclusively the Roman Church now trains her clergy. Renan can never, therefore, view Christianity save through a Roman medium, and from a Roman Catholic standpoint. Descended himself from a Jewish stock, and trained up in Roman Catholic ideas, Renan, sceptic though he be, is lost in admiration of the Papacy, because it has combined the Jewish and the ancient imperial ideas, so that Rome having taken the place which Jerusalem once occupied in the spiritual organisation, has now become the local centre of unity for the Latin Church, where Christ's vicar visibly bears sway, to whom resort can be had from every land as an authoritative guide, and whence he and he alone dispenses with more than imperial sway the gifts and graces of Divine love. Rome is for the Latin Church the centre of the earth, and upon Rome and its spiritual ruler all interest is concentrated as Christ's earthly representative and deputy. Now what London is to our own colonists, what Rome is for its adherents, such, and infinitely more, would the localised presence of Jesus Christ have been for the Christian world had not the ascension taken place. The Papacy, instead of securing the universality of the Church, strikes a deadly blow at it. The Papacy, with its centralised ecclesiastical despotism, is not the Catholic Church, it is simply the local Church of Rome spread out into all the world; just as Judaism never was and never could have been catholic in its ideal, no matter how widely spread it was, from the shores of the British Islands in the West to the far-distant regions of China in the East. Its adherents, like the eunuch of Ethiopia, never felt a local interest in their religion,—their eyes ever turned towards Zion, the city of the great King. And so would it have been with the bodily presence of Christ manifested in one spot; the Christian Church would still have remained a purely local institution, and the place where the risen Saviour was manifested would have been for Christian people the one centre towards which all their thoughts would gravitate, to the complete neglect of those home interests and labours in which each individual Church ought to find the special work appointed for it by the Master. It was expedient for the Church that Christ should go away, to deepen faith, to strengthen Christian self-reliance, to offer play and scope for the power and work of the Holy Ghost, to render life a testing-ground, and a place of probation for the higher life to come. But above all, it was expedient that Christ should go away in order that the Church might rise out of and above that narrow provincialism in which the Jewish spirit would fain bind it, might attain to a truly universal and catholic position, and thus fulfil the Master's magnificent prophecy to the woman of Samaria, when, viewing in spirit the Church's onward march, beholding it bursting all local and national bonds, recognising it as the religion of universal humanity, He proclaimed its destiny in words which shall never die—"Woman, believe Me, the hour cometh when neither in this mountain nor in Jerusalem shall ye worship the Father. God is a Spirit, and they that worship Him must worship Him in spirit and in truth." The ascension of Jesus Christ was absolutely necessary to equip the Church for its universal mission, by withdrawing the bodily presence of Christ into that unseen region which bears no special relation to any terrestrial locality, but is the common destiny, the true fatherland, of all the sons of God.[30]

V. We have now seen how the ascension was needful for the Church, by rendering Christ an ideal object of worship for the whole human race, thus saving it from that tendency to mere localism which would have utterly changed its character. We can also trace another great blessing involved in it. The ascension glorified humanity as humanity, and ennobled man viewed simply as man. The ascension thus transformed life by adding a new dignity to life and to life's duties.

This was a very necessary lesson for the ancient world, especially the ancient Gentile world, which Christ came to enlighten and to save. Man, considered by himself as man, had no peculiar dignity in the popular religious estimate of Greece and Rome. A Greek or a Roman was a dignified person, not, however, in virtue of his humanity, but in virtue of his Greek or Roman citizenship. The most pious Greeks or Romans simply despised mankind as such, regarding all other nations as barbarians, and treating them accordingly. Roman law exempted Roman citizens from degrading and cruel punishments, which they reserved for men outside the limits of Roman citizenship, because that humanity as humanity had no dignity attached to it in their estimation. The gladiatorial shows were the most striking illustration of this contempt for human nature which paganism inculcated.[31]

It is a notable evidence, too, of the firm grasp upon the popular mind this contempt had taken, of the awful depths to which the fatal infection had permeated the public conscience, that it was not till four hundred years after the Incarnation, and not till one hundred years after the triumph of Christianity, that these frightful carnivals of human blood and slaughter yielded to the gentler and nobler principles of the religion of the Cross. No name indeed in the long roll of Christian martyrs, who for truth and righteousness have laid down their lives, deserves higher mention than that of Telemachus, the Asiatic monk, who, in the year 404, hearing that the city, where the blessed Apostles Peter and Paul had suffered, was still disgraced by the gladiatorial shows, made his way to Rome, and by the sacrifice of his own life terminated them for ever within the bounds of Christendom. Telemachus rushed between the combatants in the arena, flung them asunder, and then was stoned to death by the mob, infuriated at the interruption of their favourite amusement.[32] A tragic but glorious ending indeed, showing clearly how little the Roman mob realized as yet the doctrine of the sanctity of human nature; how powerful was the sway which paganism and pagan modes of thought held as yet over the populace of nominally Christian Rome; the tradition of which even still perpetuates itself in the cruel bull-fights of Spain. From the beginning, however, Christianity took exactly the opposite course, declaring to all the dignity and glory of human nature in itself. The Incarnation was in itself a magnificent proclamation of this great elevating and civilising truth. The title Son of Man, which Christ, rising above all narrow Jewish nationalism, assumed to Himself, was a republication of the same dogma; and then, to crown the whole fabric, comes the doctrine of the ascension, wherein mankind was taught that human nature as joined to the person of God has ascended into the holiest place of the universe, so that henceforth the humblest and lowliest can view his humanity as allied with that elder Brother who in the reality of human flesh—glorified, indeed, spiritualised and refined by the secret, searching processes of death—has passed within the veil, now to appear in the presence of God for us. What new light must have been shed upon life—the life of the barbarian and of the slave—crushed beneath the popular theory of St. Paul's day![33] What new dignity this doctrine imparted to the bodies of the outcast and despised, counted fit food only for the cross, the stake, or the arena! Man might despise them and ill-treat them, yet their bodies were made like unto the one glorious Body for ever united to God, and therefore they were comforted, elevated, enabled to endure as seeing Him who is invisible. Cannot we see many examples of the consoling, elevating power of the ascension in the New Testament? Take St. Paul's writings, and there we trace the influence of the ascension in every page. Take the very lowest case. Slaves under the conditions of ancient society occupied the most degraded position. Their duties were of the humblest type, their treatment of the worst description, their punishments of the most terrible character.[34] Yet for even these oppressed and degraded beings the doctrine of the ascension transformed life, because it endowed that menial service which they rendered with a new dignity. "Servants, obey in all things your masters according to the flesh; not with eye service, as men pleasers, but in singleness of heart, fearing God." And why? Because life has been enriched with a new motive: "Whatsoever ye do, do it heartily as to the Lord, and not unto men; knowing that of the Lord ye shall receive the reward of the inheritance; for ye serve the Lord Christ." *Ye serve the Lord Christ.* That was the supreme point. The cooking of a dinner, the dressing of an imperious lady's hair, the teaching of a careless or refractory pupil—all these things were transfigured into the service of the ascended Lord. And as with the servant, so was it with their masters. The ascension furnished them with a new and practical motive, which, at first leading to kindly treatment and generous actions, would one day, by the force of logical deduction as well as of Christian principle, lead to the utter extinction of slavery. "Masters, render unto your servants that which is just and equal, knowing that ye also have a Master in heaven." The doctrine of the ascension diffused sweetness and light throughout the whole Christian system, furnishing a practical motive, offering an ever-present and eternal sanction, urging men upwards and onwards; without which neither the Church nor the world would ever have reached that high level of mercy, charity, and purity which men now enjoy. Perhaps here again the present age may see the doctrine of the ascension asserting its glory and its power in the same direction. Much of modern speculation tends to debase and belittle the human body, teaching theories respecting its origin which have a natural tendency to degrade the popular standard. If people come to think of their bodies as derived from a low source, they will be apt to think a low standard of morals as befitting bodies so descended. The doctrine of evolution has not, to say the least, an elevating influence upon the masses. I say nothing against it. One or two passages in the Bible, as Gen. ii. 7, seem to support it, appearing, as that verse does, to make a division between the creation of the body of man and the creation of his spirit.[35] But the broad tendency of such speculation lies in a downward moral direction. Here the doctrine of the ascension steps in to raise for us, as it raised for the materialists of St. Paul's day, the standard of current conceptions, and to teach men a higher and a nobler view. We leave to science the investigation of the past and of the lowly sources whence man's body may have come; but the doctrine of the ascension speaks of its present sanctity and of its future glory, telling of the human body as a body of humiliation and of lowliness indeed, but yet proclaiming it as even now, in the person of Christ, ascended into the heavens, and seated on the throne of the Most High. It may have been once humble in its origin; it is now glorious in its dignity and elevation; and that dignity and that elevation shed a halo upon human nature, no matter how degraded and wherever it may be found, because it is like unto that Body, the firstfruits of humanity, which stands at the right hand of God. Thus the doctrine of the ascension becomes for the Christian the ever-flowing fountain of dignity, of purity, and of mercy, teaching us to call no man common or unclean, because all have been made like unto the image of the Son of God.

# CHAPTER IV
# THE ELECTION OF MATTHIAS

"They prayed, and said, Thou, Lord, which knowest the
hearts of all men, shew of these two the one whom Thou
hast chosen, to take the place in this ministry and apostleship
from which Judas fell away, that he might go to his own
place. And they gave lots for them; and the lot fell upon
Matthias; and he was numbered with the eleven apostles." —
Acts i. 24-6.

We have selected the incident of this apostolic election as the central
point round which to group the events of the ten days' expectation which
elapsed between the Ascension and Pentecost. But though this election is a
most important fact, in itself and in the principles involved therein, yet there
are numerous other circumstances in this waiting time which demand and
will amply repay our thoughtful attention.

I. There is, for instance, the simple fact that ten days were allowed to
elapse between Christ's departure and the fulfilment of His promise to send
the Comforter to take His place with His bereaved flock. The work of the
world's salvation depended upon the outcome of this Divine agent. "Tarry
ye in the city till ye be endued with power from on high;" and all the time
souls were hurrying on to destruction, and society was becoming worse
and worse, and Satan's hold upon the world was daily growing in strength.
God, however, acted in this interval according to the principles we see
illustrated in nature as well as in revelation. He does nothing in a hurry. The
Incarnation was postponed for thousands of years. When the Incarnation
took place, Christ grew up slowly, and developed patiently, till the day of
His manifestation to Israel. And now that Christ's public work on earth was
done, there is no haste in the further development of the plan of salvation,
but ten days are suffered to elapse before His promise is fulfilled. What a
rebuke we read in the Divine methods of that faithless unbelieving haste
which marks and mars so many of our efforts for truth and righteousness,
and specially so in these concluding years of the nineteenth century. Never
did the Church stand more in need of the lesson so often thus impressed
upon her by her Divine Teacher. As Christ did not strive nor cry, neither
did any man hear His voice in the streets, so neither did He make haste,

because He lived animated by Divine strength and wisdom, which make even apparent delay and defeat conduce to the attainment of the highest ends of love and mercy. And so, too, Christ's Church still does not need the bustle, the haste, the unnatural excitement which the world thinks needful, because she labours under a sense of Divine guidance, and imitates His example who kept His Apostles waiting ten long days before He fulfilled His appointed promise. What a lesson of comfort, again, this Divine delay teaches! We are often inclined to murmur in secret at the slow progress of God's Church and kingdom. We think that if we had the management of the world's affairs things would have been ordered otherwise, and the progress of truth be one long-continued march of triumph. A consideration of the Divine delays in the past helps us to bear this burden, though it may not explain the difficulty. God's delays have turned out to His greater glory in the past, and they who wait patiently upon Him will find the Divine delays of the present dispensation equally well ordered.

II. Then again, how carefully, even in His delays, God honours the elder dispensation, though now it had grown old and was ready to vanish away. Christianity had none of that revolutionary spirit which makes a clean sweep of old institutions to build up a new fabric in their stead. Christianity, on the contrary, rooted itself in the past, retained old institutions and old ideas, elevating indeed and spiritualising them, and thus slowly broadened down from precedent to precedent. This truly conservative spirit of the new dispensation is manifest in every arrangement, and specially reveals itself in the times selected for the great events of our Lord's ministry—Easter, Ascension, then the ten days of expectation, and then Pentecost. And it was most fitting that it should be so. The old dispensation was a shadow and picture of the higher and better covenant one day to be unfolded. Moses was told to make the tabernacle after the pattern shown to him in the mount, and the whole typical system of Judaism was modelled after a heavenly original to which Christ conformed in the work of man's salvation.

At the first Passover, the paschal lamb was offered up and the deliverance from Egypt effected; and so, too, at the Passover the true Paschal Lamb, Jesus Christ, was presented unto God as an acceptable sacrifice, and the deliverance effected of the true Israel from the spiritual Egypt of the world. Forty days after the Passover, Israel came to the mount of God, into which Moses ascended that he might receive gifts for the people; and forty days after the last great Paschal Offering, the great spiritual Captain and Deliverer ascended into the Mount of God, that He, in turn, might receive highest spiritual blessings and a new law of life for God's true people. Then there came the ten days of expectation and trial, when the Apostles were called to wait upon God and prove the blessings of patient abiding upon Him, just as the Israelites were called to wait upon God while Moses was absent in the mount. But how different the conduct of the Apostles from that of the more carnal Jews! How typical of the future of the two religions—the Jewish and the Christian! The Jews walked by sight, and not by faith; they grew impatient, and made an image, the golden calf, to be their visible Deity. The Apostles tarried in patience, because they were walking by faith, and they received in return the blessing of an ever-present unseen Guide and Comforter to lead them, and all who like them seek His help, into the ways of truth and peace. And then, when the waiting time is past, the feast of Pentecost comes, and at Pentecost, the feast of the giving of the old law, as the Jews counted it, the new law of life and power, written not on stony tables, but on the fleshy tables of the heart, is granted in the gift of the Divine Comforter. All the lines of the old system are carefully followed, and Christianity is thus shown to be, not a novel invention, but the development and fulfilment of God's ancient purposes.[36] We can scarcely appreciate nowadays the importance and stress laid upon this view among the ancient expositors and apologists. It was a favourite taunt used by the pagans of Greece and Rome against Christianity that it was only a religion of yesterday, a mere novelty, as compared with their own systems, which descended to them from the dawn of history. This taunt has been indeed most useful in its results for us moderns, because it led the ancient Christians to pay the most careful attention to chronology and historical studies, producing as the result works like *The Chronicle of Eusebius*, to which secular history itself owes the greatest obligations.

The heathens reproached Christians with the novelty of their faith, and then the early Christians replied by pointing to history, which proved that the Jewish religion was far older than any other, maintaining at the same time that Christianity was merely the development of the Jewish religion, the completion and fulfilment in fact and reality of what Judaism had shadowed forth in the ritual of the Passover and of Pentecost.[37]

III. We notice again in this connection the place where the Apostles met, and the manner in which they continued to assemble after the ascension, and while they waited for the fulfilment of the Master's promise: "They returned unto Jerusalem, and they went up into an upper chamber." Round this upper room at Jerusalem has gathered many a story dating from very early ages indeed. The upper room in which they assembled has been identified with the chamber in which the Last Supper was celebrated, and where the gift of the Holy Ghost was first received, and that from ancient times. Epiphanius, a Christian writer of the fourth century, to whom we owe much precious information concerning the early ages of the Church, tells us that there was a church built on this spot even in Hadrian's time, that is, about the year 120 A.D.[38] The Empress Helena, again, the mother of Constantine the Great, identified or thought she identified the spot, and built a splendid church to mark it out for all time; and succeeding ages have spent much care and thought upon it. St. Cyril of Jerusalem was a writer little referred to and little known in our day, who yet has much precious truth to teach us. He was a learned bishop of Jerusalem about the middle of the fourth century, and he left us catechetical lectures, showing what pains and trouble the Early Church took in the inculcation of the fundamental articles of the Christian creed. His catechetical lectures, delivered to the candidates for baptism, contain much valuable evidence of the belief, the practice, and the discipline of the early ages, and they mention among other points the church built upon Mount Zion on the spot once occupied by this upper room. The tradition, then, which deals with this chamber and points out its site goes back to the ages of persecution; and yet it is notable how little trouble the book of the Acts of the Apostles takes in this matter. It is just the same with this upper chamber as with the other localities in which our Lord's mighty works were wrought. The Gospels tell us not where His temptations occurred, though man has often tried to fix the exact locality. The site of the Transfiguration and of the true Mount of Beatitudes has engaged much human curiosity; the scene of Peter's vision at Joppa and of St. Paul's conversion on the road to Damascus,—all these and many other divinely honoured localities of the Old as well as of the New Testament have been shrouded from us in thickest darkness, that we might learn not to fix our eyes upon the external husk, the locality, the circumstances, the time, which are nothing, but upon the interior spirit, the love, the unity, the devotion and self-sacrifice which constitute in the Divine sight the very heart and core of our holy religion.[39] They assembled themselves, too, in this upper chamber in a united spirit, such as Christianity, though only in an undeveloped shape, already dictated. The Apostles "continued steadfastly in prayer, with the women also, and Mary, the mother of Jesus." The spirit of Christianity was, I say, already manifesting itself.

In the temple, as in the synagogues to this day, the women prayed in a separate place; they were not united with the men, but parted from them by a screen. But in Christ Jesus there was to be neither male nor female. The man in virtue of his manhood had no advantage or superiority over the woman in virtue of her womanhood; and so the Apostles gathered themselves at the footstool of their common Father in union with the women, and with Mary the mother of Jesus. How simple, again, this last mention of the Blessed Virgin Mother of the Lord! how strangely and strongly contrasted the scriptural record is with the fables and legends which have grown up round the memory of her whom all generations must ever call blessed. Nothing, in fact, shows more plainly the historic character of the book we are studying than a comparison of this last simple notice with the legend of the assumption of the Blessed Virgin as it has been held since the fifth century, and as it is now believed in the Church of Rome. The popular account of this fabled incident arose in the East amid the controversies which rent the Church concerning the Person of Christ in the fifth century. It taught that the Holy Virgin, a year or so after the ascension, besought the Lord to release her; upon which the angel Gabriel was sent to announce her departure in three days' time. The Apostles were thereupon summoned from the different parts of the world whither they had departed. John came from Ephesus, Peter from Rome, Thomas from India, each being miraculously wafted on a cloud from his special sphere of labour, while those of the apostolic company who had died were raised for the occasion. On the third day the Lord descended from heaven with the angels, and took to Himself the soul of the Virgin. The Jews then attempted to burn the body, which was miraculously rescued and buried in a new tomb, prepared by Joseph of Arimathea in the Valley of Jehoshaphat. For two days the angels were heard singing at the tomb, but on the third day their songs ceased, and the Apostles then knew that the body had been transferred to Paradise. St. Thomas was indeed vouchsafed a glimpse of her ascension, and at his request she dropped him her girdle as a token, whereupon he went to his brother Apostles and declared her sepulchre to be empty. The Apostles regarded this as merely a sign of his customary incredulity, but on the production of the girdle they were convinced, and on visiting the grave found the body was gone.[40]

Can any contrast be greater or more striking between the inspired narrative, composed for the purpose of ministering to godly life and practice, and such legendary fables as this, invented to gratify mere human curiosity, or to secure a temporary controversial triumph? The Divine narrative shrouds in thickest darkness details which have no spiritual significance, no direct bearing on the work of man's salvation. The human fable intrudes into the things unseen, and revels with a childish delight in the regions of the supernatural and miraculous.

What a striking likeness do we trace between the composition of the Acts and of the Gospels in this direction! The self-restraint of the evangelical writers is wondrous. Had the Evangelists been mere human biographers, how they would have delighted to expatiate on the childhood and youth and earlier years of Christ's manhood. The apocryphal Gospels composed in the second and third centuries show us what our Gospels would have been had they been written by men destitute of an abundant supply of the Divine Spirit. They enter into the most minute incidents of our Lord's childhood, heaven." He was eminently energetic, vigorous, quick in action. But we find no traces of that despotic authority as prince of the Apostles and supreme head over the whole Church with which some would fain invest St. Peter and his successors. St. Peter steps forward first on this occasion, as again on the day of Pentecost, and again before the high priest after the healing of the impotent man, and yet again at the council of Jerusalem; for, as we have already noted, St. Peter possessed in abundance that natural energy which impels a man to action without any desire for notoriety or any wish to thrust himself into positions of undue eminence. But then on every occasion St. Peter speaks as an equal to his equals. He claims no supreme authority; no authority, in fact, at all over and beyond what the others possessed. He does not, for instance, on this occasion claim the right as Christ's vicar to nominate an Apostle into the place of Judas. He merely asserts his lawful place in Christ's kingdom as first among a body of equals to suggest a course of action to the whole body which he knew to be in keeping with the Master's wishes, and in fulfilment of His revealed intentions.

V. The address of St. Peter led the Apostles to practical action. He laid the basis of it in the book of Psalms, the mystical application of which to our Lord and His sufferings he recognises, selecting passages from the sixty-ninth and the one hundred and ninth Psalms as depicting the sin and the fate of Judas Iscariot;[41] and then sets forth the necessity of filling up the vacancy in the apostolic office, a fact of which he had doubtless been certified by the Master Himself. He speaks as if the College of the Apostles had a definite work and office; a witness peculiar to themselves as Apostles, which no others except Apostles could render. This is manifest from the language of St. Peter. He lays down the conditions of a possible Apostle: he must have been a witness of all that Jesus had done and taught from the time of His baptism to His ascension. But this qualification alone would not make a man an Apostle, or qualify him to bear the witness peculiar to the apostolic office. There were evidently numerous such witnesses, but they were not Apostles, and had none of the power and privileges of the Twelve. He must be chosen by his brother Apostles, and their choice must be endorsed by Heaven; and then the chosen witness, who had known the past, could testify to the resurrection in particular, with a weight, authority, and dignity he never possessed before. The apostolic office was the germ out of which the whole Christian ministry was developed, and the apostolic witness was typical of that witness to the resurrection which is not the duty alone, but also the strength and glory of the Christian ministry; for it is only as the ministers and witnesses of a risen and glorified Christ that they differ from the officials of a purely human association.[42]

tell us of His games, His schoolboy days, of the flashes of the supernatural glory which ever betrayed the awful Being who lay hidden beneath. The Gospels, on the other hand, fling a hallowed and reverent veil over all the details, or almost all the details, of our Lord's early life. They tell us of His birth, and its circumstances and surroundings, that we might learn the needful lesson of the infinite glory, the transcendent greatness of lowliness and humiliation. They give us a glimpse of our Lord's development when twelve years old, that we may learn the spiritual strength and force which are produced through the discipline of obedience and patient waiting upon God; and then all else is concealed from human vision till the hour was come for the manifestation of the full-orbed God-Man. And as it was with the Eternal Son, so was it with that earthly parent whom the consensus of universal Christendom has agreed to honour as the type of devout faith, of humble submission, of loving motherhood. Fable has grown thick round her in mere human narrative, but when we turn to the inspired Word, whether in the Gospels or in the Acts,—for it is all the same in both,—we find a story simple, restrained, and yet captivating in all its details, ministering indeed to no prurient curiosity, yet rich in all the materials which serve to devout meditation, culminating in this last record, where the earthly parent finally disappears from out of sight, eclipsed by the heavenly glory of the Divine Son:—"These all continued stedfastly in prayer, with the women, and Mary, the mother of Jesus."

IV. And then we have the record of the apostolic election, which is rich in teaching. We note the person who took the first step, and his character, so thoroughly in unison with that picture which the four Gospels present. St. Peter was not a forward man in the bad sense of the word, but he possessed that energetic, forcible character to which men yield a natural leadership. Till St. Paul appeared St. Peter was regarded as the spokesman of the apostolic band, just as during our Lord's earthly ministry the same position was by tacit consent accorded to him. He was one of those men who cannot remain inactive, especially when they see anything wanting. There are some men who can see a defect just as clearly, but their first thought is, What have I to do with it? They behold the need, but it never strikes them that they should attempt to rectify it. St. Peter was just the opposite: when he saw a fault or a want his disposition and his natural gifts at once impelled him to strive to rectify it. When our Lord, in view of the contending rumours afloat concerning His ministry and authority, applied this searching test to His Apostles, "But whom do ye say that I am?" it was Peter that boldly responded, "Thou art the Christ, the Son of the living God." Just as a short time afterwards the same Peter incurred Christ's condemnation when he rebuked the Saviour for the prophecy of His forthcoming death and humiliation. The character of St. Peter as depicted in the Gospels and the Acts is at unison with itself. It is that of one ever generous, courageous, intensely sympathetic, impulsive, but deficient, as impulsive and sympathetic characters often are, in that staying power, that capacity to bear up under defeat, discouragement, and darkness which so conspicuously marked out the great Apostle of the Gentiles, and made him such a pillar in the spiritual temple of the New Jerusalem. Yet St. Peter did his own work, for God can ever find employment suitable to every type of that vast variety of temperament which finds shelter beneath the roof of Christ's Church. St. Peter's impulsiveness, chastened by prayer, solemnized by his own sad personal experience, deepened by the bitter sorrow consequent on his terrible fall, urged him to take the first conscious step as the leader of the newly-constituted society. How very similar the Peter of the Acts is to the Peter of St. Matthew; what an undesigned evidence of the truth of these records we trace in the picture of St. Peter presented by either narrative! Just as St. Peter was in the Gospels the first to confess at Cæsarea, the first to strike in the garden, the first to fail in the high priest's palace, so was he the first "to stand up in these days in the midst of the brethren," and propose the first corporate movement on the Church's part.

Here again we note that his attitude at this apostolic election proves that the interviews which St. Peter held with Christ after the Resurrection must have been lengthened, intimate, and frequent, for St. Peter's whole view of the Christian organization seems thoroughly changed. Christ had continued with His Apostles during forty days, speaking to them of the things concerning the kingdom of God; and St. Peter, as he had been for years one of the Lord's most intimate friends, so he doubtless still held the same trusted position in these post-resurrection days. The Lord revealed to him the outlines of His kingdom, and sketched for him the main lines of its development, teaching him that the Church was not to be a knot of personal disciples, dependent upon His manifested bodily presence, and dissolving into its original elements as soon as that bodily presence ceased to be realized by the eye of sense; but was rather to be a corporation with perpetual succession, to use legal language, whose great work was to be an unceasing witness to Christ's resurrection. If Peter's mind had not been thus illuminated and guided by the personal instruction of Christ, how came it to pass that prior to the descent of the Spirit the Apostles move with no uncertain step in this matter, and unhesitatingly fill up the blank in the sacred college by the election of Matthias into the place left vacant by the terrible fall of Judas? The speech of St. Peter and the choice of this new Apostle reflect light back upon the forty days of waiting. No objection is raised, no warm debate takes place such as heralded the solution of the

vexed question concerning circumcision at the council of Jerusalem; no one suggests that as Christ Himself had not supplied the vacancy the choice should be postponed till after the fulfilment of the Master's mysterious promise, because they were all instructed as to our Lord's wishes by the conversations held with Christ during His risen and glorified life.

Let us pause a little to meditate upon an objection which might have been here raised. Why fill up what Christ Himself left vacant? some short-sighted objector might have urged; and yet we see good reason why Christ may have omitted to supply the place of Judas, and may have designed that the Apostles themselves should have done so. Our Lord Jesus Christ gifted His Apostles with corporate power; He bestowed upon them authority to act in His stead and name; and it is not God's way of action to grant power and authority, and then to allow it to remain unexercised and undeveloped. When God confers any gift He expects that it shall be used for His honour and man's benefit. The Lord had bestowed upon the Apostles the highest honour, the most wondrous power ever given to men. He had called them to an office of which He Himself had spoken very mysterious things. He had told them that, in virtue of the apostolic dignity conferred upon them, they should in the regeneration of all things sit upon thrones, judging the twelves tribes of Israel. He had spoken, too, of a mysterious authority with which they were invested, so that their decisions here upon earth would be ratified and confirmed in the region of heavenly realities. Yet when a gap is made by successful sin in the number of the mystical twelve who are to judge the twelve tribes, He leaves the selection of a new Apostle to the remaining eleven, in order that they may be compelled to stir up the grace of God which was in them, and to exercise the power entrusted to them under a due sense of responsibility. The Lord thus wished to teach the Church from earliest days to walk alone. The Apostles had been long enough depending on His personal presence and guidance, and now, that they might learn to exercise the privileges and duties of their Divine freedom, He leaves them to choose one to fill that position of supernatural rank and office from which Judas had fallen. The risen Saviour acted in grace as God ever acts in nature. He bestowed His gifts lavishly and generously, and then expected man to respond to the gifts by making that good use of them which earnest prayer, sanctified reason, and Christian commonsense dictated.

St. Peter's action is notable, too, in another aspect. St. Peter was undoubtedly the natural leader of the apostolic band during those earliest days of the Church's history. Our Lord Himself recognised his natural gifts as qualifying him to fulfil this position. There is no necessity for a denial on our part of the reality of St. Peter's privilege as contained in such passages as the verse which says, "I will give unto thee (Peter) the keys of the kingdom of

After St. Peter had spoken, two persons were selected as possessing the qualifications needful in the successor of Judas. Then when the Apostles had elected they prayed, and cast lots as between the two, and the final selection of Matthias was made. Questions have sometimes been raised as to this method of election, and attempts have been sometimes made to follow the precedent here set. The lot has at times been used to supersede the exercise of human judgment, not only in Church elections, but in the ordinary matters of life; but if this passage is closely examined, it will be seen that it affords no justification for any such practice. The Apostles did not use the lot so as to supersede the exercise of their own powers, or relieve them of that personal responsibility which God has imposed on men, whether as individuals, or as gathered in societies civil or ecclesiastical. The Apostles brought their private judgment into play, searched, debated, voted, and, as the result, chose two persons equally well qualified for the apostolic office. Then, when they had done their best, they left the decision to the lot, just as men often do still; and if we believe in the efficacy of prayer and a particular Providence ordering the affairs of men, I do not see that any wiser course can ever be taken, under similar circumstances, than that which the Apostles adopted on this occasion. But we must be careful to observe that the Apostles did not trust to the lot absolutely and completely. That would have been trusting to mere chance. They first did their utmost, exercised their own knowledge and judgment, and then, having done their part, they prayerfully left the final result to God, in humble confidence that He would show what was best.

The two selected candidates were Joseph Barsabas and Matthias, neither of whom ever appeared before in the story of our Lord's life, and yet both had been His disciples all through His earthly career. What lessons for ourselves may we learn from these men! These two eminent servants of God, either of whom their brethren counted worthy to succeed into the apostolic College, appear just this once in the sacred narrative, and then disappear for ever. Indeed it is with the Apostles as we have already noted in the case of our Lord's life and the story of the Blessed Virgin, the self-restraint of the sacred narrative is most striking. What fields for romance! What wide scope for the exercise of imagination would the lives of the Apostles have opened out if the writers of our sacred books had not been guided and directed by a Divine power outside and beyond themselves. We are not, indeed, left without the materials for a comparison in this respect, most consoling and most instructive for the devout Christian.

Apocryphal histories of all the Apostles abound on every side, some of them dating from the second century itself. Many of them indeed are regular romances. The Clementine Homilies and Recognitions form a religious novel, entering into the most elaborate details of the labours, preaching, and travels of the Apostle Peter. Every one of the other Apostles, and many of the earliest disciples too, had gospels forged in their honour; there was the Gospel of Peter, of Thomas, of Nicodemus, and of many others. And so it was with St. Matthias.[43] Five hundred years after Christ the Gospel of Matthias was known and repudiated as a fiction. A mass of tradition, too, grew up round him, telling of his labours and martyrdom, as some said in Ethiopia, and as others in Eastern Asia.

Clement, a writer who lived about the year 200, at Alexandria, recounts for us some sayings traditionally ascribed to St. Matthias, all of a severe and sternly ascetic tone. But in reality we know nothing either of what St. Matthias did or of what he taught. The genuine writings of apostolic times carry their own credentials with them in this respect. They are dignified and natural. They indulge in no details to exalt their heroes, or to minister to that love of the strange and marvellous which lies at the root of so much religious error. They were written to exalt Christ and Christ alone, and they deal, therefore, with the work of Apostles merely so far as the story tends to increase the glory of the Master, not that of His servants. Surely this repression of the human agents, this withdrawal of them into the darkness of obscurity, is one of the best evidences of the genuineness of the New Testament. One or two of the earliest witnesses of the Cross have their story told at some length. Peter and Paul, when compared with James or John or Matthias, figure very largely in the New Testament narrative. But even they have allotted to them a mere brief outline of a portion of their work, and all the rest is hidden from us. The vast majority even of the Apostles have their names alone recorded, while nothing is told concerning their labours or their sufferings. If the Apostles were deceivers, they were deceivers who sought their rewards neither in this life, where they gained nothing but loss of all things, nor in the pages of history, where their own hands and the hands of their friends consigned their brightest deeds to an obscurity no eye can pierce.[44] But they were not deceivers. They were the noblest benefactors of the race, men whose minds and hearts and imaginations were filled with the glory of their risen Redeemer. Their one desire was that Christ alone should be magnified, and to this end they willed to lose themselves in the boundless sea of His risen glory. And thus they have left us a noble and inspiriting example. We are not apostles, martyrs, or confessors, yet we often find it hard to take our part and do our duty in the spirit displayed by Matthias and Joseph called Barsabas. We long for public recognition and public reward. We chafe and fret and fume internally because we have to bear our temptations and suffer our trials and do our work unknown and unrecognised by all but God. Let the example of these holy men help us to put away all such vain thoughts. God Himself is our all-seeing and our ever-present Judge. The Incarnate Master Himself is watching us. The angels and the spirits of the just made perfect are witnesses of our earthly struggles. No matter how low, how humble, how insignificant the story of our spiritual trials and struggles, they are all marked in heaven by that Divine Master who will at last reward every man, not according to his position in the world, but in strict accordance with the principles of infallible justice.

# CHAPTER V
# THE PENTECOSTAL BLESSING

"And when the day of Pentecost was now come, they were all together in one place. And suddenly there came from heaven a sound as of the rushing of a mighty wind, and it filled all the house where they were sitting. And there appeared unto them tongues parting asunder (or distributing themselves), like as of fire; and it sat upon each one of them. And they were all filled with the Holy Spirit, and began to speak with other tongues, as the Spirit gave them utterance."—Acts ii. 1-4.

In these words we find the record of the event which completed the Church, and endowed it with that mysterious power which then was, and ever since has been, the source of its true life and of its highest success.

The time when the gift of the Spirit was vouchsafed is marked for us as "when the day of Pentecost was now come." Here again, as in the fact of the ascension and the waiting of the Church, we trace the outline of Christianity in Judaism, and see in the typical ceremonial of the old dispensation the outline and shadow of heavenly realities.

What was the history of the Pentecostal feast? That feast fulfilled in the Jewish system a twofold place. It was one of the great natural festivals whereby God taught His ancient people to sanctify the different portions of the year. The Passover was the feast of the first ripe corn, celebrating the beginning of the barley harvest, as again the Pentecostal loaves set forth, solemnized, and sanctified the close of the wheat harvest. No one was permitted, according to the twenty-third of Leviticus, to partake of the fruits of the earth till the harvest had been sanctified by the presentation to God of the first ripe sheaf, just as at the greatest paschal festival ever celebrated, Christ, the first ripe sheaf of that vast harvest of humanity which is maturing for its Lord, was taken out of the grave where the rest of the harvest still lies, and presented in the inner temple of the universe as the first-fruits of humanity unto God. At Pentecost, on the other hand, it was not a sheaf but a loaf that was offered to signify the completion of the work begun at the Passover. At Pentecost the law is thus laid down: "Ye shall bring out of your habitations two wave loaves of two tenth parts of an ephah: they shall be of fine flour, they shall be baken with leaven, for first-fruits unto the Lord" (Lev. xxiii. 17). Pentecost, therefore, was the harvest festival, the feast of ingathering for the Jews; and when the type found its completion in Christ, Pentecost became the feast of ingathering for the nations, when the Church, the mystical body of Christ, was presented unto God to be an instrument of His glory and a blessing to the world at large. This feast, as we have already intimated, was a fitting season for the gift of the Holy Ghost, and that for another reason. Pentecost was considered by the Jews as a festival commemorative of the giving of the law at Mount Sinai in the third month after they had been delivered from the bondage of Egypt. It was a fitting season, therefore, for the bestowal of the Spirit, whereby the words of ancient prophecy were fulfilled, "I will put My law in their inward parts, and in their heart I will write it; and I will be their God, and they shall be My people" (Jer. xxxi. 33).[45]

The time when the Spirit was poured out on the assembled body of Christians, and the Church's foundations laid deep and strong, revealed profound reverence for the old dispensation, raising by anticipation a protest against the heretical teaching which became current among the Gnostics in the second century, and has often since found place in Christian circles, as amongst the Anabaptists of Germany and the Antinomians at the time of the Reformation. This view taught that there was an essential opposition between the Old and the New Testament, some maintainers of it, like the ancient Gnostics, holding that the Old Testament was the production of a spiritual being inferior and hostile to the Eternal God. The Divine Spirit guided St. Luke, however, to teach the opposite view, and is careful to honour the elder dispensation and the old covenant, showing that Christianity was simply the perfection and completion of Judaism, and was developed therefrom as naturally as the bud of spring bursts forth into the splendid blossom and flower of summer. We trace these evidences of the Divine foreknowledge, as well as of the Divine wisdom, in these Pentecostal revelations, providing for and forecasting future dangers with which, even in its earlier days, the bark of Christ's Church had desperately to struggle. [46]

I. Now let us take the circumstances of the Pentecostal blessing as they are stated, for every separate detail bears with it an important message. The place and the other circumstances of the outpouring of the Spirit are full of instruction. The first disciples were all with one accord in one place. There was unity of spirit and unity in open manifestation to the world at large. Christ's disciples, when they received the gifts of heaven's choicest blessings, were not split up into dozens of different organizations, each of them hostile to the others, and each striving to aggrandise itself at the expense of kindred brotherhoods. They had keenly in remembrance the teaching of our Lord's great Eucharistic supplication when He prayed to His Father for His people that "they may all be one; even as Thou Father, art in Me, and I in Thee ... that the world may believe that Thou didst send Me." There was visible unity among the followers of Christ; there was interior love and charity, finding expression in external union which qualified the disciples for the fuller reception of the spirit of love, and rendered them powerful in doing God's work amongst men. The state of the Apostles and the blessing then received have an important message for the Christianity of our own and of every age. What a contrast the Christian Church—taking the word in its broadest sense as comprising all those who profess and call themselves Christians—presents at the close of the nineteenth when compared with the opening years of the first century. May not many of the problems and difficulties which the Church of to-day experiences be traced up to this woeful contrast? Behold England nowadays, with its two hundred sects, all calling themselves by the name of Christ; take the Christian world, with its Churches mutually hostile, spending far more time and trouble on winning proselytes one from the other than upon winning souls from the darkness of heathenism;—surely this one fact alone, the natural result of our departure from the Pentecostal condition of unity and peace, is a sufficient evidence of our evil plight. We do not purpose now to go into any discussion of the causes whence have sprung the divisions of Christendom. "An enemy hath done this" is a quite sufficient explanation, for assuredly the great enemy of souls and of Christ has counterworked and traversed the work of the Church and the conversion of the world most effectually thereby. There are some persons who rejoice in the vast variety of divisions in the Church; but they are shortsighted and inexperienced in the danger and scandals which have flowed, and are flowing, from them. It is indeed in the mission field that the schisms among Christians are most evidently injurious. When the heathen see the soldiers of the Cross split up among themselves into hostile organizations, they very naturally say that it will be time enough when their own divergences and difficulties have been reconciled to come and convert persons who at least possess internal union and concord. The visible unity of the Church was from the earliest days a strong argument, breaking down pagan prejudice. Then, again, not only do the divisions of Christians place a stumbling-block in the way of the conversion of the heathen, but they lead to a wondrous waste of power both at home and abroad. Surely one cannot look at the religious state of a town or village in England without realizing at a glance the evil results of our divisions from this point of view. If men believe that the preaching of the Cross of Christ is the power of God unto salvation, and that millions are perishing from want of that blessed story, can they feel contentment when the great work of competing sects consists, not in spreading that salvation, but in building up their own cause by proselytising from their neighbours, and gathering into their own organization persons who already have been made partakers of Christ Jesus? And if this competition of sects be injurious and wasteful within the bounds of Christendom, surely it is infinitely more so when various contending bodies concentrate all their forces, as they so often do, on the same locality in some unconverted land, and seem as eagerly desirous of gaining proselytes from one another as from the mass of paganism.

Then, too, to take it from another point of view, what a loss in generalship, in Christian strategy, in power of concentration, results from our unhappy divisions? The united efforts made by Protestants, Roman Catholics, and Greeks, are indeed all too small for the vast work of converting the heathen world if they were made with the greatest skill and wisdom. How much more insufficient they must be when a vast proportion of the power employed is wasted, as far as the work of conversion is concerned, because it is used simply in counteracting and withstanding the efforts of other Christian bodies. I say nothing as to the causes of dissensions. In many cases they may have been absolutely necessary, though in too many cases I fear they have resulted merely from views far too narrow and restrained; I merely point out the evil of division in itself as being, not a help, as some would consider it, but a terrible hindrance in the way of the Church of Christ. How different it was in the primitive Church! Within one hundred and fifty years, or little more, of the ascension of Jesus Christ and the outpouring of the Divine Spirit, a Christian writer could boast that the Christian Church had permeated the whole Roman empire to such an extent that if the Christians abandoned the cities they would be turned into howling deserts. This triumphant march of Christianity was simply in accordance with the Saviour's promise. The world saw that Christians loved one another, and the world was consequently converted. But when primitive love cooled down, and divisions and sects in abundance sprang up after the conversion of Constantine the Great, then the progress of God's work gradually ceased, till at last Mahometanism arose to roll back the tide of triumphant success which had followed the preaching of the Cross, and to reduce beneath Satan's sway many a fair region, like North Africa, Egypt, and Asia Minor, which once had been strongholds of Christianity. Surely when one thinks of the manifold evils at home and abroad which the lack of the Pentecostal visible union and concord has caused, as well as of the myriads who still remain in darkness while nominal Christians bite and devour one another, we may well join in the glowing language of Jeremy Taylor's splendid prayer for the whole Catholic Church, as he cries, "O Holy Jesus, King of the saints and Prince of the Catholic Church, preserve Thy spouse whom

Thou hast purchased with Thy right hand, and redeemed and cleansed with Thy blood. O preserve her safe from schism, heresy, and sacrilege. Unite all her members with the bands of faith, hope, and charity, and an external communion when it shall seem good in Thine eyes. Let the daily sacrifice of prayer and sacramental thanksgiving never cease, but be for ever presented to Thee, and for ever united to the intercession of her dearest Lord, and for ever prevail for the obtaining for each of its members grace and blessing, pardon and salvation."[47]

II. Furthermore, we have brought before us the external manifestations or evidences of the interior gift of the Spirit really bestowed upon the Apostles at Pentecost. There was a sound as of a rushing mighty wind; there were tongues like as of fire, a separate and distinct tongue resting upon each disciple; and lastly there was the miraculous manifestation of speech in divers languages. Let us take these spiritual phenomena in order. First, then, "there came from heaven a sound as of the rushing of a mighty wind, and it filled all the house where they were sitting;" a sign which was repeated in the scene narrated in the fourth chapter and the thirty-first verse, where we are told that "when they had prayed, the place was shaken wherein they were gathered together; and they were all filled with the Holy Ghost." The appearances of things that were seen responded to the movements and powers that were unseen. It was a supernatural moment. The powers of a new life, the forces of a new kingdom, were coming into operation, and, as the result, manifestations that never since have been experienced found place among men. We can find a parallel to what then happened in scientific investigations. Geologists and astronomers push back the beginning of the world and of the universe at large to a vast distance, but they all acknowledge that there must have been a period when phenomena were manifested, powers and forces called into operation, of which men have now no experience. The beginning, or the repeated beginnings, of the various epochs must have been times of marvels, which men can now only dream about. Pentecost was for the Christian with a sense of the awful importance of life and time and of the individual soul a far greater beginning and a grander epoch than any mere material one. It was the beginning of the spiritual life, the inauguration of the spiritual kingdom of the Messiah, the Lord and Ruler of the material universe; and therefore we ought to expect, or at least not to be surprised, that marvellous phenomena, signs and wonders even of a physical type, should accompany and celebrate the scene. The marvels of the story told in the first of Genesis find a parallel in the marvels told in the second of Acts. The one passage sets forth the foundation of the material universe, the other proclaims the nobler foundations of the spiritual universe. Let us take it again from another point of view. Pentecost was, in fact, Moses on Sinai or Elijah on Horeb over again, but in less terrific form. Moses and Elijah may be styled the founder and the refounder of the old dispensation, just as St. Peter and the Apostles may be called the founders of the new dispensation. But what a difference in the inaugural scene! No longer with thunder and earthquake, and mountains rent, but in keeping with a new and more peaceful economy, there came from heaven the sound as of the rushing of a mighty wind. It is not, too, the only occasion where the idea of wind is connected with that of the Divine Spirit and its mysterious operations. How very similar, as the devout mind will trace, are the words and description of St. Luke, when narrating this first outpouring of the Spirit, to the words of the Divine Master repeated by St. John, "The wind bloweth where it listeth, and thou hearest the voice thereof, but knowest not whence it cometh, and whither it goeth: so is every one that is born of the Spirit."

There appeared, too, tongues, separate and distinct, sitting upon each of them. The outward and visible sign manifested on this occasion was plainly typical of the new dispensation and of the chief means of its propagation. The personality of the Holy Ghost is essentially a doctrine of the new dispensation. The power and influence of God's Spirit is indeed often recognised in the Old Testament. Aholiab and Bezaleel are said to have been guided by the Spirit of God as they cunningly devised the fabric of the first tabernacle. The Spirit of Jehovah began to move Samson at times in the camp of Dan; and, on a later occasion, the same Spirit is described as descending upon him with such amazing force that he went down and slew thirty men of Ashkelon. These and many other similar passages present to us the Jewish conception of the Spirit of God and His work. He was a force, a power, quickening the human mind, illuminating with genius and equipping with physical strength those whom God chose to be champions of His people against the surrounding heathen. Aholiab's skill in mechanical operations, and Samson's strength, and Saul's prophesying, and David's musical art, were all of them the gifts of God. What a noble, what a grand, inspiring view of life and life's gifts and work, is there set before us. It is the old lesson taught by St. James, though so often forgotten by men when they draw a distinction between things sacred and things secular, "Every good gift and every perfect boon is from above, coming down from the Father of light." A deeper view, indeed, of the Divine Spirit and His work on the soul can be traced in the prophets, but then they were watchers upon the mountains, who discerned from afar the approach of a nobler and a brighter day. "The Spirit of the Lord is upon me, because He hath anointed me to preach the gospel to the poor." That was Isaiah's statement of his work as adopted by our Lord; and now, at the very foundation of the Church, this deeper and nobler tone of thought concerning the Spirit is proclaimed, when there appeared tongues like as of fire sitting upon each of them.

The sign of the Holy Spirit's presence was a tongue of fire. It was a most suitable emblem, pregnant with meaning, and indicative of the large place which the human voice was to play in the work of the new dispensation, while the supernatural fire declared that the mere unaided human voice would avail nothing. The voice needs to be quickened and supported by that Divine fire, that superhuman energy and power, which the Holy Ghost alone can confer. The tongue of fire pointed on the Pentecostal morn to the important part in the Church's life, and in the propagation of the gospel, which prayer, and praise, and preaching would hereafter occupy. It would have been well, indeed, had the Church ever remembered what the Holy Ghost thus taught, specially concerning the propagation of the gospel, for it would have been thereby saved many a disgraceful page of history. The human tongue, illuminated and sanctified by fire from the inner sanctuary, was about to be the instrument of the gospel's advancement,—not penal laws, not the sword and fire of persecution; and so long as the divinely-appointed means were adhered to, so long the course of our holy religion was one long-continued triumph. But when the world and the devil were able to place in the hands of Christ's spouse their own weapons of violence and force, when the Church forgot the words of her Master, "My kingdom is not of this world," and the teachings embodied in the symbol of the tongue of fire, then spiritual paralysis fell upon religious effort; and even where human law and power have compelled an external conformity to the Christian system, as they undoubtedly have done in some cases, yet all vital energy, all true godliness, have been there utterly lacking in the religion established by means so contrary to the mind of Christ. Very good men have made sad mistakes in this matter. Archbishop Ussher was a man whose deep piety equalled his prodigious learning, yet he maintained that the civil sword ought to be used to repress false doctrine; the divines of the Westminster Assembly have left their opinion on record, that it is the duty of the magistrate to use the sword on behalf of Christ's kingdom; Richard Baxter taught that the toleration of doctrines which he considered false was sinful; and all of them forgot the lesson of the day of Pentecost, that the tongue of fire was to be the only weapon permissible in the warfare of the kingdom whose rule is over spirits, not over bodies. The history of religion in England amply proves this. The Church of England enjoyed, about the middle of the last century, the greatest temporal prosperity. Her prelates held high estate, and her security was fenced round by a perfect bulwark of stringent laws. Yet her life-blood was fast ebbing away, and her true hold upon the nation was speedily relaxing. The very highest ranks of society, whom worldly policy attached nominally to her communion, had lost all faith in her supernatural work and commission. A modern historian has shown this right well in his description of the death-scene of Queen Caroline, a woman of eminent intellectual qualities, who had played no small part in the religious life of this nation during the reign of her husband George II. Queen Caroline came to die, and was passing away surrounded by a crowd of attendants and courtiers. The whole Court, permeated by the spirit of earthliness which then prevailed, was disturbed by the death of the Queen's body, but no one seems to have thought of the Queen's soul, till some one mildly suggested that, for decency's sake, the Archbishop of Canterbury should be sent for that he might offer up prayer with the dying woman. Writing here in Ireland, I cannot forget that it was just the same with us at that very period. Religion was here upheld by worldly power; the Church, which should have been viewed as simply a spiritual power, was regarded and treated as a mere branch of the civil service, and true religion sank to its lowest depths. And we reaped in ourselves the due reward of our deeds. The very men whose voices were loudest in public for the repression of Romanism were privately living in grossest neglect of the offices and laws of religion and morality, because they in their hearts despised an institution which had forgotten the Pentecostal gift, and sought victory with the weapons of the flesh, and not with those of the spirit. May God for evermore protect His Church from such miserable mistakes, and lead her to depend more and more upon the power of the blessed and ever-present Pentecostal gift!

A separate and distinct tongue, too, sat upon each individual assembled in the upper room,—significant of the individual character of our holy religion. Christianity has a twofold aspect, neither of which can with impunity be neglected. Christianity has a corporate aspect. Our Lord Jesus Christ came not so much to teach a new doctrine as to establish a new society, based on newer and higher principles, and working towards a higher and nobler end than any society ever previously founded. This side of Christianity was exaggerated in the Middle Ages. The Church, its unity, its interests, its welfare as a corporation, then dominated every other consideration. Since the Reformation, however, men have run to the other extreme. They have forgotten the social and corporate view of Christianity, and only thought of it as it deals with individuals. Men have looked at Christianity as it deals with the individual alone, and have forgotten and ignored the corporate side of its existence. Truth is many-sided indeed, and no side of truth can with impunity be neglected. Some have erred in dwelling too much on the corporate aspect of Christianity; others have erred in dwelling too much on its individual aspect. The New Testament alone combines both in due proportion, and teaches the importance and necessity of a Church, as against the extreme Protestant, on the one hand, who will reduce religion to a mere individual matter; and of a personal religion, an individual interest in the Spirit's presence, as here indicated by the tongues which sat upon each of them, as against the extreme Romanist, on the other hand, who looks upon the Church as everything, to the neglect of the life and progress of the individual. This passage does not at the same time lend any assistance to those who would thence conclude that there was no distinction between clergy and laity, and that no ministerial office was intended to exist under the dispensation of the kingdom of heaven. The Spirit, doubtless, was poured out upon all the disciples, and not upon the Twelve alone, upon the day of Pentecost, as also upon the occasion of the conversion of Cornelius and his household. Yet this fact did not lead the Apostles and early Christians to conclude that an appointed and ordained ministry might be dispensed with. The Lord miraculously bestowed His graces and gifts at Pentecost and in the centurion's house at Cæsarea, because the gospel dispensation was opened on these occasions first of all to the Jews and then to the Gentiles. But when, subsequently to the formal opening, we read of the gifts of the Spirit, we find that their bestowal is connected with the ministry of the Apostles, of St. Peter and St. John at Samaria, or of St. Paul at Ephesus. The Holy Ghost was poured out upon all the company assembled in the upper room, or in the centurion's house; yet the Apostles saw nothing in this fact inconsistent with a ministerial organization, else they would not have set apart the seven men full of faith and of the Holy Ghost to minister to the widows at Jerusalem, nor would they have laid hands upon elders in every church which they founded, nor would St. Paul have written, "He that seeketh the office of a bishop desireth a good work," nor would St. Peter have exhorted the elders to a diligent oversight of the flock of God after the model of the Good Shepherd Himself. St. Peter clearly thought that the Pentecostal gifts did not obliterate the distinction which existed between the shepherds and the sheep, between a fixed and appointed ministry and the flock to whom they should minister, though in the very initial stages of the miraculous movement the Spirit was bestowed without any human agency upon men and women alike.[48]

III. Lastly, in this passage we find another external proof of the Spirit's presence in the miraculous gift of tongues. That gift indicated to the Apostles and to all ages the tongue as the instrument by which the gospel was to be propagated, as the symbol fire indicated the cleansing and purifying effects of the Spirit.[49] The gift of tongues is one that has ever excited much speculation, and specially so during the present century, when, as some will remember, an extraordinary attempt to revive them was made, some sixty years ago, by the followers of the celebrated Edward Irving. Devout students of Scripture have loved to trace in this incident at Pentecost, at the very foundation of the new dispensation, a reversal of that confusion of tongues which happened at Babel, and have seen in it the removal of "the covering cast over all peoples, and the veil that is spread over all nations."[50] The precise character of the gift of tongues has of late years exercised many minds, and different explanations have been offered of the phenomena. Some have viewed it as a miracle of hearing, not of speaking, and maintained that the Apostles did not speak different languages at all, but that they all spake the one Hebrew tongue, while the Jews of the various nationalities then assembled miraculously heard the gospel in their own language.

The miracle is in that case intensified one hundredfold, while not one single difficulty which men feel is thereby alleviated. Meyer and a large number of German critics explain the speaking with tongues as mere ecstatic or rapturous utterances in the ordinary language of the disciples. Meyer thinks too that some foreign Jews had found their way into the band of the earliest disciples. They naturally delivered their ecstatic utterances, not in Aramaic, but in the foreign tongues to which they were accustomed, and legend then exaggerated this natural fact into the form which the Acts of the Apostles and the tradition of the Christian Church have ever since maintained.[51] It is, indeed, rather difficult to understand the estimate formed by such critics of the gift of tongues, whether bestowed on the day of Pentecost or during the subsequent ministrations of St. Paul at Corinth and Ephesus. Meyer is obliged to confess that there were some marvellous phenomena in Corinth and other places to which St. Paul bears witness. He describes himself as surpassing the whole Corinthian Church in this particular gift (1 Cor. xiv. 18), so that if St. Paul's testimony is to be relied upon,—and Meyer lays a great deal of weight upon it,—we must accept it as conclusively proving that there existed a power of speaking in various languages among the first Christians. But the explanation offered by many critics of the gift of tongues as undoubtedly exercised at Corinth reduces it to something very like those fanatical exhibitions witnessed among the earliest followers of the Irvingite movement, or, to put it plainly, to a mere uttering of gibberish, unworthy of apostolic notice save in the language of sternest censure, as being a disorderly and foolish proceeding disgraceful to the Christian community.

Meyer's theory and that of many modern expositors seems, then, to me very unsatisfactory, raising up more difficulties than it solves. But it may be asked, what explanation do you offer of the Pentecostal miracle? and I can find no one more satisfactory than the old-fashioned one, that there was a real bestowal of tongues, a real gift of speaking in foreign languages, granted to the Apostles, to be used as occasion required when preaching the gospel in heathen lands. Dean Stanley, in his commentary on Corinthians, gives, as was his wont, a clear and attractive statement of the newer theory, putting in a vigorous shape the objections to the view here maintained. I know there are difficulties connected with this view, but many of these difficulties arise from our ignorance of the state and condition of the early Church, while others may spring from our very imperfect knowledge of the relations between mind and body. But whatever difficulties attend the explanation I offer, they are as nothing compared with the difficulties which attend the modern explanations to which I have referred.[52] What, then, is our theory, which we call the old-fashioned one? It is simply this, that on the day of Pentecost Christ bestowed upon His Apostles the power of speaking in foreign languages, according to His promise reported by St. Mark (xvi. 17), "They shall speak with new tongues." This was the theory of the ancient Church. Irenæus speaks of the tongues as given "that all nations might be enabled to enter into life;" while Origen explains that "St. Paul was made a debtor to different nations, because, through the grace of the Holy Spirit, he had received the gift of speaking in the languages of all nations." This has been the continuous theory of the Church as expressed in one of the most ancient portions of the Liturgy, the proper prefaces in the Communion office. The preface for Whit Sunday sets forth the facts commemorated on that day, as the other proper prefaces state the facts of the Incarnation, the Resurrection, and Ascension. The fact which Whit Sunday celebrates, and for which special thanks are then offered, is this, that then "the Holy Ghost came down from heaven in the likeness of fiery tongues, lighting upon the Apostles, to teach them, and to lead them to all truth; giving them both the gift of divers languages, and also boldness with fervent zeal constantly to preach the gospel unto all nations."[53]

Now this traditional interpretation has not only the authority of the past on its side; we can also see many advantages which must have accrued from a gift of this character. The preface we have just cited states that the tongues were bestowed for the preaching of the gospel among all nations. And surely not merely as a striking sign to unbelievers, but also as a great practical help in missionary labours, such a gift of tongues would have been invaluable to the Church at its very birth. There was then neither time, nor money, nor organization to prepare men as missionaries of the Cross. An universal commission and work were given to twelve men, chiefly Galilean peasants, to go forth and found the Church. How could they have been fitted for this work unless God had bestowed upon them some such gift of speech? The vast diversity of tongues throughout the world is now one of the chief hindrances with which missionary effort has to contend. Years have often to elapse before any effective steps can be taken in the work of evangelisation, simply because the question of the languages bars the way. It would have been only in accordance with God's action in nature, where great epochs have been ever signalised by extraordinary phenomena, if such a great era-making epoch as the birth of the Church of Christ had been marked with extraordinary spiritual powers and developments, which supplied the want of that learning and those organizations which the Lord now leaves to the spiritual energies of the Church itself. But it is sometimes said, we never hear of this power as used by the Apostles for missionary purposes. Nothing, however, is a surer rule in historical investigations than this, "Never trust to mere silence," specially when the records are but few, scanty, fragmentary. We know but very little of the ways, worship, actions of the Apostles. Silence is no evidence either as to what they did or did not do. Some of them went into barbarous and distant lands, as history states. Eusebius (III., 1) tells us that St. Thomas received Parthia as his allotted region, while St. Andrew taught in Scythia. Eusebius is an author on whom great reliance is justly placed. He is one, too, whose accuracy and research have been again and again confirmed in our own day by discoveries of every kind. I see, then, no reason why we should not depend upon him upon this point as well as upon others. Now if the Apostles taught in Scythia and Parthia, what an enormous advantage it must have given them in their work among a strange and barbarous people if, by means of the Pentecostal blessing, they could at once proclaim a crucified Saviour. It is sometimes said, however, the gift of speaking with foreign languages was not required by the Apostles for missionary purposes, as Greek alone would carry a man all through the world, and Greek the Apostles evidently knew. But people in saying so forget that there is a great difference between possessing enough of a language to travel over the world, and speaking with such facility as enables one to preach. English will now carry a man over the world, but English will not enable him to preach to the people of India or of China. Greek might carry Apostles all over the Roman Empire, and might enable St. Thomas to be understood by the courtiers of the great kings of Parthia, where traces of the ancient Greek language and civilization, derived from Alexander's time, long prevailed. But Greek would not enable a primitive Christian teacher to preach fluently among the Celts of Galatia, or of Britain, or among the natives of Spain or of Phrygia, or the barbarians of Scythia. [54] We see from St. Paul's case how powerful was the hold which the Aramaic language had over the people of Jerusalem. When the excited mob heard St. Paul speak in the Hebrew tongue they listened patiently, because their national feelings, the sentiments which sprang up in childhood and were allied with their noblest hopes, were touched. So must it have been all the world over. The Pentecostal gift of tongues was a powerful help in preaching the gospel, because, like the Master's promise to assist their minds and their tongues in the hour of need, it freed the Apostles from care, anxiety, and difficulties, which would have sorely hindered their great work. But while I offer this explanation, I acknowledge that it has its own difficulties; but then every theory has its difficulties, and we can only balance difficulties against difficulties, selecting that theory which seems to have the fewest. The conduct, for instance, of the Corinthians, who seem to have used the gift of tongues simply to minister to the spirit of display, not to edification or to missionary work, seems to some a great difficulty. But after all is not their conduct simply an instance of human sin, perverting and misusing a divine gift, such as we often see still? God still bestows His gifts, the real outcome and work of the Spirit. Man takes them, treats them as his own, and misuses them for his own purposes of sin and selfishness. What else did the Corinthians do, save that the gift which they abused was an exceptional one; but then their circumstances, times, opportunities, punishments, all were exceptional and peculiar. The one thing that was not peculiar was this, the abiding tendency of human nature to degrade Divine gifts and blessings. There must, we again repeat, be difficulties and mystery connected with this subject, no matter what view we take. Perhaps, too, we are no fitting judges of the gifts bestowed on the primitive Church, or the phenomena manifested under such extraordinary circumstances, when everything, every power, every force, every organization, was arrayed against the company of the twelve Apostles. Surely miracles and miraculous powers seem absolutely necessary and natural in such a case.[55] We are not now sufficient or capable judges of events as they then existed. Perhaps, too, we are not sufficient judges because we do not possess that spirit which would make us to sympathise with and understand the state of the Church at that time. "They were all together in one place." The Church was then visibly united, and internally united too. A nineteenth century Christian, with the endless divisions of Christendom, is scarcely the most fitting judge of the Church and the Church's blessings when the Spirit of the Master pervaded it and the prayer of the Master for visible unity was fulfilled in it. Christendom is weak now from its manifold divisions. Even in a mere natural way, and from a mere human point of view, we can see how its divisions destroy its power and efficacy as Christ's witness in the world. But when we take the matter from a spiritual point of view, we cannot even guess what marvellous gifts and endowments, needful for the edification of His people and the conversion of the world, we now lack from want of the Divine charity and peace which ruled the hearts of the twelve as they assembled in the upper room that Pentecostal morn. We shall better understand primitive gifts when we get back primitive union.

# CHAPTER VI
# ST. PETER'S FIRST SERMON

"But Peter, standing up with the eleven, lifted up his voice, and spake forth unto them, saying, Ye men of Judæa, and all ye that dwell at Jerusalem, be this known unto you, and give ear unto my words." — Acts ii. 14.

This verse contains the opening words of St. Peter's address to the multitude who were roused to wonder and inquiry by the miraculous manifestations of Pentecost. That address is full of interest when viewed aright, freed from all the haze which the long familiarity of ages has brought with it. In this second chapter we have the report of a sermon preached within a few days of Christ's ascension, addressed to men many of whom knew Jesus Christ, all of whom had heard of His work, His life, and His death, and setting forth the apostolic estimate of Christ, His miracles, His teaching, His ascended condition and glory. We cannot realize, unless by an intellectual effort, the special worth of these apostolic reports contained in the Acts. Men are sometimes sceptical about them, asking, how did we get them at all? how were they handed down? This is, however, an easier question to answer than some think. If we take, for instance, this Pentecostal address alone, we know that St. Luke had many opportunities of personal communication with St. Peter. He may have learned from St. Peter's own mouth what he said on this occasion, and he could compare this verbal report with the impressions and remembrances of hundreds who then were present. But there is another solution of the difficulty less known to the ordinary student of Holy Scripture. The ancients made a great use of shorthand, and were quite well accustomed to take down spoken discourses, transmitting them thus to future ages. Shorthand was, in fact, much more commonly used among the ancients than among ourselves. The younger Pliny, for instance, who was a contemporary of the Apostles, never travelled without a shorthand writer, whose business it was to transcribe passages which struck his master in the books he was perpetually studying. The sermons of Chrysostom were all extemporaneous effusions. In fact, the golden-mouthed patriarch of Constantinople was such an indefatigable pulpit-orator, preaching almost daily, that it would have been impossible to have made any copious preparation. The extensive reports of his sermons which have come down to us, the volumes of his expositions on the books of Scripture which we possess, prove that shorthand must have been constantly used by his hearers.[56] Now what would we give for a few shorthand reports of sermons by Clement of Rome, by St. Luke, by Timothy, by Apollos, preached in Rome, Alexandria, or Antioch? Suppose they were discovered, like the numerous Egyptian manuscripts which have of late years come to light, deposited in the desert sands, and were found to set forth the miracles, the ministry, and the person of Christ exactly as now we preach them, what a marvellous confirmation of the faith we should esteem them! And yet what should we then possess more than we already have in the sermons and discourses of St. Peter and St. Paul, reported by an eye and ear-witness who wrote the Acts of the Apostles?

I. The congregation assembled to listen to this first Gospel discourse preached by a human agent was a notable and representative one. There were Parthians, and Medes, and Elamites, and the dwellers in Mesopotamia and in Judæa,—or, as an ancient expositor (Tertullian) puts it, in Armenia[57] and Cappadocia,—in Pontus and Asia, in Phrygia and Pamphylia, in Egypt and in the parts of Libya about Cyrene, and strangers of Rome, Jews and proselytes, Cretes and Arabians. The enumeration of the various nationalities listening to St. Peter begins from the extremest east; it proceeds then to the north, from thence to the south, terminating with Rome, which represents the west. They were all Jews or Jewish proselytes, showing how extremely wide, at the epoch of the Incarnation, was the dispersion of God's ancient people. St. Paul, in one profound passage of the Epistle to the Galatians, notes that "God sent forth His Son in the fulness of time," that is, at the exact moment when the world was prepared for the advent of the truth. This "fulness of time" may be noted in many directions. Roman roads, Roman law, commerce, and civilization opened channels of communication which bore the tidings of the gospel into every land. A sweet singer of our own time, the late Sir Samuel Ferguson, has depicted in his *Lays of the Western Gael* this diffusion of the gospel through the military organization of Rome. He represents a Celt from Ireland as present at the crucifixion. This may seem at first somewhat improbable, as Ireland was never included within the bounds of the Roman Empire; and yet the poet's song can be justified from history. Though never included formally within the Empire, Irishmen and Scotch Highlanders must often have served in the ranks of the Roman army, just as at the present day, and especially in India, men of foreign nationalities are often found serving in the ranks of the British army. In later times Irishmen most certainly formed a Roman legion all to themselves. St. Jerome tells us[58] that he had seen them acting in that capacity at Treves, in Germany. They were noted for their bravery, which, as Jerome believes, they sustained by consuming human flesh. Three hundred years earlier Irishmen may often have enlisted in the service of those British legions which the Romans withdrew from Britain and located in the East; and thus Sir Samuel Ferguson does not pass the bounds of historic credibility when he represents a certain centurion, who had been present at the crucifixion, as returning to his native land, and there proclaiming the tidings of our Lord's atoning sacrifice:—

"And they say, Centurion Altus, when he to Emania came,

And to Rome's subjection called us, urging Cæsar's tribute claim,

Told that half the world barbarian thrills already with the faith,

Taught them by the God-like Syrian, Cæsar lately put to death."[59]

The dispersion of the Jews throughout not only the Roman Empire, but far beyond its limits, served the same end, and hastened the fulness of time needed for the Messiah's appearance. We must remember, however, that the long list of varied nationalities present at this Pentecostal feast were not Gentiles, they were Jews of the dispersion scattered broadcast among the nations as far as Central Asia towards the east, as far as southern Arabia and Aden on the south, and Spain and Britain on the west. The course of modern investigation and discovery amply confirms the statement of this passage, as well as the similar statement of the eighth chapter, which represents a Jewish statesman of Abyssinia or Ethiopia as coming up to Jerusalem for the purposes of devotion. Jewish inscriptions have been found in Aden dating back long before the Christian era. A Jewish colony existed ages before Christ in the region of Southern Arabia, and continued to flourish there down to the Middle Ages.[60] At Rome, Alexandria, and Greece the Jews at this period constituted an important factor in the total population.[61] The dispersion of the Jews had now done its work, and brought with it the fulness of time required by the Divine purposes. The way of the Messiah had been effectually prepared by it. The Divine seed fell upon no unploughed and unbroken soil. Pure and noble ideas of worship and morality had been scattered broadcast throughout the world. Some years ago the Judgment of Solomon was found depicted on the ceiling of a Pompeian house, witnessing to the spread of scriptural knowledge through Jewish artists in the time of Tiberius and of Nero. A race of missionaries, too, equipped for their work, was developed through the discipline of exile. The thousands who hung upon Peter's lips needed nothing but instruction in the faith of Jesus Christ, together with the baptism of the Spirit, and the finest, the most enthusiastic, and the most cosmopolitan of agencies lay ready to the Church's hand. While, again, the organization of synagogues, which the exigencies of the dispersion had called into existence, was just the one suited to the various purposes of charity, worship, and teaching, which the Christian Church required. Whether, indeed, we consider the persons whom St. Peter addressed, or the machinery they had elaborated, or the diffusion of pure religious ideas they had occasioned, we see in this passage a splendid illustration of the care and working of Divine Providence bringing good out of evil and real victory out of apparent defeat. Prophet and psalmist had lamented over Zion's ruin and Israel's exile into foreign lands, but they saw not how that God was thereby working out His own purposes of wider blessing to mankind at large, fitting Jews and Gentiles alike for that fulness of time when the Eternal Son should be manifested.

II. The brave, outspoken tone of this sermon evidences the power and influence of the Holy Spirit upon St. Peter's mind. St. Chrysostom, in his famous lectures on the Acts of the Apostles, notes the courageous tone of this address as a clear evidence of the truth of the resurrection. This argument has been ever since a commonplace with apologists and expositors, and yet it is only by an effort that we can realize how very strong it is. Here was St. Peter and his fellow Apostles standing up proclaiming a glorified and ascended Messiah. Just seven weeks before, they had fled from the messengers of the High Priest sent to arrest their Master, leaving Him to His fate. They had seen Him crucified, knew of His burial, and then, feeling utterly defeated, had as much as possible withdrawn themselves from public notice. Seven weeks after, the same band, led by St. Peter, himself a short time before afraid to confess Christ to a maidservant, boldly stand up, charge upon the multitude, who knew all the circumstances of Christ's execution, the crime of having thus killed the Prince of Life, and appeal to the supernatural evidence of the gift of tongues, to which they had just listened, as the best proof of the truth of their message. St. Peter's courage on this occasion is one of the clearest proofs of the truth of his testimony. St. Peter was not naturally a courageous man. He was very impulsive and very sympathetic. He was the creature of his surroundings. If he found himself in the midst of Christ's friends, he was the most forward to uphold Christ's cause, but he had not much moral stamina. He was sadly deficient in staying power. His mind was very Celtic in its tone, to draw an illustration from national characteristics. The Celtic mind is very sympathetic, ardent, enthusiastic. It is swept along in moments of excitement, either of victory or of defeat, by the dominating power of numbers. How often has this quality been manifested by the French people, for instance? They are resistless when victorious; they collapse utterly and at once when defeated. St. Peter was just the same. He was sympathetic, ardent, enthusiastic, and fell, in later as well as in earlier age, into the perils which attend such temperaments. He denied his Master when surrounded by the menials of the high priest. He was ready to die for that Master a few hours before, when sitting surrounded by Christ's disciples in the secrecy of the upper room. Divine grace and the baptism of the Spirit did not at all change his natural character in this respect. Divine grace, whether granted in ancient or in modern times, does not destroy natural character, which is God's gift to man. It merely refines, purifies, elevates it. We find, indeed, a striking illustration of this law of the Divine life in St. Peter's case.

One of the most convincing proofs of the truth of the New Testament is the identity of character we behold in the representations given of St. Peter by writers who produced their books quite independently of each other. St. Paul wrote his Epistle to the Galatians long prior to any of the Gospel narratives. Yet St. Paul's picture of St. Peter in the Epistle to the Galatians is exactly the same as that drawn by the four Evangelists alike. St. Paul depicts him as the same intensely sympathetic, and therefore the same unstable person whom the Evangelists describe. The brave scene in the upper chamber, and the scene of cowardice and disgrace in the high priest's palace, were in principle re-enacted twenty years after, about the year A.D. 53, at Antioch. St. Peter was very bold in maintaining the right of Gentile freedom, and hesitated not to live like the Gentile Christians of Antioch, so long as none of the strict Jewish Christians of Jerusalem knew about it. St. Peter wished, in fact, to stand well with both parties, and therefore strove to conciliate both. He was, for the time, a type of that famous character Mr. Facing-two-ways. He lived, therefore, as a Gentile, until some of the Jerusalem brethren arrived at Antioch, when he at once quailed before them and retreated, betraying the cause of Christian freedom, and sacrificing, just as men do still, Christian principle and honesty upon the altar of self-seeking popularity. St. Peter, we therefore maintain, always remained at heart the same character. He was bold and forward for Christ so long as all went well, because he was intensely sympathetic; but he had very little of that power of standing alone which marked St. Paul, and nerved him, even though a solitary witness, when the cause of truth was involved. This somewhat lengthened argument is absolutely necessary to show the strength of our conclusion: that it must have been an overpowering sense of the awful reality of Christ's resurrection and ascension which alone could have overcome this natural weakness of St. Peter, and make him on the day of Pentecost as brave in proclaiming Jesus Christ to his red-handed murderers as he was bold to propose a new Apostle in place of the hapless traitor to the assembled disciples in the upper chamber. St. Peter evidently believed, and believed with an intense, overwhelming, resistless conviction, in the truth of Christ's resurrection and ascension, which thus became to him the source of personal courage and of individual power.

III. Again, the tone of St. Peter's sermon was remarkable because of its enlarged and enlightened spirituality. It proved the Spirit's power in illuminating the human consciousness. St. Peter was rapidly gaining a true conception of the nature of the kingdom of God. He enunciates that conception in this sermon. He proclaims Christianity, in its catholic and universal aspect, when he quotes the prophet Joel as predicting the time when the Lord would pour out His Spirit upon all flesh. St. Peter does not indeed seem to have realized all at once the full significance of his own teaching. He did not see that his words applied to the Gentiles equally with the Jews, sounding the death-knell of all national exclusiveness in religion. Had he seen the full meaning of his own words, he would not have hesitated so much about the baptism of Cornelius and the admission of the Gentiles. It has been found true, not only of St. Peter, but of teachers, reformers, politicians, statesmen, that they have not at once recognised all the vast issues and undeveloped principles which lay wrapped up in their original message. The stress and trial of life alone draw them out, at times compelling their authors to regret their earlier actions, at other times leading them to follow out with intensified vigour the principles and movements which they had themselves set in operation. Luther, when he protested against indulgences; Erasmus, when he ridiculed the ignorance of the monks and advocated the study of the Greek New Testament; John Hampden, when he refused to pay ship money; or Bishop Ken, when he declined obedience to the orders of King James II.;—none of them saw whereunto their principles would necessarily grow till time had thoroughly threshed their teaching and their actions, separating the husk of external circumstances, which are so variable, from the kernel of principle, which is eternally the same, stern, severe, inexorable, in its operations. So it was with St. Peter, and still earlier with the prophets. They sang of and preached a universal religion, as in this passage, but yet none of them realized the full scope and meaning of the words they had used, till a special revelation upon the housetop at Joppa compelled St. Peter to grasp and understand and apply the principles he had been already proclaiming.

In this respect, indeed, we recognise the greatness, the divinity of the Master Himself towering above the noblest of His followers; above even Peter himself, upon whom He pronounced such an eulogium, and bestowed such privileges. Our Lord Jesus Christ taught this universality of Christianity, and expressly recognised it. St. Peter indeed taught it in this sermon, but he did not recognise the force of his own words. Jesus Christ not only taught it, but realized the meaning of His teaching. It was indeed no part of Christ's earthly ministry to preach to the Gentiles. He came to the house of Israel alone. Yet how clearly He witnesses, how distinctly He prophesies of the future universality of His kingdom. He heals a centurion's servant, proclaiming at the same time that many shall come from the east and west, and sit down in the kingdom, while the children of the kingdom shall be cast out. He risks His life among the inhabitants of the city where He had been brought up, in order that He may deliver this truth. He repeats it to the woman of Samaria, in order that He may chase away her national superstition. He embodies it in His great eucharistic prayer for His Apostles and for His Church at large. The more carefully and the more devoutly we study Christ's words, the more lofty will be our conception of His personality and character, who from the very beginning recognised the full force of His message, the true extent of that Divine society He was about to establish. The avowed catholicity of Christ's teaching is one of the surest proofs of Christ's divinity. He had not to wait as Peter waited, till events explained the meaning of His words; from the beginning He knew all things which should happen.

Still the tone of St. Peter's sermon proved that the Spirit had supernaturally enlightened him. He had already risen to spiritual heights undreamt-of hitherto, even by himself. A comparison of a few passages proves this. In the sixteenth chapter of St. Matthew we have narrated for us the scene where our Lord extracts from St. Peter his celebrated confession, "Thou art the Christ, the Son of the living God," and then soon after bestows upon him the equally celebrated rebuke, "Get thee behind Me, Satan! thou art a stumblingblock unto Me: for thou mindest not the things of God, but the things of men." St. Peter, with his horror-struck opposition to the very idea of Christ's death and suffering, evidently cherished the same notions of the kingdom of God, which Christ had come to establish, as James and John did when they petitioned for the highest place in the Master's kingdom. This carnal conception of a temporal kingdom and earthly forces and human weapons St. Peter retained when he armed himself with a sword and prepared to defend his Master in the Garden of Gethsemane; and even later still when, after the resurrection, the Apostles, acting doubtless through Peter as their spokesman, demanded, "Dost Thou at this time restore the kingdom to Israel?" But the Spirit was vouchsafed, and new power, of which the Master had spoken, was granted, and that power raised Peter above all such low Jewish ideas, and the kingdom announced to the Jews is no longer a kingdom of earth, with its carnal weapons and its dignities. He now understood what the Master had taught when He witnessed before Pontius Pilate His good confession, "My kingdom is not of this world: if My kingdom were of this world, then would My servants fight, that I should not be delivered to the Jews: but now is My kingdom not from hence." The carnal conception passes away under the influence of the heavenly solvent, and St.

Peter proclaimed a kingdom which was a purely spiritual dominion, dealing with remission of sins and a purified interior life, through the operation and indwelling of the Holy Ghost. The power of the Holy Ghost was shown in St. Peter's case by the vast and complete change which passed at once over his spiritual ideas and outlook. The thoughts and expectations of the pious Jews of Galilee—the very class from whom St. Peter sprang—were just then shaped and formed by the popular apocalyptic literature of the period, as we have already pointed out in the second lecture. The Second Epistle of St. Peter and the Epistle of Jude prove that the Galileans of that time were careful students of works like the Assumption of Moses, the Book of Enoch, and the Ascension of Isaiah, which agree in representing the kingdom of God and the reign of the Messiah as equivalent to the triumph of the Jewish nation over all foreign dominion and bondage. St. Peter and the other eleven Apostles shared these natural ideas and expectations till the Spirit was poured out, when they learned in a profounder spiritual comprehension to estimate aright the scope and meaning of our blessed Lord's teaching. St. Peter dwells, therefore, in his sermon on Christ's person, His sufferings, His resurrection, His ascension, no longer indeed for the purpose of exalting the Jewish nation, or predicting its triumph, but to point a purely spiritual lesson. "Repent ye, and be baptized every one of you in the name of Jesus Christ unto the remission of your sins; and ye shall receive"—not honour, riches, temporal freedom, but "ye shall receive the gift of the Holy Ghost." The subject-matter of St. Peter's sermon, the change in his tone of teaching, is another great proof of a supernatural force and power imparted on the Day of Pentecost.

IV. Let us look somewhat farther into the matter of this earliest Christian sermon, that we may learn the apostolic view of the Christian scheme. Some persons have asserted that the earliest Christians were Ebionites,[62] and taught a system of doctrine akin to modern Unitarianism. This theory can best be tested by an appeal to the Acts of the Apostles. What, for instance, was the conception of Christ's life, work, and ascended state, which St. Peter presented to the astonished multitude? We must not expect, indeed, to find in this sermon a formulated and scientific system of Christian doctrine. St. Peter was as yet far too near the great events he declared, far too close to the superhuman personality of Christ, to co-ordinate his ideas and arrange his views. It is a matter of every-day experience that when a new discovery is suddenly made, when a new revelation takes place in the region of nature, men do not grasp at once all the new relations thereby involved, all the novel applications whereof it is capable. The human mind is so limited in its power that it is not till we get some distance away from a great object that we are enabled to survey it in the fulness of its outline. Inspiration assisted

St. Peter, elevated his mind, raised his tone of thought to a higher level, but it did not reverse this fundamental law under which the human mind works. Yet St. Peter's discourse contains all the great principles of Catholic Christianity as opposed to that low view which would represent the earliest Christians as preaching the purely humanitarian scheme of modern Unitarianism. St. Peter taught boldly the miraculous element of Christ's life, describing Him as "a man approved of God by mighty works and wonders and signs which God did by Him." Yet he did not dwell as much as we might have expected upon the miraculous side of Christ's ministry. In fact, the earliest heralds of the Cross did not make as much use of the argument from miracles as we might have expected them to have done. And that for a very simple reason. The inhabitants of the East were so accustomed to the practices of magic that they simply classed the Christian missionaries with magicians. The Jewish explanation of the miracles of our Lord is of this description. The Talmudists do not deny that He worked miracles, but assert that He achieved them by a special use of the Tetragammaton, or the sacred name of Jehovah, which was known only to Himself. The sacred writers and preachers refer, therefore, again and again to the miracles of our Saviour, as St. Peter does in the second chapter, as well-known and admitted facts, whatever explanation may be offered of them, and then turn to other aspects of the question. The Apostles had, however, a more powerful argument in reserve. They preached a spiritual religion, a present peace with God, a present forgiveness of sins; they point forward to a future life of which even here below believers possess the earnest and the pledge. We, with our minds steeped in ages of Christian thought and teaching, can have no idea of the convincing self-evidencing force of teaching like that, to a Jew reared up in a system of barren formalism, and still more to a Gentile, with spiritual instincts longing for satisfaction, and which he was expected to satisfy with the bloodstained shows of the amphitheatre or with the immoralities and impure banquetings of the pagan temples. To persons in that condition, an argument derived from a mere wonderful work brought little conviction, for they were well accustomed to behold very marvellous and apparently miraculous actions, such as to this day the wandering jugglers of India exhibit.[63] But when they beheld lives transfused by the love of God, and heard pure spiritual teaching such as responded to the profoundest depths of their own hearts, then deep answered unto deep. The preaching of the Cross became indeed the power of God unto salvation, because the human soul instinctively felt that the Cross was the medicine fittest for its spiritual maladies.

V. Again, this sermon shows the method of interpreting the Psalms and Prophets popular among the pious Jews of St. Peter's time. St. Peter's method of interpretation is identical with that of our Lord, of St. Paul, and of the author of the Epistle to the Hebrews. He beholds in the Psalms hints and types of the profoundest doctrines of the Creed. We can see this in both the quotations which he makes. St. Peter finds in the sixteenth Psalm a prophecy of the intermediate state of souls and of the resurrection of our Lord. "Thou wilt not leave my soul in Hades" is a text which has furnished the basis of the article in the Apostles' Creed which teaches that Christ descended into hell. It is a pity indeed that the translation which the last revisers have adopted, "Hades" instead of "Hell," was not used in the English translation of the Apostles' Creed; for the ordinary reading has misled many a thoughtful and serious soul, as if the Creed taught that the pure and sinless spirit of the Saviour had been made partaker of the horrors of eternal misery. Whereas, in truth, the doctrine of Scripture and of the Creed alike merely asserts that our Lord's spirit, when separated from the body, entered and thereby sanctified and prepared the place or state where Christian souls, while separated from their bodies, await the general resurrection of the just and the completion of their happiness. The doctrine of the intermediate state, as taught by Bishop Pearson and other great divines, is primarily based on two texts, the passage before us and the words of our Saviour to the penitent thief, "To-day shalt thou be with Me in Paradise" (Luke xxiii. 43). This doctrine accurately corresponds with the catholic doctrine of our Lord's Person. The Arian heresy denied the true deity of our Lord. The second great heresy was the Apollinarian, which denied His true and perfect humanity. The orthodox doctrine taught the tripartite nature of man, that is, that there was in man, first, a body, secondly, the animal soul which man possesses in common with the beasts, and which perishes at death, and, lastly, the human spirit which is immortal and by which he maintains communion with God. Now the Apollinarian heresy asserted that Jesus Christ possessed a body and a soul, but denied His possession of a spirit. Its theory was that the Divine nature took the place of a true human spirit in Christ, so that Christ was unlike His brethren in this respect, that when the body died, and the animal soul perished, He had no human spirit by which He might enter into Hades, or dwell in Paradise. The Divine nature was the only portion of the Incarnate Lord which then survived. Against this view the words of St. Peter testified beforehand, teaching, by his adaptation of David's prophecy, that our Lord possessed the fulness of humanity in its threefold division, whereby He was enabled to share the experience and lot of His brethren, not only in this life, but also in the intermediate state of Hades, wherein the spirits of the blessed dead await re-union with their bodies, and expect in hope the second advent of their Lord.[64]

St. Peter's interpretation again of the Psalms recognised in David's words a prophecy of the resurrection: "Neither wilt Thou give Thy Holy One to see corruption,"—a rendering of the New Testament revisers which, however literal, is not nearly as vigorous or suggestive as the old translation, "Neither wilt Thou suffer Thy Holy One to see corruption." St. Peter then proceeds to point out how impossible it was that this prediction could have been fulfilled in David. David's flesh undoubtedly did see corruption, because every one knew where his tomb was. St. Peter's speech here touches upon a point where we can confirm his accuracy out of ancient historians. David was buried, according to ancient writers, in the city of David (2 Kings ii. 10). The Rabbis went even further, they determined the time of his death. According to a writer quoted by that great seventeenth-century teacher, Dr. John Lightfoot,[65] "David died at Pentecost, and all Israel bewailed him, and offered their sacrifices the day following." After the return from Babylon the site of the sepulchre was known, as Neh. iii. 16 reports, telling us that Nehemiah the son of Azbuk repaired the wall over against the sepulchre of David; while still later Josephus[66] tells us that Hyrcanus, the high priest, and Herod the Great opened David's tomb, and removed vast treasures from it. St. Peter's words on this occasion possess an important evidential aspect, and suggest one of the gravest difficulties which the assailants of the resurrection have to face. St. Peter appealed to the evidence of David's tomb as demonstrating the fact that he was dead, and that death still held him in its power. Why did not his opponents appeal to the testimony of Christ's tomb? It is evident from St. Peter's argument that Christ's tomb was empty, and was known to be empty. The first witnesses to the resurrection insisted, within a few weeks of our Lord's crucifixion, upon this fact, proclaimed it everywhere, and the Jews made no attempt to dispute their assertions. Our opponents may indeed say, we acknowledge the fact of the emptiness of the tomb, but the body of Christ was removed by St. Peter and his associates. How then, we reply, do you account for St. Peter's action? Did conscious guilt and hypocrisy make him brave and enthusiastic? If they say, indeed, Peter did not remove the body, but that his associates did, then how are we to account for the conversations St. Peter thought he had held with his risen Master, the appearances vouchsafed to him, the close converse, "eating and drinking with him after He was risen from the dead"? St. Peter, by his appeal to David's tomb, and its bearing on the sixteenth Psalm, proves that he believed in no ideal resurrection, no phantasm,—no ghost story, to put it plainly; but that he taught the doctrine of the resurrection as the Church now accepts it.

# CHAPTER VII
# THE FIRSTFRUITS OF PENTECOST

"Now when they heard this, they were pricked in their heart, and said unto Peter and the rest of the apostles, Brethren, what shall we do? And Peter said unto them, Repent ye, and be baptized every one of you in the name of Jesus Christ unto the remission of your sins; and ye shall receive the gift of the Holy Ghost. For to you is the promise, and to your children, and to all that are afar off, even as many as the Lord our God shall call unto Him." —Acts ii. 37-39.

The sermon of St. Peter on the day of Pentecost and the sermon of our Lord present a striking contrast. Our Lord's sermons were of various kinds; they were at times consoling, yet full of instruction and direction. Such, for instance, was the Sermon on the Mount. At other times His discourses were stern, and full of sharp reproof. Such was His teaching in His parting addresses to the Jews delivered in the temple, recorded in the synoptic Gospels. Yet they apparently failed, for the time at least, in producing any great practical results. In fact, His temple discourses served only to irritate His foes, and arouse their hostility.

St. Peter delivered a sermon on the day of Pentecost which was quite as stern and quite as calculated to irritate, and yet that discourse was crowned with results exceeding those ever achieved by our Lord, though His discourses far surpassed St. Peter's in literary skill, in spiritual meaning, in eternal significance and value. Whence came this fact? It simply happened in fulfilment of Christ's own prophecy recorded by St. John, where He predicts that His Apostles shall achieve greater works than He had achieved, "because I go unto the Father" (John xiv. 12). The departure of Christ into the true Holy of Holies opened the channel of communication between the eternal Father and the waiting Church; the Spirit was poured out through Christ as the channel, and the result was conviction and conversion; leading the people to cry out, in response to St. Peter's simple statement of facts, "Men and brethren, what shall we do?"

I. One of the first qualifications absolutely necessary, if a man is to write history tellingly and sympathetically, is a historical imagination. Unless a man can, from a multitude of separate and often independent details, reconstruct the past, realize it vividly for himself, and then depict it with life and force to his readers, he will utterly fail as a historian. The same historical imagination is needed, too, if we wish to realize the full force of the circumstances we are considering. It is hard even for those who do possess such an imagination to throw themselves back into all the circumstances and surroundings of the Apostles at Pentecost; but when we succeed in doing so, then all these circumstances can only be explained on the supposition—the orthodox and catholic supposition—that there must have happened a supernatural occurrence, and that there must have been granted a supernatural power and blessing on the day of Pentecost.

The courage of St. Peter when preaching his sermon is, as we have already noticed, a proof of the descent of the Spirit. The resurrection of his Master had doubtless inspired him with all the power of a new idea. But St. Peter's history, both before the day of Pentecost and after it, amply proved that mere intellectual conviction could be united with grievous moral cowardice. We cannot doubt, for instance, that St. Peter was intellectually convinced of the justice of the Gentile claims, and their right to a full equality with the Jews, when St. Paul felt compelled to withstand him at Antioch. Yet he was possessed with no such spiritual enthusiasm on the question as that which moved St. Paul, or else he never would have fallen into such lamentable hypocrisy as he displayed on that occasion. The gift of the Spirit was needed by St. Peter before an intellectual conviction could be transformed into an overwhelming spiritual movement, which swept every obstacle from its path. Again, the conduct of the people is a proof of the descent of the Spirit. St. Peter assails their actions, charges upon them the murder of the Messiah, and proclaims the triumph of Christ over all their machinations. Yet they listen quietly, respectfully, without opposition, as mobs do not usually listen to speeches running counter to their prejudices. Some wondrous phenomena, such as the gift of tongues, combined with divinely persuasive eloquence, flinging the ægis of their protection over the preacher's defenceless person, must have so struck the minds of these fanatical Jews as to keep them quiet while St. Peter spoke. But the result of St. Peter's speech was the chiefest evidence that something extraordinary must have happened at Jerusalem in the earliest days of the Church's history. Secular history tells us, as well as the sacred narrative, that Christianity rose again from what seemed its grave at the very spot where, and at the very moment when, the crucifixion had apparently extinguished it for ever.

The evidence of the historian Tacitus is conclusive upon this point. He lived and flourished all through the time when St. Paul's ministry was most active. He was born about the year 50, and had every opportunity of becoming acquainted with the facts concerning the execution of Christ and the rise of Christianity, as they were doubtless laid up in the imperial archives at Rome. His testimony, written at a period when, as some maintain, neither the Acts of the Apostles nor the Gospels of the New Testament were in existence, exactly tallies with the account given by our sacred books. In his *Annals*, book xv., chap. 44, he writes concerning Christianity: "Christus, from whom the name of Christian has its origin, suffered the extreme penalty during the reign of Tiberius at the hands of one of our procurators, Pontius Pilate, and a most mischievous superstition, thus checked for the moment, again broke out in Judæa." So that the Pagan historian, who knew nothing about Christianity save what official pagan documents or popular report told him, agrees with the Scriptures that Christianity was checked for a moment by the death of its founder, and then gained its earliest and most glorious triumph on the very scene of its apparent defeat where—and this is a very important part of the argument—previously the most marvellous wisdom and the most striking signs and wonders had utterly failed to gain any large measure of success. Whence, then, can we explain this fact, or how account for this conscience-stricken cry, "Men and brethren, what shall we do?" unless we assume, what the narrative of our text declares, that the Holy Ghost, in all His convincing and converting power, had been poured out from on high?

And surely our own personal experience daily corroborates this view. There may be intellectual conviction and controversial triumph without any spiritual enthusiasm. Sermons may be clever, powerful, convincing, and yet, unless the Spirit's power be sought, and an unction from on high be vouchsafed, no spiritual harvest can be expected. St. Peter's sermon, if viewed from a human standpoint, could no more have been expected to succeed than the Master's. The one new element, however, which now entered into the combination, explains the difference. The Spirit was now given, and men therefore hearkened to the servant where they had turned a deaf ear to the Master. It is a lesson much needed for our generation, especially in the case of the young, and of our Sunday-school system. The religious instruction of youth is much more carefully looked after than it used to be. Primers, handbooks, elementary commentaries, catechists' manuals, are published in profusion, and many think that provided a Sunday or day school distinguishes itself in the examination list, which is now the one great educational test, religious knowledge has been secured. The contrast between St. Peter's success and our Lord's failure warns us that there is a vast difference between religious life and religious knowledge. The most irreligious people, the most bitter opponents of Christianity, have been produced by schools and systems where religious knowledge was literally crammed down the throats of the children in a hard, mechanical, unloving style. But let there be no mistake. I do not object to organised religious instruction. I think, in fact, that a vast amount of Sunday-school teaching is utterly worthless for want of such organization. Our Sunday-school system will, in fact, be thoroughly inefficient, if not useless, as a system, till every Sunday-school has its teachers' meeting, presided over by a competent instructor, who will carefully teach the teachers themselves in a well-ordered, systematic course. But after all this has been done, we must still remember that Christianity is something more than a system of doctrine, or a Divine scheme of philosophy, which can be worked up like Aristotle's *Ethics* or Mill's *Logic*. Christianity is a Divine power, a power which must be sought in faith, in humiliation, and in prayer; and till the Holy Ghost be duly honoured, and His presence be humbly sought, the finest system and the most elaborate organizations will be found devoid of any fruitful life and vigour.

II. There are many other points of interest in this passage; let us take them one by one as they offer themselves. The people, seized by conviction and in acute pain of conscience, cried out, "What shall we do?" St. Peter replied, "Repent, and be baptized." Repent is the Apostle's first rule,— contrasting very strongly with some modern systems which have been devised on a plan very different from that of our Lord and of His Apostles. The preaching of the New Testament is ever the same. John the Baptist came, and his teaching was briefly summed up thus, "Repent ye, for the kingdom of heaven is at hand." John was removed, and Christ came. The lamp ceased to shine, and then the true Light stood revealed; but the teaching was the same, and the Messiah still proclaims, "Repent, for the kingdom of heaven is at hand." The system of teaching to which I refer parries the force of our Lord's example, as well as of the Baptist's words, by saying, that was the old dispensation. Till Christ died, the new covenant did not come into force, and therefore Christ taught in His public ministry merely as a Jew, speaking on Jewish grounds to Jews. But let us see whether such an explanation, which makes void our Lord's personal teachings and commands, is tenable. A reference to this passage sufficiently settles this point. The Master departs and the Spirit is outpoured, and still the apostolic and inspired teaching is just the same. The cry of the multitude, "Men and brethren, what shall we do?" produces, from the illuminated Apostle, the same response, "Repent," coupled with a new requirement, "Be baptized, every one of you, for the remission of sins." And the same message has ever since continued to be the basis of all real spiritual work. Simon Magus is found by St. Peter with his mind intellectually convinced, but with his affections untouched and his heart spiritually dead. To Simon Magus Peter delivers the same message, "Repent of this thy wickedness, and pray God if perhaps the thought of thine heart may be forgiven thee." John Wesley was one of the greatest evangelists that ever lived and worked for God. During the whole sixty years of his continuous labours, from the time when he taught his pupils in Oxford College and the prisoners in Oxford jail down to the last sermon that he preached, his ministry and teaching were modelled upon that of the New Testament,—it was ever a preaching of repentance. He counted it utterly useless and hopeless to preach the comforts of the gospel before he had made men feel and wince beneath the terrors of the law and the sense of offended justice. Modern times have seen, however, a strange perversion of the gospel method, and some have taught that repentance was not to be urged or even mentioned to Christian congregations.

This is one of the leading points which the Plymouth Brethren specially press in the course of their destructive and guerilla-like assaults upon the communions of reformed Christendom. The apostolic doctrine of repentance finds no place in their scheme; while again their teaching on this subject, or something very like it, is often reproduced, all unconsciously it may be, by the conductors of those mission services so common throughout the country. It is as hard now to preserve a just balance in teaching, as it was in the days of St. Paul and St. James. It is no easy matter so to preach repentance as not to discourage the truly humble soul; so to proclaim God's forgiving love as not to encourage presumption and carelessness.

I have said, indeed, that the doctrine of the Plymouth body on this point is a modern one. It is modern, indeed, when compared with the genuine teaching of the New Testament; but still it is, in fact, ancient, for it dates back to the Antinomians, who, two hundred and fifty years ago, created a great sensation among the Puritan divines. A brief historical narrative will prove this. The sermons of Dr. Tobias Crisp and Fisher's *Marrow of Modern Divinity* are books whose very titles are now forgotten, and yet the diligent student will there find all those ideas about repentance, justification, and assurance which are now produced as marvellous new truths, though reprobated two centuries ago as earnestly by Churchmen, like Bull, Beveridge, and Stillingfleet, as by Howe, and Baxter, and Williams among the Nonconformists and Puritans. The denial of the necessity for Christian repentance was based, by the logical Antinomians of the olden time, upon the theory that Christ bore in His own person the literal sins of the elect; so that an elect person has nothing whatsoever to do with his sins save assure himself, by an act of faith, that his sins were forgiven and rendered completely non-existent eighteen hundred years ago. The formula which they delight in and I have heard used, even by Churchmen, is this: "Believe that you are saved, and then you are saved." The result of this teaching in every age, wherever it has appeared, is not far to seek. The main stress of all

Christian effort is devoted not to the attainment of likeness to Christ, or that pursuit of holiness without which the beatific vision of God is impossible. The great point urged by this party in every age is the supreme importance of assurance which they identify with saving faith.[67] Therefore it is that they discourage, aye, and go farther, utterly reject, all teaching of repentance. The words of one of those old writers puts the matter in its simplest form. In the reign of James II. and William III. there arose a great controversy in London touching this very point. Dr. Williams, the founder of the well-known library in Grafton Street, London, was the leader on one side, while the sermons of Tobias Crisp were the rallying-point on the other. Williams and Baxter maintained the importance of repentance and the absolute necessity of good works for salvation. On the opposite side, the views and doctrines which we have seen pressed in modern times were explicitly stated, but with far more fearlessness and logical power than are ever now used. Here are a few of the propositions which Dr. Williams felt himself bound to refute. I shall give them at some length, that my readers may see how ancient is this heresy. "The elect are discharged from all their sins by the act of God laying their sins upon Christ on the cross, and consequently that the elect upon the death of Christ ceased to be sinners, and ever since sins committed by them are none of their sins, they are the sins of Christ." Again, the Antinomians taught, in language often still reproduced, "Men have nothing to do in order to salvation, nor is sanctification a jot the way of any person to heaven. Nor can the duties and graces of the elect, nor even faith itself, do them the least good, or prevent the least evil; while, on the other hand, the grossest sins which the elect commit cannot do them the least harm, nor ought they to fear the least hurt from their own sins." While again, coming still closer to the point on which we have been insisting, they declared, according to Dr. Williams, that "the covenant of grace hath no condition to be performed on man's part, even though in the strength of Christ. Neither is faith itself the condition of this covenant, but all the saving benefits of this covenant actually and really belong to the elect before they are born, yea, and even against their will;" while as to the nature of faith, they taught "that saving faith is nothing else but our persuasion or absolute concluding within ourselves that our sins are pardoned, and that Christ is ours." Hence they derived a dogma of their own, directly and plainly contradictory of the teaching of the New Testament on the subject of repentance, "that Christ is offered to blasphemers, murderers, and the worst of sinners, that they, remaining ignorant, unconvinced, and resolved in their purpose to continue such, may be assured they have a full interest in Christ; and this by only concluding in their own minds that Christ is theirs." It is plain to any one fully acquainted with modern religious thought, that all the special doctrines of Plymouthism concerning justification, repentance, and faith, are involved in the statements which Dr. Williams set himself to refute, and which he does refute most ably, in works long since consigned to the oblivion of our great libraries, though well worthy of careful study amid the troubles of the present age.[68] Assurance, a present knowledge of a present salvation, present peace, these are the only topics pressed upon the unconverted. If the multitude at Jerusalem had asked the same question from our modern teachers which they asked from the Apostles, "Men and brethren, what shall we do?" the reply would have been, "Do you know you are saved? If not, believe that you are saved, believe that Jesus died for you." But not one of them would have given the apostolic reply, "Repent, and be baptized, and ye shall receive the gift of the Holy Ghost," because the doctrine of repentance and the value and use of the sacrament of baptism find no place in this new-fangled scheme.

III. "Repent, and be baptized every one of you in the name of Jesus Christ for the remission of your sins." These words form the basis of a well-known clause in the Nicene Creed, which says, "I acknowledge one baptism for the remission of sins." They suggest in addition some very important discussions. The position which baptism occupies in apostolic teaching is worthy of careful notice. It is pressed upon the multitude as a present duty, and as the result there were three thousand persons baptized in that one day. It was just the same with Cornelius the centurion, and with the Philippian jailer whom St. Paul converted. Baptism did not then succeed a long course of preparatory training and instruction, as now is the case in the mission field. When men in apostolic times received the rudiments of the faith, the sacrament of baptism was administered, as being the channel or door of admission into Christ's Church; and then, being once admitted into God's house, it was firmly believed that the soul's life would grow and develop at a vastly accelerated rate. A grave question here suggests itself, whether baptism of converts from paganism is not often too long delayed? The Apostles evidently regarded the Church as an hospital where the wounds of the soul were to be healed, as a Divine school where the ignorance of the soul was to be dissipated, and therefore at once admitted the converts to the sacrament upon the profession of their rudimentary faith. The Church soon reversed this process, and demanded an amount of spiritual knowledge and a development of spiritual life as the conditions of baptism, which should have been looked for as the result of admission within her sacred ranks, forgetful of that great missionary law laid down by the Master Himself, which places baptism first and teaching afterwards, "Go ye, therefore, and make disciples of all the nations, baptizing them into the name of the Father and of the Son and of the Holy Ghost: teaching them to observe all things whatsoever I have commanded you." We freely admit that there may have been a quickened spiritual vitality, a stronger spiritual life, in the case of the earliest converts, enabling them in the course of a few hours to attain a spiritual level which demanded a more prolonged effort on the part of the later disciples. When we come to the times of the later apostolic age, and inquire from such a book as the lately-discovered *Teaching of the Twelve Apostles*, what the practice of the Church was then, we see that experience had taught a more regular, a less hasty course of action.[69] The law of baptism in the *Didache*, as the *Teaching of the Twelve Apostles* is usually called, runs thus: "Now concerning baptism, thus baptize ye; having first uttered all these things, baptize into the name of the Father and of the Son and of the Holy Spirit, in running water. But if thou hast not running water, baptize in other water; and if thou canst not in cold, then in warm. But if thou hast neither, pour water upon the head thrice, into the name of the Father and Son and Holy Spirit. But before the baptism let the baptizer and the baptized fast, and whatever others can; but the baptized thou shalt command to fast for one or two days before."

From these words it is plain that the immediate baptism of converts had ceased probably with the first organization of the Church. A pause was instituted between the first conviction of the truth and the complete initiation which baptism involved, but not such a period of delay as the months and even years over which the preparation for baptism was subsequently spread. This delay of baptism sprang out of a mistaken view of this Divine sacrament. Men came to look on it as a charm, whereby not merely admission was obtained to the Divine society which our Lord had founded, but also as bringing with it a complete purgation from the sins of a careless life. Men postponed it, therefore, to the very last, so that all sins might be swept away at once. The Emperor Constantine was a good example of this mischievous extreme. He was a man who took a kind of interest in theological matters. Like our own King James I., he considered it his duty to settle the religious affairs of his empire, even as his predecessors had done in the days of paganism. He presided over Church councils, dictated Church formularies, and exercised the same control in the Church as in the State, being all the time unbaptized. He was scarce aught but a pagan too in disposition and temper. He retained pagan symbols, titles, and observances, and imbrued his hands, Herod-like, in the blood of his own family. Yet he delayed his baptism to the very last, under the notion that then there could be thus effected at one stroke the complete removal of the accumulated sins of a lifetime.

IV. The comparison of the passage just quoted from the *Teaching of the Apostles* with the words of my text suggests other topics. The Plymouth Brethren, at least in some of their numerous ramifications, and other sects, have grounded upon the words, "be baptized, every one of you, in the name of Jesus Christ," a tenet that baptism should not be conferred in the name of the Trinity, but in that of Jesus alone. It is indeed admitted that while our Lord commanded the use of the historic baptismal formula in the concluding words of St. Matthew's Gospel, the formula itself is never expressly mentioned in the Acts of the Apostles. Not merely on the day of Pentecost, but on several other occasions, Christian baptism is described as if the Trinitarian formula was unknown. In the tenth chapter Cornelius and his household are described as "baptized in the name of Jesus Christ." In the nineteenth chapter St. Paul converts a number of the Baptist's disciples to a fuller and richer faith in Christ. They were at once "baptized into the name of the Lord Jesus." But a reference to the newly-discovered *Teaching of the Twelve Apostles* explains the difficulty, offering an interesting example of the manner in which modern discoveries have helped to illustrate and confirm the Acts of the Apostles. In the *Didache*, as in the Acts, the expression "baptism in the name of the Lord" is used. The *Didache* lays down with respect to the communion, "Let no one eat or drink of your Eucharist except those baptized into the name of the Lord." Yet this does not exclude the time-honoured formula of Christendom. The same apostolic manual lays down the rule, a little before this prohibition which we have just quoted, "Baptize into the name of the Father and of the Son and of the Holy Spirit," and then in the tenth chapter describes baptism thus administered in the threefold name, as baptism in the name of the Lord; and thus it was doubtless in the case of the Acts. For the sake of brevity St. Luke speaks of Christian baptism as baptism in the name of Christ, never dreaming at the same time that this was exclusive of the divinely appointed formula, as certain moderns have taught. The Acts of the Apostles, and the *Didache* prove their primitive character, and show that they deduce their origin from the same early epoch, because they both describe Christian baptism as performed in the name of Christ; and yet this fact does not exclude, according to either, the use of the threefold Name. It is evident that, whether in the Acts or in the *Didache*, baptism in the name of the Father, Son, and Holy Ghost was regarded as baptism especially in the name of Jesus Christ, because while the Father and the Spirit were known to the Jews, the one new element introduced was that of the name of Jesus, whom God had made both Lord and Christ. Baptism in the Triune Name was emphatically baptism in the name of the Lord. This passage, when compared with the *Didache*, sheds light on another point. The mode wherein baptism should be administered has been a point often discussed. Some have maintained the absolutely binding and universal character of immersion; others have stood at the opposite extreme, and upheld the method of sprinkling. The Church of England, in union with the ancient Church, has laid down no hard-and-fast rule on the subject. She recognises immersion as the normal idea in a warm Eastern climate, but she allows pouring (not sprinkling) of water to be substituted for immersion, which has, as a matter of fact, taken the place in the Western Church of the more regular and ancient immersion.[70] The construction of the ancient Churches, with their baptisteries surrounded with curtains, and the female assistants for the service of their own sex, amply proves that in the ancient Church, as to this day in the Eastern Church, baptism was ordinarily administered by immersion. The Church proved its Eastern origin by the mode wherein its initial sacrament was at first applied. But it also showed its power of adaptation to Western nations by allowing the alternative of pouring water when she dealt with the needs of a colder climate. Yet from the beginning the Church cannot have made the validity of her sacraments depend upon the quantity of water that was used. Take the cases reported in the Acts of the Apostles, or the rules prescribed in the apostolic manual, the *Didache*. In the latter it is expressly said that pouring with water shall suffice if a larger quantity is not at hand. On the day of Pentecost it was clearly impossible to immerse three thousand persons in the city of Jerusalem. The Ethiopian eunuch baptized by St. Philip in the wilderness could not have been immersed. He came to a stream trickling along, scarce sufficient to lave his feet, or perhaps rather to a well in the desert; the water was deep down, and reached only, as in the case of Jacob's well, by a rope or chain. Even if the water could have been reached, common sense, not to speak of any higher motive, would have forbidden the pollution of an element so needful for human life. The baptism of the eunuch must have been by pouring or affusion, as must also have been the case with the Philippian jailer. The difficulties of the case are forgotten when people insist that immersion must necessarily have been the universal rule in ancient times.[71] Men and women were baptized separately, deaconesses officiating in the case of the women. When immersion was used the men descended naked, or almost so, into the baptistery, which was often a building quite separate and distinct from the church, with elaborate arrangements for changing garments.[72] The Church, in the days of earliest freedom and purity, left her children free in those points of minor detail, refusing to hamper herself or limit her usefulness by a restriction which would have equally barred entrance to her fold in the burning deserts or in the ice-bound regions of the frozen north, where baptism by immersion would have been equally impossible.

Again, the extent of the baptismal commission is indicated in this passage. "Make disciples of all the nations by baptism" are the words of our Lord. "Be baptized, every one of you, for the promise is to you and to your children, and to all that are afar off," is St. Peter's application of this passage. St. Peter's language admits of various interpretations. Like much of Scripture, the speaker, when uttering these words, meant probably one thing, while the words themselves mean something much wider, more catholic and universal. When Peter spake thus he proclaimed the world-wide character of Christianity, just as when he quoted the prophet Joel's language he declared the mission of the Comforter in its most catholic aspect, embracing Gentiles as well as Jews. "I will pour out My Spirit upon all flesh." But St. Peter never thought of the full scope of his words. He meant, doubtless, that the promise of pardon, and acceptance, and citizenship in the heavenly kingdom was to those Jews that were present in Jerusalem, and to their children, and to all of the Jews of the dispersion scattered afar off amid the Gentiles. Had Peter thought otherwise, had he perceived the wider meaning of his words, he would have had no hesitation about the reception of the Gentiles, and the baptism of Cornelius would not have demanded a fresh revelation.

We often, indeed, invest the Apostles and the writers of Holy Scripture with an intellectual grasp of a supernatural kind, which prevents us recognising that growth in Divine knowledge which found place in them, as it found place in the Divine Master Himself. We silently vote them infallible on every topic, because the Spirit's presence was abundantly vouchsafed. The inspiration they enjoyed guided their language, and led them to use words which, while expressing their own sentiments, admitted a deeper meaning and embraced a wider scope than the speaker intended. It was just the same with the Apostles' words as with their conduct in other respects. The presence and inspiration of the Spirit did not make them sinless, did not destroy human infirmities. It did not destroy St. Peter's moral cowardice, or St. Paul's hot temper, or St. Barnabas's family partiality and nepotism; and neither did that presence illumine at once St. Peter's natural prejudices and intellectual backwardness, which led him long to restrain the mercies and lovingkindness of the Lord to His ancient people, though here on the day of Pentecost we find him using language which plainly included the Gentiles as well as the Jews within the covenant of grace. A farther question concerning the language of St. Peter here arises. Do not his words indicate that children were fit subjects for baptism? Do they not justify the practice of infant baptism? I honestly confess that, apart from the known practice of the Jews, St. Peter's language would not necessarily mean so much. But then when we take the known practice of the Jews into consideration; when we remember that St. Peter was speaking to a congregation composed of Jews of the dispersion, accustomed, in their own missionary work among the heathen, to baptize children as well as adults, we must admit that, in the absence of any prohibition to the contrary, the effect of the words of

St. Peter upon his hearers must have been this; they would have acted when Christians as they had already done as Jews, and baptized proselytes of every age and condition on their admission to the Christian fold. (See Lightfoot, *Hor. Heb.*, St. Matt. iii. 6.)

V. Such was St. Peter's sermon on the day of Pentecost. The results of it in the unity of doctrine and discipline and the community of goods will come before us in subsequent chapters. One thought stands out prominent as we survey this second chapter. Here in very deed we find an ample fulfilment of our Lord's promise to St. Peter which has been so completely misused and misunderstood, "I will give unto thee the keys of the kingdom of heaven;" a passage which has been made one of the scriptural foundations of the monstrous claims of the See of Rome to an absolute supremacy alike over the Christian Church and over the individual conscience. In this respect, however, Scripture is its own best interpreter. Just reflect how it is in this matter. Christ first of all defines, in the celebrated series of parables related in the thirteenth of St. Matthew, what the kingdom of heaven is. It is the kingdom He had come to reveal, the society He was establishing, the Church and dispensation of which He is the Head and Chief. To St. Peter he gave the keys, or power of opening the doors, of this kingdom; and this office St. Peter duly executed. He opened the door of the kingdom of heaven to the Jews on the day of Pentecost, and to the Gentiles by the conversion and baptism of Cornelius. St. Peter himself recognised on one occasion the special Providence which watched over him in this matter. He points out, in his speech to the brethren gathered at the first council held at Jerusalem, that "a good while ago God made choice among you, that by my mouth the Gentiles should hear the word of the gospel;" a passage which seems a reminiscence of the earlier promise of Christ, which Peter must have so well remembered, and a humble recognition of the glorious fulfilment which that promise had received at the Divine hand.[73] The promise was a purely personal one peculiar to St. Peter, as purely personal as the revelation made to him on the housetop at Joppa, and as such received a complete fulfilment in the Church's infant days. But Rome's vaulting ambition would not be content with the fulfilment which satisfied St. Peter himself, and on this text has been built up a series of claims which, culminating in the celebrated traffic in indulgences, precipitated the great revolution involved in the German Reformation.

# CHAPTER VIII
# THE FIRST MIRACLE

"Now Peter and John were going up into the temple at the
hour of prayer, being the ninth hour. And a certain man that
was lame from his mother's womb was carried, whom they
laid daily at the door of the temple which is called Beautiful,
to ask alms of them that entered into the temple; who seeing
Peter and John about to go into the temple, asked to receive
an alms. And Peter, fastening his eyes upon him, with John,
said, Look on us. And he gave heed unto them, expecting to
receive something from them. But Peter said, Silver and gold
have I none; but what I have, that give I thee. In the name of
Jesus Christ of Nazareth, walk." —Acts iii. 1-6.

The Acts of the Apostles considered as the first history of the Church
may be viewed as typical of all ecclesiastical history. It is in this respect
a microcosm wherein, on a small scale, we see represented the triumphs
and the mistakes, the strength and the weakness, of God's elect people
throughout the ages. Thus in the incident before us, embracing the whole
of the third chapter and the greater portion of the fourth, we have set forth
a victory of the Apostles, their subsequent persecution, together with the
blessing and strength vouchsafed in and through that persecution. The time
of these events cannot be fixed with any great exactness. They occurred
probably within a few weeks or months of the day of Pentecost. That is the
nearest we can approach to a precise date. There seems indeed to have been
a pause after the excitement and success of Pentecost, and for this we think
that we can see a good reason. The Apostles must have had plenty to do
with the vast multitude gathered upon the day of Pentecost, striving to lead
them into a fuller knowledge of the faith. We are apt to imagine at first sight
that supernatural enlightenment was vouchsafed to these earliest converts,
superseding any necessity for careful and patient instruction, so that upon
their baptism the whole work was completed. But when we reflect upon
other cases in the New Testament, we can easily see that the three thousand
souls converted by St. Peter's speech must have needed and received a great
deal of teaching. The Church of Corinth was one of St. Paul's own founding,
and upon it he lavished careful attention for a year and a half; yet we see

from his Epistles to the Corinthians how much guidance was needed by them even in elementary questions of morals, how rapidly the Church fell into grossest licence when deprived of his personal ministrations. Theophilus again, to whom the Acts were addressed by St. Luke, is reminded, in the preface of the Gospel, of the catechetical instruction in Christian truth which he had received.[74] Assuredly, then, the small band of the twelve Apostles and their few male assistants must have had their hands full enough for many weeks after Pentecost, endeavouring to give their converts such an insight into the great principles of the faith as would enable them to carry back to their various distant homes a competent knowledge of the laws and doctrines of the new dispensation. A few moments' reflection will show that the newly-baptized had much to learn about Christ,—the facts of His life, His doctrines, sacraments, the constitution of His Church, and the position allotted to the Apostles,—before they could be considered sufficiently rooted and grounded in the faith. And if this was so with converts from Judaism, then how much more must such careful instruction after baptism have been found needful in the case of the Gentiles when the time came for their admission? Much preparatory work had been done for the Jews by their Old Testament training. They had not much to learn from the Apostles in practical morality; they had a right conception of God, His character, and His service. But as for the Pagans, their whole intellectual and spiritual life, all their notions and conceptions about God, and life, and morals, were all hopelessly wrong. The Apostles and the earliest teachers had then, and missionaries amongst the heathen have still, to make a clearance of the whole pagan ground, laying a new foundation, and erecting thereon a new structure, intellectual, moral, and spiritual. St. Paul recognised the vast importance of such diligent pastoral work and catechetical training after baptism when writing his pastoral Epistles, because bitter experience had taught him their value. At Corinth for more than two years, and at Ephesus for three years, he had laboured diligently in building up his converts. And notwithstanding all his exertions, how quickly the Corinthians fell away into pagan habits of unbridled licence as soon as he left them! The Acts of the Apostles by this pause in evangelistic work which we here trace, strikes a note of warning concerning the future missionary work of the Church, speaking clearly about the necessity of diligent pastoral care, and prophesying of the certain relapses into wild excesses which may be expected to occur among those who have only been just rescued from the mire of paganism. This is one explanation of the pause in apostolic work we here seem to perceive.

Again, the analogy of the faith, the laws of human nature, suggest the need of a period of restful calm after the Pentecostal excitement, and previous to any new and successful advance. So it has been in God's dealing in the past. The excitement connected with the first attempts made by Moses to rescue his people was followed by the forty years' exile in Midian, which again led to their triumphant rescue from bondage. Elijah's victory over Jezebel and her idol priests was followed by the retreat of forty days to Horeb. The excitement of our Lord's baptism was succeeded by the forty days' fast in the wilderness. The human mind cannot be ever on the strain. Excitement must be followed by repose, or else the course of action adopted will be hurried, imperfect, transient in its results. The works of God in nature are never such. As a modern poet has nobly sung:—

"One lesson, Nature, let me learn of thee;

One lesson which in every wind is blown;

One lesson of two duties kept at one,

Though the loud world proclaim their enmity;—

Of toil unsever'd from tranquillity;

Of labour, that in lasting fruit outgrows

Far noisier schemes, accomplished in repose,

Too great for haste, too high for rivalry."[75]

There is great calm and dignity in nature; and there was great calm and dignity in grace when God was laying the foundations of His kingdom by the hands of His Apostles. There never was an age which more needed this lesson of nature and grace alike than this nineteenth century.[76] The religion of the age has been infected by the Spirit of the world, and men think that the fortresses of sin and ignorance will fall, provided there be used a sufficient quantity of noise, of puffing, and of excitement. I do not wish to find the slightest fault with energetic action. The Church of Christ has been in the past perhaps a little too dignified in its methods and operations. It has hesitated, where St. Paul never would have hesitated, to adapt itself to changed circumstances, and has ofttimes refused, like a timorous lawyer, to venture on some new and untried sphere because there was no precedent. The Reformers and their first followers were an illustration of this. The utter lack of missionary spirit and effort among the Reformers is one of the darkest blots upon their history. How sadly they contrast with the Jesuit Society, which started into existence at the same period of the world's history. No one is more keenly alive to the faults and shortcomings of that world-renowned Society than I am, yet I heartily admire the energy and devotion with which, from its earliest days, the Society of Jesus flung itself into missionary work, endeavouring to repair the losses which the Papacy sustained in Europe by fresh conquests in India, China, and America. The

Reformers were so busy in bitter controversies among themselves, and so intent upon endeavouring to fathom God's decrees and purposes, that they forgot the primary duty of the Church to spread the light and truth which it has received; they were deficient in Christian energy, and thus brought upon themselves the blight and curse of spiritual barrenness. Controversy evermore brings with it the desolation of spiritual leanness. Men cease to really believe in a religion which they only know upon paper, and only think of as a thing to be discussed. Living contact with human souls and human wants saves religion, because it translates it from a mere dead dogma into a living fact. A man who has come to doubt doctrinal statements which he has never verified, will be brought back to faith by the irresistible evidence of sinful lives changed and broken hearts comforted.

The Church of England has again and again manifested this spirit. In Ireland she refused to give the nation the Liturgy and the Bible in the Irish tongue. In Wales she hesitated in condescending to vulgar wants, and long refused to bestow a native episcopate upon the Celts of England, because the evil tradition of centuries, down from the age of the Norman conquest, had ordained that no Welshman should be a bishop. But still, while I am opposed to the Church binding itself in fetters of that kind, I am equally of opinion that there is a middle course between dignified idleness and extravagant carnal sensationalism. I have heard efforts advocated for home missionary work which, I am sure, would never have met with the approbation of the first missionaries of the Cross. The Church must be energetic, but the Church need not adopt the methods of quack medicine-sellers, or of the strolling circus. Such methods were not unknown in the primitive ages of the Church.

The preachers of the stoic philosophy strove in the second century to counteract the efforts of the Christian Church by reforming paganism, and by preaching it vigorously. They adopted every means to attract the public attention and interest—eccentricity, vulgarity, coarseness; and yet they failed, and were defeated by a society which trusted, not in human devices and carnal forces, but in the supernatural power of God the Holy Ghost.[77] The Montanists again, towards the close of the second century, fell into the same error. The Montanists are in many respects one of the most interesting of the early Christian sects. They tried to retain the customs and the spirit of apostolic Christianity, but they mistook the true methods of action. They confounded physical excitement with spiritual fervour, and strove by weird dances and strange cries, borrowed from the pagans of the Phrygian mountains, to bind to themselves the sweet influences of the Heavenly Comforter. The Church of that period diligently avoided the error of pagan stoics and of Christian schismatics. As it was in the second century, so was it just after Pentecost. The Church followed close upon its Master's footsteps, of whom it was said, "He shall not strive nor cry, neither shall any man hear His voice in the streets," and developed in quietness and retirement the spiritual life of the thousands who had crowded into the door of faith which Peter had opened.

Again there is a lesson in this period of pause and seclusion, not merely for the Church in its corporate capacity, but for individual souls. The spirit of interior sanctity is nourished most chiefly during such times of retirement and obscurity. Obscurity has indeed many advantages when viewed from the standpoint of the spiritual life. Publicity and high station and multiplicity of affairs bring with them many disadvantages. They deprive us of that peace and calm which enable a man to contrast the things of time with those of eternity, and to value them in their true light. Over-activity, fussiness, even in the most spiritual matters, is a dire enemy of true heart belief, and therefore of true strength of spirit. The Master Himself felt it so. There were many coming and going, and they had no leisure so much as to eat. Then it was He said, "Come ye into the desert, that ye may rest awhile." The excitement and strain of Pentecost, and all the subsequent efforts which Pentecost entailed, must have told seriously upon the Apostles, and so they imitated the Master, that they might renew their exhausted vigour at its primal fountain. How many a man, busy in missions, or preaching, or the thousand other forms which evangelistic and religious work now takes, would be infinitely better if this apostolic lesson were duly learned. How many a terrible scandal has arisen simply from a disregard and contempt for it. If men will think they can labour, as this passage shows the Apostles could not, without thought and reflection, and interior communion with God; if they will spend all their strength in external effort and never make time and secure seasons for spiritual replenishment, they may create much noise for a time, but their toil will be fruitless, and if they are saved themselves it will only be as by fire.

The period of retirement and obscurity came however to an end at last. The Apostles never intended to form an order purely contemplative. Such an idea, in fact, never could have entered into the mind of one of those early Christians. They remembered that their Master had expressly said, "Ye are the salt of the earth," and salt is useless if kept stored up in a vessel by itself, and never applied to any object where its curative properties might have free scope. When the spirit of Eastern gnosticism, springing from the dualism of Persia, invaded the Church, and gained a permanent hold within it, then men began to despise their bodies and life, and all that life entails. Like Eastern fanatics, they desired to abstract themselves as much as possible from the things and duties of the present, and they invented, or rather adopted from the farther East, purely contemplative orders, which spent useless lives, striving, like their prototypes of India, to rise superior to the positions which God had assigned them. Such were not the Apostles. They used rest, contemplation, they did not abuse them; and when their tone and power was restored, they issued forth again upon the field of religious activity, and joined in the public worship of the crowd. "Peter and John went up together into the temple at the hour of prayer, being the ninth hour."

The action of Peter and John in thus frequenting the temple worship gives us a glimpse into the state of feeling and thought which prevailed then and for a great many years after in the Church of Jerusalem. The Church of that city naturally clung longest of all to the old Jewish connection. Eusebius, in his *Ecclesiastical History* (iv. 5), tells us that the first fifteen bishops of Jerusalem were Hebrews, and that all the members of the Church were Hebrews too. It was only, in fact, upon the final destruction of Jerusalem, which happened under Hadrian, after the rebellion of Barcochba, A.D. 135, that the Church of Jerusalem shook itself completely free from the trammels of Judaism.[78]

But in those earliest days of the Church the Apostles naturally could not recognise the course of the Divine development. They cherished the notion that Judaism and Christianity would be found compatible the one with the other. They had not yet recognised what St. Stephen first of all, and then St. Paul, and most chiefly the author of the Hebrews, came to recognise, that Judaism and Christianity as full-blown systems were absolutely antagonistic; that the Jewish dispensation was obsolete, antiquated, and must utterly and for ever fade before a nobler dispensation that was once for all to take its place. It is hard for us to realize the feelings of the Apostles at this great transition epoch, and yet it is well for us to do so, because their conduct is full of lessons specially suited for seasons of transition. The Apostles never seem to me more clearly under the direction of the Divine Spirit than in their whole course of action at this time. They proceeded in faith, but not in haste. They held firmly to the truths they had gained, and they waited patiently upon God, till the course of His providence showed them how to co-ordinate the old system with the new truths,—until He had taught them what parts of the ancient covenant should be dropped and what retained. Their conduct has instruction very suitable for the present age, when God is giving His Church fresh light on many a question through the investigations of science. Well, indeed, will it be for Christian people to have their hearts grounded, as the Apostles' were, in a spirit of Divine love, knowing personally in whom they have believed; and then, strong in that inner revelation of God to the spirit, which surpasses in might and power all other evidences, they may patiently wait the evolution of His purposes. The prophetic declaration is true for every age, "He that believeth will not make haste."

The circumstances of the first apostolic miracle were simple enough. Peter and John were going up into the temple at the hour of the evening sacrifice. They were entering the temple by the gate well known to all dwellers at Jerusalem as the Beautiful Gate, and there they met the cripple whom they healed in the name and by the power of Jesus of Nazareth. The spot where this miracle was performed was familiar to the Jews of that day, though its precise locality is still a matter of controversy. Some hold that this Beautiful Gate was one described by Josephus in his *Wars of the Jews* (v. 5, 3) as surpassingly splendid, being composed of Corinthian brass, and called the Gate of Nicanor. Others think that it was the gate Shushan, which stood in the neighbourhood of Solomon's Porch; while others identify it with the gate Chulda, which led into the Court of the Gentiles. It was most probably the first of these which was situated on the eastern side of the outermost court of the temple, looking towards the valley of Kedron.[79] Here was gathered a crowd of beggars, such as then frequented the temples of the pagans as well as of the Jews, and such as still throng the approaches of Eastern and many Western churches. Out of this crowd one man addressed Peter and John, asking an alms. This man was well known to the regular worshippers in the temple. He was a cripple, and one long accustomed to haunt the same spot, for he was above forty years old. Peter replied to his prayer in the well-known words, "Silver and gold have I none: but what I have, that give I thee. In the name of Jesus Christ of Nazareth, walk;" and then he performed one of the few miracles ascribed to the direct action of St. Peter. Here it may be asked, Why was this miracle of healing the cripple at the temple gate the only one recorded of those earliest signs and wonders wrought by apostolic hands? The answer seems to be threefold: this miracle was typical of the Church's future work; it was the occasion of St. Peter's testimony before the Sanhedrin; and it led up to the first persecution which the Jewish authorities raised against the Church.

Viewing the Acts of the Apostles as a type of what all Church history was to be, and a Divine exposition of the principles which should guide the Church in times of suffering as well as in times of action, we can see good and solid reasons for the insertion of this particular narrative. First, then, this miracle was typical of the Church's work, for it was a beggar that was healed, and this beggar lay helpless and hopeless at the very doors of the temple. The beggar typified humanity at large. He was laid, indeed, in a splendid position,—before him was extended the magnificent panorama of hills which stood round about Jerusalem; above him rose the splendours of the building upon which the Herods had lavished the riches and wonders of their gorgeous conceptions,—but he was nothing the better for all this material grandeur till touched by the power which lay in the name of Jesus of Nazareth. And the beggar of the Beautiful Gate was in all these respects the fittest object for St. Peter's earliest public miracle, because he was exactly typical of mankind's state. Humanity, Jew and Gentile alike, lay at the very gate of God's temple of the universe. Men could discourse learnedly, too, concerning that sanctuary, and they could admire its beauteous proportions. Poets, philosophers, and wise men had treated of the temple of the universe in works which can never be surpassed, but all the while they lay outside its sacred precincts. They had no power to stand up and enter in, leaping, and walking, and praising God. It is very important, in this age of material civilization and of intellectual advance, that the Church should insist vigorously upon the great truth taught by this miracle. The age of the Incarnation must have seemed to the men of that time the very acme of civilization and of knowledge; and yet the testimony of all history and of all literature is that just then mankind was in the most deplorable state of moral and spiritual degradation. The witness of St. Paul in the first chapter of the Epistle to the Romans is amply borne out by the testimony, conscious and unconscious, of pagan antiquity. A writer of the last century, now to a great extent forgotten, Dr. Leland by name, investigated this point in the fullest manner in his great work on the necessity of a Divine revelation, demonstrating that mankind, even when highly civilized, educated, cultured, lies like a beggar at the door of the temple, till touched by the hand and power of the Incarnate God.

This miracle of healing the beggar was typical of the Church's work again, because it was a beggar who thus received a blessing when the Church roused itself to the discharge of its great mission. The first man healed and benefited by St. Peter was a poor man, and the Church's work has ever led her to deal with the poor, and to interest herself most keenly in their well-being. This first miracle is typical of Christian work, because Christianity is essentially the religion of the masses. At times, indeed, Christian teachers may have seemed to rank themselves on the side of power and riches alone; but then men should take good care to distinguish between the inconsistent conduct of Christian teachers and the essential principles of Christianity. The founder of Christianity was a carpenter, and its earliest benediction pronounced the blessedness of those that are poor in spirit, and ever since the greatest triumphs of Christianity have been gained amongst the poor. Christian hagiology, Christian legend, and Christian history alike, have combined to attest this truth. The Church calendar is decorated with lists of saints, some of them of very doubtful character, while others of them have stories connected with their careers full of meaning and rich with lessons for this generation. Thus, for instance, October 25th is the feast of a martyr, St. Crispin, from whom the great trade of shoemakers is designated. "The sons of St. Crispin" is a title going back to the earliest ages of the Church's love. St. Crispin was a Roman senator, brought up and nourished amid all that luxury with which pagan Rome surrounded the children of the highest classes. Crispin became acquainted with the faith of the followers of the Carpenter of Nazareth amid the dire persecutions which marked the final struggle between Christianity and paganism under the Emperor Diocletian during the earliest years of the fourth century. He was baptized, and feeling that a life of gilded idleness was inconsistent with his Master's example, he resigned his place, position, and property, retired into Gaul, and there devoted himself to the trade of shoemaking, as being one which could be exercised in great quietness. Manual toil was at that time considered an occupation fitted only for slaves, for we ought never to forget that the dignity of labour is no human invention, nor is it part of the religions of nature. Nay, rather, the dignity of idleness was the doctrine of Greek and Roman paganism. St. Crispin recognized the great law of labour taught by Christ and taught by His Apostles, and became the most successful of shoemakers, preaching at the same time the gospel with such success that the persecutors selected him as one of their earliest victims in that district of Gaul where he resided.[80] It has been just the same in every age. The true power of the Church has been ever displayed in preaching the gospel to the children of toil. An interesting example of this may be gathered from an age which we are apt to think specially dark. In mediæval times the secular or parochial clergy became very lax and careless throughout these islands. The mendicant friars, the followers of St. Francis, came and settled everywhere in the slums of the great towns, devoting themselves to the work of preaching to the poor. And they speedily attained a marvellous power over men. The Franciscans in the thirteenth century were exactly like the early Methodists in the last century. Both societies placed their chapels among the abodes of want; there they laboured, and there they triumphed, because they worked in the spirit and power indicated by this first recorded miracle of the beggar healed at the temple gate.[81] It will be a bad day for religion and for society when the Church ceases to be the Church and champion of the weak, the down-trodden, the destitute. Here, however, lies a danger. Its work in this direction must be done in no one-sided spirit. Christianity must never adopt the language or the tone of the mere agitator. I fear that some who now pose as specially the champions of the poor are missing that spirit of mental balance and fairness which will alone enable them to be Christian champions, because seeking to do justice unto all men. It is easy enough to flatter any class, rich or poor; and it is specially tempting to do so when the class so flattered chances to hold the reins of political power. It is very hard to render to all their due, shrinking not from telling the truth, even when unpleasant, and reproving the faults of those whose side we favour. A Christianity which triumphs through appeals to popular prejudices, and seeks a mere temporary advantage by riding on the crest of popular ignorance, is not the religion taught by Christ and His Apostles.

But yet, again, the conversion of this beggar was effected through his healing; and here we see a type of the Church's future work. The Church, then, as represented by the Apostles, did not despise the body, or regard efforts after bodily blessing beneath its dignity. Spiritual work went hand in hand with healing power. This has been a lesson which Christian people, at home and abroad, have been slow enough to learn. The whole principle, for instance, of medical missions is covered by this action on the part of the Apostles. For a long time the Church thought it was its solitary duty to preach the gospel by word of mouth, and it has only been in comparatively modern days that men have learned that one of the most powerful means of preaching the gospel was the exercise of the healing art; for surely if the gift of healing, conveyed from God by supernatural means, could be an effective help towards evangelistic work, the same gift of healing, conveyed from precisely the same source by natural channels indeed, but channels none the less truly Divine, can still be effective to the same great end. The Church should count no human interest beyond its sway, and should take the keenest interest and claim a living share in every portion of life's work. At home or abroad the bodies of men are her care as well as their souls, because bodies as well as souls have been redeemed by Jesus Christ, and both alike await their perfection and glorification through Jesus Christ. Schools, hospitals, sanitary and medical science, the dwellings and amusements of the people, trade, commerce, all should be the care of the Church, and should be based on Christ's law, and carried out on Christian principles. The Incarnation of Christ has given a deeper meaning than he ever dreamt of to the pagan poet's words,—

"Homo sum; humani nihil a me alienum puto."

We think, furthermore, that this miracle has been divinely recorded because it was the occasion of St. Peter's testimony both to the people and to their rulers. Let us strive to realize the circumstances and the locality. Peter and John, going up to the temple, met this impotent beggar at the entrance to the Court of the Women, into which the Beautiful Gate led. Our modern notions about churches confuse all true conceptions concerning the temple. The vast majority of people, when they think of the temple, form to themselves an idea of a vast cathedral, when they ought instead to think of a large college, with square succeeding square and court following court.

As Peter and John ascended the temple hill they came first to the Court of the Gentiles, which served as a market, and in which a crowd of mendicants were assembled to solicit alms. Out of this Court of the Gentiles the Beautiful Gate led into the Court of the Women, which was reserved for the ordinary religious offices of the Jewish people.[82] One of the beggars addressed the Apostles, soliciting a gift; whereupon the Apostles worked the miracle of healing. Upon this a crowd collected, attracted by the excited conduct of the man who had received such an unexpected blessing. They ran together after the manner of all crowds which assemble so easily and so rapidly in a city, and then, hurrying into the cloister, called Solomon's Porch, which was a remnant of the ancient temple, heard the address of St. Peter. It must have been a spot filled with cherished memories for the Apostle. Every Jew naturally venerated this cloister, because it was Solomon's; just as men in the grandest modern cathedral still love to point out the smallest relic of the original structure out of which the modern building grew. At San Clemente, in Rome, the priests delight to show the primitive structure where they say St. Clement ministered about the year A.D. 100.[83] At York the vergers will indicate far down in the crypt the fragments of the earliest Saxon church, which once stood where that splendid cathedral now rears its lofty arches. So, too, the Jews naturally cherished this link of continuity between the ancient and the modern temples. But for St. Peter this Solomon's Porch must have had special memories over and above the patriotic ideas that were linked with it. He could not forget that the very last feast of the Dedication which the Master had seen on earth, He walked in this porch, and there in His conversation with the Jews claimed an equality with the Father which led them to make an attempt on His life.

Here, then, it was that within twelve months the Apostle Peter makes a similar claim on his Master's behalf, in a discourse which extends from the twelfth to the twenty-sixth verse of the third chapter. That discourse has two distinct divisions. It sets forth, first the claims, dignity, and nature of Christ, and then makes a personal appeal to the men of Jerusalem. St. Peter begins his sermon with an act of profound self-renunciation. When the Apostle saw the people running together, he answered and said, "Ye men of Israel, why marvel ye at this? or why look ye so earnestly on us, as though by our own power or holiness we made this man to walk?" The same spirit of renunciation appears at an earlier stage of the miracle. When the beggar solicited an alms, Peter said, "Silver and gold have I none: but what I have, that give I thee. In the name of Jesus Christ of Nazareth, walk." One point is at once manifest when St. Peter's conduct is compared with his Master's under similar circumstances. St. Peter acts as a delegate and a servant; Jesus Christ acted as a principal, a master, — the Prince of Life, as St.

Peter calls Him in the fifteenth verse of this third chapter. The distinction between the miracles of Christ and the miracles of the Apostles declares the New Testament conception of Christ's dignity and person. Compare, for instance, the narrative of the healing of the impotent man at the Pool of Bethesda, told in the fifth chapter of St. John, with that of the healing of the impotent man laid at the temple gate. Christ said, "Rise, take up thy bed, and walk." He made no appeal, He used no prayer, He invoked no higher name. He simply spake and it was done. The Apostle Peter, the rock-man, the leader of the apostolic band, takes the greatest care to assure the multitude that he had himself neither power nor efficacy in this matter, and that all the power lay in the Name of Jesus Christ of Nazareth. Now, leaving aside for the moment any question of the truth or reality of these two miracles, is it not manifest from these two parallel cases that the New Testament writings place Jesus Christ on an exalted standpoint far above that of any human being whatsoever; in a position, in fact, which from the boldness and magnificence of its claims can only be fitly described in the language of the Nicene Creed as "God of God, Light of Light, Very God of very God."

St. Peter's words teach another lesson. They are typical of the spirit which should ever animate the Christian preacher or teacher. They turn the attention of his hearers wholly away from himself, and exalt Christ Jesus alone. And such has ever been and ever must be the secret of successful preaching. Self-consciousness, in fact, injures the effect of any kind of labour. The man who does not lose himself in his work, of whatever kind—political, philanthropic, or religious—his work may be, but is ever thinking of himself and the results of his actions upon his own prospects, can never become an enthusiast; and it is only enthusiasm and enthusiastic action which can really affect mankind. And surely the preacher of Christian truth who thinks of himself rather than of the great subject of his mission, who only preaches that he may be thought clever or eloquent, debases the Christian pulpit, and must be an awful failure in that day when God shall judge the secrets of men by Jesus Christ. St. Peter here, John the Baptist in still earlier days, ought to be the models for Christian teachers. Men came to the Baptist, did him homage, yielded him respect; but he pointed them from himself to Christ. He was a lamp, but Christ was the light; and the Baptist's teaching reached its highest, noblest level when he turned his disciples' gaze away from himself, saying, "Behold the Lamb of God, which taketh away the sin of the world." Let me, however, not be mistaken. I do not mean to say that a Christian teacher, whether writer or speaker, should never allow a single reflex thought as to his own performances to rise in his mind, should never desire to preach ably or eloquently. A man who could set up such a standard must be ignorant of human nature and of Scripture alike. One cannot, for instance, read St. Paul's Second Epistle to the Corinthians without noting how sorely he was touched by his own unpopularity amongst them and the successful machinations of his opponents. Daily experience will prove that no attainments in the spiritual life will prevent a man from valuing the esteem and recognition of his fellow men. But such a desire to please and be successful must be kept in stern control. It must not be the great object of a Christian. It must never lead him to keep back one jot or tittle of the counsel of God. The natural desire to please must be closely watched. It easily leads men to idolatry, to the installation of human fame, power, influence, gold, in the place of that Eternal Saviour whose worship ought to be the great end and the true life of the soul.

St. Peter, after his act of abnegation and self-humiliation, then proceeds to set forth the claims and to narrate the history of Jesus Christ, and in doing so enters into the particulars of His trial and condemnation, which he charges boldly home upon his listeners, who, as distinguished from his audience on the day of Pentecost, were most probably the permanent residents in Jerusalem. The Apostle narrates the events of our Lord's trial just as we find them in the Gospels—His interviews with Pilate, the outcry of the people, the choice and character of Barabbas. He asserts His resurrection, and implies, without asserting, His ascension, by the words, "Whom the heavens must receive until the times of the restitution of all things." The primitive gospel of St. Peter was just like that taught by St. Paul, as he puts it forward in the fifteenth chapter of First of Corinthians, "Brethren, I declare unto you the gospel which I have received, how that Christ died for our sins according to the scriptures: and that He was buried, and that He rose again." The earliest message, proclaimed by St. Paul or St. Peter, was one and the same; it was a declaration of certain historical facts, and what it was then such it must ever remain. Whenever the historical facts are disbelieved, then men may speak beautifully of the spiritual ideas and the moral truths symbolised by Christianity, just as Hypatia and the Neo-Platonists of Alexandria could speak in picturesque language concerning the deep poetic meaning of the old pagan legends. Poetry and legends are, however, the veriest husks wherewith to support an immortal soul under the great trials of life; and when that day comes for any soul when the great historical facts set forth in the Creed are rejected, then Christianity may remain in name and appearance, but it will cease to be the gospel of joy and peace and comfort, for the human soul can only sustain itself in the supreme moments of sorrow, separation, and death by the solid realities of fact and truth.

St. Peter, again, in this sermon leaves us a type of what Christian sermons should be. He was plain spoken, yet he was tender and sympathetic. He was plain spoken. He does not hesitate to state the crimes of the Jews in the most vigorous language. God had glorified His servant Jesus, but they delivered Him up to the agents of the idolatrous Romans; they denied Him, desired a murderer to be granted in place of the Prince of Life; urged His death when even the Roman judge would have let Him go,—and all this they had done to the long-expected and long-desired Messiah. Peter is not wanting in plainness of speech. And the Christian teacher, whether clergyman or layman, whether a pastor in the pulpit, a teacher in the Sunday-school, or the editor of a newspaper at his desk, ought to cultivate and exercise the same Christian boldness and courage. The true Christian ideal will be attained by following St. Peter's example on this occasion. He combined boldness and prudence, courage and gentleness. He spoke the truth in all honesty, but he did not adopt an attitude or use language which would arouse unnecessary opposition. What courtesy, what sympathetic, charitable politeness is manifest in St. Peter's excuse, which he offers in the course of his sermon for the Jews, rulers and people alike! "And now, brethren, I wot that through ignorance ye did it, as did also your rulers." Some men think that prudence is an idea which should never enter the head of a messenger of Christ, though no one impressed more frequently the necessity of that great virtue than did the Master, for He knew how easily imprudence may undo all the good that faithfulness might otherwise attain. Wisdom like the serpent's, gentleness like the dove's, was Christ's own rule for His Apostles. Boldness, and courage, and honesty, are blessed things, but they should be guided and moderated by charity. Earthly motives easily insinuate themselves in every man's heart, and when a man feels urged on to declare some unpleasant truth, or to raise a violent and determined opposition, he should search diligently, lest that while he imagines himself following a heavenly vision and obeying a Divine command, he should be only yielding to mere human suggestions of pride, or partisanship, or uncharitableness.

# CHAPTER IX
# THE FIRST PERSECUTION

"And as they spake unto the people, the priests, and the captain of the temple, and the Sadducees, came upon them, being grieved that they taught the people, and preached through Jesus the resurrection from the dead. And they laid hands on them, and put them in hold unto the next day: for it was now eventide.... And it came to pass on the morrow, that their rulers, and elders, and scribes, and Annas the high priest, and Caiaphas, and John, and Alexander, and as many as were of the kindred of the high priest, were gathered together at Jerusalem. And when they had set them in the midst, they asked, By what power, or by what name, have ye done this?" — Acts iv. 1-3, 5-7.

The fourth chapter of the Acts brings the Apostles into their first contact with the Jewish state organisation. It shows us the secret springs which led to the first persecution, typical of the fiercest that ever raged against the Church, and displays the calm conviction and moral strength by which the Apostles were sustained. The historical and local circumstances narrated by St. Luke bear all the marks of truth.

I. The miracle of healing the lame man had taken place in Solomon's porch or portico, which overlooked the Kedron valley, and was an usual resort as a promenade or public walk, specially in winter. Thus we read, in St. John x. 22, 23, that our Lord walked in Solomon's porch, and it was winter. Solomon's porch looked towards the rising sun, and was therefore a warm and sunny spot. It was popular with the inhabitants of Jerusalem for the same reason which led the Cistercians of the Middle Ages, when building magnificent fabrics like Fountains Abbey, to place their cloister garths, where exercise was taken, on the southern side of their churches, that there they might receive and enjoy the heat and light of our winter sun.

The crowd which was collected by Peter soon attracted the attention of the temple authorities, who had a regular police under their control. The Jews were permitted by the Romans to exercise the most unlimited freedom within the bounds of the temple to secure its sanctity. In ordinary cases the

Romans reserved to themselves the power of capital punishment, but in the case of the temple and its profanation they allowed it to the Sanhedrin.

An interesting proof of this fact has come to light of late years, attesting, in a most striking manner, the accuracy of the Acts of the Apostles. Josephus, in his *Antiquities* (xv. xi. 5), when describing the Holy Place, tells us that the royal cloisters of the temple had three walks, formed by four rows of pillars, with which they were adorned. The outermost walk was open to all, but the central walk was cut off by a stone wall, on which were inscriptions forbidding foreigners—that is, Gentiles—to enter under pain of death. Now in the twenty-first chapter of the Acts we read that a supposed breach of this law was the occasion of the riot against St. Paul, wherein he narrowly escaped death.[84]

The Jews were actually about to kill St. Paul when the soldiers came upon them. To this fact, Tertullus the orator, when speaking before the governor Felix, alludes, and that without rebuke, saying of St. Paul, "Whom we took, and would have judged according to our law."[85] Here comes in our illustration of the Acts derived from modern archæological research. Some few years ago there was discovered at Jerusalem, and there is now laid up in the Sultan's Museum at Constantinople, a sculptured and inscribed stone, containing one of these very Greek notices upon which the Apostles must have looked, warning Gentiles not to enter within the sacred bounds, and denouncing against transgressors the penalty of death which the Jews sought to inflict upon St. Paul.[86] Now it was just the same about the other details of the temple worship. Inside the sacred area the Jewish law was supreme, and Jewish penalties were enacted. In order, therefore, that the temple might be duly protected the priests watched in three places, and the Levites in twenty-one places, in addition to all their other duties connected with the offering of the sacrifices and the details of public worship. These guards discharged the duties of a sacred or temple police, and their captain was called the captain of the temple, or, as he is denominated in the Talmud, "The ruler of the mountain of the House."

Much confusion has, indeed, arisen concerning this official. He has been confounded, for instance, with the captain of the neighbouring fortress of Antonia. The Romans had erected a strong square castle, with lofty walls, and towers at the four corners, just north of the temple, and connected with it by a covered way. One of these flanking towers was one hundred and five feet high, and overlooked all the temple area, so that when a riot began the soldiers could hurry to quell it. The captain of the garrison which held this tower is called, in our version, the chief captain, or, more properly, the chiliarch, or colonel of a regiment, as we should put it in modern phraseology. But this official had nothing whatever to say to questions of

Jewish law or ritual. He was simply responsible for the peace of Jerusalem; he represented the governor, who lived at Cæsarea, and had no concern with the disputes which might arise amongst the Jews. But it was quite otherwise with the captain of the temple. He was a Jewish official, took cognisance of Jewish disputes, and was responsible in matters of Jewish discipline which Roman law respected and upheld, but in which it did not interfere. This purely Jewish official, a priest by profession, appointed by the Jewish authorities, and responsible to them alone, appears prominently on three distinct occasions. In the twenty-second of St. Luke's Gospel we have the account of the betrayal by the traitor Judas. When he was meditating that action he went first to the chief priests and the captains to consult with them. A Roman commander, an Italian, a Gaul, or possibly even a Briton, — as he might have been, for the Romans were accustomed to bring their Western legionaries into the East, as in turn they garrisoned Britain with the men of Syria, — would have cared very little whether a Galilean teacher was arrested or not. But it was quite natural that a Jewish and a temple official should have been interested in this question. While again on this occasion, and once more upon the arrest of the Apostles after the death of Ananias and Sapphira, the captain of the temple appears as one of the highest Jewish officials.[87]

II. We see too the secret source whence the opposition to apostolic teaching arose. The priests and the captain of the temple and the Sadducees came upon them. The captain was roused into action by the Sadducees, who were mingled in the crowd, and heard the words of the Apostles proclaiming the resurrection of Jesus Christ, "being grieved that they taught the people, and preached through Jesus the resurrection from the dead." It is noteworthy how perpetually the Sadducees appear as the special antagonists of Christianity during these earliest years. Our Lord's denunciations of the Pharisees were so often repeated that we are apt to think of them as the leading opponents of Christianity during the apostolic age. And yet this is a mistake. There was an important difference between the Master's teaching and that of His disciples, which accounts for the changed character of the opposition. Our Lord's teaching came specially into conflict with the Pharisees and their mode of thought. He denounced mere external worship, and asserted the spiritual and inner character of true religion. That was the great staple of his message. The Apostles, on the other hand, testified and enforced above everything else the risen, the glorified, and the continuous existence in the spirit world of the Man Christ Jesus. And thus they came into conflict with the central doctrine of Sadduceism which denied a future life. Hence at Jerusalem, at least, the Sadducees were ever the chief persecutors of the Apostles, while the Pharisees were favourable to Christianity, or at least neutral. At the meeting of the Sanhedrin of which we read in the fifth chapter, Gamaliel, a Pharisee, proposes the discharge of the imprisoned Apostles. In the twenty-third chapter, when St. Paul is placed before the same Sanhedrin the Pharisees take his side, while the Sadducees are his bitter opponents. We never read of a Sadducee embracing Christianity; while St. Paul, the greatest champion of the gospel, was gained from the ranks of the Pharisees. This fact sheds light on the character of the apostolic teaching. It was not any system of evanescent Christianity; it was not a system of mere ethical teaching; it was not a system where the facts of Christ's life were whittled away, where, for instance, His resurrection was explained as a mere symbolical idea, typifying the resurrection of the soul from the death of sin to the life of holiness; for in that case the Sadducees would not have troubled themselves on this occasion to oppose such teaching. But apostolic Christianity was a system which based itself on a risen Saviour, and involved, as its fundamental ideas, the doctrines of a future life and of a spiritual world, and of a resurrection where body and soul would be again united.

Some strange representations have been from time to time put forward as to the nature of apostolic and specially of Pauline Christianity, but one of the strangest is what we may call the Matthew Arnold theory, which makes the apostolic teaching a poor, emasculated thing, devoid of any real foundation of historical fact. If Christianity, as proclaimed by St. Peter and St. Paul, was of this type, why, we ask, was it so bitterly opposed by the Sadducees? They at any rate understood the Apostles to teach and preach a Jesus Christ literally risen from the dead and ascended in the truth of human nature into that spiritual and unseen world whose existence they denied. For the Sadducees were materialists pure and simple. As such they prevailed among the rich. The poor, then as ever, furnished very few adherents to a creed which may satisfy persons who are enjoying the good things of this life. It has very few attractions, however, for those with whom life is dealing hardly, and to whom the world presents itself in a stern aspect alone. It is no wonder the new teaching concerning a risen Messiah should have excited the hatred of the rich Sadducees, and should have been welcomed by the poorer classes, among whom the Pharisees had their followers. The system of the Sadducees was a religion indeed. It satisfied a want, for man can never do without some kind of a religion. It recognised God and His revelation to Moses. It asserted, however, that the Mosaic revelation contained nothing concerning a future life, or the doctrine of immortality. It was a religion, therefore, without fear of a future, and which could never indeed excite any enthusiasm, but was very satisfactory and agreeable for the prosperous few as long as they were in prosperity and in health. Peter and John came preaching a very disturbing doctrine to this class of people. If Peter's view of life was right, theirs was all wrong. It was no wonder that the Sadducees brought upon them the priests and the captain of the temple, and summoned the Sanhedrin to deal with them. We should have done the same had we been in their position. In every age, indeed, the bitterest persecutors of Christianity have been men like the Sadducees. It has often been said that persecution on the part of a sceptic or of an unbeliever is illogical. The Sadducees were unbelievers as regards a future life. What matter to them was it, then, if the Apostles preached a future life, and convinced the people of its truth? But logic is always pushed impetuously aside when it comes in contact with deep-rooted human feeling, and the Sadducees instinctively felt that the conflict between themselves and the Apostles was a deadly one; one or other party must perish. And so it was under the Roman empire. The ruling classes of the empire were essentially infidel, or, to use a modern term, we should rather perhaps style them agnostic. They regarded the Christian teaching as a noxious enthusiasm. They could not understand why Christians should not offer incense to the deity of the emperor, or perform any act of idolatry which was commanded by state law, and regarded their refusal as an act of treason. They had no idea of conscience, because they were essentially like the Sadducees.[88] So was it again in the days of the first French Revolution, and so we find it still. The men who reject all spiritual existence, and hold a Sadducean creed, fear the power of Christian enthusiasm and Christian love, and had they only the power would crush it as sternly and remorselessly as the Sadducees desired to do in apostolic times, or as the Roman emperors did from the days of Nero to those of Diocletian.

III. The Apostles were arrested in the evening and put in prison. The temple had an abundance of chambers and apartments which could be used as prisons, or, as the Sanhedrin were accustomed to sit in a basilica erected in the court outside the Beautiful Gate, and inside Solomon's porch or cloister, there was probably a cell for prisoners connected with it. The next morning St. Peter and St. John were brought up before the court which met daily in this basilica, immediately after the hour of the morning sacrifices. We can realize the scene, for the persons mentioned as having taken part in the trial are historical characters. The Sanhedrin sat in a semicircle, with the president in the centre, while opposite were three benches for the scholars of the Sanhedrists, who thus practically learned law. The Sanhedrin, when complete, consisted of seventy-one members, comprising chief priests, the elders of the people, and the most renowned of the rabbis; but twenty-three formed a quorum competent to transact business.[89] The high priest when present, as Annas and Caiaphas both were on this occasion, naturally exercised great influence, though he was not necessarily president of the council. The sacred writer has been accused, indeed, of a historical mistake, both here and in his Gospel (iii. 2), in making Annas high priest when Caiaphas was actually occupying that office, Annas, his father-in-law, having been previously deposed by the Romans. St. Luke seems to me, on the other hand, thus to prove his strict accuracy. Caiaphas was of course the legal high priest so far as the Romans were concerned. They recognised him as such, and delivered to him the high priest's official robes, when necessary for the fulfilment of his great office, keeping them safe at other times in the tower of Antonia. But then, as I have already said, so long as the Roman law and constitutions were observed on great state occasions, they allowed the Jews a large amount of Home Rule in the management of their domestic religious concerns, and were not keen in marking offences, if only the offences were not thrust into public notice. Annas was recognised by the Sanhedrin and by the Jews at large as the true high priest, Caiaphas as the legal or official one; and they kept themselves on the safe side, as far as the Romans were concerned, by uniting them in their official consultations in the Sanhedrin. The Sadducees, doubtless, on this occasion made every effort that their own party should attend the council meeting, feeling the importance of crushing the rising sect in the very bud. We read, therefore, that with the high priest came "John, and Alexander, and as many as were of the kindred of the high priest."[90] The priestly families were at this period the aristocracy of the Jews, and they all belonged to the Sadducees, in opposition to the democracy who favoured the Pharisees. These latter, indeed, had their own representatives in the Sanhedrin, as we shall see on a later occasion,—men of light and leading, like Gamaliel; but the permanent officials of the Jewish senate were for the most part Sadducees, and we know how easily the permanent officials can pack a popular body, such as the Sanhedrin was, with their own adherents, when any special end is to be attained.

It was before such a hostile audience that the Apostles were now called to witness, and here they first proved the power of the Divine words, "When they deliver you up, take no thought how or what ye shall speak: for it shall be given you in that same hour what ye shall speak."[91] St. Peter threw himself upon God, and found that his trust was not in vain. He was at the moment of need filled with the Holy Ghost, and enabled to testify with a power which defeated his determined foes. He had a special promise from the Master, and he acted upon it. But we must observe that this promise was a special one, limited to the Apostles and to those in every age placed in similar circumstances. This promise is no general one. It was given to the Apostles to free them from care, anxiety, and forethought as to the matter and form of the addresses which they should deliver when suddenly called to speak before assemblies like the Sanhedrin. Under such circumstances they would have no time to prepare speeches suitable for ears trained in all the arts of oratory as then practised amongst the ancients, whether Jews or Gentiles. So their Master gave them an assurance of strength and skill such as none of their adversaries could equal or resist. "It is not ye that speak, but the Spirit of your Father which speaketh in you." This promise has been, however, misunderstood and abused when applied to ordinary circumstances. It was good for the Apostles, and it is good for Christian men placed under similar conditions, persecuted for the sake of their testimony, and deprived of the ordinary means of preparation. But it is not a promise authorising Christian teachers, clerical or lay, to dispense with careful thought and industrious study when communicating the truths of Christianity, or applying the great principles contained in the Bible to the manifold circumstances of modern life. Christ certainly told the Apostles not to premeditate beforehand what they should say. When relying, however, upon the promises of God, we should carefully seek to ascertain how far they are limited, and how far they apply to ourselves; else we may be putting our trust in words upon which we have no right to depend. A presumptuous trust is next door to an act of rebellion, and has often led to unbelief. Our Lord said to the Apostles, "Provide neither gold nor silver nor brass in your purses," because He would provide for them; but He did not say so to us, and if we go out into life presumptuously relying upon a passage of Scripture that does not belong to us, unbelief may overtake us as a strong man armed when we find ourselves disappointed. And so, too, with this promise of supernatural guidance which the Apostles enjoyed, and which saints of every age have proved true when placed in similar circumstances; it is a special one for them, it does not apply to us. Christian teachers, whether in the pulpit, or the Sunday school, or the home circle, must still depend as completely as the Apostles did upon the Holy Ghost as the source of all successful teaching. But in the case of the Apostles the inspiration was immediate and direct. In the case of ordinary Christians like ourselves placed amid all the helps which God's providence gives, we must use study, thought, meditation, prayer, experience of life, as channels through which the same inspiration is conveyed to us. The Society of Friends, when George Fox established it, testified on behalf of a great truth when it asserted that the Holy Ghost dwelt still, as in apostolic times, in the whole body of the Church, and spake still through the experience of Christian people. Their testimony was a great truth and a much-needed one in the middle of the seventeenth century, when Churchmen were in danger of turning religion into a great machine of state police, such as the Greek Church became under the earlier Christian emperors, and when Puritans were inclined to smother all religious enthusiasm beneath their intense zeal for cold, rigid scholastic dogmas and confessions of faith. The early Friends came proclaiming a Divine power still present, a Church of God still energised and inspired as of old, and it was a revelation for many an earnest soul. But they made a great mistake, and pushed a great truth to a pernicious extreme, when they taught that this inspiration was inconsistent with forethought and study on the part of their teachers as to the substance and character of their public ministrations. The Society of Friends teaches that men should speak forth to their assemblies just what the Holy Ghost reveals on the spot, without any effort on their own part, such as meditation and study involve. They have acted without a promise, and they have fared accordingly. That Society has been noted for its philanthropy, for the peaceful, gentle lives of its members; but it has not been noted for expository power, and its public teachers have held but a low place among those well-instructed scribes who bring forth out of God's treasures things new and old.[92]

Expositors of Scripture, teachers of Divine truth, whether in the public congregation or in a Sunday-school class, must prepare themselves by thought, study, and prayer; then, having made the way of the Lord clear, and removed the hindrances which barred His path, we may humbly trust that the Holy Ghost will speak by us and through us, because we honour Him by our self-denial, and cease to offer burnt sacrifices unto the Lord of that which costs us nothing.[93]

IV. The address of St. Peter to the Sanhedrin is marked by the same characteristics as we find in those directed to the people. It is kindly, for though the Apostles could speak sternly and severely just as their Master did at times, yet they have left in this special direction an example to public speakers and public teachers of truth in every age. They strove first of all to put themselves in sympathy as much as possible with their audience. They did not despise the art of the rhetorician which teaches a speaker to begin by conciliating the good feelings of his audience towards himself. To the people St. Peter began, "Ye men of Israel;" he recognises their cherished privileges, as well as their sacred memories,—"Ye are the children of the prophets, and of the covenant which God made with our fathers." To the bitterly hostile audience of the Sanhedrin, where the Sadducees largely predominated, Peter's exordium is profoundly respectful and courteous, "Ye rulers of the people, and elders of Israel." The Apostles and the earliest Evangelists did not despise human feelings or outrage human sentiment when setting out to preach Christ crucified. We have known men so wrong-headed that they were never happy unless their efforts to do good or spread their peculiar opinions eventuated in a riot. When evangelistic work or any kind of attempt to spread opinions evokes violent opposition, that very opposition often arises from the injudicious conduct of the promoters; and then when the opposition is once evoked or a riot caused, charity departs, passion and violent feelings are aroused, and all hope of good evaporates for the time. There was profound practical wisdom in that command of our Lord to His Apostles, "When they persecute you in this city, flee ye into another," even taking the matter only from the standpoint of a man anxious to spread his peculiar sentiments.

The Apostle's address was kindly, but it was plain-spoken. The Sanhedrin were sitting as a board of inquisitors. They did not deny the miracle which had been wrought. We are scarcely fit judges of the attitude of mind occupied by an Eastern, specially by an Eastern Jew of those earlier ages, when confronted with a miracle. He did not deny the facts brought under his notice. He was too well acquainted with magic and the strange performances of its professors to do so. He merely inquired as to the sources of the power, whether they were Divine or diabolical. "By what power or by what name have ye done this?" was a very natural inquiry in the mouth of an ecclesiastical body such as the Sanhedrin was. It was disturbed by facts, for which no explanation such as their philosophy furnished could account. It was upset in its calculations just as, to this day, the performances of Indian jugglers or the weird wonders of hypnotism upset the calculations of the hard, narrow man who has restricted all his investigations to some one special branch of science, and has so contracted his horizon that he thinks there is nothing in heaven or in earth which his philosophy cannot explain. We should mark the expression, "By what *name* have ye done this?" for it gives us a glimpse into Jewish life and practice. The Jews were accustomed in their incantations to use several kinds of names; sometimes those of the patriarchs, sometimes the name of Solomon, and sometimes that of the Eternal Jehovah Himself. Of late years vast quantities of Jewish and Gnostic manuscripts have come to light in Egypt and Syria containing various titles and forms used by the Jewish magicians and the earlier Christian heretics, who were largely imbued with Jewish notions. It is quite in keeping with what we know of the spirit of the age from other sources that the Sanhedrin should ask, "By what power or by what name have ye done this?" While again, when we turn to the book of the Acts of the Apostles itself we find an illustration of the council's inquiry in the celebrated case of the seven sons of Sceva, the Jewish priest at Ephesus, who strove to use for their own magical purposes the Divine name of Jesus Christ, and suffered for their temerity. St. Peter's reply to the question of the court proves that the Christian Church adopted in all its Divine offices, whether in the working of miracles then or of baptism and of ordination, as still, the invocation of the Sacred Name, after the Jewish model. The Church still baptizes and ordains in the name of the Father and of the Son and of the Holy Ghost. Christ Himself had adopted the formula for baptism, and the Church has extended it to ordination, pleading thus before God and man alike the Divine power by which alone St. Peter healed the cripple and the Church sends forth its ministers to carry on Christ's work in the world.

St. Peter's address was, as we have already said, very kindly, but very bold and plain-spoken in setting forth the power of Christ's name. He had learnt by his Jewish training the tremendous importance and solemnity of names. Moses at the bush would know God's name before he went as His messenger to the captive Israelites. On Sinai God Himself had placed reverence towards His name as one of the fundamental truths of religion. Prophet and psalmist had conspired together to teach St. Peter that holy and reverend was the name of God, and to impress upon him thus the power and meaning which lies in Christ's name, and indeed in all names, though names are things we count so trifling. St. Peter dwells upon this point all through his addresses. To the people he had said, "His name, through faith in His name, hath made this man strong." To the rulers it was the same. It was "by the name of Jesus Christ of Nazareth, whom ye crucified, this man doth stand here before you whole." "There is none other name under heaven whereby we must be saved." The Sanhedrin understand the importance of this point, and tell the Apostles they must not teach in this name. St. Peter pointedly refuses, and prays, when come to his own company, "that wonders may be done through the name of Thy holy servant Jesus."

St. Peter realized the sanctity and the power of God's name, whether revealed in its ancient form of Jehovah or its New Testament form of Jesus Christ. Well would it be if the same Divine reverence found a larger place amongst ourselves. Irreverence towards the sacred name is far too prevalent; and even when men do not use God's name in a profane way, there is too much lightness in the manner in which even religious men permit themselves to utter that name which is the expression to man of supreme holiness,—"God bless us," "Lord help us and save." How constantly do even pious people garnish their conversations and their epistles with such phrases or with the symbols D.V., without any real feeling that they are thereby appealing to Him who was and is and is to come, the Eternal. The name of God is still holy as of old, and the name of Jesus is still powerful to calm and soothe and bless as of old, and Christian people should sanctify those great names in their conversation with the world.[94]

St. Peter was bold because he was daily comprehending more and more of the meaning of Christ's work and mission, was gaining a clearer insight into the dignity of His person, and was experiencing in himself the truth of His supernatural promises. How could a man help being bold, who felt the Spirit's power within, and really held with intense belief that there was salvation in none other save Christ? Personal experience of religion alone can impart strength and courage and boldness to endure, to suffer, and to testify. St. Peter was exclusive in his views. He would not have suited those easy-going souls who now think one religion just as good as another, and consequently do not regard it as of the slightest moment whether a man be a follower of Christ or of Mahomet. The earliest Christians had none of this diluted faith. They believed that as there was only one God, so there was only one Mediator between God and man, and they realized the tremendous importance of preaching this Mediator. The Apostles, however, must be cleared from a misconstruction under which they have at times suffered. St. Peter proclaims Christ to the Sanhedrin as the only means of salvation. In his address to Cornelius the centurion of Cæsarea, he declares that in every nation he that feareth God and worketh righteousness is accepted of Him. These passages and these two declarations appear inconsistent. Their inconsistency is only superficial, however, as Bishop Burnet has well explained in his exposition of the Thirty-Nine Articles, a book not read very much in these times.[95] St. Peter taught exclusive salvation through Christ. Christ is the only means, the only channel and way by which God confers salvation. Christ's work is the one meritorious cause which gains spiritual blessing for man. But then, while there is salvation only in Christ, many persons may be saved by Christ who know not of Him consciously, else what shall we say or think about infants and idiots? It is only by Christ and through Christ and for His sake that any soul can be saved. He is the only door of salvation, He is the way as well as the truth and the life. But then it is not for us to pronounce how far the saving merits of Christ may be applied and His saving power extend. St. Peter knew and taught that Jesus Christ was the one Mediator, and that by His name alone salvation could be obtained. Yet he did not hesitate to declare as regards Cornelius the centurion, that in every nation he that feareth God and worketh righteousness is accepted of Him. It ought to be sufficient for us, as it was for the Apostles, to believe that the knowledge of Christ is life eternal, while satisfied to leave all other problems in the hands of Eternal Love.

# CHAPTER X
# THE COMMUNITY OF GOODS

"And the multitude of them that believed were of one heart and soul: and not one of them said that aught of the things which he possessed was his own; but they had all things common. And with great power gave the apostles their witness of the resurrection of the Lord Jesus: and great grace was upon them all. For neither was there among them any that lacked: for as many as were possessors of lands or houses sold them, and brought the prices of the things that were sold, and laid them at the apostles' feet: and distribution was made unto each, according as any one had need." —Acts iv. 32-5.

The community of goods and its results next claim our attention in the course of this sacred record of primitive Church life. The gift of tongues and this earliest attempt at Christian communism were the two special features of apostolic, or perhaps we should rather say of Jerusalem, Christianity. The gift of tongues we find at one or two other places, at Cæsarea on the first conversion of the Gentiles, at Ephesus and at Corinth. It then disappeared. The community of goods was tried at Jerusalem. It lasted there a very short time, and then faded from the ordinary practice of the Christian Church. The record of this vain attempt and its manifold results embodies many a lesson suitable to our modern Christianity.

I. The book of the Acts of the Apostles in its earliest chapters relates the story of the triumph of the Cross; it also tells of the mistakes made by its adherents. The Scriptures prove their Divine origin, and display the secret inspiration and guidance of their writers, by their thorough impartiality. If in the Old Testament they are depicting the history of an Abraham or of a David, they do not, after the example of human biographies, tell of their virtues and throw the mantle of obscurity over their vices and crimes. If in the New Testament they are relating the story of apostolic labours, they record the bad as well as the good, and hesitate not to tell of the dissimulation of St. Peter, the hot temper and the bitter disputes of a Paul and a Barnabas.

It is a notable circumstance that, in ancient and modern times alike, men have stumbled at this sacred impartiality. They have mistaken the nature of inspiration, and have busied themselves to clear the character of men like David and the holy Apostles, explaining away the plainest facts,—the lie of Abraham, the adultery of David, the weaknesses and infirmities of the Apostles. They have forgotten the principle involved in the declaration, "Elijah was a man of like passions with ourselves;" and have been so jealous for the honour of scriptural characters that they have made their history unreal, worthless as a living example. St. Jerome, to take but one instance, was a commentator upon Scripture whose expositions are of the greatest value, specially because he lived and worked amid the scenes where Scripture history was written, and while yet living tradition could be used to illustrate the sacred narrative. St. Jerome applied this deceptive method to the dissimulation of St. Peter at Antioch of which St. Paul tells us in the Galatians; maintaining, in opposition to St. Augustine,[96] that St. Peter was not a dissembler at all, and that the whole scene at Antioch was a piece of pious acting, got up between the Apostles in order that St. Paul might have the opportunity of condemning Judaizing practices. This is an illustration of the tendency to which I am referring. Men will uphold, not merely the character of the Scriptures, but the characters of the writers of Scripture. Yet how clearly do the Sacred Writings distinguish between these things; how clearly they show that God imparted His treasures in earthen vessels, vessels that were sometimes very earthy indeed, for while in one place they give us the Psalms of David, with all their treasures of spiritual joy, hope, penitence, they in another place give us the very words of the letter written by King David ordering the murder of Uriah the Hittite. This jealousy, which refuses to admit the fallibility and weakness of scriptural personages, has been applied to the doctrine of the community of goods which finds place in the passage under review. Some expositors will not allow that it was a mistake at all; they view the Church at Jerusalem as divinely guided by the Holy Spirit even in matters of temporal policy; they ascribe to it an infallibility greater and wider than any claimed for the Roman Pontiff. He claims infallibility in matters pertaining to faith and morals, when speaking as universal doctor and teacher of the Universal Church; but those writers invest the Church at Jerusalem with infallibility on every question, whether spiritual or temporal, sacred or secular, because the Holy Ghost had been poured out upon the twelve Apostles on the day of Pentecost. Now it is quite evident that neither the Church of Jerusalem nor the Apostles themselves were guided by an inspiration which rendered them infallible upon all questions. The indwelling of the Holy Spirit which was granted to them was a gift which left all their faculties in precisely the same state as they were before the descent of the Spirit. The Apostles could make moral mistakes, as Peter did at Antioch; they were not infallible in forecasting the future, as St. Paul proved when at Ephesus he told the Ephesian elders that he should not again visit their Church,[97] while, indeed, he spent much time there in after years. The whole early Church was mistaken on the important questions of the calling of the Gentiles, the binding nature of the Levitical law, and the time of Christ's second coming. The Church of Jerusalem, till the conversion of Cornelius, was completely mistaken as to the true nature of the Christian dispensation. They regarded it, not as the new and final revelation which was to supersede all others; they thought of it merely as a new sect within the bounds of Judaism.

It was a similar mistake which led to the community of goods. We can trace the genesis and upgrowth of the idea. It cannot be denied that the earliest Christians expected the immediate return of Christ. This expectation brought with it a very natural paralysis of business life and activity. We have seen the same result happening again and again. At Thessalonica St. Paul had to deal with it, as we have already noted in the second of these lectures. Some of the Thessalonians laboured under a misunderstanding as to St. Paul's true teaching: they thought that Jesus Christ was immediately about to appear, and they gave up work and labour under the pretence of preparing for His second coming. Then St. Paul comes sharply down upon this false practical deduction which they had drawn from his teaching, and proclaims the law, "If any man will not work, neither shall he eat." We have already spoken of the danger which might attend such a time. Here we behold another danger which did practically ensue and bring forth evil fruit. The first Christian Pentecost and the days succeeding it were a period of strained expectation, a season of intense religious excitement, which naturally led to the community of goods. There was no apostolic rule or law laid down in the matter. It seems to have been a course of action to which the converts spontaneously resorted, as the logical deduction from two principles which they held; first, their brotherhood and union in Christ; secondly, the nearness of Christ's second advent. The time was short. The Master had passed into the invisible world whence He would shortly reappear. Why should they not then, as brethren in Christ, have one common purse, and spend the whole time in waiting and watching for that loved presence? This seems a natural explanation of the origin of a line of policy which has been often appealed to in the practical life of modern Europe as an example for modern Christians; and yet, when we examine it more closely, we can see that this book of the Acts of the Apostles, while it tells of their mistake, carries with it the correction of the error into which these earliest disciples fell.[98] The community of goods was adopted in no other Church. At Corinth, Ephesus, Rome, we hear nothing of it in those primitive times. No Christian sect or Church has ever tried to revive it, save the monastic orders, who adopted it for the special purpose of completely cutting their members off from any connection with the world of life and action; and, in later times still, the wild fanatical Anabaptists at the Reformation period, who thought, like the Christians of Jerusalem, that the kingdom of God, as they fancied it, was immediately about to appear.[99] The Church of Jerusalem, as the apostolic history shows us, reaped the natural results of this false step. They adopted the principles of communism; they lost hold of that principle of individual life and exertion which lies at the very root of all civilisation and all advancement, and they fell, as the natural result, into the direst poverty. There was no reason in the nature of its composition why the Jerusalem Church should have been more poverty-stricken than the Churches of Ephesus, Philippi, or Corinth. Slaves and very humble folk constituted the staple of these Churches. At Jerusalem a great company of the priests were obedient to the faith, and the priests were, as a class, in easy circumstances. Slaves cannot at Jerusalem have constituted that large element of the Church which they did in the great Greek and Roman cities, simply because slavery never reached among the Jews the same development as in the Gentile world. The Jews, as a nation, were a people among whom there was a widely diffused comfort, and the earliest Church at Jerusalem must have fairly represented the nation. There was nothing to make the mother Church of Christendom that pauper community we find it to have been all through St. Paul's ministry, save the one initial mistake, which doubtless the Church authorities found it very hard afterwards to retrieve; for when men get into the habit of living upon alms it is very difficult to restore the habits of healthy independence.

II. This incident is, however, rich in teaching for the Church of every age, and that in very various directions. It is a significant warning for the mission field. Missionary Churches should strive after a healthy independence amongst their members. It is, of course, absolutely necessary that missionaries should strive to supply temporal employment to their converts in places and under circumstances where a profession of Christianity cuts them off at once from all communication with their old friends and neighbours. The primitive Church found it necessary to give such temporal relief, and yet had to guard against its abuse; and we have been far too remiss in looking for guidance to those early centuries when the whole Church was necessarily one great missionary organization. The Apostolic Canons and Constitutions are documents which throw much light on many questions which now press for solution in the mission field. They pretend to be the exact words of the Apostles, but are evidently the work of a later age. They date back in their present shape, at latest, to the third or fourth centuries, as is evident from the fact that they contain elaborate rules for the treatment of martyrs and confessors, — and there were no martyrs after that time,—directing that every effort should be made to render them comfort, support, and sympathy. These Constitutions prove that the Church in the third century was one mighty co-operative institution, and an important function of the bishop was the direction of that co-operation. The second chapter of the fourth book of the Apostolic Constitution lays down, "Do you therefore, O bishops, be solicitous about the maintenance of orphans, being in nothing wanting to them; exhibiting to the orphans the care of parents; to the widows the care of husbands; to the artificer, work; to the stranger, an house; to the hungry, food; to the thirsty, drink; to the naked, clothing; to the sick, visitation, to the prisoners, assistance." But these same Constitutions recognise equally clearly the danger involved in such a course. The wisdom of the early Church saw and knew how easily alms promiscuously bestowed sap the roots of independence, and taught therefore, with equal explicitness, the absolute necessity for individual exertion, the duty of Christian toil and labour; urging the example of the Apostles themselves, as in the sixty-third Constitution of the second book, where they are represented as exhorting, "Let the young persons of the Church endeavour to minister diligently in all necessaries; mind your business with all becoming seriousness, that so you may always have sufficient to support yourselves and those that are needy, and not burden the Church of God. For we ourselves, besides our attention to the Word of the Gospel, do not neglect our inferior employments; for some of us are fishermen, some tent-makers, some husbandmen, that so we may never be idle." In the modern mission field there will often be occasions when, as in ancient times, the profession of Christianity and the submission of the converts to baptism will involve the loss of all things.[100] And, under such circumstances, Christian love, such as burned of old in the hearts of God's people and led them to enact the rules we have now quoted, will still lead and compel the Church in its organized capacity to lend temporal assistance to those that are in danger of starvation for Christ's sake; but no missionary effort can be in a healthy condition where all, or the greater portion, of the converts are so dependent upon the funds of the mission that if the funds were withdrawn the apparent results would vanish into thin air. Such missions are utterly unlike the missions of the apostolic Church; for the converts of the apostolic age were made by men who went forth without purse or scrip, who could not give temporal assistance even had they desired to do so, and whose great object ever was to develop in their followers a healthy spirit of Christian manliness and honest independence.

III. Then, again, this passage teaches a much-needed lesson to the Church at home about the methods of poor relief and almsgiving. "Blessed," says the Psalmist, "is he that considereth the poor." He does not say, "Blessed is he that giveth money to the poor," but, "Blessed is he that considereth the poor." Well-directed, wise, prudent almsgiving is a good and beneficial thing, but indiscriminate almsgiving, almsgiving bestowed without care, thought, and consideration such as the Psalmist suggests, brings with it far more evil than it prevents. The Church of Jerusalem very soon had experience of these evils. Jealousies and quarrels soon sprang up even where Apostles were ministering and the supernatural gifts of the Spirit were present,— "There arose a murmuring of the Grecians against the Hebrews because their widows were neglected in the daily ministrations;" and it has been ever since the experience of those called to deal with questions of temporal relief and the distribution of alms, that no classes are more suspicious and more quarrelsome than those who are in receipt of such assistance. The chaplains and managers of almshouses, asylums, charitable funds, and workhouses know this to their cost, and ofttimes make a bitter acquaintance with that evil spirit which burst forth even in the mother Church of Jerusalem. Time necessarily hangs heavy upon the recipients' hands, forethought and care are removed and cease to engage the mind, and people having nothing else to do begin to quarrel. But this was not the only evil which arose: hypocrisy and ostentation, as in the case of Ananias and Sapphira, deceit, thriftlessness, and idleness showed themselves at Jerusalem, Thessalonica, and other places, as the Epistles of St. Paul amply testify. And so it has been in the experience of the modern Church. I know myself of whole districts where almsgiving has quite demoralised the poor and eaten the heart out of their religion, so that they value religious ministrations, not for the sake of the religion that is taught, but solely for the sake of the temporal relief that accompanies it. I know of a district where, owing to the want of organization in religious effort and the shattered and broken character of Protestant Christianity, the poor people are visited and relieved by six or seven competing religious communities, so that a clever person can make a very fair income by a judicious manipulation of the different visitors. It is evident that such visitations are doing evil instead of good, and the labour and money expended are worse than useless. The proper organization of charitable relief is one of the desirable objects the Church should set before it. The great point to be aimed at should be not so much the ministration of direct assistance to the people as the development of the spirit of self-help. And here comes in the action of the Christian State. The institution of the Post Office Savings Bank, where the State guarantees the safety of the depositor's money, seems a direct exposition and embodiment of the principle which underlay the community of goods in the apostolic Church. That principle was a generous, unselfish, Christlike principle. The principle was right, though the particular shape which the principle took was a mistaken one. Experience has taught the Church of Christ a wiser course, and now the system of State-guaranteed Savings Banks enables the

Church to lead the poor committed to her care into wiser courses. Parochial and congregational Savings Banks ought to be attached to all Christian organizations, so as to teach the poor the industrial lessons which they need. We have known a district in a most thriftless neighbourhood, where immense sums used to be wasted in indiscriminate almsgiving, and yet where the people, like the woman in the Gospels, were never one whit the better, but rather grew worse. We have seen such a district, in the course of a few years, quite regenerated in temporal matters, simply by the action of what is called a parochial Penny Savings Bank. Previously to its institution the slightest fall of snow brought heart-rending appeals for coal funds, blankets, and food; while a few years of its operation banished coal funds and pauperism in every shape, simply by teaching the people the magic law of thrift, and by developing within them the love and the power of self-respecting and industrious independence. And yet efforts in this direction will not be destructive of Christian charity. They tend not to dry up the springs of Christian love. Charity is indeed a blessing to the giver, and we should never desire to see the opportunity wanting for its display. Ill indeed would be the world's state if we had no longer the poor, the sick, the needy with us. Our sinful human nature requires its unselfish powers to be kept in action, or else it quickly subsides into a state of unwholesome stagnation. Poor people need to be taught habits of saving, and this teaching will require time, and trouble, and expense. The clergy and their congregations may teach the poor thrift by offering a much higher interest than the Post Office supplies, while, at the same time, the funds are all deposited in the State Savings Bank. That higher interest will often demand as much money as the doles previously bestowed in the shape of mere gifts of coal and food. But then what a difference in the result! The mere dole has, for the most part, a demoralising tendency, while the money spent in the other direction permanently elevates and blesses.[101]

IV. But there is a more important lesson still to be derived from this incident in the apostolic Church. The community of goods failed in that Church when tried under the most favourable circumstances, terminating in the permanent degradation of the Christian community at Jerusalem; just as similar efforts must ever fail, no matter how broad the field on which they may be tried or how powerful the forces which may be arrayed on their behalf. Christian legislatures of our own age may learn a lesson of warning against perilous experiments in a communistic direction from the disastrous failure in Jerusalem; and there is a real danger in this respect from the tendency of human nature to rush to extremes. Protestantism and the Reformation accentuated the individual and individual independence. The feeling thus taught in religion reacted on the world of life and action, developing an intensity of individualism in the political world which paralysed the efforts which the State alone could make in the various matters of sanitary education and social reform. In the last generation Maurice and Kingsley and men of their school raised in opposition the banner of Christian socialism, because they saw clearly that men had run too far in the direction of individualism,—so far, indeed, that they were inclined to forget the great lesson taught by Christianity, that under the new law we are members one of another, and that all members belong to one body, and that body is Christ. Men are so narrow that they can for the most part take only one view at a time, and so now they are inclined to push Christian socialism to the same extreme as at Jerusalem, and to forget that there is a great truth in individualism as there is another great truth in Christian socialism. Dr. Newman in his valuable but almost forgotten work on the Prophetical Office of the Church defined the position of the English Church as being a *Media Via*, a mean between two extremes. Whatever may be said upon other topics, the office of the Christian Church is most certainly a *Via Media*, a mean between the two opposite extremes of socialism and individualism. Much good has been effected of late years by legislation based upon essentially socialistic ideas. Reformatory and industrial schools, to take but one instance, are socialistic in their foundations and in their tendencies. The whole body of the State undertakes in them responsibilities and duties which God intended individuals to discharge, but which individuals persistently neglect, to the injury of their innocent offspring, and of society at large. Yet even in this simple experiment we can see the germs of the same evils which sprang up at Jerusalem. We have seen this tendency appearing in connection with the Industrial School system, and have known parents who could educate and train their children in family life encouraged by this well-intentioned legislation to fling their responsibilities over upon the State, and neglecting their offspring because they were convinced that in doing so they were not only saving their own pockets but also doing better for their children than they themselves could. It is just the same, and has ever been the same, with all similar legislation. It requires to be most narrowly watched. Human nature is intensely lazy and intensely selfish. God has laid down the law of individual effort and individual responsibility, and while we should strive against the abuses of that law, we should watch with equal care against the opposite abuses. Foundling hospitals as they were worked in the last century, for instance, form an object-lesson of the dangers inherent in such methods of action. Benevolent persons in the last century pitied the condition of poor children left as foundlings. There was, some sixty years ago, an institution in Dublin of this kind, which was supported by the State. There was a box into which an infant could be placed at any hour of the day or night; a bell was rung, and by the action of a turn-stile the infant was received into the institution. But experience soon taught the same lesson as at Jerusalem. The Foundling Hospital may have temporarily relieved some deserving cases and occasionally prevented some very painful scenes, but the broad results upon society at large were so bad, immorality was so increased, the sense of parental responsibility was so weakened, that the State was compelled to terminate its existence at a very large expense. Socialism when pushed to an extreme must necessarily work out in bad results, and that because there is one constant and fixed quantity which the socialist forgets. Human nature changes not; human nature is corrupt and must remain corrupt until the end, and so long as the corruption of human nature remains the best-conceived plans of socialism must necessarily fail.

Yet the Jerusalem idea of a voluntary community of goods was a noble one, and sprang from an unselfish root. It was purely voluntary indeed. There was no compulsion upon any to adopt it. "Not one of them said that aught that he possessed was his own," is St. Luke's testimony on the point. "While it remained, did it not remain thine own? And after it was sold, was it not in thy power?" are St. Peter's words, clearly testifying that this Christian communism was simply the result and outcome of loving hearts who, under the influence of an overmastering emotion, had cast prudence to the winds. The communism of Jerusalem may have been unwise, but it was the proof of generous and devout spirits. It was an attempt, too, to realize the conditions of the new life in the new heaven and the new earth wherein dwelleth righteousness, while still the old heaven and the old earth remained. It was an enthusiasm, a high, a holy, and a noble enthusiasm; and though it failed in some respects, still the enthusiasm begotten of fervent Christian love succeeded in another direction, for it enabled the Apostles "with great power to give witness to the resurrection of the Lord Jesus." The union of these two points in the sacred narrative has profound spiritual teaching for the Church of Christ. Unselfishness in worldly things, enthusiasm about the kingdom of Christ, fervent love to the brethren, are brought into nearest contact and united in closest bonds with the possession of special spiritual power over the hearts of the unbelievers. And then, again, the unselfishness existed amongst the body of the Church, the mass of the people at large. We are sure that the Apostles were leaders in the acts of self-denial. No great work is carried out where the natural and divinely-sent leaders hang back. But it is the love and enthusiasm of the mass of the people which excite St. Luke's notice, and which he illustrates by the contrasted cases of Barnabas and Ananias; and he connects this unselfish enthusiasm of the people with the possession of great power by the Apostles. Surely we can read a lesson suitable for the Church of all ages in this collocation. The law of interaction prevails between clergy and people still as it did between the Apostles and people of old. The true minister of Christ will frequently bear before the throne of God those souls with whom the Holy Ghost has entrusted him, and without such personal intercession he cannot expect real success in his work. But then, on the other hand, this passage suggests to us that enthusiasm, fervent faith, unselfish love on the people's part are the conditions of ministerial power with human souls. A people filled with Christ's love, and abounding in enthusiasm, even by a mere natural process produce power in their leaders, for the hearts of the same leaders beat quicker and their tongues speak more forcibly because they feel behind them the immense motive power of hallowed faith and sacred zeal. But we believe in a still higher blessing. When people are unselfish, brimming over with generous Christian love, it calls down a supernatural, a Divine power. The Pentecostal Spirit of love again descends, and in roused hearts and converted souls and purified and consecrated intellects rewards with a blessing such as they desire the men and women who long for the salvation of their brethren, and are willing, like these apostolic Christians, to sacrifice their dearest and their best for it.

# CHAPTER XI
# HONESTY AND PRETENCE IN THE PRIMITIVE CHURCH

"And Joseph, who by the apostles was surnamed Barnabas (which is, being interpreted, Son of exhortation), a Levite, a man of Cyprus by race, having a field, sold it, and brought the money, and laid it at the apostles' feet."—Acts iv. 36, 37.

"But a certain man named Ananias, with Sapphira his wife, sold a possession, and kept back part of the price, his wife also being privy to it, and brought a certain part, and laid it at the apostles' feet. But Peter said, Ananias, why hath Satan filled thy heart to lie to the Holy Ghost, and to keep back part of the price of the land? Whiles it remained, did it not remain thine own? and after it was sold, was it not in thy power? How is it that thou hast conceived this thing in thy heart? thou hast not lied unto men, but unto God. And Ananias hearing these words fell down and gave up the ghost; and great fear came upon all that heard it. And the young men arose and wrapped him round, and they carried him out and buried him."—Acts v. 1-6.

The exact period in the history of the apostolic Church at which we have now arrived is a most interesting one. We stand at the very first origin of a new development in Christian life and thought. Let us observe it well, for the whole future of the Church is bound up with it. Christianity was at the beginning simply a sect of Judaism. It is plain that the Apostles at first thus regarded it. They observed Jewish rites, they joined in the temple and synagogue worship, they restricted salvation and God's favour to the children of Abraham, and merely added belief in Jesus of Nazareth as the promised Messiah to the common Jewish faith. The Spirit of God was indeed speaking through the Apostles, leading them, as it led St. Peter on the day of Pentecost, to speak words with a meaning and scope far beyond their thoughts. They, like the prophets of old, knew not as yet what manner of things the Spirit which was in them did signify.

"As little children lisp, and tell of Heaven,

So thoughts beyond their thought to those high bards were given."

Their speech had a grander and wider application than they themselves dreamt of; but the power of prejudice and education was far too great even for the Apostles, and so, though the nobility and profuseness of God's mercy were revealed and the plenteousness of His grace was announced by St. Peter himself, yet the glory of the Divine gift was still unrecognised. Jerusalem, the Temple, the Old Covenant, Israel after the flesh,—these things as yet bounded and limited the horizon of Christ's Church. How were the new ideas to gain an entrance? How was the Church to rise to a sense of the magnificence and universality of its mission? Joseph, who by the Apostles was surnamed Barnabas, emerges upon the scene and supplies the answer, proving himself in very deed a son of consolation, because he became the occasion of consoling the masses of mankind with that truest comfort, the peace of God which passes all understanding. Let us see how this came about.

I. The Christian leaders belonged originally to the extreme party in Judaism. The Jews were at this time divided into two sections. There was the Hebrew party on the one hand; extreme Nationalists as we might call them. They hated everything foreign. They clung to the soil of Palestine, to its language and to its customs. They trained up their children in an abhorrence of Greek civilisation, and could see nothing good in it. This party was very unprogressive, very narrow-minded, and, therefore, unfit to recognise the developments of God's purposes. The Galileans were very prominent among them. They lived in a provincial district, remote from the influences of the great centres of thought and life, and missed, therefore, the revelations of God's mind which He is evermore making through the course of His providential dealings with mankind. The Galileans furnished the majority of the earliest Christian leaders, and they were not fitted from their narrowness to grasp the Divine intentions with respect to Christianity and its mission. What a lesson for every age do we behold in this intellectual and spiritual defect of the Galileans. They were conscientious, earnest, devout, spiritually-minded men. Christ loved them as such, and devoted Himself to their instruction. But they were one-sided and illiberal. Their very provincialism, which had sheltered them from Sadduceeism and unbelief, had filled them with blind prejudices, and as the result had rendered them unable to read aright the mind of God and the development of His purposes. Man, alas! is a very weak creature, and human nature is very narrow. Piety is no guarantee for wisdom and breadth, and strong faith in God's dealings in the past often hinders men from realizing and obeying the Divine guidance and the evolution of His purposes amid the changed circumstances of the present. The Galilean leaders were best fitted to testify with unfaltering zeal to the miracles and resurrection of Christ. They were not best fitted to lead the Church into the possession of the Gentiles.

There was another party among the Jews whom God had trained by the guidance of His Providence for this purpose. The Acts of the Apostles casts a strong and comforting light back upon the history of the Lord's dealings with the Jews ever since the days of the Babylonish Captivity. We can see in the story told in the Acts the reason why God permitted the overthrow of Jerusalem by the hands of Nebuchadnezzar, and the apparent defeat for the time of His own designs towards the chosen people. The story of the dispersion is a standing example how wonderfully God evolves good out of seeming ill, making all things work together for the good of His Church. The dispersion prepared a section of the Jews, by travel, by foreign civilization, by culture, and by that breadth of mind and sympathy which is thereby produced, to be mediators between the Hebrew party with all their narrowness, and the masses of the Gentile world whom the strict Jews would fain have shut out from the hope of God's mercy. This liberal and progressive party is called in the Acts of the Apostles the Hellenists. They were looked at askance by the more old-fashioned Hebrews. They were Jews, children of Abraham indeed, of the genuine stock of Israel. As such they had a true standing-ground within the Jewish fold, and as true Jews could exercise their influence from within much more effectually than if they stood without; for it has been well remarked by a shrewd observer, that every party, religious or political, is much more powerfully affected by movements springing from within than by attacks directed from without. An explosive operates with much more destructive force when acting from within or underneath a fortification than when brought into play from outside. Such was the Hellenistic party. No one could deny their true Jewish character, but they had been liberalized by their heaven-sent contact with foreigners and foreign lands; and hence it is that we discern in the Hellenistic party, and specially in Joseph who by the Apostle was surnamed Barnabas, the beginnings of the glorious ingathering of the Gentiles, the very first rift in the thick dark cloud of prejudice which as yet kept back even the Apostles themselves from realizing the great object of the gospel dispensation. The Hellenists, with their wealth, their culture, their new ideas, their sense and value of Greek thought, were the bridge by which the spiritual life, hitherto wrapped in Jewish swaddling clothes, was to pass over to the masses of the Gentile world. The community of goods led Joseph Barnabas to dedicate his substance to the same noble cause of unselfishness. That dedication led to disputes between Hellenists and Hebrews, and these disputes occasioned the election of the seven deacons, who, in part, at least, belonged to the more liberal section. Among these deacons we find St. Stephen, whose teaching and martyrdom were directly followed by St. Paul and his conversion, and St. Paul was the Apostle of the Gentiles and the vindicator of Christian freedom and Christian liberty. St. Barnabas and his act of self-denial and self-sacrifice in surrendering his landed estate are thus immediately connected with St. Paul by direct historic contact, even if they had not been subsequently associated as joint Apostles and messengers of the Churches in their first missionary journeys; while again the mistaken policy of communism is overruled to the world's abiding benefit and blessing. How wonderful, indeed, are the Lord's doings towards the children of men!

II. We have thus suggested one of the main lines of thought which run through the first half of this book of the Acts. Let us now look a little more particularly at this Joseph Barnabas who was the occasion of this great, this new departure. We learn then, upon consulting the sacred text, that Joseph was a Levite, a man of Cyprus by race; he belonged, that is, to the class among the Jews whose interests were bound up with the maintenance of the existing order of things; and yet he had become a convert to the belief proclaimed by the Apostles. At the same time, while we give full credit to this Levite for his action, we must not imagine that either priests or Levites or Jews at that period fully realized all the consequences of their decisions. We find that men at every age take steps blindly, without thoroughly realizing all the results which logically and necessarily flow forth from them. Men in religious, political, social matters are blind and cannot see afar off. It is only step by step that the purposes of God dawn upon them, and Joseph Barnabas, the Levite of Cyprus, was no exception to this universal rule. He was not only a Levite, but a native of Cyprus, for Cyprus was then a great stronghold and resort of the Jewish race. It continued to be a great centre of Jewish influence for long afterwards. In the next century, for instance, a great Jewish rebellion burst forth wherever the Jews were strong enough. They rose in Palestine against the power of the Emperor Hadrian, and under their leader Barcochba vindicated the ancient reputation of the nation for desperate and daring courage; while, in sympathy with their brethren on the mainland, the Jews in Cyprus seized their arms and massacred a vast multitude of the Greek and Roman settlers, numbering, it is said, two hundred and forty thousand persons. The concourse of Jews to Cyprus in the time of the Apostles is easily explained. Augustus Cæsar was a great friend and patron of Herod the Great, and he leased the celebrated copper mines of the island to that Herod, exacting a royalty upon their produce, as we learn from Josephus, the well-known Jewish historian (*Antiqq.*, xvi. iv. 5). It was only to be expected, then, that when a Jewish monarch was leaseholder and manager of the great mining industry of the island, his Jewish subjects should flock thither, and it was very natural that amongst the crowds who sought Cyprus there should be found a minister of the Jewish faith whose tribal descent as a Levite reminded them of Palestine, and of the City of God, and of the Temple of Jehovah and of its solemn, stately worship.[102] This residence of Barnabas in Cyprus accounts for his landed property which he had the right to sell just as he liked. A Levite in Palestine could not, according to the law of Moses when strictly construed, possess any private landed estate save in a Levitical city. Meyer, a German commentator of great reputation, has indeed suggested that Jer. xxxii. 7, where Jeremiah is asked to redeem his cousin's field in the suburbs of Anathoth, proves that a member of the tribe of Levi could possess landed estate in Palestine. He therefore concludes that the old explanation that the landed property of Barnabas was in Cyprus, not in Palestine, could not stand. But the simple fact is that even the cleverest German expositors are not familiar with the text of their Bibles, for had Meyer been thus familiar he would have remembered that Anathoth was a city belonging to the priests and the tribe of Levi, and that the circumstance of Jeremiah the priest possessing a right to landed property in Anathoth was no proof whatsoever that he could hold landed property anywhere else, and, above all, affords no ground for the conclusion that he could dispose of it in the absolute style which Barnabas here displayed.[103] We conclude then that the action of Barnabas on this occasion dealt with his landed estate in Cyprus, the country where he was born, where he was well known, and where his memory is even still cherished on account of the work he there performed in conjunction with St. Paul.

III. Let us see what else we can glean concerning this personage thus prominent in the early Church, first for his generosity, and then for his missionary character and success. It is indeed one of the most fruitful and interesting lines upon which Bible study can be pursued, thus to trace the scattered features of the less known and less prominent characters of Scripture, and see wherein God's grace specially abounded in them.

The very personal appearance of Barnabas can be recalled by the careful student of this book.[104] Though it lies a little out of our way, we shall note the circumstance, as it will help us to form a more lively image of Barnabas, the Son of Consolation. The two Apostles, Paul and Barnabas, were on their first missionary tour when they came to the city of Lystra in Lycaonia. There the multitude, astonished at the miracle wrought upon the cripple by St. Paul, attempted to pay divine honours to the two Christian missionaries. "They called Barnabas Jupiter, and Paul Mercurius, because he was the chief speaker." It must have been their physical characteristics as well as the mode of address used by the Apostles which led to these names; and from the extant records of antiquity we know that Jupiter was always depicted as a man with a fine commanding presence, while Mercury, the god of eloquent speech, was a more insignificant figure. Jupiter, therefore, struck the Lycaonian people as the fittest name for the taller and more imposing-looking Apostle, while St. Paul, who was in bodily presence contemptible, was designated by the name of the active and restless Mercury. His character again shines through every recorded action of St. Barnabas. He was a thoroughly sympathetic man, and, like all such characters, he was ever swept along by the prevailing wave of thought or action, without allowing that supreme place to the judgment and the natural powers which they should always hold if the feelings and sympathies are not to land us in positions involving dire ruin and loss. He was carried away by the enthusiasm for Christian communism which now seized upon the Jerusalem Church. He was influenced by the Judaizing movement at Antioch, so that "even Barnabas was carried away with the Petrine dissimulation." His sympathies got the better of his judgment in the matter of St. Mark's conduct in abandoning the ministry to which St. Paul had called him. His heart was stronger, in fact, than his head. And yet this very weakness qualified him to be the Son of Consolation. A question has, indeed, been raised whether he should be called the Son of Consolation or the Son of Exhortation, but, practically, there is no difference. His consolations were administered through his exhortations. His speech and his advice were of a consoling, healing, comforting kind. There are still such men to be found in the Church. Just as all other apostolic graces and characteristics are still manifested,—the eloquence of a Paul, the courage of a Peter, the speculative flights of a John,—so the sympathetic power of a Barnabas is granted to some. And a very precious gift it is. There are some good men whose very tone of voice and bodily attitudes—their heads thrown back and their arms akimbo, and their aggressive walk—at once provoke opposition. They are pugnacious Christians, ever on the look out for some topic of blame and controversy. There are others, like this Barnabas, whose voices bring consolation, and whose words, even when not the clearest or the most practical, speak counsels of peace, and come to us thick-laden with the blessed dews of charity. Their advice is not, indeed, always the wisest. Their ardent cry is always, Peace, peace. Such a man on the political stage was the celebrated Lucius Carey, Lord Falkland, in the days of the great civil war, who, though he adhered to the Royalist cause, seemed, as the historian tells us, to have utterly lost all heart once that active hostilities commenced. Men of this type appear in times of great religious strife. Erasmus, for instance, at the time of the Reformation, possessed a good deal of this spirit which is devoted to compromise, and ever inclined to place the interests of peace and charity above those of truth and principle, just as Barnabas would have done at Antioch were it not for the protest of his stronger and sterner friend St. Paul. And yet such men, with their sympathetic hearts and speech, have their own great use, infusing a healing, consoling tone into seasons of strife, when others are only too apt to lose sight of the sweet image of Christian love in pursuit of what they consider the supreme interests of religious or political truth. Such a man was Barnabas all his life, and such we behold him on his first visible entrance upon the stage of Church history, when his sympathies and his generosity led him to consecrate his independent property in Cyprus to his brethren's support, and to bring the money and lay it down at the Apostles' feet.

IV. Now for the contrast drawn for us by the inspired pen of St. Luke, a contrast we find oft repeating itself in Church history. Here we have the generous sympathetic Son of Consolation on the one side, and here, too, we have a warning and a type for all time that the tares must evermore be mingled with the wheat, the false with the true, the hypocrites with real servants of God, even until the final separation. The accidental division of the book into chapters hinders casual readers from noticing that the action of Ananias and his wife is set by the writer over against that of Barnabas. Barnabas sold his estate and brought the price, the whole price, and surrendered it as an offering to the Church. The spirit of enthusiastic giving was abroad, and had seized upon the community; and Barnabas sympathized with it. Ananias and Sapphira were carried away too, but their spirits were meaner. They desired to have all the credit the Church would give them for acting as generously as Barnabas did, and yet, while getting credit for unselfish and unstinting liberality, to be able to enjoy in private somewhat of that which they were believed to have surrendered. And their calculations were terribly disappointed. They tried to play the hypocrite's part on most dangerous ground just when the Divine Spirit of purity, sincerity, and truth had been abundantly poured out, and when the spirit of deceit and hypocrisy was therefore at once recognised. It was with the Apostles and their spiritual natures then as it is with ourselves and our physical natures still. When we are living in a crowded city we notice not strange scents and ill-odours and foul gases: our senses are dulled, and our perceptive powers are rendered obtuse because the whole atmosphere is a tainted one. But when we dwell in the pure air of the country, and the glorious breezes from mountain and moor blow round us fresh and free, then we detect at once, and at a long distance, the slightest ill-odour or the least trace of offensive gas. The outpoured presence of the Spirit, and the abounding love which was produced thereby, quickened the perception of St. Peter. He recognised the hypocrisy, characterized the sin of Ananias as a lie against the Holy Ghost; and then the Spirit and Giver of life, seconding and supporting the words of St. Peter, withdrew His support from the human frame of the sinner, and Ananias ceased to live, just as Sapphira, his partner in deceit, ceased to live a few hours later. The death of Ananias and Sapphira have been ofttimes the subject of much criticism and objection, on the part of persons who do not realize the awfulness of their position, the full depths of their hypocrisy, and the importance of the lesson taught by their punishment to the Church of every age. Their position was a specially awful one, for they were brought into closest contact, as no Christian can now be brought, with the powers of the world to come. The Spirit was vouchsafed during those earliest days of the Church in a manner and style which we hear nothing of during the later years of the Apostles. He proved His presence by physical manifestations, as when the whole house was shaken where the Apostles were assembled; a phenomenon of which we read nothing in the latter portion of the Acts. By the gift of tongues, by miracles of healing, by abounding spiritual life and discernment, by physical manifestations, the most careless and thoughtless in the Christian community were compelled to feel that a supernatural power was present in their midst and specially resting upon the Apostles. Yet it was into such an atmosphere that the spirit of hypocrisy and of covetousness, the two vices to which Christianity was specially opposed, and which the great Master had specially denounced, obtruded itself as Satan gained entrance into Eden, to defile with their foul presence the chosen dwelling-place of the Holy Ghost. The Holy Ghost vindicated His authority therefore, because, as it must be observed, it was not St. Peter sentenced Ananias to death. No one may have been more surprised than St. Peter himself at the consequences which followed his stern rebuke. St. Peter merely declared his sin, "Thou hast not lied unto men, but unto God;" and then it is expressly said, "Ananias hearing these words fell down, and gave up the ghost." It was a stern action indeed; but then all God's judgments have a stern side. Ananias and Sapphira were cut off in their sins, but men are every day summoned into eternity in precisely the same state and the same way, and the only difference is that in the case of Ananias we see the sin which provoked the punishment and then we see the punishment immediately following. Men object to this narrative simply because they have a one-sided conception of Christianity such as this period of the world's history delights in. They would make it a religion of pure unmitigated love; they would eliminate from it every trace of sternness, and would thus leave it a poor weak flabby thing, without backbone or earnestness, and utterly unlike all other dispensations of the Lord, which have their stern sides and aspects as well as their loving.

It may well have been that this incident was inserted in this typical Church history to correct a false idea which would otherwise have grown up. The Jews were quite well accustomed to regard the Almighty as a God of judgment as well as a God of love. Perhaps we might even say that they viewed Him more in the former light than in the latter. Our Lord was obliged, in fact, to direct some of His most searching discourses to rebuke this very tendency. The Galileans, whose blood Pilate mingled with their sacrifices, the men upon whom the tower of Siloam fell,—neither party were sinners above all that were at Jerusalem, or were punished as such. Such was his teaching in opposition to the popular idea. The Apostles were once quite ready to ascribe the infirmity of the man born blind to the direct judgment of the Almighty upon himself or upon his parents. But men are apt to rush from one extreme to another. The Apostles and their followers were now realizing their freedom in the Spirit; and some were inclined to run into licentiousness as the result of that same freedom. They were realizing, too, their relationship to God as one of pure filial love, and they were in great danger of forgetting that God was a God of justice and judgment as well, till this stern dispensation recalled them to a sense of the fact that eternal love is also eternal purity and eternal truth, and will by no means clear the guilty. This is a lesson very necessary for every age of the Church. Men are always inclined, and never, perhaps, so much as at the present time, to look away from the severe side of religion, or even to deny that religion can have a severe side at all. This tendency in religious matters is indeed simply an exhibition of the spirit of the age. It is a time of great material prosperity and comfort, when pain is regarded as the greatest possible evil, softness, ease, and enjoyment the greatest possible good. Men shrink from the infliction of pain even upon the greatest criminals; and this spirit infects their religion, which they would fain turn into a mere matter of weakly sentiment. Against such a notion the judicial action of the Holy Ghost in this case raises an eternal protest, warning the Church against one-sided and partial views of truth, and bidding her never to lower her standard at the world's call. Men may ignore the fact that God has His severe aspect and His stern dispensations in nature, but yet the fact remains. And as it is in nature so is it in grace: God is merciful and loving to the penitent, but towards the hypocritical and covetous He is a stern judge, as the punishment of Ananias and Sapphira proved.

V. This seems one of the great permanent lessons for the Church of every age which this passage embodies, but it is not the only one. There are many others, and they most important. An eminent modern commentator and expositor[105] has drawn out at great length, and with many modern applications and illustrations, four great lessons which may be derived from this transaction. We shall just note them, giving a brief analysis of each. (1) There is such a thing as acting as well as telling a falsehood. Ananias did not say that the money he brought was the whole price of his land; he simply allowed men to draw this conclusion for themselves, suggesting merely by his conduct that he was doing exactly the same as Barnabas. There was no science of casuistry in the apostolic Church, teaching how near to the borders of a lie a man may go without actually being guilty of lying. The lie of Ananias was a spiritual act, a piece of deception attempted in the abyss of the human soul, and perpetrated, or attempted rather, upon the Holy Spirit. How often men lie after the same example. They do not speak a lie, but they act a lie, throwing dust into the eyes of others as to their real motives and objects, as Ananias did here. He sold his estate, brought the money to the Apostles, and would fain have got the character of a man of extraordinary liberality and unselfishness, just like others who truly sacrificed their all, while he enjoyed in private the portion which he had kept back. Ananias wished to make the best of both worlds, and failed in his object. He sought to obtain a great reputation among men, but had no regard to the secret eye and judgment of the Almighty. Alas! how many of our actions, how much of our piety and of our almsgiving, is tainted by precisely the same vice. Our good works are done with a view to man's approbation, and not as in the sight of the Eternal God.

(2) What an illustration we find in this passage of the saying of the Apostle, "The love of money is the root of all evil; which while some coveted after, they have erred from the faith, and pierced themselves with many sorrows!" The other scriptures are full of warnings against this vice of covetousness; and so this typical history does not leave the Church without an illustration of its power and danger. Surely if at a time when the supernatural forces of the unseen life were specially manifested, this vice intruded into the special sphere of their influence, the Church of every age should be on its perpetual guard against this spirit of covetousness which the Bible characterises as idolatry.

(3) What a responsibility is involved in being brought near to God as members of His Son's Church below! There were hypocrites in abundance at Jerusalem at that time, but they had not been blessed as Ananias had been, and therefore were not punished as he. There is a reality in our connection with Christ which must tell upon us, if not for good, then inevitably for evil. Christ is either the savour of life unto life or else the savour of death unto death unto all brought into contact with Him. In a far more awful sense than for the Jews the words of the prophet Ezekiel are true, "That which cometh into your mind shall not be at all, that ye say, We will be as the heathen, as the families of the countries, to serve wood and stone;"[106] or as the poet

of the *Christian Year* has well put it in his hymn for the eighteenth Sunday after Trinity:—

"Fain would our lawless hearts escape,
And with the heathen be,
To worship every monstrous shape
In fancied darkness free.

Vain thought, that shall not be at all,
Refuse we or obey;
Our ears have heard th' Almighty's call,
We cannot be as they.

We cannot hope the heathen's doom
To whom God's Son is given,
Whose eyes have seen beyond the tomb,
Who have the key of Heaven."

(4) Lastly, let us learn from this history how to cast out the fear of one another by the greater and more awful fear of God. The fear of man is a good thing in a degree. We should have respect to the opinion of our fellows, and strive to win it in a legitimate way. But Ananias and his consort desired the good opinion of the Christian community regardless of the approval or the watchful eye of the Supreme Judge, who interposed to teach His people by an awful example that in the new dispensation of Love, as well as in the old dispensation of Law, the fear of the Lord is the beginning of wisdom, and that they and they alone have a good understanding who order their lives according to that fear, whether in their secret thoughts or in their public actions.

# CHAPTER XII
## GAMALIEL AND HIS PRUDENT ADVICE

"And now I say unto you, Refrain from these men, and let them alone: for if this counsel or this work be of men, it will be overthrown: but if it is of God, ye will not be able to overthrow them; lest haply ye be found even to be fighting against God. And to him they agreed: and when they had called the Apostles unto them, they beat them and charged them not to speak in the name of Jesus, and let them go." — Acts v. 38-40.

We have set forth in these verses an incident in the second appearance before the council of the Apostle Peter and the other Apostles, conspicuous among whom must have been James the brother of John. It is almost certain that James the son of Zebedee was at this time very prominent in the public work of the Church, for we are told in the opening of the twelfth chapter that when Herod would vex and harass and specially weaken the Church, it was neither Peter nor John he first arrested, but he laid hands on James, and placed on him the honour of being the earliest martyr from amongst the sacred band of the Apostles. Peter we may, however, be sure was the centre of Sadducean hate at this period, and one of the most conspicuous members of the Church. We should at the same time beware of exaggeration, and strive to estimate the events of these earliest days of the Church, not as we behold them now, but as they must have then appeared unto the members of the Sanhedrin. The deaths of Ananias and Sapphira seem now to us extraordinary and awe-inspiring, and sufficient to strike terror into the hearts of all unbelievers; but probably the story of them had never reached the ears of the authorities. Human life was but little accounted of among the Romans who ruled Palestine. A Roman master might slay or torture his slaves just as he pleased; and the Romans, scorning the Jews as a conquered race, would trouble themselves but little concerning quarrels or deaths among them, so long as public order and the stated business of society were not interfered with. The public miracles which St. Peter wrought, these were the things which brought matters to a crisis, and called afresh the attention of the Sanhedrin, charged as they were with all religious authority, as the miracle of healing wrought upon the impotent man had led to the arrest of the Apostles on a previous occasion.[107] It is a mistake often made, in studying the history of the past, to imagine that events which we now see to have been important and epoch-making must have been so regarded by persons living at the time when they happened. Men are never worse judges of the true value of current history than when they are placed in the midst of it. It is always the on-lookers who see most of the play. Our minds are so limited, our thoughts are so completely filled up with the present, that it is not till we have got away from the events, and can view them in their due proportion and symmetry, surrounded with all their circumstances, that we can hope to form a just appreciation of their relative importance. I have often seen a hill of a few hundred feet in height occupying a far more commanding position in men's eyes than a really lofty mountain, simply because the one was near, the other far off. The deaths of Ananias and Sapphira are recorded therefore at full length, because they bring eternal lessons of justice, judgment, and truth along with them. The numerous public miracles wrought by Peter when "multitudes came together from the cities round about Jerusalem, bringing sick folk and them that were vexed with unclean spirits, and they were healed every one," seemed to the Sanhedrin and the religious public of Jerusalem the all-important topics, though they are passed wholly over in the Scriptures as matters of no spiritual interest. If it requires a vast exercise of patience and wisdom to estimate events aright in their mere worldly aspect, it requires the operation and guidance of the Holy Ghost to form a sound judgment upon the relative spiritual value of events falling within the sphere of Church history; and there indeed it is most true that matters which seem all-important and striking to man are judged by God as insignificant and unworthy of notice. So contradictory are ofttimes the ways of God and the opinions of man.

The public miracles wrought by St. Peter had this effect,—the only one noted at length by the sacred writer: they led to the fresh arrest of Peter and the other Apostles by the High Priest and the sect of the Sadducees, and to their incarceration in the public prison attached to the temple. Thence they were delivered by an angel and sent to speak publicly in the temple, where their adversaries officially assembled; just as on a later occasion Peter, when imprisoned by himself, was released by angelic interference. Men looking back upon the history of the primitive Church, and judging of it as if it were the history of an ordinary time and age, have objected to the angelic interventions narrated here and in a few other places in the New Testament. They object because they do not realize the circumstances of the time. Dr. Jortin was a shrewd writer of the last century, now too much neglected. He remarked in one place that, suppose we admit that a special revelation of the good powers of the heavenly world was made in Christ, it was natural and fair that a special manifestation of the powers of evil should have been permitted at the time of Christ's Incarnation, in order that the triumph of good might be the greater; and thus he would account for the diabolical possessions which play such an important part in the New Testament. The principle thus laid down extends much farther indeed. The great miracle of the Incarnation, the great manifestation of God in Christ, naturally brought with it lesser heavenly manifestations in its train. The Incarnation raises for a believer the whole level of the age when it occurred, and makes it an exceptional time. The eternal gates were for a moment lifted up, and angels went in and out for a little; and therefore we accept without endeavouring to explain the words of the narrative which tells us that an angel opened the prison doors for the Apostles, bidding them go and speak in the temple all the words of this life. And then from the temple, where they were teaching early in the morning, about daybreak of the day following their arrest, they are led by the officers before the Sanhedrin which was sitting in the city. Here let us pause to note the marvellous accuracy of detail in St. Luke's narrative. The Sanhedrin used to sit in the temple, but a few years before the period at which we have arrived, four or five at most, they removed from the temple into the city, a fact which is just hinted at in the fifth verse of the fourth chapter, where we are told that the rulers, and elders, and scribes were gathered together in Jerusalem, that is, in the city, not in the temple; while again in this passage we read that when the High Priest came and convened the council and all the senate of the children of Israel, they sent their officers to bring the prisoners before them. These officers after a while returned with the information that the Apostles were preaching in the temple. If the Sanhedrin were meeting in the temple, they would doubtless have learned this fact as soon as they assembled, especially as they did not sit till after the morning sacrifice, several hours after the Apostles appeared in the temple.[108] When brought before the council the Apostles boldly proclaimed their intention to disregard all human threats, and persevere in preaching the death and resurrection of Christ. The majority would then have proceeded to extreme measures against the Apostles, and in doing so would only have acted after their usual manner.

The greater part of the Sanhedrin were Sadducees, and they, as Josephus tells us, were men of a bloodthirsty character, ever ready to proceed to punish in the most cruel manner. The simple fact is this, the Sadducees were materialists. They looked upon man as a mere animated machine, and therefore, like the pagans of the same period, they were utterly regardless of human sufferings or of the value of human life. We little recognise, reared up as we have been in an atmosphere saturated with Christian principles, how much of our merciful spirit, of our tender care for human suffering, of our reverent respect for human life, is owing to the spiritual ideas of the New Testament, teaching as it does the awful importance of time, the sanctity of the body, and the tremendous issues which depend upon life. Sadducees and pagans knew nothing of these things, because they knew nothing of the inestimable treasure lodged in every human form. Life and time would have been very different for mankind had not the spiritual principles inculcated by Pharisee and by Christian alike triumphed over the cold stern creed which strove on this occasion to stifle the religion of the Cross in its very infancy. When the Sadducees would have adopted extreme measures, the words of one man restrained them and saved the Apostles, and that one man was Gamaliel, whose name and career will again come before us. Now let us apply ourselves to the consideration of his address to the Sanhedrin. Gamaliel saw that the large public gathering to whom he was speaking were thoroughly excited and full of cruel purposes. He therefore, like a true orator, adopts the historical method as the fittest one for dealing with them. He points out how other pretenders had arisen, trading on the Messianic expectations which then existed all over Palestine, and specially in Galilee, and how they had been all destroyed without any action on the part of the Sanhedrin. He instances two cases: Judas, who lived in the days of Cyrenius and the taxing under Augustus Cæsar; and Theudas, who some time previous to that event had arisen, working upon the religious and national hopes of the Jews, as the persons now accused before them seemed also to be doing. He points to the fate of the pretenders he had mentioned, and advises the Sanhedrin to leave the Apostles to the same test of Divine Providence, confident that if mere impostors, like the others, they will meet with the same death at the hands of the Romans, without any interference on their part.

It is evident that Gamaliel must have had some special reason for selecting the risings of Theudas and Judas, beyond the fact that they were rebels against established authority. The closing years of the kingdom of Herod the Great were times when numberless rebellions took place. Josephus gives us the names of several leaders who took part in them, but, as he tells us (*Antiqq.*, XVII. x. 4), there were then "ten thousand other disorders," into the details of which he did not enter. All these risings had, however, these distinguishing features, they were all unsuccessful, and they were all quenched in blood. Gamaliel must have seen some feature common to the Christian movement and to those headed by Theudas and Judas some thirty years earlier, leading him to adduce these examples. That common feature was their Messianic character. They all alike proclaimed new hopes for Israel, and appealed to the religious expectations which then excited the people, and still are embodied in works like the book of Enoch, produced about that period; while all the other attempts were animated by a mere spirit of plunder or of personal ambition. But here we are met with a difficulty. The rationalistic commentators of Germany have urged that St. Luke composed a fancy speech and put it into the mouth of Gamaliel, and in doing so made a great historic mistake. They appeal to Josephus as their authority. He states that a Theudas arose about A.D. 44, some ten years later than this meeting of the Sanhedrin, and drew a large number of adherents after him, but was defeated by the Roman governor. On the other hand, the words of Gamaliel refer to the case of a Theudas who lived half a century earlier, and preceded Judas the Galilean. To put the matter plainly, St. Luke is accused of having composed a speech for Gamaliel, and, when doing so, of having committed a great blunder, representing Gamaliel as appealing to an incident which did not happen till ten years later.[109]

This circumstance has long attracted the notice of commentators, and has been explained in different ways. Some maintain that there was an older Theudas, who headed an abortive Messianic rebellion previous to the time of Cyrenius and the days of the taxing. This is a very possible explanation, and the identity of names constitutes no valid objection. The same names often occur in connection with the same movements, political or religious. In the third century, for instance, the Novatian heresy arose at Carthage, and thence was transferred to Rome. It was headed by two men, Novatus and Novatian, the former a Carthaginian, the latter a Roman presbyter. What a fine subject for a mythical theory, were not the facts too indisputably historical! How a German critic would revel in depicting the impossibility of two men with names so like holding precisely the same office and supporting exactly the same views in two cities so widely separated as Rome and Carthage! Or let us take two modern instances. The Tractarian movement is not yet quite sixty years old. It has not therefore yet passed out of the sphere of personal experience. It started in Oxford during the thirties, and there in Oxford we find at that very period two divines named William Palmer, both favouring the Tractarian views, both eminent writers and scholars, but yet tending finally in different directions, for one William Palmer became a Roman Catholic, while the other remained a devoted son of the Reformation. Or to come to still more modern times. There was an Irish movement in 1848 which numbered amongst its most prominent leaders a William Smith O'Brien, and there is now an Irish movement of the same character, and it also numbers a William O'Brien amongst its most prominent leaders. A Parnell leads the movement for repeal of the Union in 1890. Ninety years earlier, a Parnell resigned high office sooner than consent to the consummation of the same legislative union of Great Britain and Ireland. We might indeed produce parallel cases without number from the range of history, specially of English history, showing how political and religious tendencies run in families, and reproduce exactly the same names, and that at no distant intervals. But the very passage before us, the speech of Gamaliel and its historical argument, affords a sufficient instance. Gamaliel adduced the case of Judas the Galilean as an illustration of an unsuccessful religious movement. Every one admits that here at least Josephus and the Acts of the Apostles are at one. Judas the Gaulonite, as Josephus styles him in one place, or the Galilean as he calls him in another place, was the founder of the sect of the Zealots, who "have an inviolable attachment to liberty, and say that God is to be their only ruler and Lord" (Josephus, *Antiqq.*, XVIII., i. 6). Judas was defeated at the time of the taxing under Cyrenius, and yet more than forty-five years later we find his sons Simon and James suffering crucifixion under the Romans because they were following their father's example.[110]

Another explanation has also been offered. It has been suggested that Theudas was simply another name for one of the many rebels whom Josephus mentions, — for Simon, for instance, who had been a slave of Herod the Great, and had upon his death headed a revolt against authority. Either explanation is quite tenable, as opposed to the view which represents St. Luke as committing a gross historical error. And we are the more justified in offering these suggestions when we reflect upon the numberless instances where modern research has confirmed, and is every year confirming, the minute accuracy of this writer, who doubtless derived his information concerning what passed in the Sanhedrin, on this occasion, from St. Paul, who either as a member of the council or a favourite pupil of Gamaliel may have been present listening to the debates, or even sharing in the final decisions.[111]

Let us now turn from the purely historical side of Gamaliel's speech, and view it from a spiritual standpoint.

The address of Gamaliel was so favourable to the Apostles that it has helped to surround his name and memory with much legendary lore. It was the tradition of the ancient Greek Church from the fifth century that he was converted to Christianity and baptized, along with his son Abibus and Nicodemus, by St. Peter and St. John.[112] This story of Gamaliel's secret adherence to Christianity goes even much farther back. There is a curious Christian novel or romance, which dates back to close upon the year 200, called the *Clementine Recognitions*. We find the same tradition in the sixty-fifth chapter of the first book of these *Recognitions*.[113] But the sacred narrative itself gives us no hint of all this, contenting itself with setting forth the prudent advice which Gamaliel gave to the assembled council. It was wise advice, and well would it have been for the world if influential religious and political teachers in all ages had given similar counsel. Gamaliel was a man of large scholarship, combined with a wide mind, and he had learned that time is a great solvent, and the greatest of tests. Beneath its influence the most pretentious schemes, the most promising of structures, fade away if built upon the sand of human wisdom, while opposition only tends to consolidate and develop those that are built upon the foundation of Divine strength and power. The policy of patience recommended by Gamaliel is a wise one, either for the Church or for the state, in things spiritual and things secular alike. And yet it is one from which the natural man recoils with an instinctive repugnance. It speaks well for the Jewish Sanhedrin that on this occasion they yielded accord to the advice of their president. We are glad to recognise this spirit in these men, where we so often have to find matter for blame. Well would it have been for the Church and for the credit of Christianity had the spirit which moved even the Sadducean majority in the Jewish council been allowed to prevail; and yet how little have the men of tolerant mind been regarded in moments of temporary triumph such as the Sanhedrin just then enjoyed. Gamaliel's advice, "Refrain from these men and let them alone. If the work be of man it will be overthrown; if of God, ye will not be able to overthrow them," strikes a blow at the policy of persecution, which is essentially a policy of impatience. The intolerant man is an impatient man, not willing to imitate the Divine gentleness and long-suffering, which waits, endures, and bears with the sins and ignorance of the children of men. And the Church of Christ, when she became intolerant, as she did as soon as ever Constantine placed within her reach the sword of human power, forgot the lesson of the Divine patience, and reaped within herself, in a shallow religion, in a poorer life, in a restrained intellectual and spiritual grasp, the due reward of those who had fallen away from an imitation of the Divine example to a mere human level. It is sad to see, for instance, in the case of a man so thoroughly spiritual as St. Augustine was, how easily he fell into this human infirmity, how quickly he became intolerant when the secular arm was ranged on the side of his own opinions. The Church in his own boyhood, during the days of Julian, had to strive against the intolerance of the pagans; the orthodox, who upheld the Catholic view of the nature of the Godhead and the scriptural doctrine of the Holy Trinity, had to struggle against the intolerance of the Arians. Yet as soon as power was placed in St. Augustine's own hand he thought it right to exercise compulsion against those who differed from him.

It was exactly the same in later days. Men may take up commentators of the sixteenth and seventeenth centuries, Protestant and Roman Catholic alike. There they will find many remarks, acute, devout, heart-searching, but very few of them will be found to have arrived at the mental fairness and balance involved in those words, "Refrain from these men, and let them alone." Cornelius a Lapide was a Jesuit commentator of those times. He wrote many valuable expositions of Holy Scripture, including one dealing with this book of the Acts, filled with thoughts suggestive and stimulating. It is, however, almost ludicrous to notice how he strives to evade the force of Gamaliel's words, and to escape the application of them to his own Protestant opponents. The Sanhedrin were quite right, he thinks, in adopting Gamaliel's advice, and in showing themselves tolerant of the apostolic preaching because the Apostles worked miracles; and so, though they were unconvinced, still they had just reason to suspend their judgment. But as for the Protestants of his time, they were heretics; they were the opponents of the Church, the bride of Christ, and therefore Gamaliel's words had no application to them; as if the very question that was raised by the Protestants was not this—whether Cornelius a Lapide himself and his Jesuit brethren did not represent Antichrist, and whether the Protestants were not the true Church of God, who therefore on his own principles were quite justified in persecuting their Romish opponents. It is very difficult to get men to acknowledge their own fallibility. Every party, when triumphant, believes that it has a monopoly of truth, and has a Divine right of persecution; and every party when downcast and in adversity sees and admires the beauties of toleration. Verily societies, churches, families, as well as individuals, have good right diligently to pray, "In all time of our wealth, good Lord, deliver us," for never are men in greater spiritual danger than when prosperity leads them to vote themselves infallible, and to practise intolerance towards their fellow-men on account of their intellectual or religious opinions.

The sentiment of Gamaliel on this occasion may however be pushed to a mischievous extreme. He advised the Sanhedrin to exercise patience and self-control, but he did not apparently go any farther. He did not recommend them to adopt the noblest course, which would have been unprejudiced examination into the claims put forward by the Christian teachers. Gamaliel's advice was good, it was perhaps the best he could have given, or at least which could have been expected under the circumstances, but it was not the highest or noblest conceivable. It was the kind of advice always given by men who do not wish to commit themselves untimely, but who are waiters upon Providence, postponing their decision as to which side they shall join until they first see which side will win. Opportunists, the French call them; men who are sitting upon the fence, we in homelier phrase designate them. It is well to be prudent in our actions, because true prudence is only Christian wisdom, and such wisdom will always lead us to take the most effectual ways of doing good. But then prudence may be pushed to the extreme of moral cowardice, or at least the name of prudence may be used as a cloak for a contemptible desire to stand well with all parties, and thereby advance our own selfish interests. Prudence should be united with moral courage; it should be ready to take the unpopular side, and to champion truth and righteousness even when in a depressed and lowly condition. It was easy enough to side with Christ when the multitude cried, "Hosanna in the Highest." But the test of deepest love and unfailing devotion was when the women stood by the cross, and when the Magdalen sought out the grave in the garden that she might anoint the dead body of her loved Lord.

Finally, let us just notice the conduct of the Apostles under those circumstances. The Apostles were freed from the pressing danger of death, but they did not entirely escape. The Sanhedrin were logically inconsistent. They refrained from putting the Apostles to death, as Gamaliel advised, but they flogged them as Roman laws permitted; and a Jewish disciplinary flogging, when forty stripes save one were inflicted, was so severe that death sometimes resulted from it.[114] Man is a curiously inconsistent being, and the Sanhedrin showed on this occasion that they had their own share of this weakness. Gamaliel advised not to kill the Apostles, but let time work out the Divine purposes either of success or failure. They adopt the first part of his advice, but are not willing to allow Providence to develop His designs without their interference, and so by their stripes endeavour to secure that failure shall attend the apostolic efforts. But it was all in vain. The Apostles were living under a realized sense of heavenly things. The love of Christ, and communion with Christ and the Spirit of Christ, so raised them above all earthly surroundings that what things seemed loss and shame and grief to others were by them counted highest joy, because they looked at them from the side of God and eternity. Human threats availed nothing with men animated by such a spirit,—nay, rather as proofs of the opposition of the evil one, they only quickened their zeal, so that "every day, in the temple and at home, they ceased not to teach and to preach Jesus as the Christ." How wondrously life would be transformed for us all did we view its changes and chances, its sorrows and its pains, as the Apostles regarded them. Poverty and disgrace, undeserved loss and suffering, all alike would be transfigured into surpassing glory when endured for Christ's sake, while our powers of labour and work, and our active zeal in the holiest of causes, would be quickened, because, like them, we should walk and live and toil in the loved presence of One who is invisible.

# CHAPTER XIII
# PRIMITIVE DISSENSIONS AND
# APOSTOLIC PRECAUTIONS

"Now in these days, when the number of the disciples was multiplying, there arose a murmuring of the Grecian Jews against the Hebrews, because their widows were neglected in the daily ministration. And the twelve called the multitude of the disciples unto them, and said, It is not fit that we should forsake the word of God, and serve tables. Look ye out therefore, brethren, from among you seven men of good report, full of the Spirit and of wisdom, whom we may appoint over this business. But we will continue stedfastly in prayer, and in the ministry of the word." —Acts vi. 1-4.

The sixth chapter of the Acts, and the election of the Seven, mark a distinct advance in the career of the early Church. This sixth chapter is like the twelfth of Genesis and the introduction of Abraham upon the stage of sacred history. We feel at once as if the narrative of Genesis had come into contact with modern times, leaving the mysterious period of darkness all behind. So is it with the Acts of the Apostles. The earliest days of the primitive Church were quite unlike all modern experience. The Church had received a great blessing and a wondrous revelation, and had been enriched with marvellous powers. But just as men act when they have experienced a surpassing joy or a tremendous calamity,—they are upset for a time, they do not realize their position, they do not take all the circumstances in at once, nor can they quite settle what their future course shall be; they must get a little way distant from the joy or the sorrow before they make their future arrangements,—so was it with the Apostles during that space of time which elapsed from the Pentecostal outpouring down to the election of the Seven. We are so accustomed to think of the Apostles as inspired men, that we forget that inspiration did not destroy their natural powers or infirmities, but rather must have acted in consonance with the laws of their constitution. The Apostles must, to a certain extent, have been upset by the extraordinary events they had witnessed. They sought and found daily guidance in the power of the Spirit; but they had made no settled plans, had not compared or arranged their ideas, had formed no scheme of doctrine or teaching, had realized nothing concerning the future of the society they were unconsciously building up under the Divine leading. God had His plans; the ascended Lord had spoken to the Apostles concerning the future of the Kingdom of Heaven; but it would be making the Apostles more than men of like passions and like infirmities with ourselves to imagine that during those stirring and eventful days they had consciously realized the whole scheme of Christian doctrine and government. That period of a few months—for it could not have been more—was a period of Divine chaos, out of which the final settlement of the Church of God began slowly to evolve itself under the direction of God the Holy Ghost. How long, it may be asked, did this period of unsettlement last? A question which resolves itself into the further one bearing directly on our present subject,—what was the date of the election and subsequent martyrdom of Stephen? The answer to this throws much light on the apostolic history and the events recorded in the first five chapters of this book.

I. St. Stephen was put to death some time in the year 37 A.D., after Pontius Pilate had been recalled from the government of Palestine, and before his successor had arrived to take up the reins of power.[115] The Jewish authorities took advantage of the interregnum in order to gratify their spite against the eminent orator who was doing so much damage to their cause. Under ordinary circumstances the Jewish Sanhedrin could not put a man to death unless they had received the fiat of the Roman authorities. Now, however, during this interval, there was no supreme authority from whom this fiat could be secured, and so they seized the opportunity and executed Stephen as a blasphemer, according to the method prescribed in the law of Moses. This happened in the year 37 A.D., about four years after the Crucifixion. We must, however, observe another point. During the latter years of his administration, Pontius Pilate had been acting in a most tyrannical manner. This fact explains a circumstance which must strike the most casual reader of the Acts. We there read that the supreme Jewish council made two attempts to restrain the Apostles; the first after the healing of the cripple at the Temple Gate, and the second when Gamaliel dissuaded them from their purposes of blood. After that they allowed the Apostles to pursue their course without any hostility. This appears to the casual reader more striking, more difficult to understand, than it was in reality. We are now obliged to think of Judaism and Christianity as opposed and mutually exclusive religions; we cannot conceive of a man being a Jew and a Christian at the same time. But it was not so with the Apostles and their followers at the period of which we are writing. This may seem contradictory to what I have elsewhere stated as to the antagonistic character of the two religions. But the apparent inconsistency is easily explained. As full-blown and realized systems, Judaism and Christianity are inconsistent. The one was a bud, the other an expanded flower. The same individual bulb cannot be at the same moment a bud and a flower. But the Apostles had not as yet realized Christianity as a full-blown system, nor grasped all its consequences. There was no inconsistency when they made a conjoint profession of Judaism and Christianity. The Apostles and their followers were all scrupulous observers of the law of Moses; and no dwellers in Jerusalem were more regular attendants at the Temple worship than the persons who had as yet no distinct name, and were known only as followers of the Prophet of Nazareth. To take an illustration from modern ecclesiastical history, the Apostles and the early Jerusalem Church must have been simply known to the Jewish authorities, just as the first Methodists at Oxford were known to the Church authorities of John Wesley's earlier days, as stricter members of the Church of England than the usual run of people were. This fact alone lessens the difficulty we might find in accounting for the statements made as to the continued activity of the Apostles, and the freedom they enjoyed even after they had been solemnly warned by the Sanhedrin. Neither the Apostles themselves nor the Jewish council recognised as yet any religious opposition in the teaching of Peter and his brethren. The Apostles themselves had not yet formulated their ideas nor perceived whither their principles would ultimately lead them. No one indeed would have been more surprised than themselves had they foreseen the antagonistic position into which they would be ultimately forced; and as for the Sanhedrin, the only charge they brought against the Apostles was not a religious one at all, but merely that they were challenging the conduct and decision of the authorities concerning the execution of Jesus Christ, and, as the High Priest put it, "intend to bring this Man's blood upon us."[116] But then history reveals to us some other facts which completely explain the difficulty and vindicate the historical accuracy of the sacred narrative. St. Stephen was put to death in the year 37. At that time he may have been acting as a deacon for two, or even three, years, during which Christian teaching and views made very rapid progress, all unopposed by the Jewish authorities, simply because their attention was concentrated on other topics of much more pressing interest. Pilate was appointed governor of Palestine in 26 A.D. He ruled it for ten years, till the end of 36 A.D., when he was recalled. God causes all things to work together for good, and overrules even state changes to the development of His purposes. Pilate's whole period of rule was, as I have already said, marked by tyranny; but the concluding years were the worst. The members of the Sanhedrin were then specially excited by two actions which touched themselves most keenly. He seized on the accumulated proceeds of the Temple-tax of two drachmas, about eighteen pence, paid by every Jew throughout the world, which then amounted to a vast sum, expending it in making an aqueduct for the supply of Jerusalem. This action affected the pecuniary resources of the Jewish authorities. But he attacked them on a dearer point still, for he set up the images of the emperor in the Holy City, and thus wounded them in their religious feelings, introducing the abomination of desolation into the most sacred places.[117]

All the attention of the priests, the Pharisees, the Sadducees, and the people, was concentrated upon the violent deeds of Pilate. They had no time to think of the Apostles,—who, indeed, must themselves have shared in the national enthusiasm and universal hostility which Pilate's attempts excited. A common opposition stilled, for the time, the internal strife and controversy about the prophet of Nazareth which had, for a little, rent asunder the inhabitants of Jerusalem. Let us now repeat the dates to which we have attained. St. Stephen was executed in 37 A.D.; his election took place probably in 34 A.D. The first seven chapters of the Acts set before us, then, all we know of the history of the earliest four years of the Church's life and work; and yet though very briefly told, that history tallies with what we learn from writers like Josephus and Philo.

II. Let us now return to the text of our narrative. This sixth chapter offers a very useful glimpse into the inner life of the primitive Church. It shows us what led up to the election of the Seven in these words: "Now in these days, when the number of the disciples was multiplying, there arose a murmuring of the Grecian Jews against the Hebrews, because their widows were neglected in the daily ministration."

(a) The election sprang out of the multiplying, and the multiplying begat a murmuring among the disciples. There is here teaching for the Church of all time, plain and evident to every reader, a lesson which history has repeated from age to age. Increase of numbers does not always mean increase of happiness, increase of devotion, increase of true spiritual life, but has often brought increase of trouble and discontent alone. What a lesson of patient submission under present trials the wise man may here read. God has made all things double one against another; and when He bestows such notable increase as He granted to the apostolic Church, He adds thereto some counter-balancing disadvantage to keep His people low and make them humble. Undiluted joy, unmitigated success, is not to be the portion of God's people while tabernacling here below. How often has the lesson been repeated in their experience of the past as in our own personal experience as well!

The trial of the apostolic Church was typical of the trials which awaited future ages. The Church in the Diocletian persecution, for instance, was wasted and torn. The records of that last great trial through which the

Church passed, just prior to her final triumph over Paganism, are lighted up by the fires of the most determined attempt ever made to crush the faith of the Crucified One. How often during that last persecution God's faithful ones must have wept in secret over the ruin of the holy places and the threatened destruction of the faith! Yet the trials of the hours of adversity were as nothing compared with the dangers which beset the Church when the faith triumphed under Constantine, and the multitude of the disciples was increased and multiplied by the power of imperial patronage. The trials of the day of persecution were external, and utterly powerless to affect the spiritual life of Christ's mystical body. The trials of a multiplying and enlarging Church were internal; they arose from unbelief, and hypocrisy, and want of Christian love, and were destructive of the life of God in the human soul. The dangers of success, the subtle temptations of prosperity, making us proud, contemptuous of others, self-conscious, dependent wholly upon man and independent of God, are the lessons, ecclesiastical, social, and personal, pressed upon us by the opening words of this sixth chapter.

(*b*) These words, again, correct a popular mistake, and reproduce a warning of our Master too often forgotten. When the disciples were increasing, and the hearts of the Apostles all aglow with the success vouchsafed them, "a murmuring arose between the Grecian Jews and the Hebrews." What a glimpse we get here into the very heart and centre of early Christian social life. It is often the hardest task in historical researches to get such a glimpse as here is given. We know the outer life of societies, of families, of dynasties. We see them in their external form and symmetry: we behold them in their company dress and in their public appearances; but till we get to know and realize their common every-day life, how they ate, drank, slept, how their social intercourse was maintained, we fail to grasp the most important side of their existence. The primitive Church is often thought of and spoken of as if its social and spiritual life were wholly unlike our own; as if sin and infirmity were entirely absent, and perfect holiness there prevailed. This expression, "Now in these days there arose a murmuring," shows us that the presence of supernatural gifts, the power of working miracles and speaking with other tongues, did not raise the spiritual level of individual believers above that we find in the Church of the present day. The distribution of alms is always attended by jealousies and disputes, rendering the work one of the most unpleasant tasks which can be undertaken by any man. No matter how earnestly one strives to be fair and just, no matter how diligently one may seek to balance claim against claim and righteously to satisfy the wants of those who seek relief, still there will always be minds that will never be content, and will strive to detect injustice and wrong and favouritism, no matter how upright the intention may be. What a comfort to God's servant striving to do his duty is the study of this sixth chapter of the Acts! Fretting and worry, weary days and sleepless nights, are often the only reward which the Christian philanthropist receives in return for his exertions. But here comes in the Acts of the Apostles to cheer. It was just the same with the Apostles, for they must have been the chief almoners or distributers of the Church's common fund prior to the election of the Seven. The Apostles themselves did not escape the accusation of favouritism, and we may be well content to bear and suffer what the Apostles were compelled to endure. Let us only take heed that like them we suffer wrongfully, and that our conscience testify that we have striven to do everything in the sight of the Lord Jesus Christ; and then, disregarding all human murmuring and criticism, we should calmly proceed upon our work, in no way discouraged because the recipients of Christian bounty still act as even the primitive Christians did. This is one important lesson we gain from this passage.

(c) We may, again, learn another great truth from this incident, and that is, that the primitive Church was no ideal communion, but a society with failings and weaknesses and discontent, exactly like those which exist in the Church of our own times. The favourite argument with controversialists of the Church of Rome, when trying to draw proselytes from among Protestants, is, as logicians say, of an *à priori* type. They will enlarge upon the importance of religion and religious truth, and upon the awful consequences which will result from a mistake on such a vital question, and then they will argue that God must have constituted a living infallible guide on such an important topic, and that guide is in their opinion the Pope, as the head of the Catholic Church. The Scriptures are full of warnings— unnoticed warnings they often are, but still they are full of them—as to the untrustworthy character of all such kind of arguments. In this sixth chapter, for instance, the thoughtful and meditative student can see a specimen of these providential admonitions, and a reason for its insertion in the sacred story. Christ came to establish the Christian Church upon earth. For this purpose He lived and suffered and rose again. For this purpose He sent forth the Third Person of the Holy Trinity to lead and guide and dwell in His Church; and surely, *à priori*, we might as well conclude that in the Church so founded, so guided, so ruled by Peter and the rest of the Apostles, there would have been found no such thing as favouritism, or murmuring, or discontent,—sentiments which might exist in the unregenerate world, but which should find no place in the kingdom of the Spirit. But, when we turn to the sacred record of Christ's sayings, and the inspired history of Christ's Church, we find that all our *à priori* presumptions and all our logical anticipations are put to flight, for the Master warns us in the thirteenth of St. Matthew, when speaking His wondrous parables concerning the Kingdom of Heaven, that sin and imperfection will ever find their place in His Church; and then the history of the Acts of the Apostles comes in to confirm the inspired prophecy, and we see from this chapter how the primitive Church of Christ was torn and racked with mere earthly feelings and mere human infirmities, like the ordinary worldly societies which existed all around; "there arose a murmuring" even in the Church where Apostles taught, where the Holy Ghost dwelt, and where the Pentecostal gifts were displayed. The occasion of the murmuring, too, is noteworthy and prophetic. It was like the trial under which man fell and by which Christ was tempted. It was a mere material temptation. Even in the primitive Church, living as it did in the region and presence of the supernatural, expecting every day and hour the return of the ascended Lord, even there material considerations entered, and the world and the things thereof found a place, and caused divisions where they would seem to have been strictly excluded by the very conditions of the Church's existence. The Church and the world there touched and influenced one another; and so it must be always. There is a world indeed against which the Church must ever protest—the world of impure lusts and wicked desires, the world of which Paganism was the presiding genius; but then there is a world in which the Church must exist and with which it must deal, the world which God has created and ordained, the world of human society and human wants, feelings, desires, appetites. With these the Church must ever come in contact. Monasticism and asceticism have endeavoured indeed in the past to get rid of this world. They cut men and women off from marriage and separated them from society, and reduced human wants to a minimum; and yet nature asserted itself, and the corruptions of monasticism have been a divinely-ordered protest against foolish attempts to separate between things spiritual and things secular, between the Church founded by Christ and the world created by God.[118] The murmuring arose on this occasion because the Apostles made no such mistake, but recognised fearlessly that the Church of Christ took cognizance of such a question as the daily distribution and the temporal wants of its disciples. The apostolic Church did not disdain a mere economic question, and yet the Church of our own time has been slow enough to follow its example; but, thank God, it is learning more and more of its duty in this respect. The time has been when nothing was considered worthy of the notice of the Christian pulpit or of Church synods and Church courts save purely spiritual and doctrinal questions. The vast subjects of education, of the social life, of the amusements of the people, the methods of legislation or statesmanship, were thought outside the region of Christian activity, and were utterly neglected or else left wholly to those who made no profession at least of being guided by Christian principle. But now we have learned the important truth that the Church is a Divine leaven placed in the mass of human society to permeate it through and through; and perhaps the present danger is that the clergy should forget the apostolic warning, true for every age, that while the Church in its totality, priests and people, should take an active interest in these questions, and strive to mould the whole life of man on Christian principles, it is not at the same time "fit that the ministry should forsake the word of God and serve tables."

III. But we have not yet done with this murmuring or with the lessons it furnishes for the Church of the future. What lay at the basis of this murmuring, and of the jealousy thereby indicated? "There arose a murmuring of the Grecian Jews against the Hebrews;" a racial question developed itself, and racial, or perhaps we should rather say, in this case, social and linguistic, differences found place in the apostolic Church, and gave rise to serious quarrels even where the Spirit in fullest measure and in extraordinary power was enjoyed. There was bitter dissension between Jews and Samaritans, though they believed in the same God and reverenced the same revelation. Political circumstances in the past sufficiently explain that quarrel. There was almost, if not quite, as bitter hostility between the Grecians and the Hebrews, because they spoke different languages and practised diverse customs, and that though they worshipped in the same temple and belonged to the same nation. The origin of these differences in the Christian Church of Jerusalem goes back to a very distant period. Here comes in the use of the Apocrypha, "which the Church doth read for example of life and instruction of manners." If we wish to understand the course of events in the Acts we must refer to the books of Maccabees, where is told the romantic story of the struggle of the Jews against the Greek kings of Syria, who tried to force them into conformity with the religion of Greece, which then was counted the religion of civilization and of culture. The result was that the intensely national party became bitterly hostile to everything pertaining to Greece and its civilization. The Jews of Palestine of that period became like the purely Celtic Irish of the Reformation epoch. The Irish identified the Reformation with England and English influence, just as the Jews identified Paganism with Greece and Syria, and Greek influence; and the result was that the Irish became the most intensely ultramontane nation, and the Palestinian Jews became the most intensely narrow and prejudiced nation of their time. The Palestinian or Hebrew Jews, speaking the Aramaeic or Chaldee tongue, scorned Greek language and all traces of Greek civilization, while the Jews of the Dispersion, specially those of Alexandria, strove to recommend the Jewish religion to the Gentile world, whose civilization and culture they appreciated, and whose language they used.

The opposition of the Hebrew to the Grecian Jews was very bitter, and expressed itself in language which has come down to us in the Talmudic writings. "Cursed be he who teacheth his son the learning of the Greeks," was a saying among the Hebrews; while again, we hear of Rabban Simeon, the son of Gamaliel, St. Paul's teacher, who used to embody his hatred of the Grecians in the following story: "There were a thousand boys in my father's school, of whom five hundred learned the law and five hundred the wisdom of the Greeks; and there is not one of the latter now alive, excepting myself here and my uncle's son in Asia."[119] Heaven itself was supposed by the Hebrews to have plainly declared its hostility against their Grecian opponents. Hence, naturally, arose the same divisions at Jerusalem. There were in that city nearly five hundred synagogues, a considerable proportion of which belonged to the Grecian Jews. All classes and all the synagogues, Hebrew and Grecian alike, contributed their quota to the earliest converts won by the Apostles; and these converts brought their old jealousies and oppositions with them into the Church of Christ. The Hebrew or the Grecian Jew of yesterday could not forget, to-day, because he had embraced a belief in Jesus of Nazareth as the Messiah, all his old feelings and his old hereditary quarrels, and hence sprang the Christian dissensions of which we read, prophetic of so many similar racial and social and linguistic dissensions in the Church down to the present time. The Acts of the Apostles is a kind of magic mirror for Church history. In the olden times men dreamt of a magic mirror into which one could look and see the course of their future life depicted. We can see something of the same in this inspired book. The bitter dissensions which racial and linguistic differences have made in the Church of every age are here depicted in miniature. The quarrels between East and West, between Greeks and Latins, between Latins and Teutons, between Teuton and Celt, between Roman Catholic and Protestant, between the Whites and Negroes, between European Christians and Hindoo converts; the scandalous scenes still enacted round the Holy Place at Jerusalem, where peace is kept between nominal Christians only by the intervention of Mahometan soldiers,—all turn upon the same points and embody the same principles, and may best find solution upon the lines laid down by the Apostles. And what were these lines? They laid down that there are diversities of functions and of work in the Church of Christ; there is a ministry of the word, and there is a serving of tables. One class should not absorb every function; for if it does, the highest function of all, the ministry of the word and prayer, will inevitably suffer. Well, indeed, would it have been had this lesson been far more laid to heart. How many a schism and rent in the visible Church of Christ has been caused because no work, no spiritual function, was found for a newly-awakened layman anxious to do something for Him who had done so much for his soul. The principle here laid down in germ is a very fruitful one, suitable for every age. A new crisis, a fresh departure, an unexpected need, has arisen, and a new organization is therefore at once devised by the Apostles; and well would it have been had their example found closer imitation. We have been too much in the habit of looking upon the Church of Christ as if it were once for all stereotyped in apostolic times, and as if there were nothing to be done in the living present save to adapt these ancient institutions to our modern needs. The Roman Catholic Church has been in many respects more true to apostolic principles than the children of the Reformation. With all her intense conservatism Rome has never hesitated to develop new organizations as new needs have arisen, and that in the boldest manner. It has often been remarked that the Church of Rome would never have lost John Wesley and the Wesleyans as the Church of England did. She would have put a brown cassock upon him, and girded him with a rope, and sent him forth as the head of a new order, to do the work to which he felt impelled and for which God had qualified him. Experience has taught us, however, that we cannot safely neglect apostolic precedent; and the warning implied in the words of the Apostles, "it is not fit that we should forsake the word of God and serve tables," has been amply fulfilled. The highest ministry of the word has been injured by the accumulation of all public work in the Church on one class alone. What minister of Jesus Christ does not feel that, even with the wider and more apostolic views now prevalent, with all the recognition of the service which godly Christian laymen render, the old tradition is still strong, and clergymen are too absorbed in the mere serving of tables, to the neglect of their higher functions? The laity often complain of the poor, thin, meagre character of the preaching to which they are compelled to listen; but how can it be otherwise when they demand so much purely secular service, so much serving of tables from those whose great work is to teach? The Church of England, in her service for the ordination of priests, demands from the candidates whether they will devote themselves to the study of the Word of God, and such other studies as bear upon the same. I often wonder how her clergy are now to fulfil this solemn vow, when frequently they have not a night in the week at home, save perhaps Saturday evening, and when, from early morning to late at night, all their energies are swallowed up in the work of schools, and clubs, and charitable organizations, and parochial visitation, leaving little time and still less energy for the work of meditation and thought and study. The clergy are the Lord's prophets, watchmen upon the walls of Zion. It is their great business to explain the Lord's will, to translate the ideas of the Bible into the language of modern life, to apply the Divine principles of doctrine and discipline laid down in the Bible to the ever-varying wants of our complex modern civilization; and how can this function be discharged unless there be time for reading and for thinking, so as to gain a true notion of what are these modern wants, and to find out how the eternal principles of the Scriptures are to be applied to them? We require a great deal more organized assistance in the work of the Church, and then, when that assistance is forthcoming, we may expect and demand that the highest ministry of all, "the ministry of the Word and prayer," shall be discharged with greater efficiency and blessing. The Apostles in meeting this crisis, laid down a law of true development and living growth in the divine society. The Church of Christ is ever to have the power to organize herself in face of new departures, while at the same time they proclaim the absolute necessity and the perpetual obligation of the Christian ministry in its highest aspect; for surely if even for Apostles it was needful that their whole time should be devoted to the ministry of the word of God and prayer, and the Church of that time, with all its wondrous gifts, demanded such a ministry, there ought to exist in the modern Church also an order of men wholly separated unto those solemn duties.

IV. The Apostles having determined upon the creation of a new organization to deal with a new need, then appeal to the people for their assistance, and call upon them to select the persons who shall be its members; but they, at the same time, reserve their own rights and authority, and, when the selection has been made, claim the power of ordination and appointment for themselves. The people nominated while the Apostles appointed. The Apostles took the most effective plan to quiet the trouble which had arisen when they took the people into their confidence. The Church has been often described as the mother of modern freedom. The councils of old time were the models and forerunners of modern parliaments. The councils and synods of the Church set an example of open discussion and of legislative assemblies in ages when tyrannical authority had swallowed up every other vestige of liberty. The Church from the beginning, and in the Acts of the Apostles, clearly showed that its government was not to be an absolute clerical despotism, but a free Christian republic, where clergy and people were to take counsel together. It is a noteworthy thing indeed, that even in the Roman Catholic Church, where the exclusive claims of the clergy have been most pressed, the recognition of the rights of the laity in the matter of Church councils and debates has found place down to modern times. The representatives of the Emperor and other Christian princes took their seats in the Council of Trent, jointly with bishops and other ecclesiastics; and it was only at the Vatican Council of 1870 that this last lingering trace of lay rights finally disappeared. The Apostles laid down by their action the principle of Church freedom, and the mutual rights of clergy and people; but they also gave a very practical hint for the peaceful management of organizations, whether ecclesiastical, or social, or political. They knew what was the right thing to do, but they did not impose their will by the mere exercise of authority; they took counsel with the people, and the result was that a speedy solution of all their difficulties was arrived at. How many a quarrel in life would be avoided, how many a rough place would be made smooth, were the apostolic example always followed. Men naturally resist a law imposed from without without any appearance of consultation with them or of sanction on their part; but men willingly yield obedience to laws, even though they may dislike them, which have been passed with their assent and appeal to their reason. In Church matters especially would this rule apply, and the example of the Apostles be most profitably followed. Autocratic action on the part of the clergy in small matters has often destroyed the unity and harmony of congregations, and has planted roots of bitterness which have ruined ministerial usefulness. While steadily maintaining great fundamental principles, a little tact and thought, a wise condescension to human feeling, will often win the day, and carry measures which would otherwise be vigorously resisted.

Finally, the Apostles enunciate the principles which should guide the Church in its selection of officials, specially when they have to deal with the temporal concerns of the Society. "Look ye out therefore from among you seven men of good report." Attempts have been made to explain why the number was fixed at seven. Some have asserted that it was so determined because it was a sacred number, others because there were now seven congregations in Jerusalem, or seven thousand converts. Perhaps, however, the true reason was a more commonplace one, and that was that seven is a very convenient practical number. In case of a difference of opinion a majority can always be secured on one side or other, and all blocks avoided. The number seven was long maintained in connection with the order of deacons, in imitation of the apostolic institution. A council at Neo-Cæsarea, in the year 314, ordained that the number of seven deacons should never be exceeded in any city, while in the Church of Rome the same limitation prevailed from the second century down to the twelfth, so that the Roman Cardinals, who were the parochial clergy of Rome, numbered among them merely seven deacons down to that late period. The seven chosen by the primitive Church were to be men of good report because they were to be public functionaries, whose decisions were to allay commotions and murmurings; and therefore they must be men of weight, in whom the public had confidence. But, further, they must be men "full of the Spirit and of wisdom." Piety was not the only qualification; they must be wise, prudent, sound in judgment as well. Piety is no security for wisdom, just as in turn wisdom is no security for piety; but both must be combined in apostolic officials. The Apostles thereby teach the Church of all time what are the qualifications necessary for effective administrators and officials. Even in charitable distributions and financial organizations the Church should hold up the high standard set before her by the Apostles, and seek out men actuated by religious principle, guided by religious truth, swayed by Divine love, the outcome of that Spirit whose grace and blessing are necessary for the due discharge of any office, whether of service, of charity, or of worship, in the Church of Jesus Christ; but possessed withal of strong common sense and vigorous intellectual power, for love and zeal separated from these often fall into mistakes which make religion and its adherents a laughing-stock to the world and a hindrance to the cause of truth and holiness. God can indeed make the weak things of this world to confound the high and mighty, but it would be presumptuous in us to think that we can do the same, and therefore must seek out the instruments best suited in every way to do God's work and accomplish His purposes.

# CHAPTER XIV
# ST. STEPHEN AND THE EVOLUTION
# OF THE CHRISTIAN MINISTRY

"And the saying pleased the whole multitude: and they chose Stephen, a man full of faith and of the Holy Spirit, and Philip, and Prochorus, and Nicanor, and Timon, and Parmenas, and Nicolas a proselyte of Antioch: whom they set before the Apostles: and when they had prayed, they laid their hands on them.... Stephen, full of grace and power, wrought great wonders and signs among the people. But there arose certain of them that were of the synagogue called the synagogue of the Libertines, and of the Cyrenians, and of the Alexandrians, and of them of Cilicia and Asia, disputing with Stephen. And they were not able to withstand the wisdom and the Spirit by which he spake. Then they suborned men, which said, We have heard him speak blasphemous words against Moses, and against God."—Acts vi. 5, 6; 8-11.

The names of the seven chosen on the suggestion of the Apostles raises very naturally the question, To what office were they appointed? Did the seven elected on this occasion represent the first beginning of that office of deacon which is regarded as the third rank in the Church, bishops being first, and presbyters or priests second. It is agreed by all parties that the title of deacon is not given to them in the sixth chapter of the Acts, and yet such an unprejudiced and fair authority as Bishop Lightfoot, in his Essay on the Christian Ministry, maintains that the persons selected and ordained at this crisis constituted the first origin of the diaconate as it is now known.[120] The Seven are not called, either here or wherever else they are mentioned in the Acts, by the name of deacons, though the word διακονεῖν (serve), which cannot be exactly rendered into English, as the noun deacon has no equivalent verb answering to it, is applied to the duties assigned to them. But all the best critics are agreed that the ordination of the Seven was the occasion of the rise of a new order and a new office in the Church, whose work dealt more especially with the secular side of the ministerial function. The great German critic Meyer, commenting on this sixth chapter, puts it well, though not so clearly as we should like. "From the first regular overseership of alms, the mode of appointment to which could not but regulate analogically the practice of the Church, was gradually developed the diaconate, which subsequently underwent further elaboration." This statement is somewhat obscure, and thoroughly after the manner of a German critic; let us develop it a little, and see what the process was whereby the distributers of alms to the widows of the earliest Church organization became the officials of whom St. Laurence of Rome in the third, and St. Athanasius of Alexandria in the fourth century were such eminent examples.

I. The institutions of the synagogue must necessarily have exercised a great influence over the minds of the Apostles and of their first converts. One fact alone vividly illustrates this idea. Christians soon began to call their places of assembly by the name of churches or the Lord's houses, but the old habit was at first too strong, and so the churches or congregations of the earliest Christians were called synagogues. This is evident even from the text of the Revised Version of the New Testament, for if we turn to the second chapter of the Epistle of James we read there, "If there come into your *synagogue* a man with a gold ring,"—showing that in St. James's day a Christian church was called a synagogue. This custom received some few years ago a remarkable confirmation from the records of travel and discovery. The Marcionites were a curious Christian sect or heresy which sprang up in the second century. They were intensely opposed to Judaism, and yet so strong was this tradition that even they seem to have retained, down to the fourth century, the name of synagogue as the title of their churches, for some celebrated French explorers have discovered in Syria an inscription, still in existence, carved over the door of a Marcionite church, dated A.D. 318, and that inscription runs thus: "The Synagogue of the Marcionites."[121]

Now seeing that the force of tradition was so great as to compel even an anti-Jewish sect to call their meeting-houses by a Jewish name, we may be sure that the tradition of the institutions, forms, and arrangements of the synagogue must have been infinitely more potent with the earliest Christian believers, constraining them to adopt similar institutions in their own assemblies. Human nature is always the same, and the example of our own colonists sheds light upon the course of Church development in Palestine. When the Pilgrim Fathers went to America, they reproduced the English constitution and the English laws in that country with so much precision and accuracy that the expositions of law produced by American lawyers are studied with great respect in England. The American colonists reproduced the institutions and laws with which they were familiar, modifying them merely to suit their own peculiar circumstances; and so has it been all the world over wherever the Anglo-Saxon race has settled—they have done exactly the same thing. They have established states and governments modelled after the type of England, and not of France or Russia. So was it with the early Christians. Human nature compelled them to fall back upon their first experience, and to develop under a Christian shape the institutions of the synagogue under which they had been trained. And now when we read the Acts we see that here lies the most natural explanation of the course of history, and specially of this sixth chapter. In the synagogue, as Dr. John Lightfoot expounds it in his *Horæ Hebraicæ* (Matt. iv. 23), the government was in the hands of the ruler and the council of elders or presbyters, while under them there were three almoners or deacons, who served in the same capacity as the Seven in superintending the charitable work of the congregation. The great work for which the Seven were appointed was distribution, and we shall see that this was ever maintained, and is still maintained, as the leading idea of the diaconate, though other and more directly spiritual work was at once added to their functions by St. Stephen and St. Philip.[122] Now just as our colonists brought English institutions and ideas with them wherever they settled, so was it with the missionaries who went forth from the Mother Church of Jerusalem. They carried the ideas and institutions with them which had been there sanctioned by the Apostles, and thus we find deacons mentioned in conjunction with bishops at Philippi, deacons joined with bishops in St. Paul's Epistle to Timothy, and the existence of the institution at Corinth, and its special work as a charitable organization, implied in the description given of Phœbe to the Roman Christians in the sixteenth chapter of the Epistle to the Romans. St. Paul's directions to Timothy in the third chapter of his first Epistle deal both with deacons and deaconesses, and in each case lay down qualifications specially suited for distributers of charitable relief, whose duty called upon them to visit from house to house, but say nothing about any higher work. They are indeed "to hold the mystery of the faith in a pure conscience;" they must be sound in the faith like the Seven themselves; but the special qualifications demanded by St. Paul are those needed in almoners: "The deacons must be grave, not double-tongued, not given to much wine, not greedy of filthy lucre."

So far as to the testimony of Scripture. When we pass beyond the bounds of the canonical books, and come to the apostolic fathers, the evidence is equally clear. They testify to the universality of the institution, and bear witness to its work of distribution. Clement of Rome was a contemporary of the Apostles. He wrote an Epistle to the Corinthians, which is the earliest witness to the existence of St. Paul's Epistles to the same Church. In Clement's epistle we find express mention of deacons, of their apostolic appointment, and of the universal diffusion of the office. In the forty-third chapter of his epistle Clement writes to the Corinthians concerning the Apostles:—"Thus preaching through countries and cities they appointed bishops and deacons for those who should afterwards believe," clearly implying that deacons then existed at Rome, though we have no express notice of them in the epistle written by St. Paul to the Roman Church.

There is a rule, however, very needful for historical investigations. Silence is no conclusive argument against an alleged fact, unless there be silence where, if the alleged fact had existed, it must have been mentioned. Josephus, for instance, is silent about Christ and Christianity. Yet he wrote when its existence was a matter of common notoriety. But there was no necessity for him to notice it. It was an awkward fact too, and so he is silent. St. Paul does not mention deacons as existing at Rome, though he does mention them at Philippi. But Clement's words expressly assert that universally, in all cities and countries, this order was established wherever the Apostles taught; and so we find it even from pagan records. Pliny's letter to Trajan, written about A.D. 110, some fifteen or twenty years later than Clement, testifies that the order of deacons existed in far distant Bithynia, among the Christians of the Dispersion to whom St. Peter directed his Epistle. Pliny's words are, "I therefore thought it the more necessary, in order to ascertain what truth there was in this account, to examine two slave-girls who were called deaconesses (*ministræ*), and even to use torture." (See the article Trajanus in the *Dict. Christ. Biog.*, iv., 1040.) It is exactly the same with St. Ignatius in the second chapter of his Epistle to the Trallians, which dates about the same period. The spiritual side of the office had now come more prominently into notice, as the occasion of their first appointment had fallen into disuse; but still Ignatius recognises the origin of the diaconate when he writes that "the deacons are not deacons of meats and drinks, but servants of the Church of God" (Lightfoot, *Apost. Fathers*, vol. ii., sec. i., p. 156). While again Polycarp, in his Epistle to the Philippians, ch. v., recognises the same qualities as necessary to deacons which St. Paul requires and enumerates in his Epistle to Timothy. Justin Martyr, a little later, twenty years or so, tells us that the deacons distributed the elements consecrated in the Holy Communion to the believers that were absent (Justin, *First Apol.*, ch. lxvii.). This is most important testimony, connecting the order of deacons as then flourishing at Rome and their work with the Seven constituted by the Apostle. The daily distribution of the Apostle's time was closely connected with the celebration of the Eucharist, which indeed in its meal or food, common to all the faithful, and its charitable collections and oblations, of which Justin Martyr speaks, retained still some trace of the daily distribution which prevailed in the early Church, and occasioned the choice of the Seven. The deacons in Justin Martyr's day distributed the spiritual food to the faithful, just as in earlier times they distributed all the sustenance which the faithful required, whether in their spiritual or their temporal aspect. It is evident, from this recital of the places where the deacons are incidentally referred to, that their origin was never forgotten, and that distribution of charitable relief and help was always retained as the essence, the central idea and notion, of the office of deacon, though at the same time other and larger functions were by degrees entrusted to them, as the Church grew and increased, and ecclesiastical life and wants became more involved and complex.[123] History bears out this view. Irenæus was the disciple of Polycarp, and must have known many apostolic men, men who had companied with the Apostles and knew the whole detail of primitive Church government; and Irenæus, speaking of Nicolas the proselyte of Antioch, describes him as "one of the seven who were first ordained to the diaconate by the Apostles." Now Irenæus is one of our great witnesses for the authenticity of the Four Gospels; surely then he must be an equally good witness to the origin of the order of deacons and the existence of the Acts of the Apostles which is implied in this reference. It is scarcely necessary to go farther in Church history, but the lower one goes the more clearly we shall see that the original notion of the diaconate is never forgotten. In the third century we find that there were still only seven deacons in Rome, though there were forty-six presbyters, a number which was retained down to the twelfth century in the seven cardinal deacons of that Church.[124] The touching story of the martyrdom of St. Laurence, Archdeacon of Rome in the middle of the third century, shows that he was roasted over a slow fire in order to extort the vast sums he was supposed to have in charge for the purpose of relieving the sick and the poor connected with the Roman Church; proving that the original conception of the office as an executive and charitable organization was then vigorously retained; just as it is still set forth in the ordinal of the Church of England, where, after reciting how the deacon's office is to help the priest in several subordinate positions, it goes on to say, "Furthermore, it is his office, where provision is so made, to search for the sick, poor, and impotent people of the parish, to intimate their estates, names, and places where they dwell, unto the curate, that by his exhortation they may be relieved by the alms of the parishioners."

The only objection of any value which has been raised to this line of argument is based on a mere assumption. It has been said that the Seven were appointed for a special emergency, and to serve a temporary purpose connected with the community of goods which existed in the early Church of Jerusalem, and therefore when this arrangement ceased the office itself ceased also. But this argument is based on the assumption that the Christian idea of a community of goods wholly passed away, so that services of an order like the Seven were no longer required. This is a pure assumption. The community of goods as practised at Jerusalem was found by experience to be a mistake. The shape of the idea was changed, but the idea itself survived. The old form of community of goods passed away. The Christians retained their rights of private property, but were taught to regard this private property as in a sense common, and liable for all the wants and needs of their poor and suffering brethren. A charitable order, or at least an order charged with the care of the poor and their relief, must inevitably have sprung up among the Jewish Christians. The relief of the poor was a necessary part of the duty of a synagogue. The Jewish domestic law enforced a poor-rate, and collected it through the organization of each synagogue, by means of three deacons attached to each. Selden, in his great work on *The Laws of the Hebrews*, bk. ii., chap. vi. (*Works*, i., 632), tells us that if "any Jew did not pay his fair contribution he was punished with stripes." As soon as the Jewish Christians began to organize themselves, the idea of almoners, with their daily and weekly distributions, after the synagogue model, was necessarily developed.[125] We have an unexceptionable piece of evidence upon this point. The satirist Lucian lived at the close of the second century. He was a bitter scoffer, who jeered at every form of religion, and at Christianity above all. He wrote an account of a certain Syrian named Peregrinus Proteus, who was an impostor trading upon the religious principles of various philosophical sects, and specially on those of the Christians. Lucian tells us that the Christians were the easiest persons to be deceived, because of their opinions. Lucian's words are interesting as showing what a second-century pagan, a clever literary man too, thought of Christianity, viewing it from the outside. For this reason we shall quote a little more than the words which immediately bear upon the subject. "It is incredible with what alacrity these people (the Christians) support and defend the public cause. They spare nothing, in fact, to promote it. These poor men have persuaded themselves that they shall be immortal, and live for ever. They despise death therefore, and offer up their lives a voluntary sacrifice, being taught by their lawgiver that they are all brethren, and that, quitting our Grecian gods, they must worship their own sophist, who was crucified, and live in obedience to His laws. In compliance with them, they look with contempt on all worldly treasures, and hold everything in common—a maxim which they have adopted without any reason or foundation. If any cunning impostor, therefore, who knows how to manage matters, come amongst them, he soon grows rich by imposing on the credulity of those weak and foolish men." We can see here that the great outer world of paganism considered a community of goods as still prevailing among the Christians. Their boundless liberality, their intense devotion to the cause of their suffering brethren, proved this, and therefore, because a practical community of goods existed amongst them, an order of men was required to superintend the distribution of their liberality in the Second Century just as truly as the work of the Seven was needed in the Church of Jerusalem.

II. We thus can see that the office of deacon, as now constituted, had its origin in apostolic times, and is built upon a scriptural foundation; but here we are bound to point out a great difference between the ancient and the modern office. An office or organization may spring up in one age, and after existing for several centuries may develop into a shape utterly unlike its original. Yet it may be very hard to point out any special time when a vital change was made. All we can say is that the first occupants of the office would never recognise their modern successors. Take the papacy as an instance. There has been at Rome a regular historical succession of bishops since the first century. The succession is known and undoubted. Yet could one of the bishops of Rome of the first three centuries,—above all, could a first-century bishop of Rome like St. Clement, by any possibility recognise himself or his office in the present Pope Leo XIII.? Yet one would find it difficult to fix the exact moment when any vital change was made, or any unwonted claims put forward on behalf of the Roman See.[126] So was it in the case of deacons and their office. Their modern successors may trace themselves back to the seven elected in the primitive Church at Jerusalem, and yet the office is now a very different one in practice from what it was then. Perhaps the greatest difference, and the only one we can notice, was this. The diaconate is now merely the primary and lowest rank of the Christian ministry; a kind of apprenticeship, in fact, wherein the youthful minister serves for a year, and is then promoted as a matter of course; whereas in Jerusalem or Rome of old it was a lifelong office, in the exercise of which maturity of judgment, of piety, and of character were required for the due discharge of its manifold duties. It is now a temporary office, it was of old a permanent one. And the apostolical custom was much the best. It avoided many difficulties and solved many a problem. At present the office of the diaconate is practically in abeyance, and yet the functions which the ancient deacons discharged are not in abeyance, but are placed upon the shoulders of the other orders in the Church, already overwhelmed with manifold responsibilities, and neglecting, while serving tables, the higher aspects of their work. The Christian ministry in its purely spiritual, and specially in its prophetical or preaching aspect, is sorely suffering because an apostolic office is practically set aside. In the ancient Church it was never so. The deacons were chosen to a life-office. It was then but very seldom that a man chosen to the diaconate abandoned it for a higher function. It did not indeed demand the wholesale devotion of time and attention which the higher offices of the ministry did. Men even till a late period, both in East and West, combined secular pursuits with it. Thus let us take one celebrated instance. The ancient Church of England and of Ireland alike was Celtic in origin and constitution. It was intensely conservative, therefore, of ancient customs and usages derived from the times of persecution, when Christianity was first taught among the Gauls and Celts of the extreme West. The well-known story of the introduction of Christianity into England under St. Augustine and the opposition he met with prove this. As it was in other matters, so was it with the ancient Celtic deacons; the old customs remained; they held office for life, and joined with it at the same time other and ordinary occupations. St. Patrick, for instance, the apostle of Ireland, tells us that his father Calpurnius was a deacon, and yet he was a farmer and a decurion, or alderman, as we should say, of a Roman town near Dumbarton on the river Clyde. This happened about the year 400 of the Christian era.[127]

Here indeed, as in so many other cases, the Church of Christ needs to go back to scriptural example and to apostolic rule. We require for the work of the Church deacons like the primitive men who devoted their whole lives to this one object; made it the subject of their thoughts, their cares, their studies, how they might instruct the ignorant, relieve the poor and widows, comfort the prisoners, sustain the martyrs in their last supreme hour; and who thus using well the office of a deacon found in it a sufficient scope for their efforts and a sufficient reward for their exertions, because they thereby purchased for themselves a good degree and great boldness in the faith of Jesus Christ. The Church now requires the help of living agencies in vast numbers, and they are not forthcoming. Let her avail herself of apostolic resources, and fall back upon primitive precedents. The real diaconate should be revived. Godly and spiritual men should be called upon to do their duty. Deacons should be ordained without being called to give up their ordinary employments. Work which now unduly accumulates upon overburdened shoulders should be assigned to others suitably to their talents, and thus a twofold blessing would be secured. Christian life would flourish more abundantly, and many a rent and schism, the simple result of energies repressed and unemployed, would be destroyed in their very commencement.

We have devoted much of our space to this subject, because it is one of great interest, as touching the origin and authority of the Christian ministry, and also because it has been a subject much debated; but we must hurry on to other points connected with the first appointment to the diaconate. The people selected the person to be ordained to this work. It is probable that they made their choice out of the different classes composing the Christian community. The mode of election of the Seven, and the qualifications laid down by the Apostles, were derived from the synagogue. Thus we read in Kitto's *Cyclopædia,* art. "Synagogue:"—"The greatest care was taken by the rulers of the synagogue and of the congregation that those elected almoners should be men of modesty, wisdom, justice, and have the confidence of the people. They had to be elected by the harmonious voice of the people." Seven deacons altogether were chosen. Three were probably Hebrew Christians, three Grecian Christians or Hellenists, and one a representative of the proselytes, Nicolas of Antioch. This would have been but natural. The Apostles wanted to get rid of murmurs, jealousies, and divisions in the Church, and in no way could this have been more effectually done than by the principle of representation. Had the Seven been all selected from one class alone, divisions and jealousies would have prevailed as of old. The Apostles themselves had proved this. They were all Hebrew Christians. Their position and authority might have secured them from blame. Yet murmurings had arisen against them as distributers, and so they devised another plan, which, to have been successful, as it doubtless was, must have proceeded on a different principle. Then when the seven wise and prudent men were chosen from the various classes, the Apostles asserted their supreme position: "When the Apostles had prayed, they laid their hands on them." And as the result peace descended like a shower upon the Church, and spiritual prosperity followed upon internal peace and union.

III. "They laid their hands on them." This statement sets forth the external expression and the visible channel of the ordination to their office which the Apostles conferred. This action of the imposition of hands was of frequent use among the ancient Jews. The Apostles, as well acquainted with Old Testament history, must have remembered that it was employed in the case of designation of Joshua as the leader of Israel in the place of Moses (Num. xxvii. 18-23; compare Deut. xxxiv. 9), that it was used even in the synagogue in the appointment of Jewish rabbis, and had been sanctioned by the practice of Jesus Christ. The Apostles naturally, therefore, used this symbol upon the solemn appointment of the first deacons, and the same ceremonial was repeated upon similar occasions. Paul and Barnabas were set apart at Antioch for their missionary work by the imposition of hands. St. Paul uses the strongest language about the ceremony. He does not hesitate to attribute to it a certain sacramental force and efficacy, bidding Timothy "stir up the gift of God which is in thee through the laying on of my hands" (2 Tim. i. 6); while again when we come down a few years later we find the "laying on of hands" reckoned as one of the fundamental elements of religion, in the sixth chapter of the Epistle to the Hebrews. But it was not merely in the solemn appointment of officials in the Church that this ceremony found place. It was employed by the Apostles as the rite which filled up and perfected the baptism which had been administered by others. Philip baptized the Samaritans. Peter and John laid their hands on them and they received the Holy Ghost. The ceremony of imposition of hands was so essential and distinguishing a point that Simon Magus selects it as the one he desires above all others effectually to purchase, so that the outward symbol might be followed by the inward grace. "Give me also this power, that on whomsoever I lay my hands, he may receive the Holy Ghost," was the prayer of the arch-heretic to St. Peter; while again in the nineteenth chapter we find St. Paul using the same visible ceremony in the case of St. John's disciples, who were first baptized with Christian baptism, and then endued by St. Paul with the gift of the Spirit. Imposition of hands in the case of ordination is a natural symbol, indicative of the transmission of function and authority. It fitly indicates and notifies to the whole Church the persons who have been ordained, and therefore has ever been regarded as a necessary part of ordination. St. Jerome, who was a very keen critic as well as a close student of the Divine oracles, fixes upon this public and solemn designation as a sufficient explanation and justification of the imposition of hands in ordinations, lest any one should be ordained without his knowledge by a silent and solitary prayer. Hence every branch of the Church of Christ has rigorously insisted upon imposition of hands after the apostolic example, in the case of ordinations to official positions, with one or two apparent and very doubtful exceptions, which merely prove the binding character of the rule.

IV. The list of names again is full of profit and of warning. How completely different from human histories, for instance, is this Divine record of the first doings of the Church! How thoroughly shaped after the Divine model is this catalogue of the earliest officials chosen by the Apostles! Men have speculated whether they were Hebrews or Grecians, whether they belonged to the seventy sent forth by Christ or to the hundred and twenty who first gathered into the upper room at Jerusalem. All such speculations are curious and interesting, but they have nothing to do with man's salvation; therefore they are sternly put on one side and out of sight. How we should long to know the subsequent history of these men, and to trace their careers! yet Holy Writ tells us but very little about them, nothing certain, in fact, save what we learn about St. Stephen and St. Philip. God bestowed Holy Scripture upon men, not to satisfy or minister to their curiosity, but to nourish their souls and edify their spirits. And surely no lesson is more needed than the one implied in the silences of this passage; there is in truth none more necessary for our publicity-seeking and popularity-hunting age than this, that God's holiest servants have laboured in obscurity, have done their best work in secret, and have looked to God alone and to His judgment for their reward. I have said indeed that concerning the list of names recorded as those of the first deacons, we know nothing but of St. Stephen and St. Philip, whose careers will again come under our notice in later chapters. There is, however, a current tradition that Nicolas, the proselyte of Antioch, did distinguish himself, but in an unhappy direction. It is asserted by Irenæus in his work *Against Heresies* (Book I., ch. 26), that Nicolas was the founder of the sect of Nicolaitans denounced in the Revelation of St. John (ch. ii., 6, 16). Critics are, however, much divided upon this point. Some clear Nicolas of this charge, while others uphold it. It is indeed impossible to determine this matter. But supposing that Nicolas of Antioch was the author of this heresy, which was of an antinomian character, like so many of the earliest heresies that distracted the primitive Church, this circumstance would teach us an instructive lesson. Just as there was a Judas Iscariot among the Apostles, and a Demas among St. Paul's most intimate disciples, so was there a Nicolas among the first deacons. No place is so holy, no office so sacred, no privileges so great, but that the tempter can make his way there. He can lurk unseen and unsuspected amid the pillars of the temple, and he can find us out, as he did the Son of God Himself, amid the wilds of the desert. Official position and exalted privileges confer no immunity from temptation. Nay, rather, they bring with them additional temptations over and above those which assail the ordinary Christian, and should therefore lead everyone called to any similar work to diligent watchfulness, to earnest prayer, lest while teaching others they themselves fall into condemnation. There is, however, another lesson which a different version of the history of Nicolas would teach. Clement of Alexandria, in his celebrated work called the *Stromata* (Book II., chap. 20, and Book III., chap. 4), tells us that Nicolas was a most strictly virtuous man. He was extreme even in his asceticism, and, like many ascetics, used language that might be easily abused to the purposes of wickedness. He was wont to say that the "flesh must be abused," meaning that it must be chastised and restrained. One-sided and extreme teaching is easily perverted by the wicked nature of man, and men of impure lives, listening to the language of Nicolas, interpreted his words as an excuse for abusing the flesh by plunging into the depths of immorality and crime. Men placed in official positions and called to the exercise of the clerical office should weigh their words. Extreme statements are bad unless duly and strictly guarded. The intention of the speaker may be good, and a man's own life thoroughly consistent, but unbalanced teaching will fall upon ground where the life and intention of the teacher will have no power or influence, and bring forth evil fruit, as in the case of the Nicolaitans.

V. The central figure of this whole section of our narrative is St. Stephen. He is introduced into the narrative with the same startling suddenness which we may note in the case of Barnabas and of Elijah. He runs a rapid course, flings all, Apostles and every one else, into the shade for a time, and then disappears, exemplifying those fruitful sayings of inspiration, so true in our every-day experience of God's dealings, "The first shall be last, and the last first." "Paul may plant, Apollos may water, but it is God alone that giveth the increase." Stephen, full of grace and power, did great signs and wonders among the people. These two words, grace and power, are closely connected. Their union in this passage is significant. It was not the intellect, or the eloquence, or the activity of St. Stephen which made him powerful among the people and crowned his labours with such success. It was his abundant grace. Eloquence and learning, active days and laborious nights, are good and necessary things. God uses them and demands them from His people. He chooses to use human agencies, and therefore demands that the human agents shall give Him of their best, and not offer to Him the blind and lame of their flock. But these things will be utterly useless and ineffective apart from Christ and the power of His grace. The Church of Christ is a supernatural society, and the work of Christ is a supernatural work, and in that work the grace of Christ is absolutely necessary to make any human gift or exertion effectual in carrying out His purposes of love and mercy. This is an age of organizations and committees and boards; and some good men are so wrapped up in them that they have no time to think of anything else. To this busy age these words, "Stephen, full of grace and power," convey a useful warning, teaching that the best organizations and schemes will be useless to produce Stephen's power unless Stephen's grace be found there as well. This passage is a prophecy and picture of the future in another aspect. The fulness of grace in Stephen wrought powerfully amongst the people. It was the savour of life unto life in some. But in others it was a savour of death unto death, and provoked them to evil deeds, for they suborned men "which said, We have heard him speak blasphemous words against Moses, and against God."

We get in these words, in this false accusation, even through its falsehood, a glimpse into the character of St. Stephen's preaching. A false accusation need not be necessarily altogether false. Perhaps rather we should say that, in order to be effective for mischief, a twisted, distorted charge, with some basis of truth, some semblance of justification about it, is the best for the accuser's purpose, and the most difficult for the defendant to answer. St. Stephen was ripening for heaven more rapidly than the Apostles themselves. He was learning more rapidly than St. Peter himself the true spiritual meaning of the Christian scheme. He had taught, in no ambiguous language, the universal character of the Gospel and the catholic mission of the Church. He had expanded and applied the magnificent declarations of the Master Himself, "The hour cometh, when neither in this mountain, nor in Jerusalem, shall ye worship the Father;" "The hour cometh, and now is, when the true worshippers shall worship the Father in spirit and in truth." And then the narrow-minded Grecian Jews, anxious to vindicate their orthodoxy, which was doubted by their Hebrew brethren, distorted Stephen's wider and grander conceptions into a charge of blasphemy against the holy man. What a picture of the future of Christ's best and truest witnesses, especially when insisting on some nobler and wider or forgotten aspect of truth. Their teaching has been ever suspected, distorted, accused as blasphemous; and so it must ever be. And yet God's servants, when they find themselves thus misrepresented, can realize to themselves that they are but following the course which the saints of every age have run, that they are being made like unto the image of Stephen the first martyr, and of Jesus Christ Himself, the King of Saints, who suffered under a similar accusation. The mere popularity-hunter will, of course, carefully eschew such charges and suspicions. His object is human praise and reward, and he shapes his teaching so as to carefully avoid giving offence. But then the mere popularity-hunter seeks his reward here below, and very often gets it. Stephen, however, and every true teacher looks not for reward in this world. Stephen taught truth as God revealed it to his soul. He suffered the consequence, and then received his crown from that Almighty Judge before whose awful tribunal he ever consciously stood. Misrepresentation must ever be expected by God's true servants. It must be discounted, borne with patiently, taken as a trial of faith and patience, and then, in God's own time, it will turn out to our greater blessing. One consideration alone ought to prove sufficient to console us under such circumstances. If our teaching was not proving injurious to his cause, the Evil One would not trouble himself about it. Let us only take good heed lest our own self-love and vanity should lead us to annoy ourselves too much about the slander or the evil report, remembering that misrepresentation and slander is ever the portion of God's servants. Jesus Christ and Stephen were thus treated. St. Paul's teaching was accused of tending to licentiousness; the earliest Christians were accused of vilest practices; St. Athanasius in his struggles for truth was accused of rebellion and murder; the Reformers were accused of lawlessness; John Wesley of Romanism and disloyalty; William Wilberforce of being an enemy to British trade; John Howard of being an encourager of crime and immorality. Let us be content then if our lot be with the saints, and our portion be that of the servants of the Most High.

Again, we learn from this place how religious zeal can overthrow religion and work out the purposes of evil. Religious zeal, mere party spirit taking the place of real religion, led the Hellenists to suborn men and falsely accuse St. Stephen. They made an idol of the system of Judaism, and forgot its spirit. They worshipped their idol so much that they were ready to break the commandments of God for its sake. The dangers of party spirit in matters of religion, and the evil deeds which have been done in apparent zeal for God and real zeal for the devil, these are still the lessons, true for the future ages of the Church, which we read in this passage. And how true to life has even our own age found this prophetic picture. Men cannot indeed now suborn men and bring fatal charges against them in matters of religion, and yet they can fall into exactly the same crime. Party religion and party zeal lead men into precisely the same courses as they did in the days of St. Stephen. Partisanship causes them to violate all the laws of honour, of honesty, of Christian charity, imagining that they are thereby advancing the cause of Christ, forgetting that they are acting on the rule which the Scriptures repudiate, — they are doing evil that good may come, — and striving to further Christ's kingdom by a violation of His fundamental precepts. Oh for more of the spirit of true charity, which will lead men to support their own views in a spirit of Christian love! Oh for more of that true grasp of Christianity which will teach that a breach of Christian charity is far worse than any amount of speculative error! The error as we think it may be in reality God's own truth; but the violation of God's law implied in such conduct as Stephen's adversaries displayed, and as party zeal now often prompts, can never be otherwise than contrary to the mind and law of Jesus Christ.

# CHAPTER XV
## ST. STEPHEN'S DEFENCE AND THE DOCTRINE OF INSPIRATION

"[The Grecian Jews] stirred up the people, and the elders, and the scribes, and came upon him, and seized him, and brought him into the council, and set up false witnesses, which said, This man ceaseth not to speak words against this holy place, and the law: for we have heard him say, that this Jesus of Nazareth shall destroy this place, and shall change the customs which Moses delivered unto us."—Acts vi. 12-14.

"And the high priest said, Are these things so? And he said, Brethren and fathers, hearken."—Acts vii. 1, 2.

St. Stephen and St. Philip are the two prominent names among the primitive deacons. Stephen, however, much surpasses Philip. Devout expositors of Scripture have recognised in his name a prophecy of his greatness. Stephen is Stephanos, a garland or crown, in the Greek language. Garlands or crowns were given by the ancient Greeks to those who rendered good services to their cities, or brought fame to them by winning triumphs in the great national games. And Stephen had his name divinely chosen for him by that Divine Providence which ordereth all things, because he was to win in the fulness of time an imperishable garland, and to gain a crown of righteousness, and to render highest services to the Church of God by his teaching and by his testimony even unto death. St. Stephen had a Greek name, and must have belonged to the Hellenistic division of the Jewish nation. He evidently directed his special energies to their conversion, for while the previous persecutions had been raised by the Sadducees, as the persons whose prejudices had been assailed, the attack on Stephen was made by the Grecian Jews of the synagogues belonging to the Libertines or freedmen, in union with those from Cyrene, Alexandria, Cilicia, and Asia. The Libertines had been slaves, Jewish captives, taken in the various wars waged by the Romans. They had been dispersed among the Romans at Rome and elsewhere. There in their captivity they had learned the Greek language and become acquainted with Greek culture; and now, when they had recovered their freedom through that suppleness and power of adaptation which the Jewish race has ever displayed, they returned to Jerusalem in such numbers that a synagogue of the Libertines was formed. Their captivity and servitude had, however, only intensified their religious feelings, and made them more jealous of any attempts to extend to the Gentiles who had held them captives the spiritual possessions they alone enjoyed. There is, indeed, an extremely interesting parallel to the case of the Libertines in early English history, as told by Bede. The Saxons came to England in the fifth century and conquered the Christian Celts, whom they drove into Wales. The Celts, however, avenged themselves upon their conquerors, for they refused to impart to the pagan Saxons the glad tidings of salvation which the Celts possessed.[128] But the Libertines were not the only assailants of St. Stephen. With them were joined members of synagogues connected with various other important Jewish centres. Jerusalem was then somewhat like Rome at the present time. It was the one city whither a race scattered all over the world and speaking every language tended. Each language was represented by a synagogue, just as there are English Colleges and Irish Colleges and Spanish Colleges at Rome, where Roman Catholics of those nationalities find themselves specially at home. Among these Hellenistic antagonists of St. Stephen we have mention made of the men of Cilicia. Here, doubtless, was found a certain Saul of Tarsus, enthusiastic in defence of the ancient faith, and urgent with all his might to bring to trial the apostate who had dared to speak words which he considered derogatory of the city and temple of the great king.

Saul, indeed, may have been the great agent in Stephen's arrest. It is a nature and an intellect like his that can discern the logical results of teaching like St. Stephen's, and then found an accusation upon the deductions he makes rather than upon the actual words spoken. Saul may have placed the Church under another obligation on this occasion. To him may be due the report of the speech made by Stephen before the Sanhedrin. Indeed, it is to St. Paul in his unconverted state we feel inclined to attribute the knowledge which St. Luke possessed of the earlier proceedings of the council in the matter of the Christians.[129] After St. Paul's conversion we get no such details concerning the deliberations of the Sanhedrin as we do in the earlier chapters of the Acts, simply because Saul of Tarsus, the rising champion and hope of the Pharisees, was present at the earlier meetings and had access to their inmost secrets, while at the later meetings he never appeared save to stand his trial as an accused person. The question, How was Stephen's speech preserved? has been asked by some critics who wished to decry the historic truth of this narrative, and to represent the whole thing as a fancy sketch or romance, worked up on historic lines indeed, but still only a romance, written many years after the events had happened. Critics who ask this forget what modern research has shown in another department. The *Acts* of the martyrs are sometimes very large documents, containing reports of charges, examinations, and speeches of considerable length. These have often been considered mere fancy history, the work of mediæval monks wishing to celebrate the glory of these early witnesses for truth, and sceptical writers have often put them aside without bestowing even a passing notice upon them.

Modern investigation has taken these documents, critically investigated them, compared them with the Roman criminal law, and has come to the conclusion that they are genuine, affording some of the most interesting and important examples of ancient methods of legal procedure anywhere to be found. How did the Christians get these records? it may be asked. Various hints, given here and there, enable us to see. Bribery of the officials was sometimes used. The notaries, shorthand writers, and clerks attendant upon a Roman court were numerous, and were always accessible to the gifts of the richer Christians when they wished to obtain a correct narrative of a martyr's last trial. Secret Christians among the officials also effected something, and there were numerous other methods by which the Roman judicial records became the property of the Church, to be in time transmitted to the present age.[130] Now just the same may have been the case with the trials of the primitive Christians, and specially of St. Stephen. But we know that St. Paul was there. Memory among the Jews was sharpened to an extraordinary degree. We have now no idea to what an extent the human memory was then developed. The immense volumes which are filled with the Jewish commentaries on Scripture were in those times transmitted from generation to generation simply by means of this power. It was considered, indeed, a great innovation when those commentaries were committed to writing instead of being intrusted to tradition. It is no wonder then that St. Paul could afford his disciple, St. Luke, a report of what Stephen said on this occasion, even if he had not preserved any notes whatsoever of the process of the trial. Let us, however, turn to the consideration of St. Stephen's speech, omitting any further notice of objections based on our own ignorance of the practices and methods of distant ages.

I. The defence of St. Stephen was a speech delivered by a Jew, and addressed to a Jewish audience. This is our first remark, and it is an important one. We are apt to judge the Scriptures, their speeches, arguments, and discussions, by a Western standard, forgetting that Orientals argued then and argue still not according to the rules of logic taught by Aristotle, nor by the methods of eloquence derived from the traditions of Cicero and Quinctilian, but by methods and rules essentially different. What would satisfy Westerns would have seemed to them utterly worthless, just as an argument which now seems pointless and weak appeared to them absolutely conclusive. Parallels, analogies, parables, mystical interpretations were then favourite methods of argument, and if we wish to understand writers like the authors of the scriptural books we must strive to place ourselves at their point of view, or else we shall miss their true interpretation. Let us apply this idea to St. Stephen's defence, which has been often depreciated because treated as if it were an oration addressed to a Western court or audience. Erasmus, for instance, was an exceedingly learned man, who lived at the period of the Reformation. He was well skilled in Latin and Greek learning, but knew nothing of Jewish ideas. He hesitates not, therefore, to say in his Annotations on this passage that there are many things in Stephen's speech which have no bearing on the question at issue; while Michaelis, another German writer of great repute in the earlier days of this century, remarks that there are many things in this oration of which we cannot perceive the tendency, as regards the accusation brought against the martyr. Let us examine and see if the case be not otherwise, remembering that promise of the Master, given not to supersede human exertion or to indulge human laziness, but given to support and sustain and safeguard His persecuted servants under circumstances like those amid which Stephen found himself. "But when they deliver you up, be not anxious how or what ye shall speak; for it shall be given you in that hour what ye shall speak. For it is not ye that speak, but the Spirit of your Father that speaketh in you." What, then, was the charge brought against Stephen? He was accused of "speaking blasphemous words against Moses, and against God," or, to put it in the formal language used by the witnesses, "We have heard him say that Jesus of Nazareth shall destroy this place, and shall change the customs which Moses delivered unto us." Now Stephen, if merely a man of common sense, must have intended to reply to this indictment. Some critics, as we have just noted, think that he failed effectually to do so. We are indeed often in great danger of paying too much attention and lending too great weight to objections of this kind urged by persons who assume to themselves the office of critics; and to counteract this tendency perhaps it is as well to note that a leading German writer of a rationalistic type, named Zeller, who has written a work to decry the historical character of the Acts, finds in St. Stephen's words an oration "not only characteristic, but also better suited to the case and to the accusation raised against him than is usually supposed."

Disregarding, then, all cavils of critics whose views are mutually destructive, let us see if we cannot discern in this narrative the marks of a sound and powerful mind, guided, aided, and directed by the Spirit of God which dwelt so abundantly in him. St. Stephen was accused of irreverence towards Moses, and hostility towards the temple, and towards all the

Jewish institutions. How did he meet this? He begins his address to the Sanhedrin at the earliest period of their national history, and shows how the chosen people had passed through many changes and developments without interfering with their essential identity amid these changes. His opponents now made idols of their local institutions and of the buildings of the temple, but God's choice and God's promise had originally nothing local about them at all. Abraham their great father was first called by God in Ur of the Chaldees, far away across the desert in distant Mesopotamia. Thence he removed to Charran, and then, only after the lapse of years, became a wanderer up and down in Canaan, where he never possessed so much of the land as he could set his foot upon. The promises of God and the covenant of grace were personal things, made to God's chosen children, not connected with lands or buildings or national customs. He next takes up the case of Moses. He had been accused of blasphemy and irreverence towards the great national law-giver. His words prove that he entertained no such feelings; he respected and revered Moses just as much as his opponents and accusers did. But Moses had nothing to say or do with Canaan, or Jerusalem, or the temple. Nay, rather, his work for the chosen people was done in Egypt and in Midian and on the side of Horeb, where the presence and name of Jehovah were manifested not in the temple or tabernacle, but in the bush burning yet not consumed.

The Grecian Jews accused Stephen of irreverence towards Moses. But how had their forefathers treated that Moses whom he recognised as a divinely-sent messenger? "They thrust him from them, and in their hearts turned back again into Egypt." Moses, however, led them onward and upward. His motto was hope. His rod and his voice ever pointed forward. He warned them that his own ministry was not the final one; that it was only an intermediate and temporary institution, till the prophet should come unto whom the people should hearken. There was a chosen people before the customs introduced by Moses. There may therefore be a chosen people still when these customs cease, having fulfilled their purpose. The argument of St. Stephen in this passage is the same as that of St. Paul in the fourth chapter of Galatians, where he sets forth the temporary and intermediate character of the Levitical law and of the covenant of circumcision. So teaches St. Stephen in his speech. His argument is simply this:—I have been accused of speaking blasphemous words against Moses because I proclaimed that a greater Prophet than he had come, and yet this was only what Moses himself had foretold. It is not I who have blasphemed and opposed Moses: it is my accusers rather. But then he remembers that the accusation dealt not merely with Moses. It went farther, and accused him of speaking blasphemous words against the national sanctuary, "saying that Jesus of

Nazareth shall destroy this place." This leads him to speak of the temple. His argument now takes a different turn, and runs thus. This building is now the centre of Jewish thoughts and affections. But it is a mere modern thing as compared with the original choice and promise of God. There was no chosen dwelling-place of the Almighty in the earliest days of all; His presence was then manifested wherever His chosen servants dwelt. Then Moses made a tent or tabernacle, which abode in no certain spot, but moved hither and thither. Last of all, long after Abraham, and long after Moses, and even after David, Solomon built God an house. Even when it was built, and in all its original glory, even then the temporary character of the temple was clearly recognised by the prophet Isaiah, who had long ago, in his sixty-sixth chapter, proclaimed the truth which had been brought forward as an accusation against himself: "Heaven is My throne, and earth is My footstool; what house will ye build Me, saith the Lord, or what is the place of My rest? Hath not My hand made all these things?"—a great spiritual truth which had been anticipated long before Isaiah by King Solomon, in his famous dedication prayer at the opening of the temple: "But will God indeed dwell on the earth? Behold the heaven and the heaven of heavens cannot contain Thee; how much less this house that I have builded" (1 Kings viii. 27). After St. Stephen had set forth this undeniable truth confirmed by the words of Isaiah, which to the Pharisaic portion of his audience, at least, must have seemed conclusive, there occurs a break in the address.

One would have thought that he would then have proceeded to describe the broader and more spiritual life which had shone forth for mankind in Christ, and to expound the freedom from all local restrictions which should henceforth belong to acceptable worship of the Most High. Most certainly, if the speech had been invented for him and placed in his mouth, a forger would naturally have designed a fuller and more balanced discourse, setting forth the doctrine of Christ as well as the past history of the Jews. We cannot tell whether he actually entered more fully into the subject or not. Possibly the Sadducean portion of his audience had got quite enough. Their countenances and gestures bespoke their horror of St. Stephen's doctrine. Isaiah's opinion carried no weight with them as contrasted with the institutions of Moses, which were their pride and glory; and so, borne along by the force of his oratory, St. Stephen finished with that vigorous denunciation which led to his death: "Ye stiffnecked and uncircumcised in heart and ears, ye do always resist the Holy Ghost: as your fathers did, so do ye." This exposition of St. Stephen's speech will show the drift and argument of it as it appears to us. But it must have seemed to them much more powerful, plain-spoken, and aggressive. He vindicated himself to any right-thinking and fair mind from the accusation of irreverence towards

God, towards Moses, or towards the Divine institutions. But the minds of his hearers were not fair. He had trampled upon their prejudices, he had suggested the vanity of their dearest ideas, and they could not estimate his reasons or follow his arguments, but they could resort to the remedy which every failing though for the present popular cause possesses,—they could destroy him. And thus they treated the modern as their ancestors had treated the ancient prophets. What a lesson Stephen's speech has for the Church of every age! How wide and manifold the applications of it! The Jewish error is one that is often committed, their mistake often repeated. The Jews identified God's honour and glory with an old order that was fast passing away, and had no eyes to behold a new and more glorious order that was opening upon them. We may blame them then for their murder of St. Stephen, but we must blame them gently, feeling that they acted as human nature has ever acted under similar circumstances, and that good motives were mingled with those feelings of rage and bigotry and narrowness that urged them to their deed of blood. Let us see how this was. Stephen proclaimed a new order and a new development, embracing for his hearers a vast political as well as a vast religious change. His forecast of the future swept away at once all the privileges and profits connected with the religious position of Jerusalem, and thus destroyed the political prospects of the Jewish people. It is no wonder the Sanhedrin could not appreciate his oration. Men do not ever listen patiently when their pockets are being touched, their profits swept away, their dearest hopes utterly annihilated. Has not human experience often repeated the scene acted out that day in Jerusalem? On the political stage men have often seen it,—we ourselves have seen it. The advocates of liberty, civil and religious, have had to struggle against the same spirit and the same prejudices as St. Stephen. Take the political world alone. We now look back and view with horror the deeds wrought in the name of authority and in opposition to the principles of change and innovation. We read the stories of Alva and the massacres in the Netherlands, the bloody deeds of the seventeenth century in England and all over Europe, the miseries and the bloodshed of the American war of independence, the fierce opposition with which the spirit of liberty has been resisted throughout this century; and our sympathies are altogether ranged on the side of the sufferers,—the losers and defeated, it may have been, for the time, but the triumphant in the long run.

The true student, however, of history or of human nature will not content himself with any one-sided view, and he will have some sympathy to spare for those who adopted the stern measures. He will not judge them too harshly. They reverenced the past as the Jews of Jerusalem did, and reverence is a feeling that is right and blessed. It is no good sign for this age of ours that it possesses so little reverence for the past, thinks so lightly of the institutions, the wisdom, the ideas of antiquity, and is ready to change them at a moment's notice. The men who now are held up to the execration of posterity, the high priest and the Sanhedrin who murdered Stephen, the tyrants and despots and their agents who strove to crush the supporters of liberty, the writers who cried them down and applauded or urged on the violent measures which were adopted and sometimes triumphed for the time,—we should strive to put ourselves in their position, and see what they had to say for themselves, and thus seek to judge them here below as the Eternal King will judge them at the great final tribunal. They knew the good which the old political institutions had worked. They had lived and flourished under them as their ancestors had lived and flourished before them. The future they knew not. All they knew was that changes were proposed which threatened everything with which their dearest memories were bound up, and the innovators seemed dangerous creatures, obnoxious to God and man, and they dealt with them accordingly.

So it has been and still is in politics. The opponents of political change are sometimes denounced in the fiercest language, as if they were morally wicked. The late Dr. Arnold seems a grievous offender in this respect. No one can read his charming biography by Dean Stanley without recognising how intolerant he was towards his political opponents; how blind he was to those good motives which inspire the timorous, the ignorant, and the aged, when brought face to face with changes which appear to them thickly charged with the most dangerous results. Charity towards opponents is sadly needed in the political as well as in the religious world. And as it has been in politics so has it been in religion. Men reverence the past, and that reverence easily glides into an idolatry blind to its defects and hostile to any improvement. It is in religion too as in politics; a thousand other interests— money, office, expectations, memories of the loved and lost—are bound up with old religious forms, and then when the prophet arises with his Divine message, as Stephen arose before the Sanhedrin, the ancient proverb is fulfilled, the corruption of the best becomes the worst, the good motives mingle with the evil, and are used by the poor human heart to justify the harshest, most unchristian deeds done in defence of what men believe to be the cause of truth and righteousness. Let us be just and fair to the aggressors as well as to the aggrieved, to the persecutors as well as to the persecuted. But let us all the same take good heed to learn for ourselves the lessons this narrative presents. Reverence is a good thing, and a blessed thing; and without reverence no true progress, either in political or spiritual things, can be made. But reverence easily degenerates into blind superstitious idolatry. It was so with the Sanhedrin, it was so at the Reformation, it has ever been so with the opponents of true religious progress. Let us evermore strive to keep minds free, open, unbiassed, respecting the past, yet ready to listen to the voice and fresh revelations of God's will and purposes made to us by the messengers whom He chooses as He pleases. Perhaps there was never an age which needed this lesson of Stephen's speech and its reception more than our own. The attitude of religious men towards science and its numerous and wondrous advances needs guidance such as this incident affords. The Sanhedrin had their own theory and interpretation of God's dealings in the past. They clung to it passionately, and refused the teaching of Stephen, who would have widened their views, and shown them that a grand and noble development was quite in accordance with all the facts of the case, and indeed a necessary result of the sacred history when truly expounded. What a parable and picture of the future we here find! What a warning as to the attitude religious men should take up with respect to the progress of science! Patience, intellectual and religious patience, is taught us. The Sanhedrin were impatient of St. Stephen's views, which they could not understand, and their impatience made them lose a blessing and commit a sin. Now has it not been at times much the same with ourselves? Fifty or sixty years ago men were frightened at the revelations of geology,—they had their own interpretations of the past and of the Scriptures,—just as three centuries ago men were frightened at the revelations and teaching of modern astronomy. Prejudiced and narrow men then strove to hound down the teachers of the new science, and would if they could have destroyed them in the name of God. Patience here, however, has done its work and has had its reward. The new revelations have been taken up and absorbed by the Church of Christ. Men have learned to distinguish between their own interpretations of religion and of religious documents on the one hand and the religion itself on the other. The old, human, narrow, prejudiced interpretations have been modified. That which could be shaken and was untrue has passed away, while that which cannot be shaken has remained.

The lesson taught us by these instances of astronomy and geology ought not to be thrown away. Patience is again necessary for the Christian and for the scientist alike. New facts are every day coming to light, but it requires much time and thought to bring new facts and old truths into their due correlation, to look round and about them. The human mind is at best very small and weak. It is blind, and cannot see afar off, and it is only by degrees it can grasp truth in its fulness. A new fact, for instance, discovered by science may appear at first plainly contradictory to some old truth revealed in Scripture. But even so, we should not lose our patience or our hope taught us by this chapter. What new fact of science can possibly seem more contradictory to any old truth of the Creeds than St. Stephen's teaching about the universal character of God's promise and the freeness of acceptable worship must have seemed when compared with the Divine choice of the temple at Jerusalem? They appeared to the Sanhedrin ideas mutually destructive, though now we see them to have been quite consistent one with another. Let this historic retrospect support us when our faith is tried. Let us welcome every new fact and new revelation brought by science, and then, if they seem opposed to something we know to be true in religion, let us wait in confidence begotten of past experience that God in His own good time will clear up for His faithful people that which now seems difficult of comprehension. Patience and confidence, then, are two lessons much needed in this age, which St. Stephen's speech and its reception bring home to our hearts.

II. We have now spoken of the general aspect of the discourse, and the broad counsels we may gather from it. There are some other points, however, points of detail as distinguished from wider views, upon which we would fix our attention. They too will be found full of guidance and full of instruction. Let us take them in the order in which they appear in St. Stephen's address. The mistakes and variations which undoubtedly occur in it are well worthy of careful attention, and have much teaching necessary for these times. There are three points in which Stephen varies from the language of the Old Testament. In the fourteenth verse of the seventh chapter Stephen speaks thus: "Then sent Joseph, and called his father Jacob to him, and all his kindred, threescore and fifteen souls;" while, if we turn to the Pentateuch, we shall find that the number of the original Hebrew immigrants is placed three times over at seventy, or threescore and ten, that is in Gen. xlvi. 27, Exod. i. 5, and Deut. x. 22. This, however, is only a comparatively minor point. The Septuagint or Greek version of the Pentateuch reads seventy-five in the first of these passages, making the sons of Joseph born in Egypt to have been nine persons, and thus completing the number seventy-five, at which it fixes the roll of the males who came with Jacob. The next two verses, the fifteenth and sixteenth, contain a much more serious mistake. They run thus:—"So Jacob went down into Egypt, and died, he, and our fathers, and were carried over into Sychem, and laid in the sepulchre that Abraham bought for a sum of money of the sons of Emmor the father of Sychem." Now here there occur several grave errors. Jacob was not carried over and buried at Sychem at all, but at the cave of Machpelah, as is plainly stated in Gen. l. 13. Again, a plot of ground at Sychem was certainly bought, not by Abraham, however, but by Jacob. Abraham bought the field and cave of Machpelah from Ephron the Hittite. Jacob bought his plot at Sychem from the sons of Emmor. There are in these verses, then, two serious historical mistakes; first as to the true burial-place of Jacob, and then as to the purchaser of the plot of ground at Sychem. Yet, again, there is a third mistake in the forty-third verse, where, when quoting a denunciation of Jewish idolatry from Amos v. 25, 26, he quotes the prophet as threatening, "I will carry you away beyond Babylon," whereas the prophet did say, "Therefore I will cause you to go into captivity beyond Damascus." St. Stephen substituted Babylon for Damascus, two cities between which several hundred miles intervened. I have stated the difficulty thus as strongly as possible, because I think that, instead of constituting a difficulty, they are a real source of living help and comfort, as well as a great practical confirmation of the story. Let us take this last point first. I say that these mistakes, admitted mistakes which I make no vain attempt to explain away, constitute a confirmation of the story as given in the Acts against modern rationalistic opponents. It is a favourite theme of many of these writers that the Acts of the Apostles is a mere piece of fancy history, a historical romance composed in the second century for the purpose of reconciling the adherents of St. Paul, or the Gentile Christians, with the followers of St. Peter, or the Jewish Christians. The persons who uphold this view fix the date of the Acts in the earlier half of the second century, and teach that the speeches and addresses were composed by the author of the book and put into the mouths of the reputed speakers. Now, in the mistake made by St. Stephen, we have a refutation of this theory. Surely any man composing a speech to put into the mouth of one of his favourite heroes and champions would not have represented him as making such grave errors when addressing the supreme Jewish senate. A man might easily make any of these slips which I have noticed in the heat of an oration, and they might have even passed unnoticed, as every speaker who has much practice in addressing the public still makes precisely the same kind of mistake. But a romancer, sitting down to forge speeches suitable to the time and place, would never have put in the mouth of his lay figures grave errors about the most elementary facts of Jewish history. We conclude, then, that the inaccuracies reported as made by St. Stephen are evidences of the genuine character of the oration attributed to him. Then again we see in these mistakes a guarantee of the honesty and accuracy of the reports of the speech. The other day I read the objections of a critic to our Gospels. He wished to know, for instance, how the addresses of our Lord could have been preserved in an age when there was no shorthand. The answer is, however, simple enough, and conclusive: there was shorthand in that age.[131] Shorthand was then carried to such perfection that an epigram of Martial (xiv. 208), a contemporary poet, celebrating its triumphs may be thus translated:—

> "Swift though the words, the pen still swifter sped;
> The hand has finish'd ere the tongue has said."

While even if the Jews knew nothing of shorthand, the human memory, as we have already noted, was then developed to a degree of which we have no conception. Now, whether transmitted by memory or by notes, this address of St. Stephen bears proofs of the truthfulness of the reporter in the mistakes it contains. A man anxious for the reputation of his hero would have corrected them, as parliamentary reporters are accustomed to make the worst speeches readable, correcting evident blunders, and improving the grammar. The reporter of St. Stephen's words, on the contrary, gave them to us just as they were spoken. But then, I may be asked, how do you account for St. Stephen's mistake? What explanation can you offer? My answer is simple and plain enough. I have no other explanation to offer except that they are mistakes such as a speaker, filled with his subject, and speaking to an excited and hostile audience, might naturally make; mistakes such as truthful speakers every day make in their ordinary efforts. Every man who speaks an extemporaneous discourse such as Stephen's was, full of references to past history, is liable to such errors. Even when the memory retains the facts most accurately, the tongue is apt to make such lapses. Let a number of names be mingled up together in a speech or sermon where frequent mention has to be made of one now and of another again, how easily in that case a speaker substitutes one for another. But it may be objected that it is declared of Stephen that he was "full of the Holy Ghost and wisdom," that "he was full of faith and power," and that his adversaries "were not able to resist the wisdom and the spirit with which he spake." But surely this might be said of able, devoted, and holy men at the present day, and yet no one would say that they were miraculously kept from the most trivial mistakes, and that their memories and tongues were so supernaturally aided that they were preserved from the smallest verbal inaccuracies. We are always inclined to reverse the true scientific method of enquiry, and to form notions as to what inspiration must mean, instead of asking what, as a matter of fact, inspiration did mean and involve in the case of the Bible heroes. People when they feel offended by these mistakes of St. Stephen prove that they really think that Christianity was quite a different thing in the apostolic days from what it is now, and that the words "full of the Holy Ghost" and the presence of the Divine Spirit meant quite a different gift and blessing then from what they imply at the present time. I look upon the mistakes in this speech in quite a different light. St. Luke, in recording them exactly as they took place, proves, not merely his honesty as a narrator, but he also has handed down to us a most important lesson. He teaches us to moderate our notions and to chasten our à priori expectations. He shows us we must come and study the Scriptures to learn what they mean by the gift and power of the Holy Spirit. St. Luke expressly tells us that Stephen was full of the Holy Ghost, and then proceeds to narrate certain verbal inaccuracies and certain slips of memory to prove to us that the presence of the Holy Ghost does not annihilate human nature, or supersede the exercise of the human faculties. Just as in other places we find Apostles like St. Peter or St. Paul spoken of as equally inspired, and yet the inspiration enjoyed by them did not destroy their human weakness and infirmities, and, full of the Holy Ghost as they were, St. Paul could wax wroth and engage in bitter dissension with Barnabas, his fellow-labourer; and St. Peter could fall into hypocrisy against which his brother Apostle had publicly to protest. It is wonderful how liable the mind is, in matters of religion, to embrace exactly the same errors age after age, manifesting themselves in different shapes. Men are ever inclined to form their theories beforehand, and then to test God's actions and the course of His Providence by those theories, instead of reversing the order, and testing their theories by facts as God reveals them. This error about the true theory of inspiration and the gifts of the Holy Ghost which Protestants have fallen into is exactly the same as two celebrated mistakes, one in ancient, the other in modern times. The Eutychian heresy was very celebrated in the fifth century. It split the Eastern Church into two parts, and prepared the way for the triumph of Mahometanism. It fell, too, into this same error. It formed an *à priori* theory of God and His nature. It determined that it was impossible for the nature of Deity to be united to a nature which could feel hunger and thirst and weakness, because that God cannot be affected by any human weakness or wants. It denied, therefore, the real humanity of the Lord Jesus Christ and the reality of His human life and actions; teaching that His human body was not real, but merely a phenomenal or apparent one, and then explaining away all the statements and facts of Gospel history which seemed to them to conflict with their own private theory. In the West we have had ourselves experience of the same erroneous method of argument. The adherents of the Church of Rome argue for the infallibility of the Pope in the same way. They dilate on the awful importance of religious truth, and the fearful consequences of a mistake in such matters. Hence they conclude that it is only natural and fitting that a living, speaking, teaching, infallible guide should be appointed by God to direct the Church, and thence they conclude the infallibility of the Pope; a method of argument which has been amply exposed by Dr. Salmon in his work on the Infallibility of the Church. The Roman Catholics form their theory first, and when they come to facts which conflict with their theory, they deny them or explain them away in the most extraordinary manner.

Protestants themselves, however, are subject to the same erroneous methods. They form a theory about the Holy Ghost and His operations. They conclude, as is true, that He is Himself right, and just, and true in all His doings, and then they conclude that all the men whom He chose in the earliest age of the Church, and who are mentioned in Scripture as endued with His grace, must have been as free from every form of error as the Holy Spirit Himself. They thus fashion for themselves a mere *à priori* theory like the Eutychian and the Romanist, and then, when they apply their theory to passages like St. Stephen's speech, they feel compelled to deny facts and offer forced explanations, and to reject God's teaching as it is embodied in the divinely taught lessons of history. Let us be honest, fearless students of the Scriptures. St. Stephen was full of the Holy Ghost, and as such his great, broad, spiritual lessons were taught by the Spirit, and commend themselves as Divine teaching to every Christian heart. But these lessons were given through human lips, and had to be conveyed through human faculties, and as such are not free from the imperfections which attach themselves to everything human here below. Surely it is just the same still. God the Holy Ghost dwells with His people as of old. There are men even in this age of whom it still may be said, that in a special sense "they are full of the Holy Ghost," a blessing granted in answer to faithful prayer and devout communion and a life lived closely with God. The Holy Spirit speaks through them and in them. Their sermons, even on the simplest topics, speak with power, they teem with spiritual unction, they come home with conviction to the human conscience. Yet surely no one would dream of saying that these men are free from slips of speech and lapses of memory in their extemporaneous addresses, or in their private instructions, or in their written letters, because the Holy Ghost thus proves His presence and His power in His people as of old. The human heart and conscience easily and at once distinguish between that which is due to human weakness and what to Divine grace, according to that most pregnant saying of an Apostle himself gifted above all others, "We have this treasure in earthen vessels, that the excellency of the power may be of God and not of us." This view may be startling to some persons who have been accustomed to look to the Bible as some persons look to the Pope, as an oracle which will give them infallible guidance on every topic without the exercise of any thought or intelligence on their own part. Yet it is no original or novel notion of my own, but one that has been luminously set forth by a devout expositor of Scripture, dealing with this very passage many years ago. Dr. Vaughan, in his lectures on the Acts, preaching at Doncaster when vicar of that place, thus states his conclusions on this point:—"Now I will address one earnest word to persons who may have noticed with anxiety in this chapter, or who may have heard it noticed by others in a tone of cavil or disbelief, that in one or two minor points the account here given of Jewish history seems to vary from that contained in the narrative of the Old Testament. For example, the history in the book of Genesis tells us that the burying-place bought by

Abraham was in Mamre or Hebron, not at Sychem; and that it was bought by him of Ephron the Hittite, Jacob (not Abraham) being the purchaser of the ground at Shechem of the sons of Hamor, Shechem's father. My friends, can you really suppose that a difference of this nature has anything to do, this way or that, with the substantial truth of the gospel revelation? I declare to you that I would not waste the time in endeavouring (if I was able) to reconcile such a variance. It is to be regretted that Christian persons, in their zeal for the literal accuracy of our Holy Book, have spoken and written as if they thought that anything could possibly depend upon such a question. We all know how easy it is to get two witnesses in a court of justice to give their stories of an occurrence in the same words. We know also how instant is the suspicion of falsehood which that formal coincidence of statement brings upon them. Holy Scripture shows what I may indeed call a noble superiority to all such uniformity. Each book of our Bible is an independent witness; shown to be so, not least, by verbal or even actual differences on some trifling points of detail. And they who drink most deeply at the fountain head of Divine truth learn to estimate these things in the same manner; to feel what we might describe as a lordly disdain for all infidel objections drawn from this sort of petty, paltry, cavilling, carping, creeping criticism. Let our faith at last, God helping us, be strong enough and decided enough to override a few or a multitude of such objections. We will hear them unmoved; we will fearlessly examine them; if we cannot resolve them, then, in the power of a more majestic principle, we will calmly turn from them and pass them by. What we know not now, we may know hereafter; and if we never know we will believe still." These are wise words, very wholesome, very practical, and very helpful in this present age.

III. Let us briefly gather yet another lesson from this passage. The declaration of the Church's catholicity and the universal nature of Christian worship contained in verses 47-50 deserve our attention. What did St. Stephen say?—"But Solomon built Him a house. Howbeit the Most High dwelleth not in houses made with hands; as saith the prophet, The heaven is My throne, and the earth the footstool of My feet; what manner of house will ye build Me? saith the Lord; or what is the place of My rest? Did not My hand make all these things?" These words must have sounded as very extraordinary and very revolutionary in Jewish ears, because they most certainly struck at the root of the exclusive privilege claimed for Jerusalem, that it was the one place upon earth where acceptable worship could be offered, and where the Divine presence could be manifested. It seems no wonder that they should have roused the Sanhedrin to the pitch of fury which ended in the orator's judicial murder. But these words have been at times pressed farther than Stephen intended. He merely wished to teach that

God's special and covenanted presence was not for the future to be limited to Jerusalem. In the new dispensation of the Messiah whom he preached, that special covenanted presence would be found everywhere. Where two or three should be gathered in Christ's name there would God's presence be found. These words of Stephen have sometimes been quoted as if they sounded the death-knell of special places dedicated to the honour and glory of God, such as churches are. It is evident, however, that they have no such application. They sounded the death-knell of the exclusive privilege of one place, the temple, but they proclaimed the freedom which the Church has ever since claimed, and the Jewish Church of the dispersion, by the institution of synagogues, had led the way in claiming teaching that wherever true hearts and true worshippers are found, there God reveals Himself. But we must bear in mind a distinction. Stephen and the Apostles rejected the exclusive right of the Temple as the one place of worship for the world. They asserted the right to establish special places of worship throughout the world. They rejected the exclusive claims of Jerusalem. But they did not reject the right and the duty of God's people to assemble themselves as a collective body for public worship, and to realize Christ's covenanted presence. This is an important limitation of St. Stephen's statement. The absolute duty of public collective worship of the Almighty cannot be too strongly insisted upon. Men neglect it, and they support themselves by an appeal to St. Stephen's words, which have nothing to do with public worship more than with private worship. The Jews imagined that both public and private worship offered in the Temple had some special blessing attached, because a special presence of God was there granted. St. Stephen attacked this prejudice. His words must, however, be limited to the exact point he was then dealing with, and must not be pressed farther. Private prayer was binding on all God's people in the new and freer dispensation, and so, too, public worship has a special covenant blessing attached to it, and the blessing cannot be obtained if people neglect the duty. Public worship has been by Protestants looked at too much, as if it were only a means of their own edification, and thus, when they have thought that such edification could be as well or better attained at home, by reading a better sermon than they might chance to hear in the public congregation, they have excused their absence to their own conscience. But public worship is much more than a means of edification. It is the payment of a debt of worship, praise, and adoration due by the creature to the Creator. In that duty personal edification finds a place, but a mere accidental and subsidiary place. The great end of public worship is worship, not hearing, not edification even, though edification follows as a necessary result of such public worship when sincerely offered. The teaching of St. Stephen did not then apply to the erection of churches and buildings set apart for God's service, or to the claim made for public worship as an exercise with a peculiar Divine promise annexed. It simply protests against any attempt to localise the Divine presence to one special spot on earth, making it and it alone the centre of all religious interest. St. Stephen's words are indeed but a necessary result of the ascension of Christ as we have already expounded its expediency. Had Christ remained on earth, His personal presence would have rendered the Church a mere local and not an universal institution; just as the doctrine of Roman Catholics about the Pope as Christ's Vicar, and Rome as his appointed seat, has so far invested Rome with somewhat of the characteristics of Jerusalem and the Temple. But our Lord ascended up on high that the hearts and minds of His people might likewise ascend to that region where, above time, and sense, and change, their Master evermore dwells, as the loadstone which secretly draws their hearts, and guides their tempest-tossed spirits across the stormy waters of this world to the haven of everlasting rest.

# CHAPTER XVI
# THE FIRST CHRISTIAN MARTYRDOM

"And they cast him out of the city, and stoned him: and the witnesses laid down their garments at the feet of a young man named Saul. And they stoned Stephen, calling upon the Lord, and saying, Lord Jesus, receive my spirit. And he kneeled down, and cried with a loud voice, Lord, lay not this sin to their charge. And when he had said this, he fell asleep. And Saul was consenting unto his death." — Acts vii. 58-60; viii. 1.

The apology of Stephen struck the keynote of Christian freedom, traced out the fair proportions of the Catholic Church, while the actual martyrdom of Stephen taught men that Christianity was not only the force which was to triumph, but the power in which they were to suffer, and bear, and die. Stephen's career was a type of all martyr lives, and embraces every possible development through which Christ's Church and His servants had afterwards to pass, — obscurity, fame, activity, death, fixing high the standard for all ages.

I. We have in this passage, telling the story of that martyrdom, a vast number of topics, which have formed the subject-matter of Christian thought since apostolic times. We have already remarked that the earliest quotation from the Acts of the Apostles connects itself with this scene of Stephen's martyrdom. Let us see how this came about. One hundred and forty years later than Stephen's death, towards the close of the second century, the Churches of Vienne and Lyons were sending an account of the terrible sufferings through which they had passed during a similar sudden outburst of the Celtic pagans of that district against the Christians. The aged Pothinus, a man whose life and ministry touched upon the apostolic age, was put to death, suffering violence very like that to which St. Stephen was subjected, for we are told expressly by the historian Eusebius that the mob in its violence flung missiles at him. "Those at a distance, whatsoever they had at hand, every one hurled at him, thinking it would be a great sin if they fell short in wanton abuse against him."[132] The Church of Lyons, according to the loving usage of those early times, sent an account of all their trouble to the brethren in Asia and Phrygia, that they might read it at the celebration of the Eucharist for their own comfort and edification. They entered into great details, showing how wonderfully the power of God's grace was manifested, even in the weakest persons, sustaining their courage and enabling them to witness. The letter then goes on to note the marvellous humility of the sufferers. They would not allow any one to call them martyrs. That name was reserved to Jesus Christ, "the true and faithful Martyr," and to those who had been made perfect through death. Then, too, their charity was wonderful, and the epistle, referring to this very incident, tells how they prayed "like Stephen, that perfect martyr, Lord, impute not this sin to them." The memory of St. Stephen served to nerve the earliest Gallic martyrs, and it has ever since been bound up with the dearest feelings of Christians. The arrangements of the Calendar, with which we are all familiar, are merely an expression of the same feeling as that recorded in the second-century document we have just now quoted. Christmas Day and St. Stephen's Day are closely united,—the commemoration of Christ's birth is joined with that of the martyrdom of St. Stephen, because of a certain spiritual instinct. Christmas Day records the fact of the Incarnation, and then we have according to the order of the Calendar three holy days, St. Stephen's, St. John's, and the Holy Innocents' Day, which follow one another in immediate succession. Many persons will remember the explanation of an old commentator on the Calendar and Liturgy, of which Keble makes a very effective use in his hymns in the *Christian Year* set apart for those days. There are three classes of martyrs: one in will and deed like St. Stephen,— this is the highest class, therefore he has place next to Christ; another in will, but not in deed, like St. John the Divine, who was ready to suffer death but did not,—this is the second rank, therefore his place comes next St. Stephen; and lastly come the Holy Innocents, the babes of Bethlehem, martyrs in deed but not in will, and therefore in the lowest position. The Western Church, and specially the Church of Northern Europe, has always loved the Christmas season, with its cheerful fires, its social joys, its family memories; and hence, as it was in the Church of the second century, so with ourselves, none has a higher or dearer place in memory, doubtless largely owing to this conjunction, than the great proto-martyr. Men have delighted, therefore, to trace spiritual analogies and relationships between Stephen and Christ; fanciful perhaps some of them are, but still they are devout fancies, edifying fancies, fancies which strengthen and deepen the Divine life in the soul. Thus they have noted that Christmas Day and St. Stephen's Day are both natal days. In the language of the ancient Church, with its strong realizing faith, men spoke of a saint's death or martyrdom as his *dies natalis*. This is, indeed, one of the many traces of primitive usage which the Church of Rome has preserved, like a fly fixed in amber, petrified in the midst of her liturgical uses. She has a Martyrology which the ordinary laity scarcely ever see or use, but which is in daily use among the clergy and the various ecclesiastical communities connected with that Church. It is in the Latin tongue, and is called the *Martyrologium Romanum*, giving the names of the various saints whose memories are celebrated upon each day throughout the year, and every such day is duly styled the natal or birthday of the saint to whom it is appropriated. The Church of Rome retains this beautiful custom of the primitive Church, which viewed the death-day of a saint as his birthday into the true life, and rejoiced in it accordingly. That life was not, in the conception of the primitive believers, a life of ghosts and shadows. It was the life of realities, because it was the life of eternity, and therefore the early Christians lived for it, they longed for it, and counted their entrance upon it their true natal or birthday. The Church brought the two birthdays of Christ and Stephen into closest union, and men saw a beautiful reason for that union, teaching that Christ was born into this lower world in order that Stephen might be born into the heavenly world. The whole of that dreadful scene enacted at Jerusalem was transformed by the power of that beautiful conception. Stephen's death was no longer a brutal murder; faith no longer saw the rage, the violence, the crushed body, the mangled and outraged humanity. The birthday of Jesus Christ, the Incarnation of the Master, transfigured the death-scene of the servant, for the shame and sufferings were changed into peace and glory; the execrations and rage of the mob became angelic songs, and the missiles used by them were fashioned into messengers of the Most High, ushering the faithful martyr through a new birth into his eternal rest. Well would it be for the Church at large if she could rise to this early conception more frequently than she commonly does. Men did not then trouble themselves about questions of assurance, or their Christian consciousness. These topics and ideas are begotten on a lower level, and find sustenance in a different region. Men like Stephen and the martyrs of Vienne and Lyons lived in the other world; it was the world of all their interests, of all their passionate desires, of all their sense of realities. They lived the supernatural life, and they did not trouble themselves with any questions about that life, no more than a man in sound physical health and spirits cares to discuss topics dealing with the constitution of the life which he enjoys, or to debate such unprofitable questions as, How do I know that I exist at all? Christians then knew and felt they lived in God, and that was enough for them. We have wandered far enough afield, however; let us retrace our steps, and seek to discover more in detail the instruction for the life of future ages given us in this first martyr scene.

II. We have brought before us the cause of the sudden outburst against Stephen. For it was an outburst, a popular commotion, not a legal execution.

We have already explained the circumstances which led the Sanhedrin to permit the mob to take their own course, and even to assist them in doing so. Pilate had departed; the imperial throne too was vacant in the spring or early summer of the year 37; there was an interregnum when the bonds of authority were relaxed, during which the Jews took leave to do as they pleased, trusting that when the bonds were again drawn tight the misdeeds of the past and the irregularities committed would be forgotten and forgiven. Hence the riot in which Stephen lost his life. But what roused the listeners—Sanhedrists, elders, priests, and people alike—to madness? They heard him patiently enough, just as they afterwards heard his successor Paul, till he spoke of the wider spiritual hope. Paul, as his speech is reported in the twenty-second chapter, was listened to till he spoke of being sent to the Gentiles. Stephen was listened to till he spoke of the free, universal, spiritual character of the Divine worship, tied to no place, bounded by no locality. Then the Sanhedrin waxed impatient, and Stephen, recognising with all an orator's instinct and tact that his opportunity was over, changes his note—charging home upon his hearers the same spirit of criminal resistance to the leadings of the Most High as their fathers had always shown. The older Jews had ever resisted the Holy Ghost as He displayed His teaching and opened up His purposes under the Old Dispensation; their descendants had now followed their example in withstanding the same Divine Spirit manifested in that Holy One of whom they had lately been the betrayers and murderers. It is scarcely any wonder that such language should have been the occasion of his death. How exactly he follows the example of our Saviour! Stephen used strong language, and so did Jesus Christ. It has even been urged of late years that our Lord deliberately roused the Jews to action, and hastened His end by His violent language of denunciation against the ruling classes recorded in the twenty-third chapter of St. Matthew. There is, however, a great lesson of eternal significance to be derived from the example of St. Stephen as well as of our Lord. There are times when strong language is useful and necessary. Christ's ordinary ministry was gentle, persuasive, mild. He did not strive nor cry, neither did any man hear His voice in the streets. But a time came when, persuasion having failed of its purpose, the language of denunciation took its place, and helped to work out in a way the Pharisees little expected the final triumph of truth. Stephen was skilful and gentle in his speech; his words must at first have sounded strangely flattering to their prejudices, coming from one who was accused as a traitor to his race and religion. Yet when the gentle words failed, stern denunciation, the plainest language, the keenest phrases,—"Stiff-necked and uncircumcised in heart and ears," "Betrayers and murderers of the Righteous One,"—prove that a Christian martyr then, and Christ's martyrs and witnesses of every age, are not debarred under certain circumstances from the use of such weapons. But it is hard to know when the proper time has come for their employment. The object of every true servant and witness of Christ will be to recommend the truth as effectually as possible, and to win for it acceptance. Some people seem to invert this course, and to think that it is unworthy a true follower of Christ to seek to present his message in an attractive shape. They regard every human art and every human motive or principle as so thoroughly bad that men should disregard and despise them. Human eloquence, or motives of policy and prudence, they utterly reject. Their principles lead some of them farther still. They reject the assistance which art and music and literature can lend to the cause of God, and the result is that men, specially as they grow in culture and civilisation, are estranged from the message of everlasting peace. Some people, with a hard, narrow conception of Christianity, are very responsible for the alienation of the young and the thoughtful from the side of religion through the misconceptions which they have caused. God has made the doctrines of the cross repugnant to the corrupt natural feelings of man, but it is not for us to make them repugnant to those good natural principles as well which the Eternal Father has implanted in human nature, and which are an echo of His own Divine self in the sanctuary of the heart. It is a real breach of charity when men refuse to deal tenderly in such matters with the lambs of Christ's flock, and will not seek, as St. Stephen and the apostles did, to recommend God's cause with all human skill, enlisting therein every good or indifferent human motive. Had St. Stephen thought it his duty to act as some unwise people do now, we should never have had his immortal discourse as a model for faithful and skilful preaching. We should merely have had instead the few words of vigorous denunciation with which the address closed. At the same time the presence of these stern words proves that there is a place for such strong language in the work of the Christian ministry. There is a time and place for all things, even for the use of strong language. The true teacher will seek to avoid giving unnecessary offences, but offence sharp and stern may be an absolute duty of charity when prejudice and bigotry and party spirit are choking the avenues of the soul, and hindering the progress of truth. And thus John the Baptist may call men a generation of vipers, and Paul may style Elymas a child of the devil, and Christ may designate the religious world of His day as hypocrites; and when occasion calls we should not hesitate to brand foul things with plain names, in order that men may be awakened from that deadly torpor into which sin threatens to fling them. The use of strong language by St. Stephen had its effect upon his listeners. They were sawn asunder in their hearts, they gnashed their teeth upon the martyr. His words stirred them up to some kind of action. The Gospel has a double operation, it possesses a twofold force—the faithful teaching of it cannot be in vain. To some it will be the savour of life unto life, to others the savour of death unto death. Opposition may be indeed unwisely provoked. It may be the proof to us of nothing else save our own wilfulness, our own folly and imprudence. But if Christian wisdom be used, and the laws of Christian charity duly observed, then the spirit of opposition and the violence of rage and persecution prove nothing else to the sufferers than that God's word is working out His purposes, and bringing forth fruit though it be unto destruction.

III. Again, the locality, the circumstances, and the surroundings of Stephen's martyrdom deserve a brief notice. The place of his execution is pointed out by Christian tradition, and that tradition is supported by the testimony of Jewish custom and of Jewish writings. He was tried in the Temple precincts, or within sight of it, as is manifest from the words of the witnesses before the council, "He ceaseth not to speak against *this* holy place. We have heard him say that this Jesus of Nazareth shall destroy *this* place." The mob then rushed upon him. Under ordinary circumstances the Roman garrison stationed in the neighbouring town of Antonia, which overlooked the temple, would have noticed the riot, and have hastened to intervene, as they did many years after, when St. Paul's life was threatened in a similar Jewish outburst. But the political circumstances, as we have already shown, were now different.[133] Roman authority was for the moment paralysed in Jerusalem. People living at great centres such as Rome once was, or London now is, have no idea how largely dependent distant colonies or outlying districts like Judæa are upon personal authority and individual lives. In case of a ruler's death the action of the officials and of the army becomes necessarily slow, hesitating; it loses that backbone of energy, decision, and vigour which a living personal authority imparts. The decease of the Roman Emperor synchronising with the recall of Pontius Pilate must have paralysed the action of the subordinate officer then commanding at Antonia, who, unaware what turn events might take, doubtless thought that he was safe in restraining himself to the guardianship and protection of purely Roman interests.

The scene of Stephen's murder is sometimes located in the Valley of Jehoshaphat, near the brook Kedron, under the shadow of Olivet, and over against the Garden of Gethsemane. To that spot the gate of Jerusalem, called the Gate of St. Stephen, now leads.[134] Another tradition assigns the open country north-east of Jerusalem, on the road to Damascus and Samaria, as the place consecrated by the first death suffered for Jesus Christ. It is, however, according to the usual practice of Holy Scripture to leave this question undecided, or rather completely disregarded and overlooked. The Scriptures were not written to celebrate men or places, things temporary and transient in themselves, and without any bearing on the spiritual life.

The Scriptures were written for the purpose of setting forth the example of devotion, of love, and of sanctity presented by its heroes, and therefore it shrouds all such scenes as that of Stephen's martyrdom in thickest darkness. There is as little as possible of what is merely local, detailed, particular about the Scriptures. They rise into the abstract and the general as much as is consistent with being a historical narrative. Perhaps no spot in the world exhibits more evident and more abundant proofs of this Divine wisdom embodied in the Scriptures than this same city of Jerusalem as we now behold it. What locality could be more dear to Christian memory, or more closely allied with Christian hope, than the Holy Places, as they are emphatically called—the Church of the Holy Sepulchre and its surroundings? Yet the contending struggles of Roman Catholics, Greeks, and Armenians have made the whole subject a reproach and disgrace, and not an honour to the Christian name, showing how easily strife and partisanship and earthly passions enter in and usurp the ground which is nominally set apart for the honour of Christ Jesus. It is very hard to keep the spirit of the world out of the most sacred seasons or the holiest localities.

Stephen is hurried by the mob to this spot outside the Holy City, and then they proceed in regular judicial style so far as their fury will allow them. Dr. John Lightfoot, in his great work *Horæ Hebraicæ*, dealing with this passage, notes how we can trace in it the leading ideas and practices of Jewish legal processes. The Sanhedrin and their supporters dragged St. Stephen out of the city because it was the law as laid down in Lev. xxiv. 14—"Bring forth him that hath cursed without the camp." The Jews still retained vivid memories of their earlier history, just as students of sociology and ethnology still recognise in our own practices traces of ancient pre-historic usages, reminiscences of a time, ages now distant from us, when our ancestors lived the savage life in lands widely separated from our modern homes. So did the Jews still recognise the nomad state as their original condition, and even in the days of our Saviour looked upon Jerusalem as the camp of Israel, outside of which the blasphemer should be stoned.

Lightfoot then gives the elaborate ceremonial used to insure a fair trial, and the re-consideration of any evidence which might turn up at the very last moment. A few of the rules appointed for such occasions are well worth quoting, as showing the minute care with which the whole Jewish order of execution was regulated: "There shall stand one at the door of the Sanhedrin having a handkerchief in his hand, and an horse at such a distance as it was only within sight. If any one therefore say, I have something to offer on behalf of the condemned person, he waves the handkerchief, and the horseman rides and calls the people back. Nay, if the man himself say, I have something to offer in my own defence, they bring him back four or five times one after another, if it be a thing of any moment he has to say." I doubt, adds Lightfoot, they hardly dealt so gently with the innocent Stephen. Lightfoot then describes how a crier preceded the doomed man proclaiming his crime, till the place of execution was reached; where, after he was stripped of his clothes, the two witnesses threw him violently down from a height of twelve feet, flinging upon him two large stones. The man was struck by one witness in the stomach, by the other upon the heart, when, if death did not at once ensue, the whole multitude lent their assistance. Afterwards the body was suspended on a tree. It will be evident from this outline of Lightfoot's more prolonged and detailed statement that the leading ideas of Jewish practice were retained in St. Stephen's case; but as the execution was as much the act of the people as of the Sanhedrin, it was carried out hurriedly and passionately. This will account for some of the details left to us. We usually picture to ourselves St. Stephen as perishing beneath a deadly hail of missiles, raised upon him by an infuriated mob, before whom he is flying, just as men are still maimed or killed in street riots; and we wonder therefore when or where St. Stephen could have found time to kneel down and commend his spirit to Christ, or to pray his last prayer of Divine charity and forgiveness under such circumstances as those we have imagined. The Jews, however, no matter how passionate and enraged, would have feared to incur the guilt of murder had they acted in this rough-and-ready method. The witnesses must first strike their blows, and thus take upon themselves the responsibility for the blood about to be shed if it should turn out innocent. The culprits, too, were urged to confess their sin to God before they died. Stephen may have taken advantage of this well-known form to kneel down and offer up his parting prayers, which displaying his steadfast faith in Jesus only stirred up afresh the wrath of his adversaries, who thereupon proceeded to the last extremities.[135]

Stephen's death was a type of the vast majority of future martyrdoms, in this among other respects: it was a death suffered for Christ, just as Christ's own death was suffered for the world at large, and that under the forms of law and clothed with its outward dignity. Christianity proclaims the dignity of law and order, and supports it—teaches that the magistrate is the minister of God, and that he does a divinely-appointed work; but Christianity does not proclaim the infallibility of human laws or of human magistrates.[136] Christianity does not teach that any human law or human magistrate can dictate to the individual conscience, or intrude itself into the inner temple of the soul. Christianity indeed has, by a long and bitter experience, taught the contrary, and vindicated the rights of a free conscience, by patiently suffering all that could be done against it by the powers of the world assuming the forms and using the powers of law. Christians, I say, have taught the dignity of law and order, and yet they have not hesitated to resist and overturn bad laws, not however so much by active opposition as by the patient suffering of all that fiendish cruelty and lust could devise against the followers of the Cross. Just as it was under the forms of law that our Saviour died and Stephen was executed, and Peter and Paul passed to their rest, so was it under the same forms of law that the primitive Church passed through those ten great persecutions which terminated by seating her on the throne of the Cæsars. Law is a good thing. The absence of law is chaos. The presence of law, even though it be bad law, is better than no law at all. But the individual Christian conscience is higher than any human law. It should yield obedience in things lawful and indifferent. But in things clearly sinful the Christian conscience will honour the majesty of law by refusing obedience and then by suffering patiently and lovingly, as Stephen did, the penalty attached to conscientious disobedience.

IV. Let us now briefly notice the various points of interest, some of them of deep doctrinal importance, which gather round St. Stephen's death. We are told, for instance, that the martyr, seeing his last hour approaching, "looked up steadfastly into heaven, and saw the glory of God, and Jesus standing on the right hand of God." Surely critics must have been sorely in want of objections to the historical truth of the narrative when they raised the point that Stephen could not have looked up to heaven because he was in a covered chamber and could not have seen through the roof! This is simply a carping objection, and the expression used about St. Stephen is quite in keeping with the *usus loquendi* of Scripture. In the seventeenth of St. John, and at the first verse, we read of our Lord that "lifting up His eyes to heaven" He prayed His great eucharistic prayer on behalf of His Apostles. He lifted His eyes to heaven though He was in the upper chamber at the time. The Scriptural idea of heaven is not that of the little child, a region placed far away above the bright blue sky and beyond the distant stars, but rather that of a spiritual world shrouded from us for the present by the veil of matter, and yet so thinly separated that a moment may roll away the temporary covering and disclose the world of realities which lies behind. Such has been the conception of the deepest minds and the profoundest teaching. St. Stephen did not need a keen vision and an open space and a clear sky, free from clouds and smoke, as this objection imagines. Had St. Stephen been in a dungeon and his eyes been blind, the spiritual vision might still have been granted, and the consolation and strength afforded which the sight of his ascended Lord vouchsafed. This view of heaven and the unseen world is involved in the very word revelation, which, in its original Greek shape, apocalypse, means simply an uncovering, a rolling away of something that was flimsy, temporary, and transient, that a more abiding and nobler thing may be seen. The roof, the pillars, the solid structure of the temple, the priests and Levites, the guards and listeners, all were part of the veil of matter which suddenly rolled away from Stephen's intensified view, that he might receive, as the martyrs of every age have received, the special assistance which the King of Martyrs reserves for the supreme hour of man's need. The vision of our Lord granted at this moment has its own teaching for us. We are apt to conjure up thoughts of the sufferings of the martyrs, to picture to ourselves a Stephen perishing under a shower of stones, an Ignatius of Antioch flung to the beasts, a Polycarp of Smyrna suffering at the stake, the victims of pagan cruelty dying under the ten thousand forms of diabolical cruelty subsequently invented; and then we ask ourselves, could we possibly have stood firm against such tortures? We forget the lesson of Stephen's vision. Jesus Christ did not draw back the veil till the last moment; He did not vouchsafe the supporting vision till the need for it had come, and then to Stephen, as to all His saints in the past, and to all His saints in the future, the Master reveals Himself in all His supporting and sustaining power, reminding us in our humble daily spheres that it is our part to do our duty, and bear such burdens as the Lord puts upon us now, leaving to Him all care and thought for the future, content simply to trust that as our day is so shall our grace and our strength be. Stephen's vision has thus a lesson of comfort and of guidance for those fretful souls who, not content with the troubles and trials of the present, and the help which God imparts to bear them, will go on and strive to ascertain how they are to bear imaginary dangers, losses, and temptations which may never come upon them.

Then, again, we have the final words of Stephen, which are full of important meaning, for they bear witness unto the faith and doctrine of the apostolic Church. They stoned Stephen, "calling upon the Lord, and saying, Lord Jesus, receive my spirit;" while again a few moments later he cried, "Lord, lay not this sin to their charge." The latter petition is evidently an echo of our Lord's own prayer on the cross, which had set up a high standard of Divine charity in the Church. The first martyr imitates the spirit and the very language of the Master, and prays for his enemies as Christ himself had done a short time before; while the other recorded petition, "Lord Jesus, receive my spirit," is an echo likewise of our Lord's, when He said, "Father, into Thy hands I commend My spirit." We note specially about these prayers, not only that they breathe the spirit of Christ Himself, but that they are addressed to Christ, and are thus evidences to us of the doctrine and practice of the early Church in the matter of prayer to our Lord. St. Stephen is the first distinct instance of such prayer, but the more closely we investigate this book of the Acts and the Epistles of St. Paul, the more clearly we shall find that all the early Christians invoked Christ, prayed to Him as one raised to a supernatural sphere and gifted with Divine power, so that He was able to hear and answer their petitions. St. Stephen prayed to Christ, and commended his soul to Him, with the same confidence as Christ Himself commended His soul to the Father. And such commendation was no chance expression, no exclamation of adoring love merely. It was the outcome of the universal practice of the Church, which resorted to God through Jesus Christ. Prayer to Christ and the invocation of Christ were notes of the earliest disciples. Saul went to Damascus "to bind all that called upon the name of Jesus" (ch. ix. 14). The Damascene Jews are amazed at the converted Saul's preaching of Jesus Christ, saying, "Is not this he that in Jerusalem made havoc of them which called on this name?" (ch. ix. 21). While again Rom. x. 12 and 1 Cor. i. 2 prove that the same custom spread forth from Jerusalem to the uttermost parts of the Church. The passage to which I have just referred in the Corinthian Epistle is decisive as to St. Paul's teaching at a much later period than St. Stephen's death, when the Church had had time to formulate its doctrines and to weigh its teaching. Yet even then, he was just as clear on this point as Stephen years before, addressing his Epistle to the Church of God at Corinth, "with all that call upon the name of the Lord Jesus Christ in every place;" while again, when we descend to the generation which came next after the apostolic age, we find, from Pliny's celebrated letter written to Trajan, describing the practices and ideas of the Christians of Bithynia in the earliest years of the second century, that it was then the same as in St. Paul's day. One of the leading features of the new sect as it appeared to an intelligent pagan was this: "They sang an hymn to Christ as God." St. Stephen is the earliest instance of such worship directly addressed to the Lord Jesus Christ, a practice which has ever since been steadily maintained in every branch of the Church of Christ. It has been denied, indeed, in modern times that the Church of England in her formularies gives a sanction to this practice, which is undoubtedly apostolical. A reference, however, to the collect appointed for the memorial day of this blessed martyr would have been a sufficient answer to this assertion, as that collect contains a very beautiful prayer to Christ, beseeching assistance, similar to that given to St. Stephen, amid the troubles of our own lives. The whole structure of all liturgies, and specially of the English liturgy, protests against such an idea. The Book of Common Prayer teems with prayer to Jesus Christ. The Te Deum is in great part a prayer addressed to Him; so is the Litany, and so are collects like the prayer of St. Chrysostom, the Collect for the First Sunday in Lent, and the well-known prayer for the Third Sunday in Advent—"O Lord Jesu Christ, who at Thy first coming didst send Thy messenger to prepare Thy way."[137] The Eastern Church indeed addresses a greater number of prayers to

Christ directly. The Western Church, basing itself on the promise of Christ, "Whatsoever ye shall ask the Father in My Name, He will give it you," has ever directed the greater portion of her prayers to the Father through the Son; but the few leading cases just mentioned, cases which are common to the whole Western Church, Reformed or unreformed, will prove that the West also has followed primitive custom in calling upon the name and invoking the help of the Lord Jesus Himself. And then when Stephen had given us these two lessons, one of faith, the other of practice; when he had taught us the doctrine of Christ's divinity and the worship due to Him, and the practice of Christian charity and the forgiving spirit which flows forth from it, even towards those who have treated His servants most cruelly, then Stephen "fell asleep," the sacred writer using an expression for death indicative of the new aspect which death had assumed through Christ, and which henceforth gave the name of cemeteries to the last resting-places of Christian people.

V. The execution of St. Stephen was followed by his funeral. The bodies of those that were stoned were also suspended on a tree, but there was no opposition to their removal, as afterwards in the great persecutions. The pagans, knowing that Christians preached the doctrine of the resurrection of the body, strove to prove the absurdity of this tenet by reducing the body to ashes. The Christians, however, repeatedly proved that they entertained no narrow views on this point, and did not expect the resurrection of the identical elements of which the earthly body was composed. They took a broader and nobler view of St. Paul's teaching in the fifteenth of 1st Corinthians, and regarded the natural body as merely the seed out of which the resurrection body was to be developed. This is manifest from some of the stories told us by ancient historians concerning the Christians of the second century. The martyrs of Vienne and Lyons have been already referred to, and their sufferings described. The pagans knew of their doctrine of the resurrection of the body, and thought to defeat it by scattering the ashes of the martyrs upon the waters of the Rhone; but the narrative of Eusebius tells us how foolish was this attempt, as if man could thus overcome God, whose almighty power avails to raise the dead from the ashes scattered over the ocean as easily as from the bones gathered into a sepulchre. Another story is handed down by a writer of Antioch named John Malalas, who lived about A.D. 600, concerning five Christian virgins, who lived some seventy years earlier than these Gallic martyrs, and fell victims to the persecution which raged at Antioch in the days of the Emperor Trajan, when St. Ignatius perished. They were burned to death for their constancy in the faith, and then their ashes were mingled with brass, which was made into basins for the public baths. Every person who used the basins became ill, and then the emperor caused the basins to be formed into statues of the virgins, in order, as Trajan said, that "it may be seen that I and not their God have raised them up."[138]

But while it is plainly evident from the records of history that the earliest Christians had no narrow views about the relation between the present body of humiliation and the future body of glory, it is equally manifest that they paid the greatest attention to the mortal remains of their deceased friends, and permitted the fullest indulgence in human grief. In doing so they were only following the example of their Master, who sorrowed over Lazarus, and whose own mortal remains were cared for by the loving reverence of Nicodemus and Joseph of Arimathea. Christianity was no system of Stoicism. Stoicism was indeed the noblest form of Greek thought, and one which approached most closely to the Christian standpoint, but it put a ban upon human affection and feeling. Christianity acted otherwise. It flung a bright light on death, and illuminated the dark recesses of the tomb through the resurrection of Jesus Christ and the prospect for humanity which that resurrection opens up. But it did not make the vain attempt of Stoicism to eradicate human nature. Nay, rather, Christianity sanctified it by the example of Jesus Christ, and by the brief notice of the mourning of the Church for the loss of their foremost champion, St. Stephen, which we find in our narrative. Such a gratification of natural feeling has never been inconsistent with the highest form of Christian faith. There may be the most joyous anticipation as to our friends who have been taken from us joined with the saddest reflections as to our own bereavement. We may be most assured that our loss is the infinite gain of the departed, and for them we mourn not; but we cannot help feeling that *we* have sustained a loss, and for *our* loss we must grieve. The feelings of a Christian even now must be thus mixed, and surely much more must this have been the case when "devout men buried Stephen and made great lamentation over him."

The last results we note in this passage of Stephen's death are twofold. Stephen's martyrdom intensified the persecution for a time. Saul of Tarsus was made for a while a more determined and active persecutor. His mental position, his intellectual convictions, had received a shock, and he was trying to re-establish himself, and quench his doubts, by intensifying his exertions on behalf of the ancient creed. Some of the most violent persecutions the Church has ever had to meet were set on foot by men whose faith in their own systems was deeply shaken, or who at times have had no faith in anything at all. The men whose faith had been shaken endeavoured, by their activity in defence of the system in which they once fully believed, to obtain an external guarantee and assurance of its truth; while the secret unbeliever was often the worst of persecutors, because he regarded all religions as equally false, and therefore looked upon the new teachers as rash and mischievous innovators.

The result then of Stephen's martyrdom was to render the Church's state at Jerusalem worse for the time. The members of the Church were scattered far and wide, all save the Apostles. Here we behold a notable instance of the protecting care of Providence over His infant Church. All save the Apostles were dispersed from Jerusalem. One might have expected that they would have been specially sought after, and would have been necessarily the first to flee. There is an early tradition, however, which goes back to the second century, and finds some support in this passage, that our Lord ordered the Apostles to remain in the city of Jerusalem for twelve years after the Ascension, in order that every one there might have an opportunity of hearing the truth.[139] His protecting hand was over the heads of the Church while the members were scattered abroad. But that same hand turned the apparent trial into the Church's permanent gain. The Church now, for the first time, found what it ever after proved to be the case. "They that were scattered abroad went about preaching the word." The Church's present loss became its abiding gain. The blood of the martyrs became the seed of the Church. Violence reacted on the cause of those who employed it, as violence—no matter how it may temporarily triumph—always reacts on those who use it, whether their designs be intrinsically good or bad; till, in a widely disseminated Gospel, and in a daily increasing number of disciples, the eye of faith learned to read the clearest fulfilment of the ancient declaration, "The wrath of man shall praise God, and the remainder of wrath shalt Thou restrain."[140]

# CHAPTER XVII
# SIMON MAGUS AND THE
# CONVERSION OF SAMARIA

"And Philip went down to the city of Samaria, and proclaimed unto them the Christ.... But there was a certain man, Simon by name, which beforetime in the city used sorcery, and amazed the people of Samaria, giving out that himself was some great one: to whom they all gave heed, from the least to the greatest, saying, This man is that power of God which is called Great." — Acts viii. 5, 9, 10.

The object of the earlier part of this book of the Acts is to trace the steady, gradual development of the Church among the Jews, the evolution, never ceasing for a moment, of that principle of true catholic and universal life which the Master implanted within her, and which never ceased working till the narrow, prejudiced, illiberal little company of Galileans, who originally composed the Church, became the emancipated Church of all nations. This process of development was carried on, as we have already pointed out, through the agency of the Hellenistic Jews, and specially of the deacons who were so intimately connected with that class. We have in the last few lectures surveyed the history of one deacon, St. Stephen; we are now led to the story of another, St. Philip. His activity, as described in the eighth chapter, runs upon exactly the same lines. St. Stephen proclaims the universal principles of the gospel; St. Philip acts upon these principles, going down to the city of Samaria, and preaching Christ there. The prominent position which the deacons had for the time taken is revealed to us by two notices. Philip leaves Jerusalem and goes to Samaria, where the power of the high priest and of the Sanhedrin does not extend, but would rather be violently resisted. Here he is safe for the time, till the violence of the persecution should blow over. And yet, though Philip has to leave Jerusalem, the Apostles remain hidden by the obscurity into which they had for a little fallen, owing to the supreme brilliancy of St. Stephen: "They were all scattered abroad except the Apostles." The deacons were obliged to fly, the Apostles could remain: facts which sufficiently show the relative positions the two classes occupied in the public estimation, and illustrate that law of the Divine working which we so often see manifesting itself in the course of the Church's chequered career, the last shall be first and the first last. God, on this occasion, as evermore, chooses His own instruments, and works by them as and how He pleases.

I. This reticence and obscurity of the Apostles may seem to us now somewhat strange, as it certainly does seem most strange how the Apostles could have remained safe at Jerusalem when all others had to fly. The Apostles naturally now appear to us the most prominent members of the Jerusalem, nay, farther, of the Christian Church throughout the world. But then, as we have already observed, one of the great difficulties in historical study is to get at the right point of view, and to keep ourselves at that point under very varying combinations of circumstances. We are apt to fling ourselves back, or, if the expression be allowed, to project ourselves backwards into the past, and to think that men must always have attributed the same importance to particular persons or particular circumstances as we do. We now see the whole course of events, and can estimate them, not according to any mere temporary importance or publicity they may have attained, but according to their real and abiding influence. Viewing the matter in this light, we now can see that the Apostles were much more important persons than the deacons. But the question is, not how we regard the Apostles and the deacons, but how did the Sanhedrin and the Jews of Jerusalem in Stephen's and Philip's time view these two classes. They knew nothing of the Apostles as such.[141] They knew of them simply as unlearned and ignorant men who had been once or twice brought before the Council. They knew of Stephen, and perhaps, too, of Philip, as cultured Grecian Jews, whose wisdom and eloquence and persuasive power they were not able to resist; and it is no wonder that in the eyes of the Sadducean majority, who then ruled the Jewish senate, the deacons should be specially sought out and driven away.

The action of the Apostles themselves may have conduced to this. Here let us recur to a thought we have already touched upon. We are inclined to view the Apostles as if the Spirit which guided them totally destroyed their human personality and their human feelings. We are apt to cherish towards the Apostles the same reverential but misleading feeling which the believers of the early Church cherished towards the prophets, and against which St. James clearly protested when he said, "Elijah was a man of like passions with ourselves." We are inclined to think of them as if there was nothing weak or human or mistaken about them, and yet there was plenty of all these qualities in their character and conduct. The Apostles were older than the deacons, and they were men of much narrower ideas, of a more restricted education. They had less of that facility of temper, that power of adaptation, which learning and travel combined always confer. They may have been somewhat suspicious too of the headlong course pursued by Stephen and his fellows. Their Galilean minds did not work out logical results so rapidly as their Hellenistic friends and allies. They had been slow of heart to believe with the Master. They were slow of heart and mind to work out principles and to grasp conclusions when taught by His servants and followers. The Apostles were, after all, only men, and they had their treasure in earthen vessels. Their inspiration, and the presence of the Spirit within their hearts, were quite consistent with intellectual slowness, and with mental inability to recognise at once the leadings of Divine Providence. It was just then the same as it has ever been in Church history. The older generation is always somewhat suspicious of the younger. It is slow to appreciate its ideas, hopes, aspirations, and it is well perhaps that the older generation is suspicious, because it thus puts on a drag which gives time for prudence, forethought, and patience to come into play. These may appear very human motives to attribute to the Apostles, but then we lose a great deal of Divine instruction if we invest the Apostles with an infallibility higher even than that which Roman Catholics attribute to the Pope. For them the Pope is infallible only when speaking as universal doctor and teacher, a position which some among them go so far as to assert he has never taken since the Church was founded, so that in their opinion the Pope has never yet spoken infallibly. But with many sincere Christians the Apostles were infallible, not only when teaching, but when thinking, acting, writing on the most trivial topics, or discoursing on the most ordinary subjects.

II. Let us now turn our attention to Philip and his work, and its bearing on the future history and development of the Church. Here, before we go any farther, it may be well to note how St. Luke gained his knowledge of the events which happened at Samaria. We do not pretend indeed, like some critics, to point out all the sources whence the sacred writers gathered their information. Any one who has ever attempted to write history of any kind must be aware how impossible it often is for the writer himself to trace the sources of his information after the lapse of some time. How much more impossible then must it be for others to trace the original sources whence the sacred or any other ancient writers derived their knowledge, when hundreds and even thousands of years have elapsed. Our own ignorance of the past is a very unsafe ground indeed on which to base our rejection of any ancient document whatsoever.

It is well, however, to note, where and when we can, the sources whence information may have been gained, and fortunately this book of the Acts supplies us with instruction on this very point. A quarter of a century later the same Saul who, doubtless, helped to make St. Philip fly on this occasion from Jerusalem, was dwelling for several days beneath his roof at Cæsarea.

He was then Paul the Apostle of the Gentiles, who bore in his own person many marks and proofs of his devotion to the cause which Philip had proclaimed and supported while Paul was still a persecutor. The story of the meeting is told us in the twenty-first chapter of this book. St. Paul was on his way to Jerusalem to pay that famous visit which led to his arrest, and, in the long run, to his visit to Rome and trial before Cæsar. He was travelling up to Jerusalem by the coast road which led from Tyre, where he landed, through Cæsarea, and thence to the Holy City. St. Luke was with him, and when they came to Cæsarea they entered into the house of Philip the Evangelist, with whom they abode several days. What hallowed conversations St. Luke must there have listened to! How these two saints, Paul and Philip, would go over the days and scenes long since past and gone! How they would compare experiences and interchange ideas; and there it was that St. Luke must have had abundant opportunities for learning the history of the rise of Christianity in Samaria which here he exhibits to us.

Let us now look a little closer at the circumstances of the case. The place where Philip preached has raised a question. Some have maintained that it was Samaria itself, the capital city, which Philip visited and evangelized. Others have thought that it was a city,—some indefinite city of the district Samaria, probably Sychar, the town where our Lord had taught the Samaritan woman. Some have held one view, some the other, but the Revised Version would seem to incline to the view that it was the capital city which St. Philip visited on this occasion, and not that city which our Lord Himself evangelized. It may to some appear an additional difficulty in the way of accepting Sychar as the scene of St. Philip's ministry, that our Lord's work and teaching some five years previously would, in that case, seem to have utterly vanished. Philip goes down and preaches Christ to a city which knew nothing of Him. How, some may think, could this have possibly been true, and how could such an impostor as Simon have carried all the people captive, had Christ Himself preached there but a few short years before, and converted the mass of the people to belief in Himself? Now I maintain that it was Samaria, the capital, and not Sychar, some miles distant, that Philip evangelized, but I am not compelled to accept this view by any considerations about Christ's own ministry and its results. Our Lord might have taught in the same city where Philip taught, and in the course of five years the effect of His personal ministry might have entirely vanished.

There is no lesson more plainly enforced by the gospel story than this, Christ's own personal ministry was a comparatively fruitless one. He taught the Samaritan woman, indeed, and the people of the city were converted, as they said, not so much by her witness as by the power of Christ's own words and influence. But then the Holy Ghost was not yet given, the Church was not yet founded, the Divine society which Christ, as the risen Saviour, was to establish, had not yet come into existence; and therefore work like that done at Samaria was a transient thing, passing away like the morning cloud or the early dew, and leaving not a trace behind. Christ came not to teach men a Divine doctrine, so much as to establish a Divine society, and, till this society was established, the work done even by Christ Himself was a fleeting and evanescent thing. The foundation of the Church as a society was absolutely necessary if the doctrine and teaching of Christ was to be preserved. The article of the creed, "I believe in the Holy Catholic Church," has been neglected, slighted, and undervalued by Protestants. I have heard even of avowed expositors of the Apostles' Creed who, when they came to this article, have passed it over with a hasty notice because it did not fit into their narrow systems. And yet here again the Supreme wisdom of the Divine plan has been amply vindicated, and the experience of the New Testament has shown that if there had not been a Church instituted by Christ, and established with Himself as its foundation, rock, and chief corner-stone, the wholesome doctrine and the supernatural teaching of Christ would soon have vanished. I am here indeed reminded of the words and experience of one of the greatest evangelists who have lived since apostolic times. John Wesley, when dealing with a cognate subject, wrote to one of his earliest preachers about the importance of establishing Methodist societies wherever Methodist preachers found access, and he proceeds to urge the necessity for doing so on precisely the same grounds as those on which we explain the failure of our Lord's personal ministry, so far at least as present results were concerned. Wesley tells his correspondent that wherever Methodist teaching alone has been imparted, and Methodist societies have not been founded as well, the work has been an utter failure, and has vanished away.

So it was with the Master, Christ Jesus. He bestowed His Divine instruction and imparted His Divine doctrine, but as the time for the outpouring of the Spirit and the foundation of the Church had not yet come, the total result of the personal work and labours of the Incarnate God was simply one hundred and twenty, or at most five hundred souls. It constitutes, then, to our mind no difficulty in the way of regarding Sychar as the scene of Philip's teaching, that Christ Himself may have laboured there a few years before, and yet that there should not have been a trace of His labours when St. Philip arrived. The Master might Himself have taught in a town, and yet His disciple's preaching a few years later might have been most necessary, because the Spirit was not yet given. The plain meaning, however, of the words of the Acts is that it was to the city of Samaria, the capital city, that Philip went; and it is most likely that to the capital city a character like Simon would have resorted, and not to any smaller town, as affording him the largest field for the exercise of his peculiar talents, just as afterwards we shall find, in the course of his history, that he resorted to the capital of the world, Rome itself, as the scene most effectual for his purposes.[142]

III. St. Philip went down, then, to Samaria and preached Christ there, and in Samaria he came across the first of those subtle opponents with whom the gospel has ever had to struggle,—men who did not directly oppose the truth, but who corrupted its pure morality and its simple faith by a human admixture, which turned its salutary doctrines into a deadly poison. Philip came to Samaria, and there he found the Samaritans carried away with the teaching and actions of Simon. The preaching of the pure gospel of Jesus Christ, and the exercise of true miraculous power, converted the Samaritans, and were sufficient to work intellectual conviction even in the case of the Magician. All the Samaritans, Simon included, believed and were baptized. This is the introduction upon the stage of history of Simon Magus, whom the earliest Church writers, such as Hegesippus, the father of Church history, who was born close upon the time of St. John, and flourished about the middle of the second century, and his contemporary Justin Martyr, describe as the first of those gnostic heretics who did so much in the second and third centuries to corrupt the gospel both in faith and practice. The writings of the second and third centuries are full of the achievements and evil deeds of this man Simon, which indeed are related by some writers with so much detail as to form a very considerable romance. Here, then, we find a corroborative piece of evidence as to the early date of the composition of the Acts of the Apostles. Had the Acts been written in the second century, it would have given us some traces of the second-century tradition about Simon Magus; but having been written at a very early period, upon the termination of St. Paul's first imprisonment, it gives us simply the statement about Simon Magus as St. Luke and St. Paul had heard it from the mouth of Philip the Evangelist. St. Luke tells us nothing more, simply because he had no more to tell about this first of the celebrated heretics. When we come to the second century Simon's story is told with much more embellishment. The main outlines are, however, doubtless correct. All Christian writers agree in setting forth that after the reproof which, as we shall see, Simon Peter the Apostle bestowed upon the magician, he became a determined opponent of the Apostles, especially of St. Peter, whose work he endeavoured everywhere to oppose and defeat. With this end in view he went to Rome, as Justin Martyr says, in the reign of Claudius Cæsar, and as other writers say, in the time of Nero.

There he successfully deceived the people for some time. We have early notices of his success in the Imperial city. Justin Martyr is a writer who came close upon the apostolic age. He wrote an Apology for the Christians, which we may safely assign to some year about 150 A.D. At that time he was a man in middle life, whose elder contemporaries must have been well acquainted with the history and traditions of the previous century. In that first Apology Justin gives us many particulars about Christianity and the early Church, and he tells us, concerning Simon Magus, that his teaching at Rome was so successful in leading the Roman people astray that they erected a statue in his honour, between the two bridges. It is a curious fact, and one, too, which confirms the accuracy of Justin, that in the year 1574 there was dug up on the very spot indicated by Justin, the island in the Tiber, a statue bearing the inscription described by Justin, "Semoni Sanco Deo Fidio." Critics, indeed, are now pretty generally agreed that this statue was the one seen by Justin, but that it was originally erected in honour of a Sabine deity, and not of the arch-heretic as the Apologist supposed; though there are some who think that the appeal of Justin to a statue placed before men's eyes, and about which many at Rome must have known all the facts, could not have been made on such mistaken grounds. It is not altogether safe to build theories or offer explanations based on our ignorance, and opposed to the plain, distinct statements of a writer like Justin, who was a contemporary with the events of which he speaks. It seems indeed a plausible explanation to say that Justin Martyr mistook the name of a Sabine deity for that of an Eastern heretic. But there may have been two statues and two inscriptions on the island, one to the heretic, another to the ancient Sabine god. Later writers of the second and third centuries improved upon Justin's story, and entered into great details of the struggles between Simon and the two Apostles, St. Peter and St. Paul, terminating in the death of the magician when attempting to fly up to heaven in the presence of the Emperor Nero. His death did not, however, put an end to his influence. The evil which he did and taught lived long afterwards. His followers continued his teaching and proved themselves active opponents of the truth, seducing many proselytes by the apparent depth and subtlety of their views. Such is the history of Simon Magus as it is told in Church history, but we are now concerned simply with the statements put forward in the passage before us.[143] There Simon appears as a teacher who led the Samaritans captive by his sorcery, which he used as the basis of his claim to be recognised as "that power of God which is called Great." Magic and sorcery have always more or less prevailed, and do still prevail, in the Eastern world, and have ever been used in opposition to the gospel of Christ, just as the same practices, under the name of Spiritualism, have shown themselves hostile to Christianity in Western Europe and in America. The tales of modern travellers in India and the East, respecting the wondrous performances of Indian jugglers, remind us strongly of the deeds of Jannes and Jambres who withstood Moses, and illustrate the sorcery which Simon Magus used for the deception of the Samaritans. The Jews, indeed, were everywhere celebrated at this period for their skill in magical incantations—a well-known fact, of which we find corroborative evidence in the Acts. Bar-Jesus, the sorcerer who strove to turn the proconsul of Cyprus from the faith, was a Jew (Acts xiii. 6-12). In the nineteenth chapter we find the seven sons of Sceva, the Jewish priest, exercising the same trade of sorcery; while, as is well known from references in the classical writers, the Jews at Rome were famous for the same practices.

These statements of writers sacred and secular alike have been confirmed in the present age. There has been a marvellous discovery of ancient documents in Egypt within the last twelve or fifteen years, which were purchased by the Austrian government and duly transferred to Vienna, where they have been investigated. They are usually called the Fayûm Manuscripts.[144] They contain some of the oldest documents now existing, and embrace among them large quantities of magical writings, with the Hebrew formulæ used by the Jewish sorcerers when working their pretended miracles. So wondrously does modern discovery confirm the statements and details of the New Testament!

It is not necessary now to discuss the question whether the achievements of sorcery and magic, either ancient or modern, have any reality about them, or are a mere clever development of sleight of hand, though we incline to the view which admits a certain amount of reality about the wonders performed, else how shall we account for the doings of the Egyptian magicians, the denunciations of sorcery and witchcraft contained in the Bible, as well as in many statements in the New Testament? A dry and cold age of materialism, without life and fire and enthusiasm, like the last century, was inclined to explain away such statements of the Scriptures. But man has now learned to be more distrustful of himself and the extent of his discoveries. We know so little of the spirit world, and have seen of late such strange psychological manifestations in connection with hypnotism, that the wise man will hold his judgment in suspense, and not hastily conclude, with the men of the eighteenth century, that possession with devils was only another name for insanity, and that the deeds of sorcerers were displays of mere unassisted human skill and subtlety.[145] As it was with the Jews, so was it with the Samaritans. They were indeed bitterly separated the one from the other, but their hopes, ideas, and faith were fundamentally alike. The relations between the Samaritans and the Jews were at the period of which we treat very like those which exist between Protestants and Roman Catholics in Ulster,—professing different forms of the same faith, yet regarding one another with bitterer feelings than if far more widely separated. So it was with the Jews and Samaritans; but the existing hostility did not change nature and its essential tendencies, and therefore as the Jews practised sorcery, so did Simon, who was a native of Samaria; and with his sorcery he ministered to the Messianic expectation which flourished among the Samaritans equally as among the Jews. The Samaritan woman testified to this in her conversation with our Lord, and as she was a woman of a low position and of a sinful character, her language proves that her ideas must have had a wide currency among the Samaritan people. "The woman saith unto Him, I know that Messiah cometh, which is called Christ: when He is come, He will declare unto us all things." Simon took advantage of this expectation, and gave himself out to be "that power of God which is called Great;" testifying by his assertion to the craving which existed all through the Jewish world for the appearance of the long-expected deliverer, a craving which we again find manifesting itself in the many political pretenders who sprang up in the regions of more orthodox Judaism, as Josephus amply shows. The world, in fact, and specially the world which had been affected with Jewish ideas and Jewish thought, was longing for a deeper teaching and for a profounder spiritual life than it had as yet known. It was athirst for God, yea, even for the living God; and when it could find nothing better, it turned aside and strove to quench the soul's desires at the impure fountains which magic and sorcery supplied.

IV. Philip the Evangelist came with his teaching into a society which acknowledged Simon as its guide, and his miracles at once struck the minds of the beholders. They were miracles worked, like the Master's, without any secret preparations, without the incense, the incantations, the muttered formulæ which accompanied the lying wonders of the magician. They formed a contrast in another direction too,—no money was demanded, no personal aims or low objects were served; the thorough unselfishness of the evangelist was manifest. Then, too, the teaching which accompanied the miracles was their best evidence. It was a teaching of righteousness, of holy living, of charity, of humility; it was transparently unworldly. It was not like Simon's, which gave out that he himself was some great one, and treated of himself alone; but it dealt with "the kingdom of God and the name of Jesus Christ;" and the teaching and the miracles, testifying the one to the other, came home to the hearts of the people, leading them captive to the foot of the Cross. It has often been a debated question whether miracles alone are a sufficient evidence of the truth of a doctrine, or whether the doctrine needs to be compared with the miracles to see if its character be worthy of the Deity. The teaching of the New Testament seems to be plainly this, that miracles, in themselves, are not a sufficient evidence. Our Lord warns His disciples that deceivers shall one day come working mighty signs and wonders, so as to lead astray, if it be possible, even the very elect; and He exhorts His disciples to be on their guard against them. But while miracles alone are no sufficient evidence of the truth of a doctrine, they were a very needful assistance to the doctrines of the gospel in the age and country when and where Christianity took its rise. Whether the sorcery and magic and wonders of Simon, and the other false teachers against whom the Apostles had to contend, were true or false, genuine or mere tricks, still they would have given the false teachers a great advantage over the preachers of the gospel, had the latter not been armed with real divine supernatural power which enabled them, as occasion required, to fling the magical performances completely into the shade. The miraculous operations of the Apostles seem to have been restricted in the same way as Christ restricted the working of His own supernatural power. The Apostles never worked miracles for the relief of themselves or of their friends and associates. St. Paul was detained through infirmity of the flesh in Galatia, and that infirmity led him to preach the gospel to the Galatian Celts. He did not, perhaps he could not, employ his miraculous power to cure himself, just as our Lord refused to use His miraculous power to turn stones into bread. St. Paul depended upon human skill and love for his cure, using probably for that purpose the medical knowledge and assistance of St. Luke, whom we find shortly afterwards in his company.[146] Miraculous power was bestowed upon the first Christian teachers, not for the purposes of display or of selfish gratification, but simply for the sake of God's kingdom and man's salvation.

And as it was with St. Paul so was it with his companions. Timothy was exhorted to betake himself to human remedies to cure his physical weakness, while when another apostolic man, Trophimus, was sick, he was left behind by the Apostle at Miletus till he should get well (2 Tim. iv. 20). Miracles were for the sake of unbelievers, not of believers, and for this purpose we cannot see how they could have been done without, under the circumstances in which the gospel was launched into the world. Man's nature had been so thoroughly corrupted, the whole moral atmosphere had been so permeated with wickedness, the whole moral tone of society had been so terribly lowered, that the Apostles might have come preaching the purest morality, the most Divine wisdom, and it would have fallen on ears so deaf, and eyes so blind, and hearts so seared and hardened, that it would have had no effect unless they had possessed miraculous power which, as occasion demanded, served to call attention to their teaching. But when the preliminary barriers had been broken down, and the miracles had fulfilled their purpose, then the preaching of the kingdom of God and the name of Jesus Christ did their work. Here again a thought comes forward on which we have already said a little. The subject matter of Philip's preaching is described in the fifth verse as Christ, "Philip went down to the city of

Samaria, and proclaimed unto them the Christ," and then in the twelfth verse it is expanded for us into "the kingdom of God and the name of Jesus Christ." These two subjects are united. The kingdom of God and the name of Jesus Christ. The Apostles taught no diluted form of Christianity. They preached the name of Jesus Christ, and they also taught a Divine society which He had established and which was to be the means of completing the work of Christ in the world. Our Lord Jesus Christ and His Apostles recognised the great truth, that a mere preaching of a philosophical or religious doctrine would have been of very little use in reforming the world. They therefore preached a Church which should be the pillar and ground of the truth, which should gather up, safeguard, and teach the truth whose principles the Apostles set forth. To put it in plain language, the Evangelist St. Philip must have taught the doctrine of a Church of Jesus Christ as well as of a doctrine of Jesus Christ. Had the doctrine of Jesus Christ been taught without and separate from the doctrine of a Church, the doctrine of Christ's person and character might have vanished, just as the doctrine of Plato or Aristotle or that of any of the great ancient teachers vanished. But Jesus Christ had come into the world to establish a Divine society, with ranks, gradations, and orderly arrangements; He had come to establish a kingdom, and they all knew then what a kingdom meant. For the Greek, Roman, or Jewish mind, a kingdom meant more even than it does for us. It meant in their conceptions a despotism where the king ordered and did just what he liked. The Romans, in fact, abominated the name king, and invented the term emperor instead, because for them the word king connoted what it does not connote for us, the possession and exercise of absolute power. Yet, for all this, the Apostles preached Christ as a King and His society as a kingdom, because in that new society which He had called into existence, the graces, the gifts, the offices of the society are totally dependent upon and entirely subservient to Jesus Christ alone.

How wondrously the life, the activity, the fervour and power of the Church would have been changed had this truth been always recognised. The Church of Jesus Christ, as regards its hidden secret life, is a despotism. It depends upon Christ alone. It depends not upon the State, not upon man, not upon wealth or position or earthly influences of any kind: it depends upon Christ alone. The Church has often forgot this secret of its strength. It has trusted in the arm of flesh, and has relied upon human patronage and power, and then it has grown, perhaps, in grandeur and importance as far as the world is concerned; but, as it has grown in one direction, it has lost in the other, and that the only direction worthy a Church's attention. The temptation to rely on the help of the world alone has assailed the Church in various ways. It assails individual Christians, it assails congregations, it assails the Church at large. All of them, whether individuals, congregations, or churches, are apt to imagine that power and prosperity consist in wealth, or worldly position, or the number of adherents, forgetting that Christ alone is the source of power to the Church or to individual souls, and that where He is wanting, no matter what may be the outward appearance, or the numerical increase or the political influence, there indeed all true life has departed.

V. The results of Philip's teaching and work in Samaria were threefold.

(1) The Samaritans believed Philip, and among the believers was Simon. There are some people who teach faith and nothing else, and imagine that if they lead men to exercise belief then the whole work of Christianity is done. This incident at the very outset of the Church's history supplies a warning against any such one-sided teaching. The Samaritans believed, and so did Simon the Magician, who had for long deceived them. The very same word is used here for the faith exercised by the Samaritans and by Simon, as we find used to describe the belief of the three thousand on the day of Pentecost, or of the Philippian jailer who accepted St. Paul's teaching amid all the terror of the earthquake and the opened prison. They were all intellectually convinced and had all accepted the Christian faith as a great reality. Intellectual faith in Christ is the basis on which a true living faith which works by love is grounded. A faith of the heart which is not based on a faith of the head is very much akin to a superstition. Of course we know that there are people whose faith is deep-rooted and fruitful who cannot state the grounds of their belief, but they are well aware that others can thus state it, that their faith is capable of being put into words and defended in argument. Intellectual faith in Christianity must ever be regarded as a gift of the Holy Ghost, according to that profound word of the Apostle, "No man can say, Jesus is Lord, but in the Holy Ghost." But intellectual faith in the truth and reality of Christ's mission may exist in a heart where there is no sense of sin and of spiritual want, and then belief in Christ avails nothing. There were cravings after righteousness and peace in Samaritan bosoms, but there was none in one heart, at least, and that heart was therefore unblessed. The results of St. Philip's work teach us that faith is not everything in the Christian life.

(2) Again we find that another result was, that the Samaritans were all baptized, including their arch-deceiver Simon. Philip, then, in the course of his preaching of Christ, must have told them of Christ's law of baptism. The preaching of the name of Jesus Christ and of the kingdom of God must have included a due setting forth of His laws and ordinances. We do no honour to Christ when we neglect any part of His revelation. If God has

revealed any doctrine or any practice or any sacrament, it must be of the very greatest importance. The mere fact of its revelation by Him makes it of importance, no matter how we, in our short-sighted wisdom, may think otherwise. Philip set forth therefore the whole counsel of God, and as the result all the Samaritans were baptized, including Simon; but then again, as Simon's case taught that faith by itself availed not to change the heart, so Simon's case teaches that baptism, neither alone nor in conjunction with intellectual faith, avails to convert the soul and purify the character. God offers His graces and His blessings, faith and baptism, but unless there be receptivity, unless there be consent of the will, and a thirst of the soul and a longing of the heart after spiritual things, the graces and gifts of the Spirit will be offered in vain.

(3) And then, lastly, the final and abiding result of Philip's work was, there was great joy in that city. They rejoiced because their souls had found the truth, which can alone satisfy the cravings of the human heart and minister a joy which leaves no sting behind, but is a joy pure and exhaustless. The joys of earth are always mixed, and the more mixed the more unsatisfying. The joy of a Christian soul which knows Christ and His preciousness, which has been delivered by Christ from deceit and impurity and vice, as these Samaritans had, and which feels and enjoys the new light thrown on life by Christ's revelations, that joy is a surpassing one, ravishing the soul, satisfying the intellect, purifying the life. There was great joy in that city, and no wonder, for as the poet has well sung, contrasting the "world's gay garish feast" with God's sacred consolations bestowed upon holy souls,—

> "Who, but a Christian, through all life
> That blessing may prolong?
> Who, through the world's sad day of strife,
> Still chant his morning song?

> "Such is Thy banquet, dearest Lord;
> O give us grace, to cast
> Our lot with Thine, to trust Thy word,
> And keep our best till last."[147]

# CHAPTER XVIII
# THE APOSTLES AND CONFIRMATION

"Now when the Apostles which were at Jerusalem heard that Samaria had received the word of God, they sent unto them Peter and John: who, when they were come down, prayed for them, that they might receive the Holy Ghost: for as yet He was fallen upon none of them: only they had been baptized into the name of the Lord Jesus. Then laid they their hands on them, and they received the Holy Ghost." — Acts viii. 14-18.

In the last lecture we noticed the work of Philip in Samaria, the present one will deal with the mission of the Apostles Peter and John to complete and perfect that work.

The story, as told in the sacred narrative, is full of instruction. It reveals the ritual of the apostolic Church, the development of its organization and practice, the spiritual lessons which the earliest gospel teachers imparted and the latest gospel teachers will find applicable. Philip converted the Samaritans and laid the basis of a Christian Church. Word was at once brought of this new departure to the Apostles at Jerusalem, because it was a new step, a fresh development which must have given a great shock to the strict Jewish feeling, which regarded the gospel as limited by the bounds of orthodox Judaism. The Apostles may have felt some surprise at the news, but they evidently must have acknowledged the Samaritans as standing on a higher level than the Gentiles, for they do not seem to have raised any such objections to their baptism as were afterwards urged against St. Peter when he preached to and baptized Cornelius. "Thou wentest in to men uncircumcised," was the objection of the Jerusalem Church urged against St. Peter as regards Cornelius. The Samaritans were circumcised, and therefore this objection did not apply. The Jews, indeed, of Judæa and of Galilee hated the Samaritans with a perfect hatred, but neither hatred nor love is ever guided by reason. Our feelings always outrun our judgment, and the judgment of the Jews compelled them to recognise the Samaritans as within the bounds of circumcision, and therefore the Apostles tolerated, or at least did not except against, the preaching of the gospel to the Samaritans, and their admission by baptism into the Messianic kingdom. It is a phenomenon we often see repeated in our own experience. A brother or a relation alienated is harder to be won and is more bitterly regarded than a total stranger with whom we may have quarrelled, though, at the same time, reason, perhaps even pride and self-respect and regard for consistency, compel us to recognise that he occupies a different position from that of a perfect stranger. The conversion of the Samaritans must be viewed as one of the divinely-appointed steps in the plan of human unification, one of the divinely-appointed actions gently leading to the final overthrow of the wall of partition between Jew and Gentile which the earlier chapters of this book trace for us. How beautiful the order, how steady and regular the progress, that is set before us! First we have the call of the strict Jews, then that of the Hellenistic Jews, next that of the Samaritans, and then the step was not a long one from the admission of the hated Samaritans to the baptism of the devout though uncircumcised Gentile, Cornelius. God does His work in grace, as in nature, by degrees. He teaches us that changes must come, and that each age of the Church must be marked by development and improvement; but He shows us here in His word how changes should be made,—not rashly, unwisely, impetuously, and therefore uncharitably, but gently, gradually, sympathetically, and with explanations abundantly vouchsafed to soothe the feelings and calm the fears of the weaker brethren. This method of the Divine government receives an illustration in this passage. God led the Church of the first age very gradually, and therefore we see the apostolic college steadily, though perhaps blindly and unconsciously, advancing on the road of progress and of Christian liberality.

We have in this section of primitive Church history a two-fold division: the action of the Apostles on one side, the attitude and conduct of Simon Magus on the other. Each division has quite distinct teaching. Let us in this chapter take note of the Apostles.

I. The Apostles who were at Jerusalem heard of the conversion of Samaria, and they at once sent thither Peter and John to supervise the work. The deacons had, for a time, appeared to supersede the Apostles before the world, but only in appearance. The Apostles retained the chief government in their own hands, though to the men of the time others seemed the more prominent workers. The Apostles gave free scope to the gifts entrusted to their brilliant subordinates, but none the less they felt their own responsibility as rulers of the Divine society, and never for a moment did they relinquish the authority over that society which God had entrusted to them. They felt that Christ had instituted an organized society with ranks and offices duly graduated, with officials—of whom they were themselves the chief—assigned to their appointed tasks, and never did they surrender to any man their divinely-given power and authority. Philip might preach in Samaria; but though he was successful in winning converts, the Apostles claimed the right of inspecting and controlling his labours. They successfully solved a problem which has often proved a very troublesome one. They combined the exercise of power with the free play of enthusiasm, and the result was that the enthusiasm was shielded from mistakes, and the power was vivified by the touch of enthusiasm and prevented from falling into that cold, heartless, ice-like thing which autocratic rule, in Church and State alike, has so often become. What a picture and guide we here behold for the Church of all ages! What a needed lesson is here taught! What errors and schisms would have been avoided throughout the long ages which have since elapsed, had the example of the apostolic Church been more closely followed, had power been more sympathetic with enthusiasm, and enthusiasm more loving, obedient, and submissive as regards authority!

The Apostles recognised their own responsibility and acted upon their own sense of authority, and they sent forth Peter and John to minister in Samaria and supply what was wanting as soon as they heard of the work done by St. Philip. The persons whom the college of Apostles thus despatched are worthy of notice, and have a direct bearing on some of the great theological and social problems of this age. They sent Peter and John. Peter, then, was the messenger of the Apostles, — the sent one, not the sender. We can find nothing of the supremacy of Peter in these early apostolic days of which men began to dream in later years. The supreme authority in the Church and the burden of the Christian ministry were laid upon the twelve Apostles as a whole, and they, as a body of men entrusted with co-equal power, exercised their functions. They knew nothing of Peter as the prince of the Apostles; nay, rather, when occasion demanded, they sent Peter as well as John as their delegates. The choice of these two men, just as their previous activity, depended again upon spiritual grounds, upon their love, their zeal, their Christian experience, not upon any official privilege or position which they enjoyed above the other Apostles.

Surely in this view again the Acts of the Apostles may be regarded as a mirror of all Church history. The pretended supremacy of St. Peter above his brethren has been the ground on which the claim of Roman supremacy over all other Christian Churches has been urged. That claim has been backed up by forgeries like the False Decretals, where fictitious letters of Popes dating from the first century downwards have been used to support the papal assertions. But plain men need not go into abstruse questions of Church history, or into debates upon disputed texts. We have one undoubted Church history, admitted by all parties who profess and call themselves Christians. That history is the Acts of the Apostles, and when we examine it we can find nothing about St. Peter, his life or his actions, answering in the remotest degree to that imperial and absolute authority which the papacy claims in virtue of its alleged descent from that holy Apostle. The Acts knows of St. Peter sometimes as the leader and spokesman of the Apostles, at other times as their delegate, but the Acts knows nothing and hints nothing of St. Peter as the ruler, the prince, the absolute, infallible guide of his fellow Apostles and of the whole Church.

Peter and John were the persons despatched as the apostolic delegates to complete the work begun by Philip. We can see spiritual reasons which may have led to this choice. Peter and John, with James his brother, had been specially favoured with Christ's personal communications, they had been admitted into His most intimate friendship, and therefore they were spiritually eminent in the work of Christ, and peculiarly fitted to do work like that which awaited them in Samaria,—pointing Christian men to the great truth, that eminence in Christ's Church and cause will evermore depend, not upon official position or hierarchical or ministerial authority, but upon spiritual qualifications and the vigour of the interior life. How wonderfully has the prophecy involved in the pre-eminence of Peter, James, and John been fulfilled. When we look back over the ages of Christian labour which have since elapsed, whose are the foremost names? Whose fame as Christian workers is the greatest? Not popes or princes, or bishops of great cities, but an Augustine, the bishop of an obscure African see; an Origen, a presbyter of Alexandria; a Thomas à Kempis whom no man knows; or presbyters like John Wesley, or George Herbert, or Fletcher of Madeley, or John Keble;—men like them, holy and humble of heart, obscure in station or in scenes of labour, they have lived much with God and they have gained highest places in the saintly army, because they were specially the friends of Jesus Christ. The world knew nothing of them, and the men of affairs and the children of time, whose thoughts were upon rank, and place, and titles, knew nothing of them; and such men had their reward perhaps, they gained what they sought; but the despised ones of the past have had their reward as well, for their names have now become as ointment poured forth, whose sweet fragrance has filled the whole house of the Lord.

II. And now why were Peter and John sent to Samaria from Jerusalem? They were doubtless sent to inspect the work, and see whether the apostolic approval could be given to the step of evangelizing the Samaritans. They had to form a judgment upon it; for no matter how highly we may rate the inspiration of the Apostles, it is clear that they had to argue, debate, think, and balance one side against another just like other people. The inspiration they enjoyed did not save them the trouble of thinking and the consequent danger of disputation; it did not force them to adopt a view, else why the debates we read of concerning the baptism of Cornelius, or the binding character of circumcision? It is clear, from the simple fact that controversy and debate held a prominent place in the early Christian Church, that there was no belief in the existence of infallible guides, local and visible, whose autocratic decisions were final and irreversible, binding the whole Church. It was then believed that the guidance of the Holy Spirit was vouchsafed through the channel of free discussion and interchange of opinion, guided and sanctified by prayer. Peter and John had to go down to Samaria and keenly scrutinize the work, so as to see whether it bore the marks of Divine approval, completing the work by the imposition of their hands and prayer for the gifts of the Holy Ghost. The Apostles duly discharged their mission, and by their ministry the converts received the gift of the Holy Spirit, together with some or all of those external signs and manifestations which accompanied the original blessing on the day of Pentecost at Jerusalem. This portion of our narrative has been always regarded by the Church, whether in the East or the West, as its authority for the practice of the rite of confirmation. The assertion of the Church of England, in one of the collects appointed for use by the bishop in the Confirmation Service, may be taken as expressing on this point the opinion of the Churches—Roman, Greek, and Anglican. "Almighty and everliving God, who makest us both to will and to do those things that be good and acceptable unto Thy Divine Majesty; We make our humble supplications unto Thee for these Thy servants, upon whom (after the example of Thy holy Apostles) we have now laid our hands, to certify them (by this sign) of Thy favour and gracious goodness towards them." Let us reflect for a little on these words. The reference to apostolic example in this collect is not, indeed, merely to this incident at Samaria. The example of St. Paul at Ephesus, as narrated in the nineteenth chapter, is also claimed as another case in point. There we find that St. Paul came to a place where he had previously laboured for a short time. He discovered in Ephesus some disciples who had received the imperfect and undeveloped form of teaching which John the Baptist had communicated. A sect had apparently been already formed to continue John's teaching, such as we still find perpetuated amid the wilds of distant Mesopotamia, in the shape of the semi-Christian society which there practises daily baptism as a portion of its religion.[148] St. Paul explains to them the richer and fuller teaching of Christ, commands them to be baptized after the Christian model, by one of his attendants, and then, like Peter and John, completes the baptismal act by the imposition of hands and prayer for the gift of the Spirit. These two apostolic incidents are not, however, the only scriptural grounds which can be alleged for the continued use of confirmation. It might be said that the practice of the Apostles was not sufficient to justify or authorize confirmation as a scriptural rite, unless it can be shown that the imposition of hands, after baptism and as its completion, passed into the ordinary usage of the early

Church. Let me here make a brief digression. The New Testament cannot be used as a guide-book to the whole life and practice of the early Church, because it was merely a selection from the writings of the Apostles and of their companions. If we possessed everything that the Apostles wrote, we doubtless should have information upon many points of apostolic doctrine and ritual concerning which we now can only guess, some of which would doubtless very much surprise us. Thus, to take an example, we should have been left without one single reference to the Holy Communion in all the writings of St. Paul, had not the disorders at Corinth led to grave abuses of that sacrament, and thus caused St. Paul incidentally to mention the subject in the tenth and eleventh chapters of his first epistle to that Church.

Or to take another case. The *Teaching of the Twelve Apostles* has been already referred to and described. It is manifestly a manual dealing with the Church of apostolic times, and there we find reference to customs which were practised in the Apostolic Church, to which no reference, or at least very slight reference, is made in the Epistles or other books of the New Testament. The Apostles practised fasting as a preparation for important Church actions, as we learn from the account of the ordination of Paul and Barnabas at Antioch. The *Teaching of the Apostles* shows us that this practice, derived from the Jews, was the rule before baptism (of this we read nothing in the New Testament), as well as before ordination (of this we do read something), and that not only by the persons to be baptized, but by the ministers of baptism as well.[149] It mentions Wednesday and Friday fasts as instituted in opposition to the Monday and Thursday fasts of the Jews; it shows us how the lovefeasts of the Primitive Church were celebrated, and sheds much light upon the Order of prophets and their activity, to which St. Paul barely alludes. If we could regain the numberless writings of the Apostles and other early Christians which have perished, we should doubtless possess information upon many other practices and customs of early Church life which would much surprise us. The New Testament cannot then be used as an exhaustive account of the Primitive Church; its silence is no conclusive argument against apostolic origin or sanction as regards any practice, any more than the Old Testament is to be regarded as an exhaustive history of the Jewish nation. And yet, though we speak thus, confirmation or laying on of hands upon the baptized as the completion of the initial sacrament is not left without notice in the Epistles. The imposition of hands as the complement of baptism did not cease with the Apostles and was not tied to them alone, any more than did the use of water in the sacrament of baptism itself cease with the Apostles, as some of the Society of Friends have contended, or the imposition of hands in ordination terminate with apostolic times, as others have argued. This appears from two passages. St. Paul, in the twenty-second verse of the fifth chapter of 1 Timothy, when dealing with Timothy's conduct in the usual pastoral oversight of the Church, lays down, "Lay hands suddenly on no man." These words referred not to ordination, for St. Paul had passed from that subject and was treating of Timothy's ministerial conduct towards the ordinary members of his flock, directing how he was to care for their souls, reproving publicly the notorious transgressor, and putting him to open shame. We admit, indeed, at once that this notice of the imposition of hands may refer to another use of it which was practised in the early Church. St. Paul may be referring to the imposition of hands when a lapsed or excommunicated member was readmitted into the Church; or both uses of the ceremony, in confirmation as well as in absolution, may be included under the one reference. But in any case we have another distinct, though incidental, mention of this rite, and that at a time, in a manner, and in a book which clearly proves the practice to have passed into the general custom of the Church. Let us see how this is.

The Epistle to the Hebrews was written by one of the second generation of Christians, one of the generation who could look back to and wonder at the miracles and gifts of the apostolic age. The writer of the Hebrews tells us himself that he was in this position; for when speaking, in the opening of the second chapter, concerning the danger of neglecting the Gospel message, he describes it as a "great salvation; which having at the first been spoken through the Lord, was confirmed unto us by them that heard; God also bearing witness with them, both by signs and wonders, and by manifold powers, and by gifts of the Holy Ghost, according to His own will." So that it is evident that the Church of the Hebrews was the composition of a man who belonged to a time when the Church had passed out of the fluid state in which we find it in the earlier chapters of the Acts. It had passed into a condition when rites and ceremonies and Church government and ecclesiastical organisations had crystallised, and when men repeated with profoundest reverence the forms and ceremonies which had become associated with the names and persons of the earliest teachers of the faith; names and persons which now were surrounded with all that sacred charm and halo which distance, and above all else, death, lend to human memories. There is an interesting passage in Tertullian which shows how this feeling worked among the early Christians, making them anxious in divine worship to repeat most minutely and even absurdly the circumstances of the Church's earliest days. In Tertullian's works we have a treatise on Prayer, in which he expounds the nature of the Lord's Prayer, going through it petition by petition, proving conclusively that Tertullian and the Christians nearest the apostolic age knew nothing of that modern absurdity which asserts that the

Lord's Prayer should not be used by Christians. He then proceeds to explain certain useful customs, and to reprove certain superstitious ceremonies practised by the Christians of his day. He approves and explains the custom of praying with hands outstretched, because this is an imitation of our Lord, whose hands were outstretched upon the cross.[150] He disapproves of the practice of washing the hands before every prayer, which Tertullian says was done in memory of our Lord's Passion, when water was used by Pilate to wash his hands, and designates as superstitious the custom of sitting down upon their couches or beds after they had prayed, in imitation of Hermas who wrote the *Shepherd*, of whom it was said, that after finishing his prayer, he sat down on his bed.[151] Now this last instance exactly illustrates what must have happened in the case of the second generation of Christians, to whom the Epistle to the Hebrews was directed. Men at the end of the second century, when Tertullian lived, looked back to the Shepherd of Hermas with the same profound reverence as to the Apostles. They imitated, therefore, every action and ceremony practised by the Shepherd, whom they regarded as inspired, reading his writings with the same reverence as those of the Apostles.

Human nature is ever the same. The latest sect started in the present generation will be found acting on the same principles as the Christians of the apostolic age. The practices and ceremonial of their first founders become the model on which they shape themselves, and every departure from that model is bitterly resented. Human nature is governed universally by principles which are essentially conservative and traditional.[152] So it must have been with the immediate followers of the Apostles; they conformed themselves as exactly as they could to everything—rite, ceremony, form of words—which the Apostles delivered or practised. And the Apostles certainly delivered precepts and laid down rules on various liturgical questions, of which we have now no written record. St. Paul expressly refers to traditions and customs which he had delivered or intended to deliver, some of which we know, others of which we know not.[153] Now wherefore have we made this long excursion into the dim regions of primitive antiquity? Simply to show that it is *à priori* likely that the writer of the Epistle to the Hebrews, and men like him of the second and third generation of Christians, would have followed the example of the Apostles, and practised imposition of hands together with prayer for the gift of the Spirit in the case of those baptized into Christ, merely because the Apostles had beforetime practised it. And then, when we come to the actual study of the Epistle to the Hebrews, and read the sixth chapter, we find our anticipations fulfilled. In the first two verses of that chapter the writer lays down the first principles of Christ, the foundation doctrines of the Christian system, which he takes for granted as known and acknowledged by every one; they are, repentance from dead works, faith towards God, the teaching of baptisms, and of laying on of hands, and of the resurrection of the dead and of eternal judgment. Here the imposition of hands cannot refer to ordination, because, as all the other points are matters of personal religion and individual practice, not of ecclesiastical organisation, so we must restrict the imposition of hands referred to as a principle of the Christian religion, to some imposition of hands needful for every Christian, not for the few merely who should be admitted to the work of the ministry. While, again, its close connection with baptism clearly points to the imposition of hands in Confirmation, which the Apostles practised and the primitive Christians adopted from their example. And then, when we pass to ecclesiastical antiquity and study the works of Tertullian, the earliest writer who enters into the details of the practices and ritual established in the Churches, we find imposition of hands connected with baptism exactly as stated in the Epistle to the Hebrews, and viewed as the channel by which the gift of the Holy Ghost is conveyed,[154] not in the shape of miraculous gifts, but in all that edifying, consoling, and sanctifying power which every individual needs, and in virtue of which the New Testament writers, in common with Tertullian, call baptized men temples of the Holy Ghost and partakers of the Holy Ghost.[155]

# CHAPTER XIX
## ST. PETER AND SIMON MAGUS

"Now when Simon saw that through the laying on of the Apostles' hands the Holy Ghost was given, he offered them money, saying, Give me also this power, that on whomsoever I lay my hands, he may receive the Holy Ghost." — Acts viii. 18, 19.

We have in the last exposition endeavoured to explain the origin of the rite of Confirmation and to connect its development in the second century with the first notice of its rise in germ and principle at Samaria. There have been from time to time modifications and changes in the ordinance. The Church has availed itself of the power she necessarily possesses to insist upon different aspects of Confirmation at different periods. The Church of England at the Reformation brought out into prominence the human side of Confirmation as we may call it, which views the rite as a renewal and strengthening of the baptismal vows of renunciation, faith, and obedience, which had fallen too much out of sight, while still insisting on the Divine side as well, which regards Confirmation as a method of Divine action, a channel of Divine grace, strengthening and blessing the soul. Yet no one can imagine that the Reformers invented a new ordinance because they insisted on a forgotten and latent side of the old rite. So it was during the second century and in Tertullian's time. The exigencies of the Christian Church of that age had led to certain modifications of apostolic customs, but the central idea of solemn imposition of hands continued, and was regarded as of apostolic appointment. If we descend a little lower this is plain enough. St. Cyprian, the contemporary and disciple of Tertullian, expressly attributes the institution of the rite to the action of the Apostles at Samaria, a view which is subsequently attested by those great lights of the ancient Church, St. Jerome and St. Augustine.[156] As my object is, however, not to write a treatise on Confirmation, but to trace the evolution and development of apostolic customs and ritual, and to show how they were connected with the Church of the second century, I restrain myself to Tertullian alone.

I cannot see how this argument is to be evaded without rejecting the testimony of Tertullian and denying what we may call the historic memory and continuity of the Church at the close of the second century. Upon the testimony of Tertullian we very largely depend for our proof of the canonicity of the books of the New Testament. Men when impugning or rejecting Tertullian's witness on this or any similar question, should bear in mind what the results of their teaching may be; for surely if Tertullian's clear evidence avails not to prove the apostolic character of confirmation, it cannot be of much use to establish the still more important question of the canon of the New Testament or the authorship of the Gospels and Acts. We think, on the other hand, that Tertullian's references to this practice are naturally and easily explained by our theory that the Churches established by the Apostles followed their example. The first converts that were made after the Apostles had founded a Church were treated by the resident bishop and presbyters exactly as the Apostle had treated themselves. Timothy at Ephesus acted as he had seen St. Paul do. Timothy completed his converts' baptism by the imposition of hands, and then his successor followed the example of Timothy, and so confirmation received that universal acceptance which the writings of the Fathers disclose.

I. Let us now return to the consideration of the actual doings of Peter and John at Samaria, and the lessons we may draw from thence as touching the manner in which men should follow the example left by them at this crisis in Church history. The Apostles prayed for those that had been baptized into the name of the Lord Jesus, and then they laid their hands upon them, and the baptized received the Holy Ghost. Prayer went before the imposition of hands, to show that there was nothing mechanical in their proceedings; that it was not by their own power or virtue that any blessing was granted, but that they were only instruments by whom the Lord worked. The Apostles always acted, taught, ordained, confirmed, in the profoundest confidence, the surest faith that God worked in them and through them. St. Paul in his address to the elders of Miletus and Ephesus, whom he had himself ordained, spoke of their ordination, not as the work of man, but of the Holy Ghost. He pierced the veil of sense and saw, far away and behind the human instrument, the power of the Divine Agent who was the real Ordainer. "Take heed unto yourselves and to all the flock, in the which the Holy Ghost hath made you bishops." And so again in his words to Timothy there was not a shadow of doubt when he bid him "stir up the gift of God, which is in thee through the laying on of hands:" a gift which was doubtless no miraculous power, but the purely spiritual endowment, needful now as in ancient times for the edification and strengthening of human souls. As it was in ancient times so is it still, the Church of Christ unites prayer with imposition of hands. She cannot recognise any difference in the methods of God's dealing with human souls in apostolic times and in modern ages. Human wants are the same, human nature is the same, the promises of God and the ministry of God are the same; and therefore as in Samaria, so in England, the work of baptism is completed when further prayer is offered, and the imposition of hands by the chief ministers of God's Church signifies her holy confidence in the abiding presence and work of the Divine Spirit.

We desire to insist upon this devotional side of confirmation, because the rite of confirmation has been too often treated as a mere mechanical function, just indeed as men in times of spiritual deadness and torpor come to regard all spiritual functions in a purely mechanical aspect. The New Testament brought to light a religion of the spirit; but human nature ever tends to become formal in its religion, and therefore has persistently striven, and still persistently strives, to turn every external function and office in a mechanical direction. The Apostles prayed and then laid their hands upon the Samaritan converts, and we may be sure that these prayers were intense personal supplications, dealing directly with the hearts and consciences of the individuals. Confirmation, united with fervent prayer, public and private, with searching addresses directed to the conscience, with personal dealing as regards individual hearts, followed by public imposition of hands,—surely every one must acknowledge that such a solemnisation and sanctification of the great crisis when boyhood and girlhood pass into manhood and womanhood must have very blessed effects. Experience has, indeed, proved the wisdom of the ancient Church concerning this ordinance. Confirmation has not developed itself exactly in the East as we know it in the West. In the Eastern Church, as amongst the Lutherans of Germany, confirmation can be administered by a presbyter as well as by a bishop, to whom alone the Western Church limits the function. But whether in the East or West, confirmation is regarded as the transition step connecting baptism and the Eucharist. Christian bodies which have rejected the ancient customs have felt themselves obliged to adopt a similar method. Preparation for first Communion has taken the place of confirmation. There has been the same earnest dealing with conscience, the same fuller instruction in Christian truth and life, and the one thing lacking has been that following of the apostolic example in solemn imposition of hands, which would have thrown back the young mind to the days of the Church's earliest life, and helped it to realize something of the continuity of the Church's work and existence.

Many, as I know, ministering in societies where confirmation after the ancient model has been rejected, have bitterly lamented its disuse as depriving them of a solemn appointed time when they should have been brought into closer contact with the lives, the feelings, and the consciences of the lambs of Christ's flock. I am bound to confess, at the same time, that no one is more alive than I am to the many defects and shortcomings in the modes and fashions in which confirmation is sometimes viewed and conferred. The mere mechanical view of it is far too prevalent. Careful and prayerful preparation, systematic instruction in the field of Christian doctrine, is still in many cases far too little thought of. Confirmation offers a splendid opportunity when an earnest pastor may open out to young minds eager to receive truth, a fuller acquaintance with the deep things of God. Alas! how miserably such earnest young minds are sometimes met. It is stated that it was by injudicious treatment at such a time that the ardent, enthusiastic mind of the late Charles Bradlaugh was alienated from Christian truth. Intelligent sympathy is what the young desire and crave for at such seasons. Then it is that the man who has kept his mind fresh and active by wide and generous study finds the due reward of his labours. He does not attempt to meet doubts and difficulties by foolish denunciations. He knows that such doubts are in the air; that they meet the young in the newspapers, magazines, conversations of the day. He proves by his instructions that he knows of them and enters into them. He encourages frank discussion of them, and thus often proves himself at a very trying time the most helpful and consoling friend to the young and troubled spirit.

Confirmation, if viewed merely from the purely human side, and if we say nothing at all about a Divine blessing, offers a magnificent opportunity for a wise pastor of souls. He will, indeed, treat different ranks in different ways. A class of ploughboys or of village lads and girls need plain speaking on the great facts of life and of the Gospel, while the higher and more educated or sharper inhabitants of cities and towns require teaching which will embrace the problems of modern thought, as well as the foundation truths of morals. A perfunctory repetition of the Church Catechism, as in some parishes, or a brief study of a portion of the Greek Testament, as in some of our public schools, is a miserable substitute for that careful preparation embracing devotional as well as intellectual preparation, which such an important function demands.[157] Then, again, the method in which confirmation is administered calls for improvement and change. The confirmation of immense crowds at central churches tends to confirm the mere mechanical idea about confirmation. Parochial confirmations, a confirmation of the young of each congregation in presence of the congregation itself, that is the standard at which we should aim. The Church of Rome can give us wise suggestions on this point. Some time ago I noticed an account of a Roman Catholic confirmation in the west of Ireland. It was held in a town of twelve or fifteen thousand inhabitants. The bishop took a week for the confirmations in that town, examining all the children beforehand, bringing them thus into direct contact with himself as their supreme pastor, and assuring himself of the sufficiency of their preparation.

II. We have now noted some of the defects connected with modern confirmations; but the conduct of Simon Magus and this incident at Samaria remind us that defects and shortcomings must ever exist, as they existed in the Church of the Apostles. We note here Simon's offer and St. Peter's address. Simon Magus had believed, had been baptized, and doubtless had also been confirmed by the Apostles. In the case of some of the Samaritans, at least, the presence of the Holy Ghost must have been proved by visible or audible signs, for we are told that when Simon *saw* that through the imposition of apostolic hands the Holy Ghost was given, he offered them money to enable him to do the same. His offer sufficiently explains the nature of his faith. He was convinced intellectually of the truth of certain external facts which he had seen. He knew nothing of spiritual want, or the power of sin, or a desire for interior peace and sanctity. He looked upon the Apostles as cleverer jugglers and sorcerers than himself, accessible to precisely the same motives, and therefore he offered them money if they would endow him with the knowledge and power they possessed and exercised. The Acts of the Apostles, as a mirror of all Church history, thus selects for our instruction an event which sounds a warning needful for every age.

Simon Magus had a mere intellectual knowledge of the truth, and that mere intellectual knowledge, apart from a moral and spiritual conception of it, plunged him into a deeper fall than otherwise might have been the case. Simon Magus was a typical example of this, and successive centuries have offered many notable imitations. Julian the Apostate was brought up as a Christian clergyman, and used to read the lessons in Church, whence he would adjourn to join in the polluting rites of paganism; and so it has been from age to age, till in our own time some of the bitterest opponents of Christianity, at home or in the mission field, have been those who, like Simon, knew of the Gospel facts but had tasted nothing of the Gospel life.

We may derive from this incident guidance in a difficult controversy which has of late made much stir. Men have asserted that Christian missionaries were giving far too much time to mere intellectual training of pagans, instead of devoting themselves to evangelistic work. A writer who has never visited the mission-field has no right to pass judgment on such a matter. But cannot we read in this passage a warning against such a tendency? Intellectual conviction does not mean spiritual conversion. Of course we know that no human effort can ensure spiritual blessings, but if intellectual training of clever pagan youths, and not spiritual work, be regarded as the great object of Christian missions; if the Holy Ghost be not honoured by being made the supreme lord of heart and life and work, we cannot expect any blessed results to follow. We read very little in the earliest ages of the Church about educational missions. The work of education was not despised. The school of Alexandria from the earliest times held high the standard of Christian scholarship. But that school, though open, like all ancient academies, to every class, was primarily intended for the training of Christian youth, placing before all other studies the Divine science of theology.

The offer, again, of Simon Magus has given a name to a sin which has been found prevalent in every age and in every country. The sin has, indeed, taken different shapes. Simony, throughout the Middle Ages, was a common vice against which some of the more devout popes strove long and vigorously. In England and according to English law simony means still the purchase of spiritual office or spiritual functions. It would be simoniacal for a bishop to receive money for conferring holy orders or for appointment to a living. It would be an act of simony for a man to offer or give money to attain either holy orders or a living. How then, it may be said, does the unhallowed traffic in Church livings continue to flourish? Simply because, through colourable evasions, men bring themselves to break the spirit of the law while they keep within its strict letter. Simony, however, is a much more extensive and far-reaching corruption than the purchase of ecclesiastical benefices. Simony can take subtler shapes and can adapt itself to conditions very different from those which prevail under an established Church. Every one recognises, in word at least, the scandalous character of money traffic in Church offices. Even those who really practise it, hide from themselves, by some device or excuse, the character of their action. But the simoniacal spirit, the essence of Simon's sin, is found in many quarters which are never suspected. What is that essence? Simon desired to obtain spiritual power and office, not in the Divine method, but in low earthly ways. Money was his way because it was the one thing he valued and had to offer; but surely there are many other ways in which men may unlawfully seek for spiritual office and influence in the Church of Christ. Many a man who would never dream of offering money in order to obtain a high place in the Church, or would have been horrified at the very suggestion, has yet resorted to other methods just as effective and just as wrong. Men have sought high position by political methods. They have given their support to a political party, and have sold their talents to uphold a cause, hoping thereby to gain their ends. They may not have given gold which comes from the mine to gain spiritual position, but they have all the same given a mere human consideration, and sought by its help to obtain spiritual power; or they preach and speak and vote in Church synods and assemblies with an eye to elections to high place and dignity. An established Church, with its legally-secured properties and prizes, may open a way for the exercise of simony in its grosser forms. But a free Church, with its popular assemblies, opens the way for a subtler temptation, leading men to shape their actions, to suppress their convictions, to order their votes and speeches, not as their secret conscience would direct them, but as human nature and earthly considerations would tell them was best for their future prospects. How many a speech is spoken, how many a sermon is preached, how many a vote is given, not as the Holy Ghost directs, but under the influence of that unhallowed spirit of sheer worldliness which led Simon to offer money that he too might be enabled to exercise the power which the unworldly Apostles possessed. The spirit of simony may just as really lead a man to give a vote or to abstain from voting, to make a speech or keep silence, as it led men in a coarser and plainer age to give bribes for the attainment of precisely the same ends. In this respect, again, as warning against the intrusion of low earthly motives in the concerns of the Divine society, the Acts of the Apostles proves itself a mirror of universal Church history.

Then we have the address of St. Peter to this notorious sinner. It is very plain-spoken. The Apostle had been himself a great sinner, but he had not been harshly or roughly dealt with, because he had become a great penitent. St. Peter was most sympathetic, and could never have spoken so sharply as he did to Simon Magus had he not perceived with quick spiritual insight the inborn baseness and hollowness of the man's character. Still he does not cut him off from hope. He speaks plainly, as Christ's ministers should ever do when occasion requires. Simon Magus was a man of great influence in Samaria, but there was no "fear of man which bringeth a snare" about the Apostles, and so St. Peter fearlessly tells Simon his true position. "He was in the gall of bitterness and bond of iniquity." He indicates to him, however, the steps which, whether then or now, a person in that position should take if he desires to escape from the due reward of his deeds. "Repent therefore of this thy wickedness." Repentance, then, is the first step which a man whose heart is not right in God's sight has to take. There was no hesitation, as we have already remarked when speaking of St. Peter's preaching at Jerusalem, about pressing upon men the duty of hearty, sincere repentance, embracing sorrow for sin and genuine amendment of life. Then having exhorted to repentance, the Apostle proceeds, "And pray the Lord, if perhaps the thought of thy heart shall be forgiven thee." Prayer is the next step. First comes repentance, then prayer, and then forgiveness. There was nothing in St. Peter's teaching which lends the least countenance to the modern error which teaches that an unconverted man should not pray, that his one duty is to believe, and, till he does so, that his prayer is unacceptable to God. Simon Magus was as estranged from God as a human soul could well have been, yet St. Peter's word to him then, and his word to every sinner still, would be an exhortation to diligent prayer. "Pray God if perhaps the thought of thine heart shall be forgiven thee." The exhortation of Peter was blessed, for the time, to the sinner. It awoke a temporary sense of sin, though it wrought no permanent change. It has left, however, an eternal blessing and a permanent direction to the Church of Christ. In his preaching on the day of Pentecost to the Jews of Jerusalem, he shows us how to deal with those who are not as yet partakers of the Christian covenant. "Repent ye, and be baptized every one of you in the name of Jesus Christ," was his message to the devout Jews of Jerusalem; "Repent and pray" is his message to the sinner who has been brought, all unworthy, into the kingdom of light and grace, but knows nothing of it in heart and life. St. Peter valued the blessings of belief in Christ and admission by baptism into His kingdom, but he knew that these benefits only intensified a man's condemnation if not realized in heart and lived in practice. St. Peter's visit to Samaria in company with St. John has much to teach the Church on many other points, as we have pointed out, but no lesson which can be derived from it is so important as that which declares the true road for the returning sinner to follow, the value of repentance, the efficacy of heartfelt prayer, the supreme importance of a heart right in the sight of God.

# CHAPTER XX
## EVANGELISTIC WORK IN THE PHILISTINES' LAND

"But an angel of the Lord spake unto Philip, saying, Arise, and go toward the south unto the way that goeth down from Jerusalem unto Gaza: the same is desert. And he arose and went: and behold, a man of Ethiopia, a eunuch of great authority under Candace, queen of the Ethiopians, who was over all her treasure, who had come to Jerusalem for to worship; and he was returning and sitting in his chariot, and was reading the prophet Isaiah." — Acts viii. 26-8.

"And it came to pass, as Peter went throughout all parts, he came down also to the saints which dwelt at Lydda." — Acts ix. 32.

I have united these two incidents, the conversion of the Ethiopian eunuch and the mission of St. Peter to the people of Lydda, Sharon, and Joppa, because they relate to the same district of country and they happened at the same period, the pause which ensued between the martyrdom of St. Stephen and the conversion of St. Paul. The writer of the Acts does not seem to have exactly followed chronological order in this part of his story. He had access to different authorities or to different diaries. He selected as best he could the details which he heard or read, and strove to weave them into a connected narrative. St. Luke, when gathering up the story of these earliest days of the Church's warfare, must have laboured under great difficulties which we now can scarcely realize. It was doubtless from St. Philip himself that our author learned the details of the eunuch's conversion and of St. Peter's labours. St. Luke and St. Paul tarried many days with St. Philip at Cæsarea. Most probably St. Luke had then formed no intention of writing either his Gospel or his apostolic history at that period. He was urged on simply by that unconscious force which shapes our lives and leads us in a vague way to act in some special direction. A man born to be a poet will unconsciously display his tendency. A man born to be a historian will be found, even when he has formed no definite project, note-book in hand, jotting down the impressions of the passing hour or of his current studies. So probably was it with St. Luke. He could not help taking notes of conversations he heard, or making extracts from the documents he chanced to meet; and then when he came to write he had a mass of materials which it was at times hard to weave into one continuous story within the limits he had prescribed to himself. One great idea, indeed, to which we have often referred, seems to have guided the composition of the first portion of the apostolic history. St. Luke selected, under Divine guidance, certain representative facts and incidents embodying great principles, typical of future developments. This is the golden thread which runs through the whole of this book, and specially through the chapters concerning which we speak in this volume, binding together and uniting in one organic whole a series of independent narratives.

I. The two incidents which we now consider have several representative aspects. They may be taken as typical of evangelistic efforts and the qualifications for success in them. Philip the deacon is aggressive, many-sided, flexible, and capable of adapting himself to diverse temperaments, whether those of the Grecian Jews at Jerusalem, the Samaritans in central Palestine, or the Jewish proselytes from distant Africa. Peter is older, narrower, cannot so easily accommodate himself to new circumstances. He confines himself, therefore, to quiet work amongst the Jews of Palestine who have been converted to Christ as the result of the four years' growth of the Church. "As Peter went throughout all parts, he came down also to the saints which dwelt at Lydda." This incident represents to us the power and strength gained for the cause of Christ by intellectual training and by wider culture. It is a lesson needed much in the great mission field. It has hitherto been too much the fashion to think that while the highest culture and training are required for the ministry at home, any half-educated teacher, provided he be in earnest, will suffice for the work of preaching to the heathen. This is a terrible mistake, and one which has seriously injured the progress of religion. It is at all times a dangerous thing to despise one's adversary, and we have fallen into the snare when we have despised systems like Buddhism and Hindooism, endeavouring to meet them with inferior weapons.[158] The ancient religions of the East are founded on a subtle philosophy, and should be met by men whose minds have received a wide and generous culture, which can distinguish between the chaff and the wheat, rejecting what is bad in them while sympathising with and accepting what is good. The notices of Philip and Stephen and their work, as contrasted with that of St. Peter, proclaim the value of education, travel, and thought in this the earlier section of the Acts, as the labours of St. Paul declare it in the days of Gentile conversion. The work of the Lord, whether among Jews or Gentiles, is done most effectually by those whose natural abilities and intellectual sympathies have been quickened and developed. A keen race like the

Greeks of old or the Hindoos of the present, are only alienated from the very consideration of the faith when it is presented in a hard, narrow, intolerant, unsympathetic spirit. The angel chose wisely when he selected the Grecian Philip to bear the gospel to the Ethiopian eunuch, and left Peter to minister to Æneas, to Tabitha, and to Simon the tanner of Joppa; simple souls, for whom life glided smoothly along, troubled by no intellectual problems and haunted by no fearful doubts.

II. Again, we may remark that these incidents and the whole course of Church history at this precise moment show the importance of clear conceptions as to character, teaching, and objects. The Church at this time was vaguely conscious of a great mission, but it had not made up its mind as to the nature of that mission, because it had not realized its own true character, as glad tidings of great joy unto *all* nations. And the result was very natural: it formed no plans for the future, and was as yet hesitating and undecided in action. It was with the Church then as in our every-day experience of individuals. A man who does not know himself, who has no conception of his own talents or powers, and has formed no idea as to his object or work in life, that man cannot be decided in action, he cannot bring all his powers into play, because he neither knows of their existence, nor where and how to use them. This is my explanation of the great difference manifest on the face of our history as between the Church and its life before and after the conversion of Cornelius. It is plain that there was a great difference in Church life and activity between these two periods. Whence did it arise? The admission of the Gentiles satisfied the unconscious cravings of the Church. She felt that at last her true mission and her real object were found, and, like a man of vigorous mind who at last discovers the work for which nature has destined him, she flung herself into it, and we read no longer of mere desultory efforts, but of unceasing, indefatigable, skilfully-directed labour; because the Church had at last been taught by God that her great task was to make all men know the riches hidden in Christ Jesus. We have in this fact a representative lesson very necessary for our time. Men are now very apt to mistake mistiness for profundity, and clearness of conception for shallowness of thought. This feeling intrudes itself into religion, and men do not take the trouble to form clear conceptions on any subject, and they lapse therefore into the very weakness which afflicted the Church prior to St. Peter's vision. The root of practical, vigorous action is directly assailed if men have no clear conceptions as to the nature, the value, and the supreme importance of the truth. If, for instance, a man cherishes the notion, now prevalent in some circles, that Mahometanism is the religion suited for the natives of Africa, how will he make sacrifices either of time, of money, or of thought, to make the Gospel known to that great continent? I do not say that we should seek to have sharp and clear conceptions on all points. There is no man harder, more unsympathetic with the weak, more intolerant of the slightest difference, more truly foolish and short-sighted, than the man who has formed the clearest and sharpest conceptions upon the profoundest questions, and is ready to decide offhand where the subtlest and deepest thinkers have spoken hesitatingly. That man does not, in the language of John Locke, recognise the length of his own tether. He wishes to make himself the standard for everyone else, and infallibly brings discredit on the possession of clear views on any topics. There are vast tracts of thought upon which we must be content with doubt, hesitancy, and mistiness; but the man who wishes to be a vigorous, self-sacrificing servant of Jesus Christ must seek diligently for clear, broad, strong conceptions on such great questions as the value of the soul, the nature of God, the person of Jesus Christ, the work of the Spirit, and all the other truths which the Apostles' Creed sets forth as essentially bound up with these doctrines. Distinct and strong convictions alone on such points form for the soul the basis of a decided and fruitful Christian activity; as such decided convictions energised the whole life and character of the blessed apostle of love when writing, "We know that we are of God, and the whole world lieth in the evil one."

III. Now turning from such general considerations, we may compare the two incidents, St. Philip's activities and St. Peter's labours, in several aspects. *We notice a distinction in their guidance.* Greater honour is placed on Philip than upon Peter. An angel speaks to Philip, while St. Peter seems to have been left to that ordinary guidance of the Spirit which is just as real as any external direction, such as that given by an angel, but yet does not impress the human mind or supersede its own action, as the external direction does. Dr. Goulburn, in an interesting work from which I have derived many important hints,[159] suggests that the external message of the angel directing Philip where to go may have been God's answer to the thoughts and doubts which were springing up in His servant's mind. The incident of Simon Magus may have disturbed St. Philip. He may have been led to doubt the propriety of his action in thus preaching to the Samaritans and admitting to baptism a race hitherto held accursed. He had dared to run counter to the common opinion of devout men, and one result had been that such a bad character as Simon Magus had crept into the sacred fold. The Lord who watches over His people and sees all their difficulties, comes therefore to his rescue, and by one of His ministering spirits conveys a message which assures His fainting servant of His approval and of His guidance. Such is Dr. Goulburn's explanation, and surely it is a most consoling one, of which every true servant of God has had his own experience. The Lord even still deals thus with His people. They make experiments for Him, as Philip did;

engage in new enterprises and in fields of labour hitherto untried; they work for His honour and glory alone; and perhaps they see nothing for a time but disaster and failure. Then, when their hearts are cast down and their spirits are fainting because of the way, the Lord mercifully sends them a message by some angelic hand or voice, which encourages and braces them for renewed exertion.

An external voice of an angel may, in the peculiar circumstances of the case, have directed St. Philip. But the text does not give us a hint as to the appearance or character of the messenger whom God used on this occasion. The Old and New Testament alike take broader views of Divine messengers, and of angelic appearances generally, than we do. A vision, a dream, a human agent, some natural circumstance or instrument, all these are in Holy Scripture or in contemporary literature styled God's angels or messengers. Men saw then more deeply than we do, recognised the hand of a superintending Providence where we behold only secondary agents, and in their filial confidence spoke of angels where we should only recognise some natural power. Let me quote an interesting illustration of this. Archbishop Trench, speaking, in his *Notes on the Miracles*, of the healing of the Impotent Man at Bethesda, and commenting on St. John v. 4, a verse which runs thus, "For an angel of the Lord went down at certain seasons into the pool, and troubled the water: whosoever then first after the troubling of the water stepped in was made whole, with whatsoever disease he was holden," thus enunciates the principle which guided the ancient Christians, as well as the Jews, in this matter. He explains the origin of this verse, and the manner in which it crept into the text of the New Testament. "At first, probably, a marginal note, expressing the popular notion of the Jewish Christians concerning the origin of the healing power which from time to time the waters of Bethesda possessed, by degrees it assumed the shape in which we now have it." The Archbishop then proceeds to speak of the Hebrew view of the world as justifying such expressions. "For the statement itself, there is nothing in it which need perplex or offend, or which might not find place in St. John. It rests upon that religious view of the world which in all nature sees something beyond and behind nature, which does not believe that it has discovered causes when, in fact, it has only traced the sequence of phenomena, and which everywhere recognises a going forth of the immediate power of God, invisible agencies of His, whether personal or otherwise, accomplishing His will."[160] The whole topic of angelic agencies is one that has been much confused for us by the popular notions about angels, notions which affect every one, no matter how they imagine themselves raised above the vulgar herd. When men speak or think of angelic appearances, they think of angels as they are depicted in sacred pictures. The conception of young men clad in long white and shining raiment, with beautiful wings dependent from their shoulders and folded by their sides, is an idea of the angels and angelic life derived from mediæval painters and sculptors, not from Holy Writ. The important point, however, for us to remember is that Philip here moved under external direction to the conversion of the eunuch. The same Spirit which sent His messenger to direct Philip, led Peter to move towards exactly the same south-western quarter of Palestine, where he was to remain working, meditating, praying, till the hour had come when the next great step should be taken and the Gentiles admitted as recognised members of the Church.

IV. This leads us to the next point. Philip and Peter were both guided, the one externally, the other internally; but whither? They were led by God into precisely the same south-western district of Palestine. Peter was guided, by one circumstance after another, first to Lydda and Sharon, and then to Joppa, where the Lord found him when he was required at the neighbouring Cæsarea to use the power of the keys and to open the door of faith to Cornelius and the Gentile world. Our narrative says nothing, in St. Peter's case, about providential guidance or heavenly direction, but cannot every devout faithful soul see here the plain proofs of it? The book of the Acts makes no attempt to improve the occasion, but surely a soul seeking for light and help will see, and that with comfort, the hand of God leading St. Peter all unconscious, and keeping him in readiness for the moment when he should be wanted. We are not told of any extraordinary intervention, and yet none the less the Lord guided him as really as He guided Philip, that his life might teach its own lessons, by which we should order our own. And has not every one who has devoutly and faithfully striven to follow Christ experienced many a dispensation exactly like St. Peter's? We have been led to places, or brought into company with individuals, whereby our future lives have been ever afterwards affected. The devout mind in looking back over the past will see how work and professions have been determined for us, how marriages have been arranged, how afflictions and losses have been made to work for good; so that at last, surveying, like Moses, life's journey from some Pisgah summit, when its course is well-nigh run, God's faithful servant is enabled to rejoice in Him because even in direct afflictions He has done all things well. A view of life like that is strictly warranted by this passage, and such a view was, and still is, the sure and secret source of that peace of God which passeth all understanding. Nothing can happen amiss to him who has Almighty Love as his Lord and Master. St. Peter was led, by one circumstance after another, first to Lydda, which is still an existing village, then, farther, into the vale of Sharon, celebrated from earliest time for its fertility, and commemorated for its roses in the Song of Solomon

(Cant. ii. 1, Isa. xxxiii. 9), till finally he settles down at Joppa, to wait for the further indications of God's will.

But how about Philip, to whom the Divine messenger had given a heavenly direction? What was the message so imparted? An angel of the Lord spake unto Philip, saying, "Arise, and go toward the south, unto the way that goeth down from Jerusalem unto Gaza: the same is desert." Now we should here carefully remark the minute exactness of the Acts of the Apostles in this place, because it is only a specimen of the marvellous geographical and historical accuracy which distinguishes it all through, and is every year receiving fresh illustrations. Gaza has always been the gateway of Palestine. Invader after invader when passing from Egypt to Palestine has taken Gaza in his way. It is still the trade route to Egypt, along which the telegraph line runs. It was in the days of St. Philip the direct road for travellers like the Ethiopian eunuch, from Jerusalem to the Nile and the Red Sea. This man was seeking his home in Central Africa, which he could reach either by the Nile or by the sea, and was travelling therefore along the road from Jerusalem to Gaza. The Acts, again, distinguishes one particular road. There were then, and there are still, two great roads leading from Jerusalem to Gaza, one a more northern road, which ran through villages and cultivated land as it does to this day. The other was a desert road, through districts inhabited then as now by the wandering Arabs of the desert alone. Travellers have often remarked on the local accuracy of the angel's words when directing Philip to a road which would naturally be taken only by a man attended by a considerable body of servants able to ward off attack, and which was specially suitable, by its lonely character, for those prolonged conversations which must have passed between the eunuch and his teacher. Cannot we see, however, a still more suggestive and prophetic reason for the heavenly direction? In these early efforts of the Apostles and their subordinates we read nothing of missions towards the east. All their evangelistic operations lay, in later times, towards the north and north-west, Damascus, Antioch, Syria, and Asia Minor, while in these earlier days they evangelised Samaria, which was largely pagan, and then worked down towards Gaza and Cæsarea and the Philistine country, which were the strongholds of Gentile and European influence,—the Church indicated in St. Luke's selection of typical events; the Western, the European destiny working strong within. It already foretold, vaguely but still surely, that, in the grandest and profoundest sense,

"Westward the course of Empire takes its way;"

that the Gentile world, not the Jewish, was to furnish the most splendid triumphs to the soldiers of the Cross. Our Lord steadily restrained Himself within the strict bounds of the chosen people, because His teaching was for them alone. His Apostles already indicate their wider mission by pressing close upon towns and cities, like Gaza and Cæsarea, which our Lord never visited, because they were the strongholds and chosen seats of paganism. [161] The providential government of God ordering the future of His Church and developing its destinies can thus be traced in the unconscious movements of the earliest Christian teachers. Their first missionary efforts in Palestine are typical of the great work of the Church in the conversion of Europe.

V. St. Philip was brought from Samaria, in the centre, to the Gaza road leading from Jerusalem to the coast; and why? Simply in order that he might preach the Gospel to one solitary man, the eunuch who was treasurer to Candace, Queen of the Ethiopians. Here again we have another of those representative facts which are set before us in the earlier portion of this book. On the day of Pentecost, Jews from all parts of the Roman Empire, and from the countries bordering upon the east of that Empire, Parthians, Medes, Elamites, and Arabians, came in contact with Christianity. Philip had ministered in Samaria to another branch of the circumcision, but Africa, outside the Empire at least, had as yet no representative among the firstfruits of the cross. But now the prophecy of the sixty-eighth Psalm was to be fulfilled, and "Ethiopia was to stretch out her hands unto God." We have the assurance of St. Paul himself that the sixty-eighth Psalm was a prophecy of the ascension of Christ and the outpouring of the Holy Ghost. In Eph. iv. 8 he writes, quoting from the eighteenth verse, "Wherefore He saith, when He ascended up on high, He led captivity captive, and gave gifts unto men." And then he proceeds to enumerate the various offices of the apostolic ministry, with their blessed tidings of peace and salvation, as the gifts of the Spirit which God had bestowed through the ascension of Jesus Christ. And now, in order that no part of the known world might want its Jewish representative, we have the conversion of this eunuch, who, as coming from Ethiopia, was regarded in those times as intimately associated with India.

Let us see, moreover, what we are told concerning this typical African convert. He was an Ethiopian by birth, though he may have been of Jewish descent, or perhaps more probably a proselyte, and thus an evidence of Jewish zeal for Jehovah. He was an eunuch, and treasurer of Candace, Queen of the Ethiopians. He was like Daniel and the three Hebrew children in the court of the Chaldæan monarch. He had utilised his Jewish genius and power of adaptation so well that he had risen to high position. The African queen may have learned, too, as Darius did, to trust his Jewish faith and depend upon a man whose conduct was regulated by Divine law and principle. This power of the Jewish race leading them to high place amid foreign nations and in alien courts has been manifested in their history from the earliest times. Moses, Mordecai and Esther, the Jews in Babylon, were types and prophecies of the greatness which has awaited their descendants scattered among the Gentiles in our own time. This eunuch was treasurer of Candace, Queen of the Ethiopians. Here again we find another illustration of the historical and geographical accuracy of the Acts of the Apostles. We learn from several contemporary geographers that the kingdom of Meroë in Central Africa was ruled for centuries by a line of female sovereigns whose common title was Candace, as Pharaoh was that of the Egyptian monarchs. [162] There were, as we have already pointed out, large Jewish colonies in the neighbourhood of Southern Arabia and all along the coast of the Red Sea. It was very natural, then, that Candace should have obtained the assistance of a clever Jew from one of these settlements. A question has been raised, indeed, whether the eunuch was a Jew at all, and some have regarded him as the first Gentile convert. The Acts of the Apostles, however, seems clear enough on this point. Cornelius is plainly put forward as the typical case which decided the question of the admission of the Gentiles to the benefits of the covenant of grace. Our history gives not the faintest hint that any such question was even distantly involved in the conversion and baptism of the Ethiopian. Nay, rather by telling us that he had come to Jerusalem for the purpose of worshipping God, it indicates that he felt himself bound, as far as he could, to discharge the duty of visiting the Holy City and offering personal worship there once at least in his lifetime. Then, too, we are told of his employment when Philip found him. "He was returning, and sitting in his chariot read Esaias the prophet." His attention may have been called to this portion of Holy Scripture during his visit to the temple, where he may have come in contact with the Apostles or with some other adherents of the early Church. At any rate he was employing his time in devout pursuits, he was making a diligent use of the means of grace so far as he knew them; and then God in the course of His providence opened out fresh channels of light and blessing, according to that pregnant saying of our Lord, "If any man will do God's will, he shall know of the doctrine." The soul that is in spiritual perplexity or darkness need not and ought not to content itself with apathy, despair, or idleness. Difficulties will assault us on every side so long as we remain here below. We cannot escape from them because our minds are finite and limited. And some are ready to make these difficulties an excuse for postponing or neglecting all thoughts concerning religion. But quite apart from the difficulties of religion, there are abundant subjects on which God gives us the fullest and plainest light. Let it be ours, like the Ethiopian eunuch, to practise God's will so far as He reveals it, and then, in His own good time, fuller revelations will be granted, and we too shall experience, as this Ethiopian did, the faithfulness of His own promise, "Unto the righteous there ariseth up light in the darkness." The eunuch read the prophet Esaias as he travelled, according to the maxim of the rabbis that "one who is on a journey and without a companion should employ his thoughts on the study of the law." He was reading the Scriptures aloud, too, after the manner of Orientals; and thus seeking diligently to know the Divine will, God vouchsafed to him by the ministry of St. Philip that fuller light which he still grants, in some way or other, to every one who diligently follows Him.

And then we have set forth the results of the eunuch's communion with the heaven-sent messenger. There was no miracle wrought to work conviction. St. Philip simply displayed that spiritual power which every faithful servant of Christ may gain in some degree. He opened the Scriptures and taught the saving doctrine of Christ so effectually that the soul of the eunuch, naturally devout and craving for the deeper life of God, recognised the truth of the revelation. Christianity was for the Ethiopian its own best evidence, because he felt that it answered to the wants and yearnings of his spirit. We are not told what the character of St. Philip's discourse was. But we are informed what the great central subject of his discourse was. It was Jesus. This topic was no narrow one. We can gather from other passages in the Acts what was the substance of the teaching bestowed by the missionaries of the Cross upon those converted by them.[163] He must have set forth the historic facts which are included in the Apostles' Creed, the incarnation, the miracles, death, resurrection, and ascension of Christ, and the institution of the sacrament of baptism as the means of entering into the Church. This we conclude from the eunuch's question to Philip, "See, here is water; what doth hinder me to be baptized?" Assuredly Philip must have taught him the appointment of baptism by Christ; else what would have led the eunuch to propound such a request? Baptism having been granted in response to this request, the eunuch proceeded on his homeward journey, rejoicing in that felt sense of peace and joy and spiritual satisfaction which true religion imparts; while Philip is removed to another field of labour, where God has other work for him to do. He evangelised all through the Philistine country, preaching in all the cities till he came to Cæsarea, where in later years he was to do a work of permanent benefit for the whole Church, by affording St. Luke the information needful for the composition of the Acts of the Apostles.[164]

VI. Let us in conclusion note one other point. Our readers will have noticed that we have said nothing concerning the reply of Philip to the eunuch's question, "What doth hinder me to be baptized?" The Authorized Version then inserts ver. 37, which runs thus: "And Philip said, If thou believest with all thy heart, thou mayest. And he answered and said, I believe that Jesus Christ is the Son of God." While if we take up the Revised Version we shall find that the Revisers have quite omitted this verse in the text, placing it in the margin, with a note stating that some ancient authorities insert it wholly or in part. This verse is now given up by all critics as an integral part of the original text, and yet it is a very ancient interpolation, being found in quotations from the Acts as far back as the second century. Probably its insertion came about somehow thus, much the same as in the case of John v. 4, to which we have already referred in this lecture. It was originally written upon the margin of a manuscript by some diligent student of this primitive history. Manuscripts were not copied in the manner we usually think. A scribe did not place a manuscript before him and then slowly transcribe it, but a single reader recited the original in a scriptorium or copying-room, while a number of writers rapidly followed his words. Hence a marginal note on a single manuscript might easily be incorporated in a number of copies, finding a permanent place in a text upon which it was originally a mere pious reflection. Regarding this thirty-seventh verse, however, not as a portion of the text written by St. Luke, but as a second-century comment or note on the text, it shows us what the practice of the next age after the Apostles was. A profession of faith in Christ was made by the persons brought to baptism, and probably these words, "I believe that Jesus Christ is the Son of God," was the local form of the baptismal creed wherever this note was written. Justin Martyr in his first *Apology*, chap. 61, intimates that such a profession of belief was an essential part of baptism, and this form, "I believe that Jesus Christ is the Son of God," may have been the baptismal formula used in the ritual appointed for these occasions. Some persons indeed have thought that this short statement represented the creed of the Church of the second century. This raises a question which would require a much longer treatment than we can now bestow upon it. Caspari, an eminent Swedish theologian, has discussed this point at great length in a work which the English student will find reviewed and analysed in an article by Dr. Salmon published in the *Contemporary Review* for August 1878, where that learned writer comes to the conclusion that the substance of the Apostles' Creed dates back practically to the time of the Apostles. And now, as I am concluding this volume, an interesting confirmation of this view comes to us from an unexpected quarter. The *Apology* of Aristides was a defence of Christianity composed earlier even than those of Justin Martyr. Eusebius fixes the date of it to the year 124 or 125 A.D. It was at any rate one of the earliest Christian writings outside the Canon. It has been long lost to the Christian world. We knew nothing of its contents, and were only aware of its former existence from the pages of the Church History of Eusebius. Two years ago it was found by Professor J. Rendel Harris, in Syriac, in the Convent of St. Catharine on Mount Sinai, and has just been published this month of May 1891 by the Cambridge University Press. It is a most interesting document of early Christian times, showing us how the first Apologists defended the faith and assailed the superstitions of paganism. Professor Harris has added notes to it which are of very great value. He points out the weak points in paganism which the first Christians used specially to assail. Aristides' *Apology* is of peculiar value in this aspect. It shows us how the first generation after the last Apostle was wont to deal with the false gods of Greece, Rome, and Egypt. It is, however, of special importance as setting forth from a new and unexpected source how the early Christians regarded their own faith, how they viewed their own Christianity, and in what formularies they embodied their belief. Professor Harris confirms Dr. Salmon's contention set forth in the article to which we have referred. In the time of Aristides the Christians of Athens, for Aristides was an Athenian philosopher who had accepted Christianity, were at one with those of Rome and with the followers of Catholic Christianity ever since. Aristides wrote according to Eusebius in 124 A.D., according to Professor Harris in the earliest days of Antoninus Pius, that is, before 140 A.D.; but still we can extract from his *Apology* all the statements of the Apostles' Creed in a formal shape. Thus Professor Harris restores the Creed as professed in the time of Aristides, that is, the generation after St. John, and sets it forth as follows:—

> We believe in one God Almighty,
> Maker of Heaven and Earth:
> And in Jesus Christ His Son,
>
> Born of the Virgin Mary.
>
> He was pierced by the Jews,
> He died and was buried:
> The third day He rose again:
> He ascended into Heaven.

He is about to come to judge.[165]

This *Apology* of Aristides is a most valuable contribution to Christian evidence, and raises high hopes as to what we may yet recover when the treasures of the East are explored. The *Diatessaron* of Tatian was a wondrous find, but the recovery of the long-lost *Apology* of Aristides endows us with a still more ancient document, bringing us back close upon the very days of the Apostles. As this discovery has only been published when these pages are finally passing through the press, I must reserve a farther notice of it for the preface to this volume.

# INDEX

Burgess, Rev. H. W., LL.D.

Burnet, Bishop *Commentary on the Thirty-Nine Articles*

Butler, Bishop

Bzovius *Continuation of Baronius' Annals*

Calvin

Candace

Capes, Rev. W. W., M.A. *The Age of the Antonines*

Cardinals, College of

Cato *de Re Rustica*

Cave *Lives of Fathers*

Charteris, Dr.

Chrysostom, St.

Cicero *Tusc. Disp.*

Cistercians

Clarke, Adam

Clement of Alexandria

Clement of Rome

Clementine literature

Coke, Thomas

Columbanus, St.

Confirmation, rite of, chaps. xviii . xix .
*Contemporary Review*

Conybeare and Howson *Life and Epistles of St. Paul*

Coptic Church

Cornelius à Lapide

Court of the Gentiles

Crisp, Tobias, Dr. *Sermons*

Crispin, St.

Cyprian, St.

Cyprus

Cyril, St., of Jerusalem


Darby, J. N.

David, tomb of, opened

Deacons, choice and work of, chaps. xiii . xiv .
De Vogüe *Le Temple de Jérusalem*

*Dictionary of Christian Biography,*

— — — — *Antiquities*

— — — — *Greek and Roman Geography*

*Didache*

Douket, in *Rev. des Quest. Hist.*

Friends, Society of

Fuller, Rev. J. M.


Gamaliel

Gate of Temple (Chulda)

Gaza

Gibbon *History*

Golden Gate

Goulburn, Dean *Acts of the Deacons*

Gwynn, Dr.


Hadrian, Emperor

Hall, S. C.

Harnack *Texte u. Untersuch.*,

Harris, Professor,

Helena, Empress

Herzog *Encyclopædia*

Hippolytus,

Hook, Dean

Howard, John

Hyreanus

Indich

Irenæus

— — *Adv. Hær.*

Irish longevity

Irvingites

Jason and Papiscus

Jerome, St.,

Jesuits

John, St. *Acts of*

Jortin

Josephus *Antiqq.*

— — *Wars*

*Jubilees, Book of*

Judas Iscariot

Julian the Apostate

Justin Martyr,

Keble, John *Christian Year*

Kingsley, Charles

Kitto *Bib. Cyclop.*

Marcion

Marnas, the God of Gaza

Martial *Epigrams*

*Martyrologium Romanum*

Matthias, election of

Maurice, F. D.

Mechitarites

Mede, Joseph *Works of*

Meroë

Metaphrastes, Simeon

Meyer on the Acts

Mill, J. S. *Logic*

Milles, Bishop *Works of St. Cyril*

Milman *History of the Jews*

Mithraism

Mivart, St. George *Genesis of Species*

Moll, Dr. A., on *Hypnotism*

Montanists

*Monumenta Franciscana*

*Muratorian Fragment*

Nelson *Fasts and Festivals*

Neo-Cæsarea

Nestorianism

New Testament, Canon of

Newman, Cardinal

Newton, Robert

Nicanor, Gate of

Nicodemus

Nicolas, proselyte of Antioch

Northcote *Epitaphs of the Catacombs*

Novatianus

Novatian heresy

Novatus


Origen

Otto *Corp. Apologet.,*

Overbeck


Palmer, William

Pantænus

Vaughan, C. J., D.D. *The Church of the First Days*

Victor I., Pope

Watson, Richard

Wesley, John

Wilberforce, William

Williams, Dr.

Zeller *Acts of the Apostles*

# FOOTNOTES:

[1] See the treatise on the Christian Ministry in his *Philippians*, p. 186.

[2] Dr. Goulburn, in his *Acts of the Deacons*, suggested this view of the Acts of the Apostles nearly thirty years ago.

[3] For an account of Simeon Metaphrastes the English reader should consult Dr. Schaff's valuable *Encyclopædia of Historical Theology*.

[4] See Professor Ramsay on "The Tale of Saint Abercius" in the *Journal of Hellenic Studies*, vol. iii., p. 338, for a full account of this new source of early Church history which his travels and excavations have brought to our notice.

[5] Ceillier, *Hist. des Auteurs Ecclésiastiques*, i., 403.

[6] Mr. Harris's discovery is not the first find of this ancient apologist in modern times. The Armenian Mechitarites of Venice published what they called two sermons of Aristides in 1878; which Cardinal Pitra, the learned librarian of the Vatican, reprinted in 1883, in his *Analecta Sacra*, t. iv., pp. x, xi, 6-11, 282-86. One of these sermons was a fragment of the *Apology* of Aristides, which the Mechitarites scarcely at first recognised as such. M. Rénan, in his *Origines de Christianisme*, vol. vi., p. vi (Paris, 1879), scoffed at this fragment, declaring that, from the technical theological terms, such as Theotokos, therein used, it was evidently posterior to the fourth century. Doulcet, in the *Revue des Questions Historiques* for October 1880, pp. 601-12, made an effective reply with the materials at hand at the time, but Mr. Harris's publication of the complete work triumphantly demonstrates that M. Rénan's objections were worthless (see Harris, pp. 2, 3, 27). It is another proof that Christians have everything to hope and nothing to fear from such discoveries of early documents. Mr. Harris's preface is specially interesting, because it shows that we have had the *Apology* of Aristides all the time, though we knew it not, as it was worked in the quasi-oriental tale of Barlaam and Joasaph printed among the works of St. John of Damascus.

[7] The apologists of the second century will be found in a collected shape in Otto's *Corpus Apologetarum*, in nine vols. (Jena, 1842-72). Most of those mentioned above will be found in an English shape in Clarke's Ante-

Nicene Library. See also Harnack in *Texte und Untersuchungen*, bd. i., hft. i. (Leipzig, 1882).

[8] St. Jerome, in *Ep.* 70, addressed to Magnus, a Roman rhetorician, expressly says that Justin Martyr imitated Aristides. The *Cohortatio ad Græcos* attributed to him is much liker the treatise of Aristides than Justin's admitted first and second apologies.

[9] Overbeck, Zeller, and Schwegler fix the composition of the Acts between 110 and 130, the very date of the *Apology* of Aristides. See Zeller's *Acts of the Apostles*, p. 71 (London: Williams & Norgate, 1875).

[10] For an account of the Jewish controversy in the second century see Gebhardt and Harnack's *Texte*, bd. i., hft. 3 (Leipzig, 1883), where Harnack seeks to critically restore the substance of the dialogue between Jason and Papiscus. An article on "Apologists" in the *Dictionary of Christian Biography*, vol. i., pp. 140-47, and another on "Theophilus" (13) in the same work, vol. iv., p. 1009, should be consulted.

[11] See a copious account of this strange second-century forgery in Dr. Gwynne's article on Thecla in the fourth volume of the *Dictionary of Christian Biography*. Dr. Salmon, in his *Introduction to the N.T.*, chap. xix., gives a most interesting description of the apocrypha Acts of the Apostles, which even the unlearned can enjoy.

[12] The Irish people are very Oriental in the tenacity with which they retain ancient traditions, transmitting them intact to posterity. Abundant instances have proved this, the traditions having been perpetuated in some cases for five hundred years or more. The following case has come under the writer's notice in his own neighbourhood. There is near Dublin a village called Finglas, celebrated for its ancient Abbey. A cross stood there which had been venerated from the earliest times. When Cromwell's soldiers were advancing to attack Dublin about the year 1648, their iconoclastic fame reached the inhabitants of Finglas, who took the ancient cross and buried it in one of the glebe fields. Some one hundred and sixty years later a vicar of Finglas of antiquarian tastes heard traditions of this event. He learned from an extremely old man that his grandfather when a boy had been present at the burial of the cross, and had shown him the spot where it was concealed. The vicar made excavations, and duly found the cross, which he re-erected some time about 1810, in a spot where it is still to be seen. This instance will show how two long lives could cover the space between St. Paul's middle age and Tertullian's mature years. See *Fingal and its Churches*, by Rev. R. Walsh, D.D., pp. 147-49. Dublin, 1888. St. Jerome, *De Vir. Illust.*, 53, mentions a similar case in his time. St. Jerome knew an old man who when young had

himself known one of St. Cyprian's secretaries. St. Jerome wrote about A.D. 400, St. Cyprian died in 257; the difference exactly between Tertullian and St. Paul.

[13] See two articles on St. Columbanus and his library in the *Expositor* for June and August 1889.

[14] Dr. Salmon, in his *Introd. N.T.*, pp. 48-54, describes the Muratorian Fragment.

[15] See Dr. Sanday's *The Gospels in the Second Century*, and Dr. Salmon's *Introd. N.T.*, pp. 204-208.

[16] The latest enquiries and discoveries confirm this view, which may be deduced from a study of the apostolic Fathers, with which should be compared the new second-century documents belonging to Ephesus and Rome discussed in *Texte u. Untersuch.* of Gebhardt and Harnack for 1888. Their titles are the tract *De Aleatoribus*, by Pope Victor I., and the *Martyrdoms* of Carpus and Papylus, Companions of St. Polycarp. Pope Victor gives a long extract from the *Shepherd of Hermas*, and calls it "Divine Scripture;" which shows that the canon was not closed at Rome in the last fifteen years of the second century.

[17] An interesting account of this second-century document will be found in the *Texts*, edited by Gebhardt and Harnack, or in the *Dict. Christ. Biog.* under "Scillitan Martyrs." Every scrap of second century evidence is of the greatest importance for biblical criticism.

[18] See Butler's *Analogy*, Part II., chap. vi.

[19] J. Keble, "The Sixth Sunday after Epiphany."

[20] The book of Enoch was translated into English by Archbishop Laurence, and was first published about seventy years ago. There is an exhaustive article on the subject in the second volume of the *Dictionary of Christian Biography*, written by Professor Lipsius of Jena.

[21] The book of Jubilees has never been published in English. An interesting account of it will be found in the later editions of Kitto's *Biblical Cyclopædia*. The reader will find another account of the book of Jubilees in the *Dict. Christ. Biog.*, iv., 507. The Psalms of Solomon are contained in the *Cod. Pseud. Vet. Test.* of J. A. Fabricius. There is a brief notice of them in the *Dict. Chris. Biog.*, iv., 508, under the title "Pseudepigrapha."

[22] The strongest argument, from a mere literary point of view, for the existence of a supernatural element in Christianity and primitive Christian literature will be derived from a contrast between the Jewish literature of

the period of the Christian era and the New Testament. Take, for instance, the book of Jubilees. It was written about the time of our Lord, and probably in Galilee. It represents the current tone of Jewish religion, and shows us, with its narrowness and absurdities, what the New Testament would have been had it been the product of unassisted human nature. The book of Jubilees or of Enoch is the strongest argument for the inspiration of the New Testament. I cannot even imagine what explanation can be offered of the difference in tone between the Christian and the Jewish writings save that of the inspiration of the Christian.

[23] The most curious instance of the essential identity of the nature deities of the West and East will be found in Mithraism. The worship of Mithras was originally the worship of the sun. It started from India, passed into Persia, thence found its way to Asia Minor, and about 70 B.C. was introduced into Rome, where it became, about A.D. 200, the great rival of Christianity, imitating the sacraments of baptism and holy communion in rites of its own. Mithraism easily combined with the worship of Apollo, or the Sun-God. Apollo, Mithras, and Baal were fundamentally one and the same. Tertullian, Justin Martyr, and Origen call Mithraism a demoniacal imitation of Christianity. See more on this point in the article on Mithras in the *Dictionary of Christian Biography*, vol. iii., p. 925.

[24] The miraculous gifts of the Spirit possessed by the Apostles did not guard them against mistakes as to the future, nor override the exercise of private judgment and common sense, nor enable them to work miracles or cure sicknesses for their own purposes. St. Paul, for instance, was obliged to depend upon the assistance of St. Luke when he was ill. The miraculous powers were restrained, as in our Lord's example, to cases where God's glory was specially advanced by their exercise.

[25] See my *Ireland and the Celtic Church* for the traditions about St. Joseph of England.

[26] The line of argument followed in this chapter was originally suggested to me by a sermon for the First Sunday in Advent, printed in a volume of *Sermons at the Octagon Chapel, Bath*, by the Rev. W. C. Magee, B.D., now Archbishop of York. London, Hatchards, 1858.

[27] The incarnation and the ascension are, in this respect, very much on a level in St. Paul's writings. The incarnation and birth of our Lord are referred to incidentally, but only incidentally, in Rom. i. 3; Gal. iv. 4; 1 Tim. iii. 16; yet the facts of the birth and incarnation must have occupied a great share of St. Paul's attention, if we are to judge of his teaching by the Gospel of St. Luke, his disciple and companion. The Apostle never formally states

the doctrine of the incarnation as St. Luke set it forth, because it was well known by all to whom he wrote as the very foundation of his system. A bare reference was therefore enough. It was just the same with the doctrine of the ascension.

[28] See Archbishop Trench on the Draw-net in *Notes on the Parables*, p. 145, 10th ed.

[29] We now live so fast that it may perhaps be necessary to explain that the *Unseen Universe* was a book written some ten or eleven years ago by two eminent scientists, showing how that it was needful, on the principles, of modern science, to postulate the existence of an unseen universe, out of which the seen universe has been derived, and into which it is in turn passing.

[30] The line of thought here worked out was originally suggested to me by Canon Liddon's sermon on "Our Lord's Ascension the Church's Gain," in his first series of University sermons.

[31] The gladiatorial shows form an interesting standard by which we may compare the practical effects of Christian and the very highest pagan sentiment. Tertullian denounced them in the strongest language in his treatise *De Spectaculis*. Cicero, in the *Tusculan Disputations*, ii. 17, defends them warmly as the best discipline against fear of pain and death.

[32] The original authority for the story of Telemachus is Theodoret's *Eccles. Hist.*, v. 26. It is vigorously told by Gibbon in the thirtieth chapter of his *Decline and Fall*.

[33] The doctrine of the sanctity of human life was unknown under paganism. Tacitus tells us, about the year A.D. 61, how that Pedianus Secundus, prefect of the city, having been murdered by one of his slaves, the whole body of his slaves, numbering more than four hundred persons, of every age and sex, were put to death (*Annals*, xiv., 42-45).

[34] We have no idea of the frightful character of pagan slavery. The worst form which negro slavery ever took never approached it. The following story will give our readers some idea of it. Cato, the censor, wrote a treatise, very little read or known, called *De Re Rustica*, treating of farming operations. In this he gives directions concerning the economical management of slaves, and among other things tells how wine for their winter consumption was to be prepared. "Put into a cask ten amphoræ of sweet wine, two amphoræ of sour vinegar, and as much wine boiled down by two-thirds. Add fifty amphoræ of pure water. Mix all together with a stick three times a day for five consecutive days. After this add sixty-four amphoræ of stale salt and water."

[35] See St. George Mivart, *Genesis of Species*, p. 282. The whole chapter (xii.) on Theology and Evolution is well worth careful study.

[36] See on this point Dr. John Lightfoot's *Horæ Hebraicæ*, Acts ii. 1; and a sermon by the learned Joseph Mede of Cambridge on Deut. xvi. 16, 17, in his *Works*, vol. i., p. 350 (London, 1664).

[37] See this point worked out in Dr. Salmon's article *Chronica*, in the first volume of the *Dict. Christ. Biog.*, and in the opening of his article on *The Chronicle of Eusebius* in the second volume of the same work. A brief extract from one of the earliest and most learned apologists, who lived about the middle of the second century, will show how the Christians elaborated this argument. Tatian, in ch. xl. of his *Oration to the Greeks*, speaks thus: "Therefore from what has been said it is evident that Moses was older than the ancient heroes, wars, and demons. And we ought rather to believe him, who stands before them in point of age, than the Greeks, who, without being aware of it, drew his doctrines as from a fountain. For many of the sophists among them, stimulated by curiosity, endeavoured to adulterate whatever they learned from Moses, and from those who philosophised like him, first that they might be considered as having something of their own, and secondly, that covering up by a certain rhetorical artifice whatever things they did not understand, they might misrepresent the truth as if it were a fable. But what the learned among the Greeks have said concerning our polity and the history of our laws, and how many and what kind of men have written of these things, will be shown in the treatise against those who have discoursed of Divine things."

[38] Epiphanius, *On Weights and Measures*, ch. xiv.

[39] The traditions about the upper chamber are given at length in Fr. Quaresmius, *Terræ Sanctæ Elucidatio*, t. ii., p. 119 (Antwerp, 1639), with which may be compared Bingham's *Antiquities*, bk. viii., ch. i., sec. 13; Mede's *Discourse Of Churches* in his *Works*, vol. i., p. 408; and Bishop Milles' notes on Cyril's *Catech.*, xvi. 2, in his edition of that writer, p. 225.

[40] See, for a fuller account, Salmon's *Introduction N. T.*, 4th ed., pp. 384-86, and the references there given.

[41] Peter may have learned this mystical mode of interpretation from our Lord Himself in His conversations. See Luke xxiv. 44-9.

[42] The intimate connection between the Christian ministry and the miraculous facts of Christianity has been powerfully argued by Charles Leslie in his *Short and Easy Method with the Deists*. He contends that the existence of the Christian ministry is a standing evidence of the supernatural facts of the gospel which can alone explain that existence.

If the facts never happened, how did the Christian ministry arise? Hence he concludes the perpetual character and obligation of the ministry for Christians, or, to quote his own words, "Now the Christian priesthood, as instituted by Christ Himself, and continued by succession to this day, being as impregnable and flagrant a testimony to the truth of the matter of fact of Christ as the sacraments or any other public institutions; besides that, if the priesthood were taken away, the sacraments and other public institutions which are administered by their hands, must fall with them: therefore the devil has been most busy, and bent his greatest force, in all ages, against the priesthood, knowing that if that goes down, all goes with it." —Leslie's *Works*, vol. i., p. 27.

[43] The literature of the apocryphal Gospels is very extensive. Those who wish to pursue this subject will find abundant materials in an article on "Gospels, Apocryphal" in the second volume of the *Dictionary of Christian Biography*, written by Professor Lipsius of Jena; or in Dr. Salmon's *Introduction to the New Testament*, Lect. XI. Origen mentioned the Gospel of Matthias, while again Eusebius (*H. E.*, iii., 25) describes it as heretical. See Fabricius, *Cod. Apoc. N. T.* p. 782. The apocryphal Acts of Andrew and Matthias may be seen in Tischendorf's *Acta Apoc.*, p. 132. Nelson's *Fasts and Festivals* tells, in a convenient shape, the traditions about St. Matthias and the other Apostles.

[44] The dignified self-restraint of the Acts is nowhere more manifest than in its reference to Judas Iscariot. The only notice bestowed upon him is connected with the election of Matthias. Papias was a writer of the beginning of the second century. He knew some of the Apostles and early disciples, and gathered diligently every tradition about the Church's early days. Papias made an attempt to harmonise the account of the death of Judas given by St. Peter with that told in St. Matthew, which has been preserved for us by two Greek commentators, Œcumenius, who lived in the tenth, and Theophylact, who flourished in the eleventh century. The difficulty is this. St. Matthew says that Judas hanged himself; St. Peter says that he burst asunder. Papias harmonises the two by telling that Judas first of all hanged himself on a fig-tree, but the halter broke. He was then seized with a terrible dropsy, and swelled up to an enormous size, so that when endeavouring to pass where a waggon could go he burst asunder. The narrative of Papias is given in Theophylact on Matt. xxvii., and Œcumenius on Acts i. Dr. Routh, in his *Reliquiæ Sacræ*, vol. i., pp. 9, 25, points out that the horrid details of the story, which cannot be here printed, are due to the Greek commentators enlarging on the simple facts stated by Papias. Origen, with characteristic daring, suggests that Judas committed suicide as soon as he saw that our Lord was condemned, in order that he might arise in the region of the dead

before Him, and there seek His forgiveness. There is a curious Latin book, published in 1680, which gives all the traditions about the traitor. Its title is Kempius, *On the Life and Fate of Judas Iscariot*.

[45] In the last lecture I have already given the reference to Lightfoot's and Mede's works where this point is fully worked out.

[46] The same view has practically been taught by some modern sects, who have proclaimed that all of the Old Testament and the whole of our Lord's teaching till He died were intended for Jews only, and have no relation to Christians. It is hard to say how such persons regard the Old Testament and the greater part of the four Gospels, save as interesting fossils to be hung up in a museum of comparative religion.

[47] Prayer for all estates of men in the Holy Catholic Church, in Jeremy Taylor's *Holy Living*, chap. iv., sec. vii.

[48] In the primitive Church the gift of preaching or prophesying seems to have been widely diffused and exercised among what we should call the laity, while at the same time a fixed and appointed ministry exercised the pastoral office, including therein the celebration of the sacraments and the exercise of Church discipline. This seems the explanation of the phenomena we behold in St. Paul's Epistles, in the manual called the *Teaching of the Twelve Apostles*, and in that curious production of the primitive Church called the *Shepherd of Hermas*. But though preaching and prophesying were at first very freely exercised, the disorders which arose at Corinth and other places quickly taught the necessity for fixed rules. It was just the same in the synagogue. The ritual and worship was conducted by the officials. Preaching was free and open to all, but subject to the control and direction of the ruler of the Synagogue, as the case of St. Paul at Antioch in Pisidia proves (Acts xiii. 15).

[49] Lightfoot, *Horæ Hebraicæ*, Acts, chap. ii., ver. 3, notes that "there is a form of prayer in the Jewish writings which was used on the solemn fast of the ninth month Ab, one clause of which illustrates the Divine symbol, 'Have mercy, O God, upon the city that mourneth, that is trodden down and desolate, because Thou didst lay it waste by fire, and by fire wilt build it up again.'"

[50] Isa. xxv. 7. See Lightfoot, *Horæ Heb.*, on Acts ii.

[51] Meyer on *Acts* (ii. 4), vol. i., pp. 67, 68. Clark's translation.

[52] The speculations and discussions now rife concerning hypnotism ought to teach modesty of assertion as to what is or is not possible. On the 28th of March there appeared in an eminent medical authority, the *Lancet*

newspaper, a review of a number of works on hypnotism, acknowledging the wonders of the subject, and containing this expression of opinion: "It is quite impossible to assign any limits to the influence of mind upon body, which is probably much more potent and far-reaching than we are usually prepared to admit." Now among the works reviewed in that article was one by Dr. Albert Moll of Berlin, published in the "Contemporary Science Series." That book makes statements about hypnotism which would quite cover Scripture miracles at which even devout people have stumbled, such as the miracles wrought by the shadow of St. Peter, or by handkerchiefs brought from the body of St. Paul (Acts v. 15, and xix. 12), which Meyer regards as mere legendary accretions to the genuine story. Moll, however, makes quite as wondrous statements about hypnotism. On page 1 he thus begins his *History of Hypnotism*: "In order to understand the gradual development of modern hypnotism from actual magnetism we must distinguish two points: firstly, that there are human beings who can exercise a personal influence over others, either by direct contact or even from a distance; and, secondly, the fact that particular psychical facts can be induced in human beings by certain physical processes. This second fact especially has long been known among the Oriental peoples, and was utilized by them for religious purposes. Kiesewetter attributes the early soothsaying by means of precious stones to hypnosis, which was induced by steadily gazing at the stones. This is also true of divination by looking into vessels and crystals, as the Egyptians have long been in the habit of doing, and has often been done in Europe: by Cagliostro, for example. These hypnotic phenomena are also found to have existed several thousand years ago among the Persian magi, as well as up to the present day among the Indian yogis and fakirs, who throw themselves into the hypnotic state by means of fixation of the gaze." The phenomena mentioned in the Acts, whether as to the tongues or to miracles worked through inanimate objects, may be compared with Moll's statements.

[53] The proper preface in the Book of Common Prayer is longer and more minute than the corresponding one in the Missal. The Reformers extended the ancient form, inserting a special reference to the gift of tongues.

[54] It is a completely mistaken notion, which no one would cherish who had read history with a full-orbed mental eye, realizing the past with its circumstances, that Latin and Greek superseded all other languages throughout the empire. Local dialects and languages continued to flourish all the time, save amongst the official classes. Else how did Welsh survive to this day in England? How did Celtic survive in France side by side with Latin? The two celebrated cases of Gregory of Tours and of St. Patrick show that their Latin was of a very rude and corrupt kind; their real spoken

language was Celtic, the tongue of the mass of the people. In a learned work just published I note a confirmation of this view. Professor Ramsay, in his *Historical Geography of Asia Minor*, p. 24, avows how his mind has changed on this question in regard to Asia Minor. "Romans governed Asia Minor, because with their marvellous governing talent they knew how to adapt their administration to the people of the plateau. It is true that the great cities (of Asia Minor) put on a Western appearance, and took Latin or Greek names. Latin and Greek were the languages of government, of the educated classes, and of polite society. Only this superficial aspect is attested in literature and in ordinary history, and when I began to travel the thought had never occurred to me that there was any other. The conviction has gradually forced itself on me that the real state of the country was very different. Greek was not the popular language of the plateau, even in the third century after Christ; the mass of the people spoke Lycaonian, and Galatian, and Phrygian, although those who wrote books wrote Greek, and those who governed spoke Latin." See for much more on the same subject, showing the prevalence of the native languages of Asia Minor down to the year A.D. 500.

[55] Christians often give their sceptical opponents an advantage over them by allowing them to state the difficulties of Christianity and never retorting the difficulties of scepticism. There is no historical fact of the distant past that cannot be encumbered with numerous difficulties, deduced, in most cases, from our own ignorance. No difficulty on our side is so great as that which the sceptic has to meet in undertaking to explain, on purely natural grounds, the rise and success of Christianity on the very spot and at the very time its Author had been crucified. The Christian story is simple and natural; the sceptical explanation forced, unnatural, and surrounded by a thousand appalling difficulties.

[56] I read the other day the report of an eminent Unitarian divine who was lecturing upon the Gospels. He was upholding the view that it was impossible that reports of the discourses of Christ and of His Apostles could have been handed down in anything like their shape as given in the New Testament, because it was an age without shorthand. The lecturer is an eminent metaphysical and philosophical critic, but he is evidently not versed in the social life of the ancients. Had the lecturer but referred to Prof. J. E. B. Mayor's edition of Pliny's *Letters*, Book iii., p. 96, he would have found abundant references proving that shorthand was a usual accomplishment among educated men long prior to the Christian era.

[57] Tertullian, *Against the Jews*, chap. vii.

[58] *Adv. Jovin.*, lib. ii., cap. 7, in Migne's *Pat. Lat.*, t. xxiii., col. 296.

[59] I have worked out this point at some length in *Ireland and the Celtic Church*, chap. i., pp. 14-20.

[60] The history of the Jewish settlement in the south of Arabia is very little known by the average student of the Acts, and yet it is a wonderful confirmation of its accuracy both here and in the account of the Ethiopian eunuch. This colony existed in Arabia long before the Christian era. They claimed, indeed, to have been a portion of the Jews of the Captivity. They established an independent kingdom in Southern Arabia, which bitterly persecuted the Christians about the year 500. A full account of this little-known persecution, and of the Homerite martyrs who suffered in it, will be found by those curious in such matters in that great monumental work the *Acta Sanctorum* of the Bollandists, vols. x. and xii. for October, under the names of St. Arethas and St. Elesbaan. Large quantities of manuscripts about this Jewish colony were discovered some years ago in the mosques of Southern Arabia. A considerable number of Jews still find a place there. See, for an account of the Jewish kingdom in Arabia, an article on Elesbaan, in vol. ii. of the *Dictionary of Christian Biography*. Gibbon in his forty-second and fiftieth chapters has much about it.

[61] The Jewish cemeteries discovered at Rome date back to the time of our Lord, or even before it. They were the models on which the Christians made the catacombs. The symbols of Judaism appear in the Christian tombs. See Northcote's *Epitaphs of the Catacombs*, and Brownlow and Northcote's *Roma Sotteranea*.

[62] The term Ebionite is thus well explained by the Rev. J. M. Fuller in the *Dict. Christ. Biog.*, vol. ii., p. 25: "The term Ebionism expresses conveniently the opinions and practices of the descendants of the Judaizers of the apostolic age, and is very little removed from Judaism. Judaism was for them not so much a preparation for Christianity as an institution eternally good in itself, and but slightly modified in Christianity. Whatever merit Christianity possessed, was possessed as the continuation and supplement of Judaism. The divinity of the old covenant was the only valid guarantee for the truth of the new. Hence the tendency of this class of Ebionites to exalt the old at the expense of the new, to magnify Moses and the prophets, and to allow Jesus Christ to be 'nothing more than a Solomon or a Jonas' (Tertull., *De Carne Christi*, c. 18); 'Legal righteousness was to them the highest type of perfection; the earthly Jerusalem, in spite of its destruction, was an object of adoration, as if it were the House of God' (Irenæus, *Adv. Hær.*, i., 26); its restoration would take place in the millennial kingdom of Messiah, and the Jews would return there as the manifested chosen people of God."

[63] See Moll's *Hypnotism*, p. 216, in the "Contemporary Science Series."

[64] See the article on "Apollinaris the Younger" in the *Dict. Christ. Biog.*, vol. i., for a concise account of the Apollinarian heresy.

[65] *Horæ Hebraicæ* on Acts ii. 29.

[66] See Josephus, *Antiqq.*, XIII., viii., 4; XVI., vii., 1; *Wars*, I., ii., 5.

[67] This point has been admirably discussed by Dr. Salmon in his sermon on "Present Salvation" in his volume of sermons styled *The Reign of Law*, pp. 295-99.

[68] This controversy between the Antinomian party and the London Nonconformists of the orthodox sort is now almost unknown, and yet it created great excitement in religious circles, conformist and nonconformist, in the time of William III. Bishop Stillingfleet of Worcester, the aged Baxter, and many of the leading divines, joined in it. The echoes of it will be found resounding in the more modern controversy between John Wesley and Fletcher on the one side, and Rowland Hill and Lady Huntingdon on the other, about the year 1770. A brief account of Dr. Daniel Williams will be found in Schaft's edition of Herzog's *Cyclopædia*; see also Calamy's *Life* i., 323.

[69] As some readers may not know what the work called the *Teaching of the Twelve Apostles* is, let me explain its history in a few words. Early Christian writers, from the year A.D. 200, speak of a work called the *Teaching of the Twelve Apostles* in the highest terms. It was evidently, as known by them, a manual used in the catechetical instruction of the young. This manual was known to all the early ages, but disappeared from the view of the Western Church during the middle ages. Nearly twenty years ago it was discovered in Constantinople by the learned Greek Bishop Bryennios, and published by him about ten years ago. It is assigned by some critics to the concluding years of the first century. A convenient and cheap edition of it will be found in the second volume of the Apostolic Fathers in Griffith and Farran's "Ancient and Modern Library." It is called the *Teaching of the Twelve Apostles*, or else the *Didache*, using a Greek title, which has the advantage of being shorter.

[70] The method of sprinkling is completely unknown to the Church ancient or modern, and should be absolutely rejected, as tending to a disuse of the element of water at all.

[71] The case of Perpetua and Felicitas, and the other famous martyrs of Carthage in the beginning of the third century, proves that pouring with water must have sufficed for baptism in a Church so intensely conservative as the Church of North Africa. Tertullian in his writings often reproves its members for the superstitious extremes to which they pushed their

conservative feelings, imitating every ancient Christian custom, rational or irrational. Felicitas and her friends were baptized in prison, where they were thrust into a noisome dungeon. How could they have been immersed in such a place? This case is good evidence for the practice of the second century as well.

[72] See the articles on Baptism and Baptistery in Smith and Cheetham's *Dictionary of Christian Antiquities*, vol. i.

[73] See Dr. John Lightfoot's *Horæ Hebraicæ*, St. Matt. xvi. 19.

[74] The apostolic manual called the *Teaching of the Twelve Apostles*, to which we have already referred, proves that the Church of the Apostles' day required catechisms and introductory formularies just as much as we do.

[75] Sonnet by Matthew Arnold on Rural Work.

[76] This line of thought has been already touched upon in Lect. IV., pp. 61-3.

[77] This episode in the history of paganism in the second century is very little known. It has been well depicted in an interesting little book, *The Age of the Antonines*, by the Rev. W. W. Capes, M.A., which only costs a couple of shillings. Chap. VIII. should specially be consulted.

[78] See the article on Barcochba in the *Dict. Christ. Biog.*, vol. i.

[79] See Lightfoot's *Horæ Hebraicæ*, Acts iii. 2. De Voguë in his great work on the Temple of Jerusalem, fully gives the traditions which attached themselves to this gate. In the fourth century it was celebrated by the Christian poet Prudentius, and in the fifth or sixth a gate called the Golden Gate was erected on its site. This gate still remains, and De Voguë in his plates vii. to xii. gives a series of views of it.

[80] The story of St. Crispin is told at length by the Bollandists in the *Acta Sanctorum* for October, vol. xi., pp. 495 to 540. St. Chrysostom in one of his orations paints a vigorous picture of two imaginary cities, one where all the people were rich, with an abundance of slaves, and therefore dependent on others for all the necessaries and conveniences of life; the other city inhabited by none but poor freemen, where everyone laboured at manual toil and provided for his wants by his own exertions. He then asks which is the happier; unhesitatingly giving the palm to the city of poverty, labour, and freedom.

[81] The analogy I have drawn between the early Methodists and the Franciscans will be amply borne out if one will take the trouble, in any of our large towns, to notice where the Franciscans have left traces of their

existence. The name Francis Street and the ruins of Franciscan foundations will almost always be found just outside the original walls, among the slums of the people. This point is noticed by Mr. Brewer in his interesting introduction to the *Monumenta Franciscana*, in the Rolls Series. He says, on p. xvii, "In London, York, Warwick, Oxford, Bristol, Lynn, and elsewhere, the Franciscan convents stood in the suburbs and abutted on the city walls. They made choice of the low, swampy, and undrained spots in the large towns, amongst the poorest and most neglected quarters." The Franciscans proved that splendid material structures are not necessary for great spiritual triumphs. An investigation of the topography of our older towns would show exactly the same great truth about early Methodist chapels. They were almost always placed in poor localities, as the name of Preaching Lane, often still connected with them, shows. See my *Ireland and the Anglo-Norman Church*, pp. 331-34, for more on this point.

[82] See Lightfoot on the Court of the Women in his *Chorography of the Holy Land*, chap. xix. in his *Works*, vol. ii., p. 29. The best modern description will be found in Count de Vogüe's *Le Temple de Jérusalem*, pp. 53-6 (Paris, 1864), with which may be compared a paper on the site of the Temple by Colonel Warren in the *Transactions* of the Society of Biblical Archæology, vol. vii., pp. 308-30.

[83] In the new edition of *Clement of Rome*, by Bishop Lightfoot, vol. i., pp. 92, 93, there is an account of this ancient church.

[84] "Moreover he brought Greeks also into the temple, and hath defiled this holy place. For they had before seen with him in the city Trophimus the Ephesian, whom they supposed that Paul had brought into the temple" (Acts xxi. 28, 29).

[85] Acts xxiv. 6.

[86] I have never seen a notice of this interesting biblical discovery in any English magazine or journal. There is an account of it in the *Revue Archéologique* for 1885, series iii., t. v., p. 241, by Clermont-Ganneau, its original discoverer. He calls it an authentic page of the New Testament.

[87] See more on this point in Dr. John Lightfoot's *Horæ Hebraicæ*, Luke xxii. 4 and Acts iv.

[88] Pliny in his *Letters*, x., 97, writes to the Emperor Trajan expressing this view when telling how he dealt with the Christians of Bithynia: "I asked them whether they were Christians: if they admitted it, I repeated the question twice, and threatened them with punishment; if they persisted, I ordered them to be at once punished: for I was persuaded, whatever the nature of their opinions might be, a contumacious and inflexible obstinacy

certainly deserved correction." A philosopher could not understand a man keeping a conscience in opposition to the law. The martyrs vindicated the freedom of the Christian conscience.

[89] It would take more space than we can now afford to explain the constitution of the Sanhedrin. There is an admirable and concise article on the subject in Schaff's edition of Herzog's *Cyclopædia*, and another in Kitto's *Biblical Cyclopædia*. Dr. John Lightfoot describes it in his *Horæ Hebraicæ*, which we so often quote. The most extensive and minute account of it will, however, be found in Latin in Selden's treatise *De Synedriis*, illustrated with plates.

[90] Dr. John Lightfoot, in his *Horæ Hebraicæ*, chap. iv., verse 6, identifies John mentioned in this passage with Rabban Jochanan ben Zaccai, the priest who lived till after the destruction of Jerusalem, and prophesied of that event forty years before it occurred. He was, however, a Pharisee, though the vast majority of the priests were Sadducees. Lightfoot tells the following story of him from the ancient Jewish books: "Forty years before the destruction of the city, when the gates of the temple flew open of their own accord, Rabban Jochanan ben Zaccai said, O Temple, Temple, why dost thou disturb thyself? I know thy end, that thou shalt be destroyed, for so the prophet Zechary hath spoken concerning thee, Open thy doors, O Lebanon, that the fire may devour thy cedar." He lived to be one hundred and twenty years old. He was permitted by Titus to remove the Sanhedrin to Jabneh on the destruction of the city, where he presided over it.

[91] St. Matt. x. 19.

[92] The decay in the numbers of the Society of Friends may be traced to several causes. The Society has done its work. Its testimony has borne its appointed fruit, and, like other systems which have sufficiently acted their part, it is passing away. One of the most evident causes of its decline is the decay of preaching consequent upon their notion of immediate inspiration. The advance of general education has told on their members, who cannot endure the unprepared and undigested expositions which satisfied their fathers. The decay in the preaching power of the Evangelical party in the Church of England may, in many cases, be traced to much the same source. No Church or society can now hope to retain the allegiance of its educated members which does not recognise that the help of the Holy Spirit is vouchsafed through the ordinary channels of study and meditation.

[93] As a Sunday school teacher for more than thirty years I feel bound to say that half the teaching in Sunday schools is useless from want of preparation on the part of teachers. A large proportion of them never think of opening their Bibles beforehand and studying the appointed lessons,

jotting down a number of leading questions to assist their memories. The result is, that after a few questions suggested by the text, the teacher turns to read a story or indulge in gossip with his pupils. A well-prepared teacher will never find an hour too long for the work appointed. I have already said something on pp. 131, 132, above, upon this subject, which is an extremely important and practical one.

[94] The primitive Christians had a profound reverence for the names of our Saviour, which they delighted to depict in different ways, some of them so secret as to defy the curiosity of the pagans. They used the symbol I.H.S., which I have known to arouse the susceptibilities of suspicious Protestants, though nothing but a Latin or Western adaptation of the three first letters of the Greek word IHΣOYΣ written in capitals. The fish, again, was a favourite symbol, because each letter of the Greek word ιχθύς stood for a different title of our Lord, Ἰησοῦς, Χριστός, Θεός, Υἱός, Σωτήρ, or Jesus, Christ, God, Son, Saviour.

[95] See Burnet's exposition of the eighteenth Article in his commentary on the Thirty-Nine Articles.

[96] See an interesting letter from St. Augustine to St. Jerome on this question in the *Letters* of St. Augustine (Clark's edition), vol. i., pp. 30-2. With which compare Bishop Lightfoot on *Galatians*, p. 128.

[97] *Cf.* Acts xx. 25; 1 Tim. i. 3, iii. 14, iv. 13; 2 Tim. i. 18. St. Paul's address to the Ephesian elder was delivered in the spring of 58 A.D. He twice revisited Ephesus, six years later, in 64 A.D. See Lewin's *Fasti Sacri*, pp. 314, 334,—a book of marvellous learning and research, which every critical student of the Acts should possess, together with the same author's *Life of St. Paul.*

[98] The communism of the early Christians was not a novel notion. The Essenes, a curious Jewish sect of that time, had long practised it; see Bishop Lightfoot's essay on the Essenes in his commentary on Colossians, 3rd ed., p. 416. Josephus, in his *Antiqq.*, XVIII., i., 5, and in his *Wars*, II., viii., 3, describes the communism of the Essenes in language that would exactly apply to that of the early Christians. Thus in the latter place he says: "These men are despisers of riches, and so very communicative as raises our admiration. Nor is there to be found any one among them who hath more than another; for it is a law among them, that those who come to them must let what they have be common to the whole order; insomuch that among them all there is no appearance of poverty or excess of riches, but every one's possessions are intermingled with every other's possessions, and so there is, as it were, one patrimony among all the brethren."

[99] The thirty-eighth Article of the Church of England is directed against the Anabaptist theory. A paralysis of ordinary life and action was temporarily produced at Jerusalem after the day of Pentecost. This quickly led to the community of goods, with its evil results. The paralysis produced at Jerusalem by the excitement and expectation of those early days was reproduced in this century at the time when Irvingism and Plymouthism took their first rise, some sixty years ago. The best illustration of the practical effects of such one-sided spiritual expectation will be found in a book forgotten by this generation, *The Letters and Papers of Lady Powerscourt*, published in 1838. She was eminent in the religious world of her day, and was intimately mixed up with the prophetical movement out of which Irvingism and Plymouthism were developed. The fundamental doctrine of both these sects was the immediate personal appearance and reign of Christ on earth. Lady Powerscourt's correspondence shows the results on an ardent mind of such an idea. She gave up society, separated herself from the world in a hermit's cottage at Lough Bray in the deepest recesses of the Wicklow Mountains, and there occupied herself in writing to her friends exhortations to cease from life's work, such as the following, which we find on p. 235: "There is much seemingly to be said for the things of this world being sanctified to heavenly uses; yet I cannot help feeling more and more assured every day that a divorce must take place,—that God and the world cannot be joined,—that it behoves us to make plain that we are the risen ones by our portion not being in any degree from hence,—that we are not struggling upwards through mire and dirt, but we are as let down from heaven. We take our stand in the kingdom of heaven, looking from above at earth, not from earth at heaven." When people begin to "look from above at earth," the step to communism is not a long one. Vast numbers of persons never recovered themselves from the strain of that time (A. D. 1830), but remained all their lives in a state of dreamy disappointment. I have enlarged on this subject in an article on J. N. Darby in the *Contemporary Review* for 1885.

[100] An interesting illustration of ancient missionary work and its likeness to modern efforts turned up a few years ago among the Fayûm papyri. It was a document containing the curse pronounced by a pagan mother upon her son who had turned Christian, solemnly cutting him off from his kith and kin. It will be found in a translated shape in the *Transactions* of the Society of Biblical Archæology for 1884, Part I. Modern converts, too, just like the ancient, have often to suffer the loss of all things for Christ's sake.

[101] It is not generally known that the Post Office offers special facilities for the establishment of such Penny Savings Banks as I advocate. The Post

Office will supply books for depositors and permit a deposit account to be opened without any limit. I have seen in my own parish the beneficial working of such an institution, increasing annually in its results for the last twenty years.

[102] Philo was a contemporary of the Apostles. He has left us many works dealing with this period. He speaks of the Jews of Cyprus in the account of his embassy to the Emperor Caius Caligula. See Milman's *History of Jews*, iii., 111, 112, and Conybeare and Howson's *Life of St. Paul*, chap. v.

[103] See Lightfoot's *Horæ Heb.*, Acts iv. 36; *cf.* Josh. xxi. 18.

[104] The early history of Barnabas is thus described by Metaphrastes, an ancient Greek writer. Barnabas was born in Cyprus, of rich parents, who sent him to be trained at Jerusalem under Gamaliel. There he formed an early friendship with St. Paul. He was a witness of our Lord's miracles, and was converted by the healing of the impotent man at Bethesda. He then was the means of converting his sister Mary and her son Mark, who was the young man with the pitcher of water whom our Lord commanded His disciples to follow when He was sending them to prepare the Passover. Mary's house was the place where the upper room was situated, and continued to be the meeting-place of the Christians, as we find from Acts xii. Metaphrastes had formerly a very bad reputation as regards truthfulness, but modern investigation has shown that his *Lives* contain some very ancient documents, going back to the second century at least. See Bishop Lightfoot's address to the Carlisle Church Congress in *Expositor* 1885, vol. i., p. 3; Prof. Ramsay in *Expositor* 1889, vol. ix., p. 265 and refs., and Cave's *Lives of the Primitive Fathers*, p. 35.

[105] C. J. Vaughan, D.D., *The Church of the First Days*, pp. 105-12.

[106] Ezek. xx. 32.

[107] Acts v. 12-16 states that St. Peter wrought many miracles, and further that men sought to place their sick in such a position that even his shadow might fall upon them, thinking that it brought healing with it. This statement has been spoken of as a demonstrative proof of legendary growth by Zeller in his work on the Acts, and is weakly apologised for by Meyer. But the analogy of hypnotism at the present time, when cures are wrought and extraordinary influence exercised without corporeal contact, is quite sufficient to vindicate St. Luke's account from the charge of legend. If moderns can produce marvellous results without immediate touch; if, for instance, hypnotised patients when blindfolded can read a book by means of their stomachs or their noses (Moll, p. 366, already quoted), or blisters can be raised by a piece of white paper merely by suggestion, as stated by Moll,

pp. 114-22, surely the statement of St. Luke is no necessary proof of legend and old wives' fables. See my remarks above.

[108] See Dr. John Lightfoot, *Horæ Hebraicæ*, on the Acts, iv. 5. *Cf.* his remarks on St. Mark xv. 1, where that learned Hebraist seems to support this view, though admitting that there is something to be said on the other side, viz., that the council met in the temple as of old.

[109] See, for instance, Zeller on the Acts of the Apostles, vol. i., p. 228 (Norgate and Williams: London, 1875), where he says: "We must therefore maintain the possibility that our author, after the fashion of ancient historians, freely invented Gamaliel's speech; and it is a question how much of it belongs to history at all, and especially whether Gamaliel delivered the discourse in favour of the Christian cause;" with which statement the whole context, should be compared. The report of Gamaliel's speech is due of course to St. Paul, who was doubtless present during its delivery.

[110] The family of Gamaliel himself illustrates the principle for which we are contending, viz., that families have a tendency to reproduce exactly the same political and religious tendencies. Gamaliel himself was grandson of the Jewish patriarch Hillel I., who presided over the Sanhedrin long before the Christian era. Gamaliel's grandson, Gamaliel II., was president of the Sanhedrin during the first twenty years of the second century. He was distinguished by the same liberal principles as characterised his grandfather. Gamaliel II. was succeeded by his son Simon. So that the presidency of the Sanhedrin continued in the same family for nearly two centuries. It is a notable fact, and not without its bearing on some modern controversies, that the Jewish canon of the Old Testament was not finally closed till the time of the presidency of Gamaliel II., that is, about the year 117 A.D. "Up to this time the members of the Sanhedrin themselves, in whom was vested the power to fix the canon, disputed the canonicity of certain portions of the Hebrew Scriptures. Thus the school of Shammai excluded Ecclesiastes and the Canticles from the text of Holy Writ, declaring that they proceeded from Solomon's uninspired wisdom. It was the Sanhedrin at Zabne which decided that these books are inspired, and that they form part of the canon."—See Mr. Ginsburg's article on Gamaliel II. in the *Dictionary of Christian Biography*, vol. ii., p. 607.

[111] Upon the question of the historical accuracy of the Acts of the Apostles, the appendix to the late Bishop Lightfoot's collected essays on *Supernatural Religion* (London, 1889) should be consulted. The opening paragraph bears directly upon our point. "In a former volume M. Renan declared his opinion that the author of the third Gospel and the Acts was verily and indeed (*bien réellement*) a disciple of St. Paul.... Such an expression

of opinion, proceeding from a not too conservative critic, is significant; and this view of the authorship, I cannot doubt, will be the final verdict of the future, as it has been the unbroken tradition of the past. But at a time when attacks on the genuineness of the work have been renewed, it may not be out of place to call attention to some illustrations of the narrative which recent discoveries have brought to light. No ancient work affords so many tests of veracity, for no other has such numerous points of contact in all directions with contemporary history, politics, topography, whether Jewish, or Greek, or Roman."

[112] We learn this from the *Bibliotheca* of Photius, Cod. 171. Photius was a very learned Greek patriarch of the ninth century. He was a diligent student, and made an analysis of every book he read. These extracts have been gathered into one volume called his *Bibliotheca* or *Library*, and can now be consulted in any collection of the Greek fathers. Photius reports his story about Gamaliel and Nicodemus from two earlier writers, Chrysippus and Lucian, presbyters of Jerusalem.

[113] For an account of the Clementine *Recognitions* see Dr. Salmon's Introduction to the N. T., 4th ed., pp. 14-19, 373-75. Translations, both of the *Recognitions* and *Homilies*, can be consulted in Clark's Ante-Nicene Library.

[114] St. Paul, as he tells us in 2 Cor. xi. 24, was five times flogged by the Jews. When the Jews inflicted this punishment the culprit was tied to a pillar in the synagogue; the executioner, armed with a scourge of three distinct lashes, inflicted the punishment; while an official standing by read selected portions of the law between each stroke. Thirteen strokes of the threefold scourge was equivalent to the thirty-nine stripes. This was the flogging the Apostles suffered on this occasion.

[115] See the authorities for the chronology of this period as given in Lewin's *Fasti Sacri*, pp. 247-53.

[116] The Church during its earliest years called itself merely the Way, not recognising the term Christian at all. This is brought out clearly in the Revised Version, as in Acts ix. 2, xix. 9, 23, xxiv. 14. The adoption of the name Christian probably marked the more distinct separation of the Church from the synagogue.

[117] See Josephus, *Antiqq.*, XVIII., iii., 1, 2.

[118] The term world is one that has very various meanings in Scripture, and good people have often made serious practical mistakes by confounding these meanings. I once met a serious young man disposed to the views of the "Brethren," who gravely told me that he thought it wrong to admire beautiful scenery because it was written, "Love not the world, neither

the things that are in the world." There are three distinct uses of the term "world" in Scripture: as expressing, (1) the material earth, Psalm xxiv. 1, "The earth is the Lord's, and the fulness thereof; the world, and they that dwell therein;" (2) the people on the earth, John iii. 16, "God so loved the world, that He gave His only begotten Son" for it; (3) the impure lusts and desires which found full scope under paganism, and still intrude themselves into the kingdom of Christ, 1 John ii. 15, 16, "Love not the world, neither the things that are in the world.... For all that is in the world, the lust of the flesh, and the lust of the eyes, and the vainglory of life, is not of the Father, but is of the world." It is evident that if we take the bad meaning of world in this last passage and apply it to the other two we shall end in the old Manichean view that the material world and the men on it are the handiwork of a bad or inferior deity, and therefore should be entirely rejected. I know that some very grave and serious people have fallen into this confusion, and have thus banished all sweetness and light from their own lives and from those of their families. It is a curious circumstance, too, that we read in ancient writers that the Manichean heresy always recommended itself to persons of a similar temperament, who in consequence led lives of a very strict and puritanical type. They looked upon the world and all that was in it as the devil's creation. How then could they smile upon, love, or enjoy anything therein? See the article "Manicheans" in the *Dict. Christ. Biog.*

[119] Lightfoot's *Horæ Heb.*, Acts vi. 1, where there is a long and learned discussion, extending over several pages, upon the distinction between the Hebrew and the Grecian Jews.

[120] Bishop Lightfoot, commenting on Philippians, says: "I have assumed that the office thus established represents the later diaconate; for though this point has been much disputed, I do not see how the identity of the two can reasonably be called in question. If the word deacon does not occur in the passage, yet the corresponding verb and substantive, διακονεῖν and διακονία, are repeated more than once. The functions, moreover, are substantially those which devolved on the deacons of the earliest ages, and which still in theory, though not altogether in practice, form the primary duties of the office. Again, it seems clear, from the emphasis with which St. Luke dwells on the new institution, that he looks on the establishment of this office, not as an isolated incident, but as the institution of a new order of things in the Church. It is, in short, one of those representative facts of which the earlier part of his narrative is almost wholly made up."

[121] See Le Bas and Waddington's *Voyage Archéologique*, vol. iii., p. 583, *Inscriptions*, No. 2558; and Dr. Salmon's article on Marcion in Smith's *Dict. Christ. Biog.*, iii., 819. There is one passage in the Epistles which shows that

not merely the name but the organization of synagogues was adopted by the early Church. In 1 Cor. vi. 1 it is written, "Dare any of you, having a matter against his neighbour, go to law before the unrighteous, and not before the saints?" This verse cannot be rightly understood unless we remember that every synagogue had its own judicial tribunal, composed of ten men, who decided on Mondays and Thursdays every controversy among the Jews, inflicting immediate corporal punishment on the condemned. The Romans permitted and supported this domestic jurisdiction, just as the Turkish Empire, which has inherited so many of the Roman traditions, allows the Greek and other Eastern Churches to exercise jurisdiction over their own members in all questions touching religion, supporting their decisions by force if necessary. St. Paul, in this passage, wishes the members of the Christian synagogues to act like those of the Jewish, and avoid the scandal of Christians going to law with their brethren before pagans.

[122] Bishop Lightfoot, in his well-known Essay on the Christian Ministry, from which we have already quoted, does not admit any likeness between the office of the diaconate in the Church and any similar office in the synagogue. He refuses to recognise the Chazzan or sexton of the synagogue as in any sense typical of Christian deacons. But he has not noticed the three almoners or deacons attached to every synagogue, whom his seventeenth-century namesake, Dr. John Lightfoot, in his tract on synagogues (*Horæ Hebr.*, St. Matt. iv. 23), considers the origin of the Christian deacons.

[123] The community of goods may have evolved itself naturally enough out of the celebration of the Eucharist. Just let us realize what must have happened, say, on the day of Pentecost and the few succeeding days. The Apostles seem to have been living a common life during the ten days of expectation. They dwelt in the house where the upper room was. The day after Pentecost there must have been a great deal to do, in prayer, baptism, and celebration of the Eucharist. Their converts would join with them in the eucharistic feast, from day to day celebrated after the primitive fashion at the end of a common meal. Some enthusiast may then have suggested that, as the Master might at any moment appear, they should always live and eat in common. After a time, as the numbers increased, this arrangement had to be modified, and a daily distribution was substituted for daily common meals. The community of goods may thus have been developed out of the spiritual feast of the Eucharist, which they took in common. When the daily distribution terminated by the exhaustion of the funds, the Agape or lovefeast took its place, remaining as a fragment or relic of the earlier custom. Pliny in his letter mentions the Agape, and rightly distinguishes it from the worship of the Christians which was celebrated in the early morning.

"After these ceremonies they used to disperse, and assemble again to share a common meal of innocent food."

[124] In the twelfth century the number of cardinal deacons was fixed at fourteen, at which it has ever since remained.

[125] See Kitto's *Biblical Cyclopædia*, articles on Synagogue and Deacon, or Schaff's edition of Herzog's *Cyclopædia*, article on Synagogues.

[126] The College of Cardinals offers another illustration of this. The Cardinals were originally the parochial clergy of Rome. As Rome's ecclesiastical ambition increased, so did that of her parochial clergy, who came to imagine that, standing so close to the Pope, who was the door, they were themselves the hinges (cardines) on whom the door turned. I wonder if one of the original presbyters of Rome would be able to recognise his office in that of a modern cardinal claiming princely rank and precedence!

[127] I have expanded this subject in *Ireland and the Celtic Church*, ch. ii., viii., ix.; and in *Ireland and the Anglo-Norman Church*, pp. 352-70.

[128] See Bede's *Ecclesiastical History*, Book ii., chap. 2.

[129] I have already said something on p. 181 of the meetings of the council, but not perhaps quite enough to explain St. Paul's relation to St. Luke as far as the Acts of the Apostles is concerned. The Sanhedrin sat in a semicircle. In the centre of the arc the president was placed; at either extremity there sat a scribe, while the disciples or pupils of the Sanhedrists were arranged in three rows appropriate to their respective attainments. In Selden's *Works*, i., 1323, in his treatise on the *Assemblies of the Hebrews*, the reader can see a plan of the Sanhedrin when sitting. St. Paul, as a favourite pupil of the President Gamaliel, would have the best place among the disciples, if he were not actually one of the council. Selden says that the disciples were arrayed in this prominent position not only that they might be instructed in law, but also might be available for serving on the council if any member died suddenly or was taken ill. St. Paul probably made numerous notes of the speeches delivered before him, and could supply St. Luke with notices written and verbal. The article in Schaff's *Theological Cyclopædia* on Sanhedrin should be consulted for more information and references on this point, as well as the other references.

[130] M. Le Blant is one of the greatest living authorities on ancient art and history. He has been head of the French Archæological School at Rome. He has published an extremely able work on the subject of the *Acts* of the martyrs, in which he treats them in a strictly scientific manner. He confronts them with the processes of Roman law, the facts of chronology and history, and triumphantly shows the vast amount of truth contained

in these documents. He also explains how the Christians got possession of the Roman magistrates' notes, which they then inserted in the local Church records, and dispersed amid other Churches, after the manner of the Epistle of the Lyonnese Church, to which reference has been already made. Le Blant of his memoir, quotes one ancient document, which incidentally mentions that "inasmuch as it was necessary to collect all the records of the martyrs' confessions, the Christians paid one of the javelin men two hundred denarii for the privilege of transcribing them." We are apt to forget that both Jews and Romans conducted all their persecutions under strict judicial forms. We sometimes think that the persecutions were mere outbursts of popular rage, managed after the manner of a street riot. The examples of the magistrates at Corinth and Ephesus in the Acts of the Apostles ought to dispel this illusion. The Romans had a perfect horror of civil commotions, and sternly repressed them. If a sect was to be put down, it should be put down in a legal manner, with questions and answers and due records of the proceedings.

[131] See above, where I have touched on this point.

[132] Epistle of the Church of Lyons in Eusebius, *Eccles. Hist.*, v. 1. This letter relates the earliest Celtic martyrdoms of which we have any knowledge. They took place at the annual Convention of the Celtic tribes of Gaul, which assembled at Lyons and Vienne. These conventions were much the same as the assembly at Tara in Meath, where St. Patrick began the work of converting Ireland. See my *Ireland and the Celtic Church*, chap. iv.

[133] See chap. xiii., above.

[134] See *Survey of Western Palestine*, iii., 126 and 383-88, where an account is given of the ruins of the ancient church erected in honour of St. Stephen by the Empress Eudocia, about A.D. 440. It is on the north side of Jerusalem.

[135] Dr. John Lightfoot in his *Horæ Hebraicæ* on Acts vii. 58, when dealing with this incident, enters into copious details as to the Jewish method of execution by stoning.

[136] The termination of St. Clement's Epistle to the Corinthians, discovered some few years ago, is most instructive on this point. It is a litany or liturgical prayer used in the primitive Roman Church. Bishop Lightfoot, in his new edition of Clement, vol. i., p. 382, commenting on it, has some very interesting thoughts on the relation between early Christianity and the Roman State.

[137] See on this point a note in Liddon's *Bampton Lectures*, 14th edition, pp. 531-43, on the worship of Jesus Christ in the services of the Church of England.

[138] See Malalas' *Chronographia*, lib. xi., and the article on Malalas in the *Dict. Christ. Biog.*, where this story is given at length.

[139] See Eusebius, v. 18; Clem. Alex., *Strom.*, vi. 5.

[140] St. Augustine, in his sermons on the festival of St. Stephen, concisely puts the matter thus: "Si Stephenus non nasset, ecclesia Paulum non haberet" ("If St. Stephen had not prayed, the Church would not have had St. Paul").

[141] The very name Apostle connotes for us an extraordinary office and dignity, placing the Twelve upon an exalted plane far above all others. But the Jewish Council knew nothing of this. The term Apostle was in common use amongst the Jews. To us it seems almost presumptuous to apply the name to any but the Twelve, though the New Testament applies it more widely. The title Apostle was given among the Jews to the legate or Church officer who attended on every synagogue and discharged its commands. It was also specially bestowed upon the messengers of the Jewish high priest or patriarch who collected the temple tax while the temple existed, and afterwards the poll tax or tribute paid by every Jew throughout the world towards the support of the patriarch and the Sanhedrin. The name Apostle is found in this sense in the Theodosian Code down to so late a period as the fifth century. Our Lord and the early Church simply adopted this title Apostle from the synagogue, as they adopted so many other rites and usages, baptism, holy communion, the various orders of the ministry, and a liturgical service.

[142] Samaria, the capital, was at this period called by the Romans Sebaste. Herod the Great rebuilt it in honour of the emperors, and erected a splendid temple there, which he inaugurated with games and gladiatorial shows. It was a suitable spot for the peculiar talents of a man like Simon Magus, as in turn it would have been specially repugnant for every reason to a strict Jew. But a Divine instinct was leading Philip on to the revelation of God's purposes of love and mercy. See Joseph., *Antiqq.*, XV., viii., 5; Stanley's *Sinai and Palestine*, p. 245.

[143] The story of the quarrels between Simon Magus and St. Peter has been used by the Tübingen school of critics in Germany to support their theory of a fundamental opposition between St. Paul and St. Peter. See Dr. Salmon's *Introduction*, chap. xix., for a full statement of this strange view.

[144] See about the Fayûm MSS. and their contents a series of articles in the Records of the *Contemporary Review* from December 1884, and in the *Expositor* for 1885 and 1888. These Fayûm documents go back to the remotest times, one of them being dated so long ago as 1200 B.C. It is very

curious that this extraordinary discovery has been apparently overlooked by the great majority of English learned societies.

[145] Moll's work on hypnotism, which we have already several times quoted, admits the reality of Eastern magic, accounting for the mango trick which Indian jugglers perform, and which every Indian resident has seen, on the ground that even vegetables can be hypnotised. It may be hard for us to admit it, but such books compel us to allow that there may be more in heaven and earth than is dreamt of in our philosophy. The presence of the grand heathen temple at Sebaste or Samaria would have made it the fitter scene for Simon's magical incantations. Magic and Paganism always flourished side by side, as we see at Ephesus.

[146] See Acts xvi. 6-10, compared with Gal. iv. 13.

[147] *The Christian Year*, 2nd Sunday after Epiphany.

[148] See about this curious sect of the Hemero-baptists Lightfoot's *Colossians*, pp. 402-407.

[149] The order for adult baptism in the Book of Common Prayer was drawn up by the divines of the Restoration. They must have been well skilled in Christian antiquity, for they lay down expressly the same rule as the *Teaching of the Apostles*. They order that notice shall be given of an adult's baptism a week at least beforehand, that the persons to be baptized may be duly exhorted to prepare themselves by prayer and fasting for that holy ordinance.

[150] There is no ceremony which proves more conclusively the identity between the ritual of apostolic ages and, say, of the year 200, than this custom of standing at public prayer with hands outstretched. St. Paul, writing to Timothy (1 Tim. ii. 8), says, "I desire therefore that the men pray in every place, lifting up holy hands," and then he prescribes rules for the women. This passage will not be understood in its full force till one grasps the notion of an early Christian at prayer, as described by Tertullian in the treatise on Prayer to which I have referred. Tertullian lays down, with other writers of the second century, that Christians should pray in public on the Lord's Day standing with the hands lifted up and the arms stretched out horizontally. On this point the practices of the East and West alike were identical, and had not changed one atom from St. Paul's to Tertullian's time. From the way some people speak one would think that the Christians of the second century were wild revolutionaries, who were only too anxious to change the ritual derived from apostolic days. Tertullian's works prove that they were, on the other hand, almost too slavish in their adherence to ancient customs. Human nature is the same in every age, and a moment's reflection

will show us that whether in England, Scotland, or Ireland, the ritual of old-fashioned congregations of every denomination is the same to-day as in the seventeenth century. A few instances occur to me which illustrate this. Dean Hook, in a letter dated April 5th, 1838, tells us that the old Presbyterian way of administering the Holy Communion, carrying the elements to the communicants sitting in their pews, still existed in the parish church of Leeds. The custom had been introduced early in the seventeenth century, and never was discontinued, notwithstanding a plain rubric forbidding it. I have read that the same custom prevailed at St. Mary's in Oxford, when Newman became Vicar. Again, down to a few years ago, in the country parts of Ulster and Connaught, the separation between the sexes in public worship continued among the Methodists, in obedience to John Wesley's law made one hundred and twenty years before. It is two hundred years since Sternhold and Hopkins' version of the Psalms was authoritatively laid aside, and Tate and Brady substituted. Yet I have within the last ten years seen Prayer-books in use at Bolton Abbey in Yorkshire, with Sternhold and Hopkins attached to them. Surely the early Christians were at least as Conservative as their modern followers.

[151] See Tertullian on Prayer, in his Works, vol. i., pp. 188-92, as translated in Clark's Ante-Nicene Library.

[152] I was much struck the other day with a modern instance of this. The Plymouth Brethren boast themselves as the least traditional of sects. They are, however, just at present split all the world over into two divisions, the great subject of debate being the writings of a Mr. Raven. He has ventured upon some perilous speculations concerning the nature of Christ's person. I have seen a formal indictment drawn out by his opponents, in which his opinions are contrasted with statements in the writings of their founder, the late J. N. Darby, which are evidently the final authority and standard of appeal for them.

[153] Thus in 1 Cor. xi. 2 St. Paul says, "Now I praise you that ye remember me in all things, and hold fast the traditions, even as I delivered them to you," and then goes on to discuss the question of veiling of women, showing the character of the traditions thus delivered. With this verse may be compared similar references in 1 Cor. vii. 17, 2 Thess. ii. 15 and iii. 9.

[154] See Tertullian on Baptism, chap. vi., where he says, "Not that in the waters we obtain the Holy Spirit, but in the water, under the influence of the angel, we are cleansed, and thus prepared for the Holy Spirit." And again, in chap. viii. he describes the course followed after baptism thus: "In the next place the hand is laid on us, invoking and inviting the Holy Spirit through the words of benediction." To pass from Tertullian to a very

different witness, we may note that Calvin in his commentary on Heb. vi. 2 says, "This one place abundantly testifies that the origin of this ceremony (imposition of hands on the baptized) came from the Apostles." He differs from Tertullian, however. Calvin does not view it so much as a channel of Divine grace as a rite for profession of faith and solemn prayer, and as such would have confirmation continued as a necessary complement of infant baptism.

[155] Compare 1 Cor. vi. 19 with Heb. vi. 4, 5.

[156] The evidence from these writers will be found in a collected shape in Bingham's *Antiquities*, book xii., chap. iii., sec. vi. St. Augustine, in his Tract VI., on 1 St. John iii., expressly deals with the objection that because the Apostles imparted miraculous gifts by the imposition of hands, therefore their conduct forms no precedent for us. "In the first age the Holy Ghost fell on them that believed; and they spake with tongues which they had never learned, as the Spirit gave them utterance. These were signs proper for that time; for then it was necessary that the Holy Ghost should be thus demonstrated in all kinds of tongues, because the gospel was to run throughout the whole world in all sorts of languages. But this demonstration once made, it ceased." I have above called Cyprian the disciple of Tertullian, because we learn from St. Jerome that Cyprian when asking for the works of Tertullian always said, "Da Magistrum," "Give me the master."

[157] It seems to me a great pity that, owing to the modern public school system, the confirmation of boys of the upper and middle classes is almost entirely passing from their own home pastors to the masters of public schools, and not always with happy results. This tends to increase the hard mechanical view of confirmation against which I protest.

[158] The primitive Church never made this mistake. The great missionaries who dealt with the heathen in the second century were profoundly skilled in philosophy, several of them being philosophers by profession. Aristides, whose long-lost *Apology* has just been recovered, Justin Martyr, and Tatian were Christian philosophers in the second century, and consecrated their powers to missionary labours. Pantænus, Clement, and Origen, profound scholars of Alexandria, took the greatest trouble to understand Greek paganism before they proceeded to refute it. I think that candidates in training for foreign missions might be taken with great advantage through a course of the second century apologists. Clement and Origen never poured indiscriminate abuse on the system they opposed; their teaching was no bald negative controversy; they always strove, like St. Paul at Athens, to ascertain what was good and true in their opponents'

position, and to work from thence. See above, where much the same line of thought has been insisted upon.

[159] *The Acts of the Deacons*, p. 276. This work discusses Philip's dealings with the eunuch at very great length. The reader desirous of seeing the spiritual teaching of that incident fully drawn out should consult it.

[160] The verse John v. 4 of the Authorised Version has now been relegated to the margin of the Revised Version.

[161] See Dean Stanley's *Sinai and Palestine*, p. 263, where this thought is further worked out. It is curious that notwithstanding the preaching of St. Philip and St. Peter in its neighbourhood, Gaza remained true to paganism longer than any other city of Palestine. The old Philistine opposition to Israel seems to have perpetuated itself in a pagan opposition to Christianity. Even in the fifth century, when St. Jerome boasted that Bethlehem was so completely Christian that the very ploughmen sang psalms and hymns as they laboured, Gaza still remained devoted to idol-worship. The inhabitants of Gaza, in union with those of Askelon, even rose in rebellion in defence of paganism towards the end of the fourth century (see Neander's *Church History*, iii., 105, Bohn's ed.). An interesting illustration of its obstinate paganism has come to light of late years. There were in Gaza eight public temples of idols, including those of the Sun, Venus, Apollo, Proserpine, Hecate, Fortune, and Marnas, dedicated to the Cretan Jupiter, believed by the people to be more glorious than any other temple in the world. All these temples were destroyed by the influence of the Empress Eudoxia, about A.D. 400; the words of the edict which overthrew the temples of Gaza can be read in the Theodosian Code, book xvi., title x., law 16. The statue of Marnas was then hidden by the pagans in the sand outside the city, where it was discovered in 1880. It is now figured and described in the *Survey of Western Palestine*, Memoirs, vol. iii., p. 254. It is especially interesting to us Christians, as being a statue which was almost certainly seen by St. Philip. See Selden, *De Dis Syris*, p. 215, and Murray's *Handbook for Palestine*, pp. 271-73.

[162] See the article "Meroë" in Smith's *Dictionary of Greek and Roman Geography*, for a long account of the land whence the eunuch came.

[163] Justin Martyr's *Dialogue* with Trypho the Jew was written about a hundred years after the eunuch's conversion. It is a good specimen of the methods adopted by the early Church in dealing with the Jews. St. Philip's teaching was doubtless of much the same kind. Justin upheld the application to Christ and its fulfilment in Him alone of the fifty-third of Isaiah, repeatedly quoting large portions of it, in the *Dialogue*, as, for

instance, in chap. xiii. The apology of St. Stephen furnished the model upon which all subsequent missionaries to the Jews framed their arguments. They all dealt largely with the transitory and typical character of the Levitical law. The apologies addressed to the Gentiles were quite different, as was natural. They dealt with the true nature of God, the conceptions men ought to form of Him, and the immoralities of the pagan deities. The newly-discovered *Apology* of Aristides, which I have described in the preface, dating from about 124 A.D., set a fashion which we find reproduced in Justin Martyr, Tatian's *Oration to the Greeks*, and in Tertullian's Apology and Address, *Ad Nationes*. The moral proofs of Christianity and its adaptation to the soul's wants are their leading topics. I have treated more of this point in the preface.

[164] The eunuch's name, according to Ethiopian tradition, was Indich or Indicus. He is believed by the Abyssinians to have converted Queen Candace, and then to have departed into India, where he taught in Ceylon. See Ludolf's *History of Ethiopia*, book iii., chaps. i. and ii.; and Bzovius' continuation of Baronius' *Annals*, A.D. 1524, where there is a long correspondence between the pope and the king of Abyssinia in that year. The Abyssinians retain to this day a great many Jewish customs mixed with their Christianity. The Abyssinian tradition is incorrect, however. Modern Abyssinia is not the same as the ancient Meroë. The conversion of Abyssinia is due to the labours of a shipwrecked merchant in the time of St. Athanasius, and derived its faith from Egypt. The Coptic Church retains still many Jewish rites. See "Ethiopian Church" in *Dict. Christ. Biog.*, vol. ii.

[165] *Texts and Studies*, edited by J. A. Robinson, M.A. (Cambridge: University Press, 1891). There are several passages in Justin's *Dialogue* with Trypho which seem to be extracts from the primitive Creed. Thus in chap. xvii. we read the following words of Justin to Trypho: "For after you had crucified Him ... when you knew that He had risen from the dead and ascended into heaven." In chap. xxxviii. Trypho objects to Justin: "For you utter many blasphemies, in that you seek to persuade us that this crucified Man was with Moses and Aaron, and spoke to them in the pillar of the cloud; that He became man, was crucified, and ascended up to heaven, and comes again to earth and ought to be worshipped." The date of the *Apology* of Aristides is fixed by the Armenian version of the *Chronicle* of Eusebius at 124 A.D. The *Paschal Chronicle* apparently assigns it to 134 A.D.